Praise for DRU

From The Viscount Trenchard, grandson .... who was appointed as the first chief of staff of the new RAF. He became the first Marshal of the Royal Air Force and was elevated to the peerage:

> *"Your book offers a unique insight into the history of air weapons development in Britain and the United States. It is written in an easy fluent style and will be essential reading both for air historians and for those whose interest is less academic but just want to understand more about such an important period in the history of airpower."*

From a letter to the author from Andrew Boyle, biographer of Lord Trenchard, *Father of the Royal Air Force*, and of Leonard Cheshire, bomber pilot, one of the few to be awarded the Victoria Cross:

> *"I was greatly intrigued and impressed by the first chapters of* Druids' Circle. *Apart from writing well and intelligently, you clearly know your stuff. Even the highly technical material doesn't intrude..."*

From Vice Admiral John T. "Chick" Hayward USN (Ret), famous WW II carrier pilot with a Silver Star, the Legion of Merit, four Distinguished Flying Crosses and five Air Medals. Latterly he was president of the U.S. Naval War College and added two Distinguished Service Medals to his awards:

> *"With congratulations on a very marvelous story and hope it will be read by many, of those stirring days. I certainly enjoyed the book and read it several times. Here is hoping for success for your most interesting story of your very exciting life."*

From Rear Admiral Eugene B. Fluckey USN (Ret), recipient of the Congressional Medal of Honor and four Navy Crosses. The most successful American submariner in WW II and author of *Thunder Below*:

> *"I enjoyed the pages you sent and must congratulate you on your outstanding work and writing. Your excerpts are truly interesting."*

DRUIDS' CIRCLE

Aircraft Flight-Testing and Armament in World War II

DRUIDS' CIRCLE

Aircraft Flight-Testing and Armament in World War II

GROUP CAPTAIN H.W. DEAN A.F.C.
Legion of Merit (Officer Class)
RAF (Retired)

PER ARDUA BOOKS, WESTBURY, WILTS

DRUIDS' CIRCLE
Aircraft Flight Testing and Armament in World War II

All rights reserved.
Copyright © 2001 M.K. Dean

First U.K. edition 2001 published by
PER ARDUA BOOKS,
30 Eden Vale, Westbury, Wiltshire

ISBN: 0 9523023 3 0
Library of Congress Catalogue Number: 95-71570

Reproduction in any manner, in whole or part,
in English or any other languages without written
permission from the publisher is forbidden.

Printed and bound by Redwood Books, Trowbridge, Wiltshire

July 6, 1935. King George V reviews the whole RAF at Mildenhall, accompanied by The Prince of Wales and The Duke of York. The prince came back to this base a year later, as Edward VIII, to inspect 99(B) and 38(B) Squadrons. The duke, who succeeded him as George VI, visited Boscombe Down in June 1941. All three visits are recalled in person in this memoir.

This account of one small facet of technical development during World War II is dedicated to the people who were really behind it all—the boffins—the scientists and technicians on our side, especially those in Britain and the United States with whom I was privileged to work.

And of all these, in particular, to that merry band of men at the California Institute of Technology involved with the development of aircraft rockets. Under Dr. Charles Lauritsen, who brought a breath of fresh air into our lives.

Such mighty minds bent to such absurd tasks.

Foreword

World War II was surely the worst of times and yet, in some odd ways, it was the best of times. Before Group Captain Dixi Dean came to our nuclear physics laboratory, the Will Keith Kellogg (the corn flakes king) Radiation Laboratory, we had already changed it into a defense lab for the design and development of land, sea, and air-fired rocket ordnance. We worked primarily for the U.S. Navy but also for the Army and the Army Air Corps. We removed one of our accelerators to the reservoir back of Morris Dam near Pasadena, where it was used as a pressure vessel to push torpedoes down a long cylindrical tube in order to launch them at well-determined angles and velocities into the water.

It was the *best* of times because we thought the war against Hitler and Tojo was a just war. We did not wonder whether a war could be just. We still do not know the answer.

In 1944, Dixi brought us real savvy (forgive the navy term) about the installation and operation of rockets on combat aircraft. He had the advantage of ten years of experience with aircraft guns and cannon and three years with aircraft rockets.

He could transmit his expertise to the boffins, as he called us, without raising the hackles of even those who thought they knew it all from drawing board experience alone. We came to trust him, and because he was friendly and congenial, we came to like him.

Now in reading *Druids' Circle* it becomes clear to me that we at Caltech shared only a small part of Dixi's activities during World War II. *Druids' Circle* tells the full story of those activities. It is a story by and about an officer, a gentleman, and a scholar. It's a tale about a pilot's love for his aircraft. Primarily it is devoted to the development and testing of aircraft armament, but it mirrors the full picture of war—the triumphs, the failures, the joys, and the sorrows. Men lived to make their beastly devices work, and men died in the doing. All of the horrors were not at the front lines. Wars require armament as well as men. The reader will find *Druids' Circle* a sometimes shocking but always fascinating account of the development of aircraft rocket ordnance.

It is more than that in many ways, but reference to one of these must suffice. Group Captain Dixi Dean spent considerable time in America during World War II on official assignments in several capacities. It is a delight to read about a British officer coming to know our land and its people in ways that his training and background had never led him to expect. He came to understand us, to share our aspirations and ideals, to join in our love of work and our love of play. But most of all, in his own way of telling, he came to see, in spite of the many differences, that America as well as Britain is a great democracy.

William A. Fowler
Nobel Laureate in Physics 1983
Officer, Légion d' Honneur

Preface

An old Roman road ran behind the house where we grew up in Princes Risborough, Buckinghamshire. It is said that the village was so called because the Black Prince, son of Edward II, had stables there and came out for weekends from London. It was the Prince's *Rising Borough*—round about 1350, I suppose. Ruins of the stables are still there to be seen.

Straight as an arrow lay the old Roman road, running in part along an older British path, the Icknield Way. From our house we could walk along the ancient, grass-covered cobblestones on up the scarp of the Chiltern Hills. A farther climb of a couple of hundred feet or so led to a large white cross cut through the deep sod, revealing the chalk that lay beneath, dazzling white in the sunlight. Whiteleaf Cross has been there for centuries to guide pilgrims to Monk's Risborough, a monastery at the foot of the hills.

Such traces of an ancient past are abundant in "this scepter'd isle" and often seem to be taken for granted. But they are the stuff that girds the loins when mortal danger rises. It is a heritage sensed and guarded by all souls, whether behind weapons or behind the scenes.

The following memoir tells of the struggles of some "backroom boys" who bent their efforts for many years to stem the predations of the Hun, yet again, in the Second World War. It is a personal account of one area of weapons development for the Royal Air Force and the Fleet Air Arm, from early small-caliber machine guns to huge cannon and on to forward-firing aircraft rockets.

All in our land were involved in the mortal struggle. Nor were the early Druids, the priests of Celtic Britain, to be left out. The megalithic circle at Stonehenge is believed to have been built by early Bronze-Age astronomers almost four thousand years ago. Their structure was used much later by the Druids, who worshipped the sun; and Stonehenge does seem to be oriented for a midsummer rite. It became a key part of our testing program. By diving each forward-firing test aircraft at the center of the circle, we measured (using a cinecamera) how accurately the aircraft could be aimed and how suitable it was as a gunnery platform. The "Druids' circle" beame the target for one of our most crucial tests.

History and tradition seem to support us in every way when our need is dire.

Acknowledgments

A book of this sort is made by many contributors whose ideas and valuable information are gratefully acknowledged. However, my flying logbook is the armature around which the basic clay of the story is molded. RAF pilots are imbued with a reverential awe to maintain an accurate and complete flying log and thus my major debt is to that impeccable record—so long after the events.

Thanks to Carol Jose, talented writer, my guide in the morass of marketing; to Julia Lee Dulfer, my editor and her delicate art of word and comma clipping; to Marguerite, my wife, for ten years of shared struggle.

I bow to many in various prestigious institutions: to Peter Hartley, Secretary in the Lord Chamberlain's Office at Buckingham Palace, for gracious permission to reproduce, under the Palace letterhead, His Majesty King George V's message to the RAF after the Royal Review of the RAF on 6 July 1935; to the Ministry of Defense, London: Sqdn Ldr P.H.R. Singleton, Air Historical Branch, for help and permission to use the Frontispiece; Mr. S.H. Clarke, Publications

Clearance Branch, for good advice; Clive Rowsell, Copyright Administrator, Crown Copyright MoD, for a generous gift of clearance for many valuable photographs. All ©British Crown copyright/MoD photographs and material so noted are reproduced with the permission of Her Britannic Majesty's Stationery Office.

My gratitude goes to the United States Naval Historical Center, notably for the courtesy shown me in supplying new prints of the many classic photos of the early days of the Naval Ordnance Test Station in California; the help I have had from Leroy L. Doig III, Command Historian at the now Naval Air Warfare Center Weapons Division, China Lake, is beyond any call of duty. My thanks to the U.S. Marine Corps and to the National Archives for the kind use of their photos.

I thank the archives of the California Institute of Technology and of the Imperial College of Science, Technology and Medicine, London, for portraits of Professor William A. Fowler and Sir Henry Tizard, respectively.

The important war museums in England: the Imperial War Museum, the RAF Museum and the Fleet Air Arm Museum all gave unstinting help which is much appreciated.

THE WHITE HOUSE
WASHINGTON

CITATION FOR THE LEGION OF MERIT
Degree of Officer

Group Captain Hubert William Dean, Royal Air Force, during the period of active hostilities in World War II, rendered exceptionally meritorious service in scientific development. Specialized in the field of aircraft armament, in the United States he aided development of rockets by facilitating the exchange of important technical and operational information, and at the time of the European invasion, joining a detachment of American personnel in England who equipped the first fighter squadron for firing the new HVAR rocket, he was untiring in the training of pilots and crews. Through his energy, special abilities and cooperative attitude, Group Captain Dean contributed substantially to the Allied war effort.

Harry Truman

Part One

One

What a beautiful day to wake up to, that brisk September 3 morning on Martlesham Heath in Suffolk, England. The tang of the North Sea to the east exhilarates and bids the spirit rise to enjoy it. But it's a sad day, too—it might be our last. Two days ago Britain fired off an ultimatum to Germany and a second, final ultimatum went off early this morning, due to expire an hour before noon.

For the past nine months of 1939 I've been aide to Squadron Leader Dru Drury, experimental gunnery officer at the Royal Air Force armament research station at Martlesham. We have been testing all new aircraft gun installations for squadron use.

GLOBAL UPDATE
September 1938–September 1939

In September 1938 Britain and France ignobly agree to the return of the important Czech Sudetenland to Germany in a foolish belief that this is the last in a string of hitherto hopeless appeasements. Hitler guarantees "peace in our time," but only a year later invades innocent Poland, knowing full well we have a mutual defense pact with his victim. We call his bluff at last and today, 3 September 1939, our deadline ends.

We assemble just before 1100 hours in the anteroom of the officers' mess to hear Mr. Chamberlain speak to the nation over the wireless. Suddenly the heavy static ceases. "This is the BBC London. Please stand by for the Honorable Neville Chamberlain, the prime minister, who will speak from 10 Downing Street."

After an endless static-filled pause, Mr. Chamberlain comes on the air. He speaks in a quiet, sad voice outlining the events leading up to this terrible moment from which there is no return, and concludes, "We are honorably allied with Poland by formal treaties against aggression and will stand by those agreements! As of this moment, therefore, we must consider ourselves at war with the German Reich."[1]

We are stunned. Although we had sensed for some time that war with the Nazis must surely come, we always hoped for some miracle to prevent it. Relief from past uncertainty now gave way to nameless fear; war is finally and irrevocably upon us. As we prepare to go in to lunch, the voice of the CO comes over the loud howler. "All personnel report to their posts without delay, in preparation for an immediate evacuation of the station."

"There goes our grub," said Dru as we pick up our caps and head for our office over at A hangar. The phone jangles as I follow him into our sanctum. "It's for you," he said, passing it over.

1935—Private venture "Britain First" built by Bristol Aircraft Company for Lord Rothermere. A light day bomber military version came soon after to be named BLENHEIM.

"Dixi, this is Hetty," comes the voice of Squadron Leader Hyde, OC, A Flight, the armament fighters. "I see you're qualified on twins. There's a Blenheim[2] on the tarmac in front of your office, ready to go. Get your gear and leave right away for Boscombe Down on Salisbury Plain. And don't say where you're going. Oh! And stay *low!*"

I protest that I've never piloted a Blenheim, but it falls on deaf ears. "Too bad!" says Hetty, hanging up.

We are airborne within an hour after the deadline falls away into history—fleeing over the treetops and putting as much distance as possible between Germany and ourselves. All experimental aircraft are leaving Martlesham, one after another, headed for Boscombe. The engine fitter of the Blenheim, one Aircraftman Rogers, is new to me. He sits alongside in the second pilot's seat and takes care of raising the undercart and adjusting the engine revs; details he knew about and I didn't. Together we ad-lib the show quite well and make a good team.

Aircraftman Narroway, the rigger, sits in the rear gun position with his eyes peeled for enemy pursuit. His gun isn't loaded. He doesn't know how to use it anyway, but I get a crick in my neck looking nervously over my shoulder as we skim the hedgerows.

The English countryside in early fall is beautiful, especially from the air; this time I hardly see it. We're too low, and I have little heart for it. Before long we begin to run into the haze of outer London. We lift up a little into clearer air, and the miles peel away like a good fly cast running out.

"Look out, sir!" yells Rogers as within moments we flash low over Windsor Castle. This is lese majesty indeed. Normally a court-martial offense, at least. Oh, well! I think to myself. Too bad! As Hetty had just told me.

How much father can it possibly be? "Where the hell are we?" I asked Rogers out loud, although I'm hogging the only air chart. "Got to be nearly there, sir," he replies, more to comfort me, I think, than to make an accurate navigational statement. As he spoke, lo and behold, an airfield looms straight ahead and we land right on our guesstimated time of arrival.

We stop at the watch office building and I scramble out.

"Hang on," I tell Rogers. "Keep her ticking over."

There's something very wrong. We are the only bloody aircraft there. Surely we can't have beaten everyone else to it though we've run like a very scared rabbit. I go into the watch office and see the NCO on duty reading the daily rag. He gets up.

"Afternoon, sir!"

I glance over the sergeant's shoulder looking for the signature on the daily routine orders pinned on the board. It says: "...by order of the officer commanding, Royal Air Force Station, Upavon." So that's were we are—Upavon! We've plonked down ten miles north of Boscombe. A trifle humiliating.

"Just a precautionary landing. We'll be off again now." I tell the duty pilot. "Good day."

I climb the flimsy metal ladder hanging from the belly of the Blenheim, and we're soon back in the air heading south for another five minutes. There we are! Beautiful, shy Boscombe. We've been at nought feet, true, but how the devil could we have missed such a vast field covered with a conglomerate of all kinds of aircraft landing pell-mell, taxiing every which way. Absolute chaos.

We manage a passable landing. The first one at Upavon was only practice, of course. Rogers does most of it again, a good lad to have aboard. We taxi over to where large cards on stakes point to "A Flight, Armament Testing." The marshals stop us on a spot miles from anywhere, on an undulation that leaves us pointing uphill at twenty degrees.

"Switches off!"

At last we collect our small bags and disperse to get something to eat.

War! My God, *War!* Is it really true?

The heavy night-bomber squadrons at Boscombe have left this same noon and by now have taken our place on the east coast. At least they've left the mess batmen behind, and one by one we trickle in for lunch, albeit somewhat late.

"Hey! Come and sit down." It's Dru, halfway through a plate of rare, juicy roast beef. "Look at that damned cheese!" he points out, and I follow his knife aimed at an enormous wheel of Stilton wrapped in a white damask napkin, a silver scoop stuck in the top. "Those bloody bomber boys live well, don't they?" It is a delicious cheese, and I'm glad Dru seems to have forgotten that I was in bombers, myself, for several years. Or is he putting me on? I quickly finish eating and go back outside.

The whole place is in utter confusion. We can't get on with our gun testing until the ground crews turn up, and they have a lot to get together before they can hit the road. We've no ammo or any place to fire the guns, anyway, or a camera section to make our recordings. Nothing! We are a most disconsolate group, with so many things waiting to be done and no way of even starting.

I look around in disbelief. How did we get into this pickle?

I think back over the years leading up to this unreal moment: back to my childhood—my school days...

How the hell did it all happen?

GLOBAL UPDATE
October 1919–April 1933

It is 1919. World War I, the war to end all wars is over and a League of Nations, the brainchild of United States President Wilson, is formed to bind the world in peace. Alas this dream is abandoned by its true father on the doorstep of Europe, where it was born and soon will die. Cynicism replaces faith, leniency is the order of the day. As the Treaty of Versailles comes formally into effect Hitler is planting the dragon's teeth that will yield him the most powerful military machine the world has ever known. Appeasement by the victorious Allies in the new peace is destined to be as futile as their recent blind acceptance of trench warfare as the only solution in winning that war.

By 1933, a false satanic party leads a recrudescent Germany. Much revered president Hindenburg names Hitler to be chancellor and in so doing unwittingly unleashes his nominee's prison-writ plans for world domination. Dachau, the first concentration camp, is opened in March 1933. Boycotts against Jews start in April. The knell of dying peace is tolling.

In September, 1920, I was eight and a half and could neither have known of nor understood the exquisite irony of the happenings in Munich after World War I. I was sent away to boarding school far enough so I couldn't sneak home to mother and was as miserable there as most young schoolboys seem to be. There's a scurrilous story that in England children are buried at about age three and dug up again at eighteen. Not entirely true—perhaps—but a sojourn at a boys' private boarding school has all the elements of being buried alive. After seven years I could quote the odd ode from Horace but had no skill in conversing with the outside world. Science was different. Happily, I had almost full time in the chem lab for a final year and it was my first love.

I became an articled apprentice to a public analyst in London for two years. The consequent training in bacteriological and chemical analyses laid the foundation for my life-to-be. The scientific approach to solving problems stood me in great stead for the experimental work I would do in the war—lurking round the corner. The work varied from a simple measurement of the water content in a sample of wheat grain, for example, to finding out what killed several members of the Marylebone Police Force. As part of the chemical analysis of some ham they'd all eaten I tested for poisonous metals. I quickly came down with a more-than-mild dose of paratyphoid, which our bio lab was just finding out had been the real culprit in the deaths.

With apprenticeship over, in spite of two years of priceless training from an eminent chemist, I found getting a job without an academic degree was like whistling for the moon., At the Royal College of Science I took my degrees of Bachelor of Science in Chemistry (with honors) and Associate of His Royal College of Service in 1932.

At college in 1929 I became good friends with a German exchange student who spent a month of the summer vacation with us. The next year I visited him in Germany. His father owned a pub in Friedrichshafen, a delightful little port on the shores of Lake Constance. There zeppelins were still being built, and Dornier flying boats hung at anchor off the shore. We had a great time, including happy evening parties where we sang rousing student tavern songs.

My friend's brother, a local intern, drove us out to a nearby *Gasthof.* His huge Mercedes Benz convertible was fantastic. It sported a triangular red pennant on the radiator cap with two little black lightning flashes depicted on it. "What's that flag you are flying there, Franz?" I asked the budding doctor.

"Oh, nothing," he shrugged, turning away. "Just a club."

We sat on the floor of the inn and sang our hearts out. We toasted our two countries swearing that never ever again would England and Germany go to war against each other...and meant it.

I was not to know the significance of that innocent-looking pennant of the *S.S. Club* until a few years later when I learned it was the badge of the dreaded *Schutzstaffel,* the Black Shirts. My God! Perfidious Albion—as Napoleon was wont to call us—had nothing on the dissimulation of my friend's brother. My eyes were by then opened to the seriousness of the growing menace in Germany. Perhaps Franz really did believe that Germany and England would never go to war, no matter what else came to pass. God knows what Hitler was teaching him.

In 1929 a few of us designed and built a simple glider in our college basement. As aeronautic students we were inspired by the news that filtered in about the great success the Germans were having at the Wasserkuppe, their gliding Mecca in the Rhön mountains. Robert Kronfeld was one of the stars we admired and with whom we flew—vicariously—as we heard of his wonderful, soaring exploits. Little did we know that this was the training ground for the secret German air force, the budding Luftwaffe.

Our recently formed Imperial College Gliding Club went to Dunstable Downs in the summer of 1929 to fly our new contraption. We assembled the glider at the top of a long, steep slope facing into a spanking wind. The glider was to be launched by means of a one-inch diameter elastic rope made into a giant V, like a catapult. The glider sat at the crotch of the V, waiting to be hurled into the air. A steel hook pointed down from the nose of the skid of the glider and slipped into a steel ring at the center of the rope.

Paul Adorjan, our captain, sat down in the little bucket seat perched over the front skid and buckled on the seat belt. He was ready to make the maiden flight. As the launching crew on the elastic rope took up the slack, he noticed the ring had dropped off the hook and was inching away from him. "Hold it!" he shouted, undoing the belt. He jumped out and ran to capture the errant ring. As he left the seat, the glider, now freed of his weight and anxious to be off, lifted into the air and flipped over onto its back, disintegrating into a pile of matchwood. It was just as well it was our captain who had done such a fell deed; but that sanctimonious thought didn't get us a new glider. We raked all the broken bits together, loaded the glider-trailer and folded our tents. We left quickly, away from the unrequited caress of the thermal uplifts. It was a sad moment.

After the tragedy of losing our precious glider before it had even flown—its brief inverted solo trajectory being the epitasis of a classic Greek drama—we had to look for a replacement. We could never build another, there's a limit to the blood one can give, and it would have to be a used model. We learned of a club in the Welsh mining hills that had gone broke in those fearful days of economic depression, asking only twenty-five pounds for their scarce-used glider.[3] Robbins, a club member, and I volunteered to collect our loot. Of course it was daylight robbery but not a deliberate act of international piracy. Hauling a glider-trailer into the wild Black Mountains in a Welsh blizzard made for quite a trip. I broke a half-shaft in the back axle of our Bullnose Morris car trying to use the engine as a brake coming down the final snow-covered hill into town, and the damage held us up for a while. From inquiring about a propeller we saw hanging over the fireplace in the local pub, we found the club also owned a small light aeroplane with a smashed lower wing. They said we could have it if we wanted and twenty-five pounds seemed their price for anything. We inspected the log book. The little gem sitting in the field behind our repair garage was the famous Avro Avian,[4] originally owned by Australian Bert Hinkler, a test pilot for Avros. In this beauty he had won the Grosvenor Cup, a well-known British amateur air race in the mid 1920s. He had also flown it from

London to Darwin in Australia in 1928. It was all there in black and white in the log. We were sorely tempted to buy it on the spot as well and rename our club the Imperial College Flying Club. They agreed to let us take the log back to London and broach the matter with our rector. If he agreed, we had a deal.

A weak winter sun managed to make the drab coal-mining valley beautiful in the snow. The raw mountain peaks looked down beneficently on our deal masking the pain of the impoverished men. We explored this remote, grim region and saw the growing unemployment in the mines. Young men stood on the street corners, cold, gloomy, upset, railing against a fate over which they had no control. They felt hemmed in by the environment. The beauteous ring of mountains formed walls of economic imprisonment for them.

We felt sad, feeling their misfortune. We had a glider our new-found friends could no longer afford; we might also buy their graceful Avian because all were broke in the once-busy valley. Not that we were much better off, but we still had some clothes—and some hope.

"Come in, Dean. What've you got there?" Henry Tizard asked, taking the Avian log from me. He sat down at his desk to examine it. "This book is wonderful," he beamed. "Let me take a closer look at it. You go and find out how much Avros will charge to repair the crumpled wing and come back and see me."

Alas, Avros wanted one thousand pounds sterling—a favor as we were students. "...Bye-bye, Bluebird." I retrieved the log book from the rector, who seemed reluctant to let it go. "What a shame. That would have been a lot of fun," he said. And I was left to mail the book back to that unhappy valley, trapped in mountains so aptly named.

By the next year we flew at every opportunity. I accumulated about two hours total flying time in some thirty flights but the memory of my very first will last forever—the supreme thrill of becoming airborne, alone, only my temple hairs spell-

1931—DAGLING primary glider. Imperial College Gliding Club captain, Paul Adorjan, is launched near cliffs at Rottingdean, Brighton, Sussex.

ing out the speed of the wind. Mastery of a new element was mine; now with Beeching I could cry, "See, see, bird, I fly!" We all caught the disease for which there is no cure: virus Daedali— flying. Most of us went on to spend our lives in aviation, actively flying, designing aircraft, or running air lines. An incurable disease but not, in truth, an unpleasant malady.

Late 1930 I caught typhoid and went to the coast to recover. On the local golf course, I met John Dowling. He was there to recuperate from a minor crash in an RAF fighter and not, like me, from a Dark-Ages disease. Naturally, our conversation gravitated to flying. Put two people together who have flown and they will soon be talking about it, with emphatic hands to help. I don't think the extent of my flying experience meant anything to Flying Office Dowling, but the fact that it was all time in the air with no engine did impress him. For my part, I was fascinated by his yarns of life as an officer in the RAF. He'd also found it hard to find a decent job at that time of worldwide depression and had taken a short-service commission—five years, with an option to renew for five more. He qualified for a fighter squadron and was now at an airfield just south of London. "Why don't you come over and have a jug of beer with me when his hooky is over?" he suggested.

"I'd love to," I told him. "I really would."

I made some sort of effort to find a job, but the hunt was not any more successful, than three years before. I went down to see John Dowling at Biggin Hill in Kent. Over the promised pint of bitter, he filled me in on the drill to apply for a short service commission. I couldn't wait.

Quietly and without any fanfare, the British government had, unto a bleak future, introduced this clever device to build up a strong reserve of flying officers for the RAF, somewhat on the cheap, of course. Young chaps were given commissions, fully trained as pilots, given service in front-line squadrons, and then put into the reserve—with weekend flying practice—for an indefinite period. I thought it was a great idea. I liked what I'd seen at John's station. I applied for and was granted a commission, starting September 1932. I know my father was disgusted with me. "Five years of specialized training being thrown away," he grumbled, "to flit off after a will-o'-the-wisp; or just a short-term solution to unemployment. Utterly stupid!"

My previous gliding experience was not only ignored by my new RAF flying instructors, but I was told it was a bloody hindrance, something to be unlearned, quickly. In the end, after an exhilarating year in light trainers (Tiger Moth)[5] and then in service aircraft (Atlas)[6] by September 1933 I could really fly. I sewed on my RAF wings and joined an elite corps of proud professionals.

1932—Primary RAF Trainers. DeHavilland TIGER MOTHS at No. 3 Flying Training School. Grantham, Lincs.

1933—RAF service trainer. Armstrong Whitworth ATLAS. Pilot Officer Dean (acting, on probation) makes first solo flight in this squadron aircraft type.

1933—RAF service trainers. Armstrong Whitworth ATLAS army-coop at Grantham, Lincs. Formation flying training.

1933—Armstrong Whitworth SISKIN. Two-seat day fighter for dual training. Being started up by a Ford Model T "Hucks" starter. Grantham, Lincs.

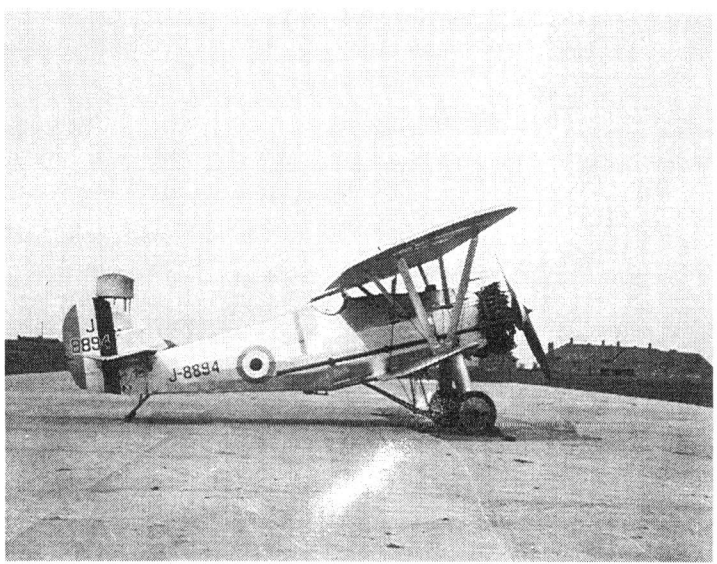

1933—Armstrong Whitworth SISKIN. Single-seat day figher for advanced flying training on squadron type.

1933—Trainee Pilot Officer Ellesborough spins in through a hangar roof from slipstream of a plane ahead. He is "given a bowler hat"—discharged from service.

GLOBAL UPDATE
August 1933–July 1937

Marshal Paul von Hindenberg dies on 3 August 1934; with him dies all decency in power in Germany. The Third Reich is proclaimed and the terms of the Versailles Treaty, scornfully shredded, are tossed as a gauntlet before the world. Massive rearmament for the domination of Europe is started in great secrecy but by the end of 1934 can no longer be hidden; only futile verbal protest is made. By 1936 Hitler is ready and marches back into the prohibited Rhineland yet only angry words are offered to stop him. Mussolini joins the game of poker by annexing Ethiopia, also without let or hindrance.

What have been ugly rumors are now stark realities chilling the blood, the more each day. Winston Churchill's lone warnings ignored for so many years are now heard as clarion calls to arms. The Sleeping Lion of England stirs at last.

Rearmament accelerated in Britain particularly in the RAF which is seen as the main bulwark of home defense—easy to maintain at a high state of readiness, flexible and immediate. Our island nation must own the air overhead to survive. The fighter airplane will be our umbrella. The Air Defense of Great Britain is a new organization to play a major role in national security.

Hawker Aircraft, originally the Sopwith Aviation Company, has made single-seat fighters since 1913. Tough thoroughbreds from this illustrious company include the Sopwith Camel and the Snipe and now in 1935 their biplane, the Hawker Fury,[7] in service with our front-line squadrons. It was the quintessence of day fighter design of the time; graceful, responsive, and with great hidden Rolls-Royce power, but its archaic armament harked back to World War I. According to the sacred formula, two of the latest British Vickers machine guns[8] were mounted in the upper fuselage where the pilot could reach to free them from frequent jams. Since they fired through the spinning propeller, a mechanism was included to stop each gun firing when the prop blade was in front of the barrel—to avoid shooting the wrong contestant. But rate of fire—the number of bullets per second being hurled at the enemy—was seriously reduced by the necessary interruption.

A radically new gun appeared from the U.S. so reliable in operation it didn't need to be within the reach of the loving hand of the pilot and could now be mounted out in the wing. The revolutionary gun had twice the rate of fire of the Vickers, and out in the wing its much superior performance would not be interrupted by the fan blades. It was the Browning gun.[9]

With their usual foresight Hawkers advanced plans in 1934 for a Fury replacement, a monoplane with a retractable undercart and an enclosed cockpit. It had much of the Fury pedigree in its design and looked much like it with the upper mainplane removed. She was even prechristened the Fury Monoplane. The Air Ministry was putting out specs for a new fighter with an extraordinarily high flight performance and an unprecedented armament of eight machine guns. After consulting Hawkers, new specs were written around their private venture and the design changed to mount four Brownings in each wing. Approved in January 1935, a prototype flew on 6 November. She was named Hurricane.[10]

GLOBAL UPDATE
June 1934–August 1938

The Germany Air Ministry also issues a new requirement for a single-seat fighter in 1934. Four manufacturers[11a] are given contracts for prototypes and all but one chose to install the British Rolls-Royce Kestrel engine, workhorse of the latest RAF aircraft and the most powerful and reliable engine available at the time. Flight trials are in October 1935 and the winner is the Bf 109,[11b] built by Bayrische Flugzeugwerke to Willy Messerschmitt's design. It first flies only a few weeks before the debut of the

Hurricane. The Bf 109, more commonly called the Me 109, is a small low-wing monoplane with a much thinner wing than the Hurricane but not much faster. Initially it is armed with two small machine guns[12] mounted in the upper fuselage decking, firing through the airscrew, but hearing about the unbelievable British requirement for eight guns, a third machine gun is installed to fire through the center of the propeller boss. This is the first production model, the Me 109B.

The first three blissful years or so after getting my wings were spent in squadron life, flying heavy bombers by day and by night, and raising hell in between. We were to be, as we firmly convinced ourselves, the cutting edge of the Air Force spear. We trained for strategic bombing, a policy articulated when the RAF was formed as an independent force on 1 April 1918 by our first chief, Marshal of the Royal Air Force Lord Trenchard. Known affectionately as "Boom" Trenchard, he was a real cannon.

1933—Handley-Page HINAIDI heavy night bomber of 99(B) Squadron at operational practice camp. Catfoss, Yorks.

1933—HINAIDI heavy bomber loading up with live HE bombs for long night bombing mission to bomb the target in the local danger area.

After a year of flying huge, obsolescent Hinaidi[13] heavy bombers shaped like railway boxcars, we reequipped with the latest Heyford[14] heavy bomber. It had been given the grandiose name of "high-speed bomber," but the term referred to the speed its bombs could be loaded aboard and not to its velocity through the air.

No. 99(B) Squadron was a black sheep. We were generally at the bottom of the list in the bombing exercises, and our rating in gunnery was not much better. Their Airships in the ministry had a solution: we were the first to get the new bomber. We also got a new wing commander, a notorious martinet named "Black Jack" Linnell, and in November of 1934 we were posted to a brand-new, unfinished airfield at Mildenhall in the fen district of Suffolk. All of us were excited with this "promotion." Our discipline improved, and our flying became more professional. We played Rugby football against all the colleges at Cambridge, beating most of them because they only fielded their

1934—New Handley-Page HEYFORD heavy night bomber for remounting 99(B) Squadron is verified by local HART day bomber from same base at Upper Heyford, Oxon.

1934—In November, all HEYFORD bombers of 99(B) Squadron fly 100 miles east to their new, but only half-complete base at RAF Station, Mildenhall, Suffolk.

1934—99(B) Squadron HEYFORDS landing at their new base.

Extra A teams for us. We explored the countryside, tried out golf courses and pubs, and made lots of new friends. We excelled at everything.

The next year the British government put on a brave show of force, probably a shaking of the mailed fist for the benefit of the obnoxious German führer. A royal review of His Majesty's air force was to be held at our splendid new airfield on 6 July 1935. Almost every aircraft we possessed was set out in very precise review order before our king—some 350 from squadrons of all types all over the British Isles. A gallant-looking force maybe, but in truth, pitifully small. The king drove past every single aircraft, each in turn.

The armada took off squadron-by-squadron and flew in formation past the king, now under a bedecked and handsome pavilion at nearby Duxford airfield. I am not sure if the Nazis were suitably impressed. I know I was. I had been given the use of a couple of aircraftmen, a couple of flags on posts, a pail of

DRUIDS' CIRCLE

1935—Flg Off Willis makes a positive night landing in center white chalk ID ring marker of the field.

1935—New crew commander Flg Off Dean lands with full war load at night in rain. Exits field. Burst tire brings aircraft back through fence onto flare path—downwind.

whitewash, and a length of string in order to paint 350 straight lines in exactly the right places all over our vast, grassy airfield so each aircraft could toe the line properly for the ground parade. Our legs ached as we covered and re-covered those interminable miles of measuring and marking.

Young RAF officers had to serve at least three years before being allowed to marry. In 1935 I married Pat Lewis, my fiancé since 1931, in the lovely old church in Barton Mills near Mildenhall. In the same village we rented a small antique house known as the Lord Mayor's Cottage, with a long garden running down to the river Lark—a large stream really. Some of the huge, highly curved horizontal beams in the cottage were rumored to have come from an old Viking ship, and walking over the uneven floors, I swear one could still feel the motion of the high seas. I loved the story, but it didn't seem very likely; the Lark had barely enough water to float a canoe.

Photographic reconnaissance was part of our bombing training. Besides many pinpoints such as the Old Man of Cerne Abbas in Dorset, we took hundreds of mosaic overlaps of the countryside from high altitude. My curiosity was aroused, so I hied me over the photo section and dug out overlaps of our village. I could easily recognize the Lark. The old established stream still vented into the original river Ouse to the west as it had before Dutchmen came over, on contract, to drain the fens in 1691. Under Cornelius Vermuyden much valuable land was reclaimed, but the old rivers had shrunk almost to nothing. Photos of the Lark showed it had been much wider as indicated by the different shading of the crops in the alluvial soil on its banks. The Lark was obviously navigable for much of its length in the late 900s, before the land was reclaimed. Vikings could easily have sailed for miles inland to pillage. They must have left a longship in the silt of the Lark at Barton Mills; and some time after it was drained, the remains were found. Some of the ship's main curving walnut timbers now formed the long lateral beams in our half-timbered cottage.

DRUIDS' CIRCLE

THE KING'S MESSAGE TO

To: The Secretary of State for Air

I warmly congratulate all ranks of the Royal Air Force on the magnificent display which I have had the pleasure of seeing today.

I was greatly impressed both by their smartness on the ground and their efficiency in the air, which leave no doubt that

THE ROYAL AIR FORCE

they will prove fully equal to any task which they may be called upon to fulfill.

Please express to all ranks my appreciation of their labours in making the Review such an unqualified success, together with my best wishes for the future welfare of the Royal Air Force.

July 6, 1935. The Royal Review. Mildenhall.

©British Crown copyright/MOD. Reprinted by permission.

28 DRUIDS' CIRCLE

July 6, 1935. The Royal Review. Mildenhall.

©British Crown copyright/MOD. Reprinted by permission.

1935—Winning HEYFORD bomber crew. Flt Lt Parks (Pilot and Flg Off Dean (Bomb Aimer and Navigator).

1936—King Edward VIII inspects 99(B) and new 38(B) Squadrons at Mildenhall. Off Dean's aircraft is third from the right, code lettered U.

They were black with age, preserved in the quiet mud of the river to a hardness of steel. No nail could now be driven in on which to hang some woven motto, or perhaps a tankard.

A long garden had been cultivated by many loving hands over the years. Its rich asparagus beds went much to seed, so prolific was the growth. Apples and pears abounded. It was heaven, or to be more exact, Eden. We doffed a hat to Mr. Barton, a much earlier owner who later in life moved to London to become its lord mayor. He left a wonderful legacy.

Toward the end of that bucolic year I took a selection exam for a permanent commission and this set the seal on my wild ambitions for the future. Shortly after the German reoccupation of the Rhineland in July 1936, I was posted to be a Specialist Armament Officers School at Eastchurch, an old establishment on an island in the Thames estuary, originally in 1914 the HQ of the new Royal Naval Air Service. Like all gunnery and bombing camps, it was a remote, deserted spot—chosen for those very reasons. There we could fire off our guns and drop small bombs without hindrance from the mass of the great British public. I left for Eastchurch ahead of Pat to find a place to rent while she went into production of our first child. Soon after appeared Penelope Ann Dean to occupy her waiting cradle and bring great fun to our house.

There were only five chaps on the course—also open to officers of the Royal Air Forces of New Zealand, Australia and Canada as needed. We had one Canadian and one Australian. In the relaxed atmosphere of the arcane training session, we had time to think and talk about affairs abroad. We worried about the bullying noises coming out of Germany. If Hitler didn't lay off soon, we all agreed, it would be better to take him on right away, before his growing forces became too large and while we, with our air forces in preponderance, could still teach him a lesson.

We were excited and impressed by a visit to the secret Aeroplane and Armament Experimental Establishment at Martlesham Heath and saw for ourselves that the British gov-

32 **DRUIDS' CIRCLE**

1935—Prototype SPITFIRE No. K 5054 at Martlesham. With wooden, fixed-pitch airscrew.

1935—French Air Force DEWOITINE single-seat day fighter with single 20 mm cannon firing through prop boss. We bought the airplane to acquire the cannon.

1935—Prototype Vickers WELLINGTON medium twin-engined night bomber. Geodetic construction. Defensive gun turrets came later.

ernment and the Air Ministry were taking the German menace very seriously. During the classified visit, we were shown the prototype of the Spitfire fighter,[15] supposedly built to the same specs as the Hurricane. She was designed by Reginald Mitchell, chief designer of Supermarine. On 26 March 1936, this beautiful new thoroughbred flew for the first time at a top speed of 350 mph—truly great.

Like the Hurricane, the Spitfire came from a long line of very superior aircraft. Its recent forebear was the Supermarine S.6B which won the International Seaplane Schneider Trophy outright for Britain in 1931 and went on to raise the world air speed record to 406.99 mph, almost 50 mph faster than the record set by its immediate predecessor two years earlier. The Spitfire was smaller than the Hurricane, lighter, and with a less heavily loaded wing, more maneuverable. As we later found out, however, it was not as rugged or versatile as to the weapons it could carry, but she was more mettlesome by far.

Martlesham also had a French Air Force fighter, a Dewoitine, with an automatic Hispano-Suiza 20 mm cannon[16] firing through the propeller boss. We bought this quaint aircraft for the sole purpose of getting our hands on its huge cannon. If we liked it enough, we would try installing it in our own fighters. It had a long barrel with a commensurately high muzzle velocity, giving it a very long range.

Next came the prototype of the new Wellington heavy bomber,[17] tucked in a hangar away from prying eyes. The Wellington was a giant stride forward from the biplane Heyford bomber I'd flown with 99(B) Squadron a few months before.

I felt much happier to see we were getting ready for the worst and our new designs were far ahead of anything else we knew of. The Hurricane and Spitfire were outstanding, and their eight-gun armament was incredibly powerful. I'd been a bomber pilot for some years, and the new heavy bomber in particular pleased and comforted my black little heart.

GLOBAL UPDATE
January 1937–March 1938

There is still no indication that the Germans plan to build heavy bombers. The doctrine of the German air force stemming from World War I is to operate almost exclusively in support of the army with dive bombers (the Stuka[18] notably) to clear the way for the tanks and medium or light bombers to interdict traffic and communications within the battlefield.

Hitler promises in January there will be no more "surprises," as he put it, and the rest of 1937 seems peaceful. In truth, he is busy building and training his troops and blooding his new air force in the Condor Legion, supporting general Franco in the Spanish Civil War. At first the Germans fly obsolescent Heinkel He 51 biplane fighters and are chewed up by Russian Polikarpof I-15 and I-16 fighters supplied to the Republicans.

The new Me 109B is ready in time and is more than a match

for the Russians though the armament is inadequate. The Germans try to replace the machine gun in the prop boss with a 20 mm cannon[19] without success. The Me 109C, with more guns is also tried and though better than the earlier model still has only half the number of similar guns in the Spitfire.

After the armament course I was posted to North Coates, an air observers school in Lincolnshire's coastal fen area, just south of the large fishing port of Grimsby. It was like being banished to a desert—a damp, cold Siberian desert.

Pat and assistant Ann packed up our bungalow and I ordered road transport to follow with the household goods. They sent an airplane down to collect me to meet a new course just starting. After checking in with Wing Commander Huskinson, CO of the camp, and meeting my new students I made a few calls and went out to discover a place for us to live. As luck would have it, a local farmer was finishing work on an attractive stone cottage and agreed to rent it to us. It was perfect for the three of us and far enough from base to escape all but dire emergency calls; and there was room for some outdoor pets and farming experiments.

My job was to teach NCO candidates the gentle art of bomb aiming as the major part of qualifying them as air observers. They had a different teacher for classroom instruction in air gunnery. After passing the course, each sewed over his left breast pocket the coveted "Flying Arsehole"—a single wing supporting a large "O" for observer—a relic of the famous Royal Flying Corps and the glamorous days before 1918.

I also had my own "command." I was CO of the ranges which occupied some three miles of dismal, lonely coastline at a spot called Donna Nook five seagull-miles south of the main station. I was happy to have the use of a small Tiger Moth—the same as my first RAF trainer—to fly down to work in style. I called up the head honcho, Warrant Officer Rainsbury, and warned him I'd fly over that afternoon to inspect the place. "I'll have the range partly drawn up for you, sir, alongside the landing strip," he replied.

It was a little disconcerting, landing for the first time almost on top of my new charges. The WO called his thirty men to attention and marched across to where my aircraft was just wheezing its last breath after switch-off.

With a guardsman's salute, he offered, "Don't look too close at the buttons, sir. The sea air turns 'em dull in no time."

I was lucky to have such a fine ramrod veteran of World War I in charge. "Don't worry, Mr. Rainsbury," I told him, "I'll be looking for things a bit more important than that." He grinned back—we had a deal.

They were good troops. Smart and tidy, obviously not too bored with their isolation. Sid Rainsbury had soccer games organized, and there was a good library. The men were well-trained in the complicated business of recording bomb strikes and marking the gunnery targets. Very pleasing, and boding well for the whole purport of the ranges. After he had dismissed the men back to their huts, Sid asked if his mess could buy me a beer.

"You bet!" I said. That little conference sealed a lasting friendship and a good mutual confidence. Sid was a real pro and had his unit in excellent shape. He was also a good father to his men.

We strolled back to the Tiger Moth, and I hopped in while Sid pulled the prop through to start her up.

Back at North Coates I ran into Flight Lieutenant O'Hagan, a wild Irishman who'd been in 99(B) Squadron when I was there. It was good to be together again. "Haggis," as he was known, had lost an arm in an accident. He was on special duty and didn't do any more active flying. When I told him I was now chief bombing instructor and just back from an inspection of the ranges, he said he'd be glad to lend a hand, overseeing nighttime bombing practices, for instance. He went on to regale me with a story about the range in which he'd just been involved.

The bombing target was a large triangle on stilts out in the shallows just off shore. At night it was lighted by a string of lamps along the three sides. Bombing control signals were located half a mile away from the target by the control tower where spotting theodolites were housed. The signals comprised a broad, short arrow, about the same size as the target and pointing at it. The arrow was equipped with strings of lights on the arms. The signals for controlling the action comprised two balls—that could be illuminated—at the base of the arrow, one on each side. The mnemonic for the budding bombardiers to read the code was:

One ball alight: Wait! Not enough strength to play yet.
Both balls alight: Go ahead! You're strong enough now.
No balls at all: Go home! You're no use to anyone.

Haggis watched an aircraft approaching overhead, obviously on a bombing run, and saw the bright flash—"bombs gone"—signal from the aircraft much too early.

"He's bombing the signals by mistake!" he yelled to the two spotters, "Run! Run!"

"I've always been taught an officer leads his men," he told me. "I led those chaps by a hundred yards!"

"That's quite a yarn, Haggis," I said, and to myself added, and very Irish!

It was an interesting job. The NCO pupils were a keen bunch and if they passed they became air crew sergeants immediately; a great incentive and "...a consummation devoutly to be wish'd."

In my duties at North Coates, I had to handle any demolitions or bomb disposal jobs that just might turn up. Not long after taking over I was taken aback when one did rear its ugly head.

It was a Saturday afternoon. Jimmie Ashfold and I were in the middle of a hard game of squash when we were interrupted by the duty dog—orderly officer—bursting abruptly into the court.

"Sir, the Grimsby Coastguards are on the phone with something very urgent! Sorry to bother you, sir."

"That's okay." I wiped the sweat off my hands, wondering

what the hell the flap was all about. Obviously it wasn't anything about a war starting up. Not coming from the CGs.

"Jim," I said, "let's call it a day. Finish you off later." I went out and caught up the dangling phone.

"Flight Lieutenant Dean here."

"This is Coastguards in Grimsby. We've a lulu here and need your help in a hurry!" came an urgent voice. "A fishing boat's just come in, and they've trawled up a peculiar torpedo-like thing. We don't like the look of it at all! It might be from your place...one of your old live buggers, eh? Can you come over and do something?"

"Sure, we'll be right over. Sounds nasty. You'd better seal off the harbor. And don't let anyone near it or mess about with it!"

"Aye, aye, sir. Understood."

"Where's the boat?"

"She's the *Tetney Lass*, tied up at Pier 4. Thanks very much, sir. Much obliged."

This could be my first demolitions job. I really didn't like it a bit. "Oh, damnation!" I said, half aloud. "Hope I don't make a complete ballocks of it!"

I got hold of the duty armorer on the phone at the range. Luckily it was Sergeant Thwaites. Thank God, I thought, just the guy I need for this shenanigan.

I explained the problem. "And, Sergeant, round up at least six chaps. Get the best you can find, good strong lads. Tell them they don't have to come if they don't want to. Could be a mess. Call me back in fifteen."

"Very good, sir."

The phone jangled suddenly and made me jump.

"Yes!"

"Thwaites, sir. I can only find four people here. It's a weekend, and most are out on pass."

"Never mind, laddie; I'll rustle up a couple from main camp. Load your truck—ropes, hoisting tackle; and put in a thick mattress for this baby. Meet me at the main gate as soon as poss."

While I waited I pulled out the armament technical manual and swatted up demotion. Flaming hell! Why me? What have I done wrong? My ready promise of a couple of volunteers was not so easy to keep. The chaps I asked had one excuse or another for not coming. The office clerks were not strong enough; the aircraft fitters had wives who'd object; and so on. By the time Thwaites appeared I'd only been able to pick up one volunteer.

"We'll make do," I told him. "We haven't time to frig around. It's too late. Let's go!"

I took the wheel of the truck and set off cross-country to Grimsby harbor with the pedal down to the floorboard.

"If we find what I'm afraid of," I said to Thwaites, "we won't be able to make this speed going back." We drove straight to the docks and started to hunt for the *Tetney Lass*. The tide was right out, making the search more difficult. All that could be seen of the moored fishing vessels were masts or funnels sticking up above the quayside.

"Aw, come on! Where is this bugger?" came a voice from the back of the truck.

At last, almost at the end of the line, we found her hiding way down below. There was a hand swabbing the afterdeck in a desultory sort of fashion. I addressed myself to him:

"Is that the *Tetney Lass,* my man?"

"Aye, lad, it is an' all," he answered. "Does thee want owt?"

"Yes, I do. Are you the captain?"

"Nay, lad, ee's belaw." Peering down a hatch, he bellowed, "Aye, Tarm, theer's a yung lad yonder wants to see thee." After some delay, the captain, or so I deemed him—he was the only one in a peaked cap—appeared wiping his mouth with the back of his hand.

"What the heck does thee want?" he called up to me, rather ungraciously, I thought.

"I understand you've found an aerial torpedo, and we've

come to collect it."

"Nay, that's diff'runt." His manner had suddenly changed. "Get thee sel' darn 'ere, an' thee can 'ave it reet quick."

We negotiated the slippery iron rungs down the seaweed-covered pilings and shook hands. The skipper took us across the deck and there, lashed to the foot of the masts, was the thing. It was a rusty, barnacled cylinder about eighteen inches across, five feet long, and pointed at both ends. The skipper gave it a friendly kick and said, "Theer it is, lad. Browt us reet gran' luck, it did an' all."

I bent down to inspect it and felt a bit queasy.

"Ah dorn't suppause it's owt. It's full o' sarnd," opined the skipper, opening a large clasp knife. Before I could stop him, he had thrust the blade into the side of the object, into a small cavity from which the steel had long since crumbled away.

"For God's sake, don't do that, you bloody fool!" I yelled. "You could easily make a spark and finish us all off!"

The bits he had scraped out did look like sand, but the color was too light; it was too crystalline and translucent. I collected the scrapings onto a piece of paper and moved to the side of the boat. They all followed closely. Holding the paper out over the side, I got Thwaites to put a match to the edge of it. As the flame spread, the grains of "sand" crackled and melted and turned dark brown. Suddenly it flared up. I quickly let go, and the hissing mess fluttered down into the tide below.

"Amatol," I said firmly, looking across at the captain, "An RAF high explosive bomb filling."

The captain had put his knife away. No one seemed anxious to go near the thing anymore. I assured them as calmly as I could it was quite safe if we handled it gently. They were reluctant, but we slung plenty of ropes around it and ran them up to the block and tackles on the truck. It was a real pain in the neck, and it seemed to weigh a ton. As the strain came on the ropes, it slithered across the wet deck and fetched up in the scuppers with a dreadful thud. Ever one of us let out an audible gasp. Up and over the side of the trawler it rose, swinging free, higher and higher. With almost predictable perversity, it twisted round and round before fouling the underside of the dock. We got it over the edge and into the truck and laid to bed on the thick mattress.

"Sleep well!" muttered Thwaites, voicing our thoughts.

We crept slowly back over forty interminable miles to the ranges, red flags flying bravely fore and aft. We drove it into a gully in the sand dunes for the night.

We had to wait until an hour before the next afternoon's low tide so we could get well out over the shallow, barely shelving beach for the disposal—burial or cremation—whatever was the mot suitable term for our unwelcome task.

In the old bomb manuals I found one that resembled our object. It was almost certainly an obsolete six-hundred-pound, World War I light-case bomb. The stabilizing fins shown on the drawings were rusted away, and the smaller arming fins for the detonators were gone. It was impossible to tell whether the old bomb was safe or had been armed. It was certainly a live bomb—we'd seen the amatol filling. Until it was destroyed, it was a real bloody menace.

How did it come to be at the bottom of the sea off Spurn Head where the avaricious trawler netted it? I personally wished it were still there. We all did.

When I arrived at the ranges, Mr. Rainsbury had all the men lined up on the landing strip. I jumped out of the Tiger Moth and called for eight volunteers for the burial ceremony, except those who'd already been on the job. All thirty stepped forward, including yesterday's bunch—a bit embarrassing; but I had to tell Thwaites he was already picked. "Sorry," I added. For the other lucky seven, we drew lots. I was glad to see Corporal Foster got one. He was an old hand and a tower of strength. Pullen and Fawcett I knew well enough; good men, too.

We found a handcart strong enough to take the bomb and hauled and pushed our unpleasant load out across the wet sands until the dunes were half a mile behind. Although the sun was going down by now, it was hot work. This was far enough.

"Okay, chaps!" I shouted. "This'll do. Let's get going!"

We set to work to dig a hole to confine the explosion. Anyone who's made castles in wet sand knows how futile it is to try to dig a deep hole. In no time at all we had a fine, wide pool with about a foot of water in it.

There was nothing else we could do, so we rolled "Horace," as the boys had by now nicknamed the bomb, into the middle of the hole, where only the upper part of his fat belly showed above water. I laid a guncotton slab on the part that showed, packing it in place with wet sand. The last thing was to connect an electric detonator to the two wires of the cable we had brought and push it into the prepared socket in the guncotton.

We set off at a spanking pace back toward the shore, paying out the wires from the drum on the now splendidly agile handcart. The tide was turning. We reached the dunes and crowded into the concrete bombproof shelter through a short labyrinth tunnel into the small, musty room within. From here it would be safe to blow up Horrible Horace. There were horizontal slits at eye level to watch the fun.

I unlocked the exploder box and looked round to see that we were all inside. There they were; eight puffing, steaming figures crouched at the slits waiting for the bomb to poof. I connected the wires and pushed the plunger into the box with a firm, determined motion, just as the manual said.

"Go on, sir," said Foster, over his shoulder. "Give old 'Orace the works."

My heart sank; nothing had happened. I raised the plunger and shoved it in again—hard. Still nothing.

Thwaites read my thoughts. "No go, sir; lousy luck!" We all stood poised, not quite sure what to do next. I closed the exploder box and locked it, pocketing the key.

"You all stay inside while I go change the det," I ordered.

"Let me go, sir. I'm faster than you," pleaded Foster. But there was no time to argue, and it wasn't his job, anyway.

Blood pounded in my ears as I ran flatfooted across the damp sand. A seagull swooped past and out to sea, passing over our distant pool in a trice. I wished I could cover the rest of the way as easily and swiftly. As I reached the pool, an incoming wave splashed in. The water level had risen to an inch below the guncotton. The bright red end of the detonator gleamed at me like some baleful eye. I waded through the water and changed the det, even though the original one looked good to me. Stop fussing about the cost, you idiot. Dammit, it only cost a few pence to change, anyway. If the det was okay, then there might be a break in the wires somewhere—a nasty thought.

Time was nearly up. Horace must be blown up before the tide was in. We'd have a difficult job finding him at the next low tide, and there was no joy in the idea of digging him out.

I picked up the twin cable and let it run through my hand, inspecting every foot of it on the way to the dunes. It was a back-breaking job, and the friction of the sand made my palm very raw. The salt water began to sting. I was in something of a panic, coming near to the high water mark, when suddenly something sharp ran into my finger; and there it was—a broken wire!

I tied my handkerchief to mark the break and stumbled on toward the shelter, shouting for the exploder box. Pullen came running out with it. I explained that I had to blow the bomb at the break in the cable. There was no time left to test the rest of it.

I sent those who'd crowded out back into the shelter, lugged the box out to the break, and quickly connected the broken ends. I rammed down the plunger again, and for a moment nothing seemed to happen. My glance rose toward the sea, and I saw a huge, blackish brown column, twenty-feet across, rising and expanding from the spot where Horace had been laid to rest. I watched, fascinated. There came a quick, gently puff of air that moved my hair backward and then forward, followed by a whoomph that made my ears sing as the blast wave rocked me on my heels. It must have been the blast wave that brought me to my senses. I threw myself flat on my face.

"Too late, you stupid bloody fool!" I recoiled at the fury in my own voice. Ages later it seemed, I raised my head to see the column of sand, mud, and water start to fall back into the flooding tide. There was a quick hiss nearby, followed by another, and something landed quite close to me. It was a small piece of tortured steel, blue at the torn edges, and still warm as I picked it up.

It was all over. The damned job was done.

Thank goodness I'd not been hit, but I'd been careless, a tad panicky, and very lucky. We found out later that it was all that was left of a Royal Navy aircraft lost at sea while on live bombing exercises years before from North Coates.

Two

GLOBAL UPDATE
March 1938–March 1939

"To talk peace and prepare secretly for war" is the incisive observation William L. Shirer makes of Hitler's winning tactic. The führer has the cunning of a Teutonic wild boar, he is the ultimate con man. Between each successful deceit he bends to stoke the furnace of his burgeoning military industry as tanks and aircraft of the latest design pour off production lines. He wins more than a river bank in taking back the Rhineland—we are the first to drop our eyes, an important preconditioning for the future. After fomenting riot and disturbance in Austria for over a year, Hitler summons Dr. Kurt von Schuschnigg, the courtly chancellor, to his private psychological torture chamber on the Obersalzberg and forces him to turn over the Austrian government to the Nazis. We and the French back off once more.

Between courses early in 1938 I had a chance for a spot of leave. My younger brother, Pip, had recently skied in the Austrian Alps and was so wildly enthusiastic Pat and I decided we must see his mountains too. We planned to take the car over, drive down through France and Germany, and on into Austria. We would park baby Ann with my parents at Risborough while we were gone.

In Austria a few days earlier Hitler had seized total power. They were about to hold a plebiscite to approve the *Anschluss,* or political union, of the two countries to give some faint air of legality to an obvious aggression. Naturally, the election would be carefully controlled; and none would dare say nay.

Moolenaar, my father's ad agent, was visiting at the time. Hearing where we were planning to go, he tempted us with a harebrained scheme that could have landed us in a nasty Nazi dungeon if by some mischance my normal good luck had been asleep at the switch. He wanted us to go on to Vienna, just annexed and occupied by the Huns, to pick up a "small parcel" for a good friend of his who had escaped to England with only his shirt a few days before.

"You'll be doing me more than just a favor," he told us, "You will be saving a fortune for my very dear friend who at the moment is absolutely penniless. Besides, we'll pay for your whole trip."

Moolenaar went on to detail the scenario for his fell plot. On arrival in Vienna, he told me first to book in at the Mariahilfe Hotel. I was then to call a certain telephone number on an outside line for further instructions. Wow! My pulse already pounded in my throat before I'd even left England.

"Are you sure it's wise to be going there just now, dear?"

Mother cautioned. "Do be careful, won't you?"

But it was a hopeless plea. Like some addicted idiot, I couldn't pass up such an obvious temptation and agreed to take a stab at liberating the loot.

When we arrived at the old Austrian frontier, the customs guardhouse was deserted, and we drove straight through. There was a real mess on the roads because the unwelcome conquerors were still busy changing the signs for driving on the right. The Austrians had been driving on the left, which I thought was the proper side, anyway, as in the U.K.

We got to Vienna and soon found the hotel. The streets were choc-a-bloc with German military motorcycles with clumsy sidecars roaring up and down, much to no purpose it seemed, except to exhibit their flags, suitably colored blood red. They drove too fast, carelessly indifferent. Jackbooted, steel-helmeted thugs. *Kultur* had come to lovely Vienna. It was more real and frightening than all the secondhand news I'd been listening to for months out in the Lincolnshire fens. It brought home the truth with sickening conviction. It was awful.

I made a sortie to a public phone outside the hotel to call Moolenaar's people. A voice answered first in German, then switched to broken English, giving me an address to come to in an hour's time.

I walked a bit and then took a taxi, getting out a block away from the apartment, going the final distance again on foot. What a fool thing to be doing, I remember thinking. Trying to emulate some cheap, sinister novel? And I wasn't even in a trench coat.

I took the heavy wrought-iron lift to the fourth floor, feeling very vulnerable in the open cage. I knocked on the door of the apartment. The doorknob turned very slowly, and a solitary, unfriendly eye examined me through the crack. I was let in and the door closed and locked. It was a dark, musty flat with heavy velvet curtains drawn against the noonday light—and the curious. A small gathering of frightened gentlemen greeted me warmly, but they were very ill at ease.

I accepted the oilskin-wrapped package, some twelve-by-four inches wide and an inch thick, heavily sealed. No offer of coffee—in Vienna of all places. Their eyes just wanted me gone. *Gruss Gott* they wished me with fervor.

I hid the package behind the windshield wiper mechanism of our little car, and we set off for the German border. Our route took us along a passage of great beauty through the Austrian Alps. We climbed the Gross Glockner to a height of over ten thousand feet; but even here the driving snow could not blot out the shame of the recent invasion, the forced union of this little country with its now resurgent, predatory neighbor. Indeed an infamous *Anschluss*. Only in the transparent quiet of the mountainous countryside was the spirit of these warm, southern people still patently alive. Simple roadside shrines bore witness to their enduring faith.

At the border I'd almost forgotten about my unwelcome piece of baggage, but I need not have worried. Seeing the Royal Air Force rank on my passport, the guards were at some pains to show due deference to the British Luftwaffe. Never was such a lowly flight lieutenant saluted so smartly.

Safely back in England, I handed my conniving friend the red-hot bundle. "This'll pay for your whole trip," he remarked with a fleeting smile. "Remember?"

"What's in the bloody thing?" I demanded, dying of curiosity.

"I really don't know," he temporized, "but it's worth a lot of dough, and my friend will be forever grateful. Think of it as loot you 'liberated' from under the noses of the most recent Vandals in Austria." The package, it turned out, contained most of the escapee's fortune; but whether in precious negotiable paper or jewels I never learned. It was too light for gold.

I didn't care if my small blow for democracy remained unsung forever; the huge satisfaction of delivering the blow, itself, was enough. At any rate we were certainly relieved to have it over with.

Sickened profoundly by witnessing the aftermath of the wicked rape of Austria, I plugged on at the North Coates school more determined than ever to turn out the best and the most accurate bomb aimers possible. We needed them ready for action in the strategic bombing role we believed to be the basic mission of the RAF in the battle we sensed ahead.

The news we heard out in the sticks by the lonely North Sea was limited mostly to columns in the press. No government source at that time told us anything of import. We learned only bits and pieces about the pace of our own rearmament or of any new developments in the air. I survived mostly on the new information I'd been privileged to glean at Martlesham in late 1936—a real breath of fresh air and an inspiration.

We had staff pilots to fly the Westland-built Wallace light bombers to train air NCO students, but I insisted on flying many of the bombing missions myself. I haunted the flight line and often ousted the staff pilots from their cockpits without warn-

1938—Westland WALLACE light day bomber used for bombing gunnery training. North Coates Observers School.

ing. I wanted to keep tabs on how well my pupils were learning to be good—nay superior—bomb aimers. It was also an advantage for them to have a pair of sympathetic hands at the aircraft controls. After all, I'd done my stint in heavy bombers and having gone through the learning hoops myself, I knew where and how they were likely to stumble. Ordering me to fly the bomber on the track they needed to hit the target, having me make course corrections at their beck and call made them realize who really was in charge during the vital bombing run. It put me on my mettle, too. I shared their good results with blatant pride.

GLOBAL UPDATE
October 1938

> We read ad nauseam about Neville Chamberlain's return flight on 1 October 1938 from the Munich capitulation. There are pictures of him standing by his airplane, smugly waving a copy of the infamous paper that condemns gallant Czechoslovakia to death. Western cynics aver valuable time has been bought by the Allies against the impending war, but Germany gains much more from the extra time bought in Czech blood.

My own immediate fate was a much happier one. A good friend at court, Wing Commander Bill Wynter-Morgan, telephoned. "How would you like to go to Martlesham and do experimental gunnery?" I couldn't believe my ears. What a priceless posting! What a pal. "We'll get you out of those marshes by the New Year. Take some leave in December."

Pat and I once more packed up our home, this time the stone farmhouse we'd been renting. We would miss the perks of fresh milk and eggs, some of which came from a couple of raucous geese, and the rows of our homegrown veggies. We lived well but always knew our house was built on sand. We were forever on campaign even in peacetime; Pat and now Ann were but camp followers. The move was easier than the last one from

Eastchurch. With some leave in between, we were able to go down together and rent a small place perched on a rise just behind the airfield.

I reported to RAF Martlesham Heath on 10 January 1939 to be aide to Squadron Leader Dru Drury, the experimental gunnery officer, or EGO as he was known. I'd met Dru three years ago at Eastchurch when he was taking the advanced armament course under Professor Black, the great mathematician. I remembered Dru well for his outstanding intelligence and ability. He was tallish, lean, and dark—and a nervous fellow. Quick to smile but with little patience for the overly slow-of-wit.

It was with some trepidation I reported to his office built under the wall of A Flight hangar, a nostalgic old World War I building. I pushed open the door, and there he sat, writing carefully in a neat file, recording what he had just done during an experimental flight. He was copying from notes made on a dirty piece of white cardboard.

"Hello," he said, "You're Dean, I suppose. About time you got here. I've been waiting too long for some help. Come on, let's get going!"

And this set the tone of our association. I found Dru to be a most meticulous observer. He taught me well, but rarely told me twice. If I forgot a detail or was unclear what he had in mind I think I was at first too scared to ask—ashamed to feel so dumb. It was a tough boot camp; but like such trials, after a healing time, one tends to view the ordeal with some degree of affection. Indeed, I think of Dru as one of the most brilliant officers I have served under and a pilot with great panache.

After lunch that first day we flew a Hawker Hart[1] over to Orfordness on the coast, ten miles or so to the east. We landed on a grass field, hard by the gunnery and bombing ranges. Terns rose from the marshes as we swooped down on this wild, forlorn spot. A raw breeze keening in from the sea made us pull up our greatcoat collars and face away.

Dru showed me a scaffolding for supporting large sheets of

1939—Hawker HART light day bombers. Formation training.

plywood we would use as targets in our gun trials. The sheets were large enough to catch all the bullets fired from our new gun installations and show us the overall size of the group of shots. He referred to these records as "jump-cards"—a nice name.

When a machine gun is fired, all the bullets do not hit the same place. The kick of the gun, the vibration, the movement of the mounting, all cause the shots to wander from the original aiming point. Before being fitted into an aircraft, a new type of gun was test fired from a rigid mounting. The pattern in the plywood showed the inherent "spread" of the shots. With that gun in an aircraft later on, we measured the overall spread again and noted the difference; if it was too large, we had to stiffen the mounting. Testing a new gun installation followed a regular sequence: ground firing to make sure the wings didn't fall off and the feed system from the ammo boxes worked properly; then air firing progressively in level flight—one gun in each wing, then two and so on until all guns were fired in salvo.

Back at Martlesham, we taxied to the tarmac and climbed out. "Have you ever flown a Hart?" Dru asked me.

"No, sir," I replied.

"Well, now's your chance!"

After I'd settled into the aircraft, this time in the front cockpit, Dru leaned in and showed me the "taps." And that was it.

"Off you go!" was all he said.

The Hart, a light day bomber, was a joy to fly as are all Hawker aircraft. She was heavier than the Hawker Fury fighter I enjoyed for air gunnery at the air armament school but had the same docile, sure response.

The new Hawker Hurricane[2] fighter I'd heard about had already been passed by Dru, and squadrons were being remounted—five by September 1938. By this time the original Browning machine gun had been thoroughly anglicized, more than three years after being received from the U.S. and installed in the first Hurricane prototype. It had been modified for British ammunition and redesigned for the breech to remain open between bursts.[3] But it was still the same basic, magnificent Browning: twice the rate of fire of the old Vickers, a higher muzzle velocity, and infinitely more reliable.

Another Hurricane came in for test. When I flew this frightening airplane for the first time, I found its acceleration startling and the ground run minimal. The most worrisome piece of juggling needed with that early model came in raising the undercart after takeoff. It was my first time ever to operate a retractable gear. The apparatus to lift and lower both the under carriage and the flaps was located in the bottom starboard corner of the cockpit, only just within reach. The throttle was about elbow level on the port wall and required the full attention of the pilot's left hand. The control column—or joystick, as the RFC would insist—was firmly in the right hand for takeoff. Raising the undercart as soon as possible after clearing the ground called for a neat switch of hands that in my case produced some hairy in-flight bucking. The next problem came when it was time to tame the beast for landing. With the undercart up, the wild thing put on speed at an alarming rate that was then difficult to lose. Only by judiciously reducing the power, dropping the wheels, and furtively tapping in a little flap as we skimmed the boundary hedge did I win her consent to land within the airfield confines.

I enjoyed my next Hurricane flight much more for two main reasons. I no longer feared the great gladiator, and this time I had the extra thrill of firing all the ammo from all the guns in salvo as one of the final tests of the Martin-Baker ammo boxes,[4] newly designed to increase the number of rounds per gun. Having settled our differences, the Hurricane and I became more than good friends. We were bosom buddies for several years because no other modern fighter with its speed had the strength and space to mount all the brutal flight-trial armament we eventually loaded into this wonderful workhorse.

Dru leaned round the door of our office. "Dix, there's a box of a new kind of ammo for the Brownings just come in for trial. It's called De Wilde and is top secret.[5] The bullets are filled with high explosive," he explained. "Mix it in with the belts for your air test this afternoon and fire against the fuselage target on the ground at Orford. Get movies of the strikes as well. It's very urgent!"

The results were excellent. The secret bullets burst on impact with healthy flashes that were clearly visible from the air during the attack and of great assistance for aiming. They blew nasty holes in the target's thin aluminum sheeting. The bullets were much more effective than the standard lead-filled ammo; but still the caliber was too small for the heavier aircraft structures and the armor plate we knew were bound to come.

GLOBAL UPDATE
March–July 1939

President Emil Hasha of Czechoslovakia surrenders the remainder of his country to Germany on 14 March. The next day Hitler's armies pour into Moravia and Bohemia culminating in the triumphant march through Prague previously denied him by the temporizing Munich pact five months before. Chamberlain suddenly awakens and announces British and French guarantees for Poland if attacked. Hitler's manic response is a most secret directive, "Case White," for an invasion of Poland any time after the first of September. The die is cast. One month later Mussolini moves his forces into Albania. England and France guarantee Rumania and Greece. Italy declares an alliance with Germany and the Pact of Steel is forged (of low-grade alloy, as it turns out).

We had been considering a special test ever since the unprecedented eight-gun armament had been accepted and put into production in the Hurricane and Spitfire; it was to be a tactical rather than a functional trial.

The new eight-gun fighters came with a unique problem in gun alignment. The guns lay in the wings from twelve to twenty feet apart in the Spit and from ten to thirteen feet in the Hurricane. Concentration of fire is axiomatic to fighter success. This infers all guns must be toed-in on one spot at a chosen range. Some pilots are born aces, with instinctive judgment. Others become top scorers because they learn to hold their fire until the target fills the windshield and they have all their guns aligned on a spot at very short range. This is not suitable, however, for the raw pilots who in their twitchy anxiety start firing four or five hundred yards out—much too far away. In traversing that excessive range the bullets—which are toed-in by gun alignment to be concentrated on a spot at much less than half that range—will have crossed over and opened up again to a wasteful scatter. We had to be ready for the fighter war to start with very few natural aces available.

Our whiz kids suggested a gun alignment that was bound to shock any ace,[6] but we were asked to test it in the air. Only the two inner gun barrels were aimed point blank. All the others were deliberately offset from the center mark by a third of a degree, spread evenly around in a circle—a "fuzzy focusing" of the guns at best. Theoretically, such dispersion would give a better bullet density for a wide variety of combat conditions, including faulty range estimation, and give the new pilot a "better chance of not missing" altogether. Now we had to check it out for real.

"I'll take the Hurricane over to Orford after lunch," Dru told me. "You get cracking now with Tomlins and the ground crew and get the plywood boards up on the target's framework. Warn the Coastguards to close the firing range for the afternoon. Get hold of Mr. Williams in the photo section and tell him we'll want a shot of our thirty-foot-square target after firing. Oh! And get him to come over under his own steam at about 1630 hours." That's how my morning started.

Tomlins, our armorer, collected the ammunition we would need, spare gun parts, and tools while the crew loaded trestles, ropes, and pickets into the lorry. As we took off for the range, I started to worry about what I might have left behind. I need not have fussed. The boys had done it all before and knew exactly what we needed.

Just before the creek that divides the mainland from the long Orford peninsula, there was a low, ramshackle building—a hut really—on the right-hand side. Dru mentioned that I should pull in there on the way to the range, so I was looking out for it.

"Stop here!" I said to Tomlins, who was driving. "We have some important business to do." Of course they knew what was up.

We went inside, and there was no doubt at all that Dru had been right! The fresh oysters that were fished out for us from the seawater tank below the floor were absolutely delicious. I managed a couple of dozen and coveted more.

"Come on, chaps! Let's get cracking," I said, as I paid the very reasonable tab, "We can't spend all day here."

While Tomlins erected the plywood target and pasted a black ten-foot aiming cross in the middle, the crew set a tail trestle at the one hundred yards combat range over toward the mainland and drove screw pickets in all round it. The sound of Dru's engine reached us just before he flashed into sight, low over our heads, to swing up and around and drop gently into the field. He taxied up to the trestle and hopped out.

"Good show! Great!" was all he said, but it was enough to put us all in a good mood.

The Hurricane was already operating with half a dozen front-line squadrons, and we had to have practical proof of the effectiveness of the special gun alignment proposed by the boffins before making any recommendations to the field. We had to confirm the gun pattern by firing all of them together, first on the ground and then in the air.

The crew hoisted the tail of the fighter, and we all helped to shove it back over the trestle. With the tail high in the air, it was now positioned in flying attitude, pointed toward the sea, right on target. I climbed into the cockpit and shouted down to the chaps below to shift the aircraft up, down, or sideways to bring the gunsight—aligned parallel to the line of flight at full speed—to bear on the middle of the black cross. We made no allowance for gravity drop: it would be less than one foot anyway and in the air might be in any direction. The aircraft was now made fast to the pickets, and one of the armorers scrambled up and opened the gun bays in the tops of the wings to load the ammo.

Tomlins hung a drawing of the boffins mathematic diagram over the center of our aiming cross on the target and then came back to line up each of the eight guns on the appropriate mark on the diagram. He used a unique tool to do this; it was a telescope small enough to slip into the breech of the gun. It had a little right-angled mirror so that he could accurately view what the barrel had its eye on.

We simultaneously fired a burst of twenty rounds from all

eight guns. The tips of the bullets in each gun had been dipped in a different colored paint and allowed almost to dry. They applied their own color coding as they passed through the target.

Dru had an inspired way to record the results for our official report. He collected a number of the cardboard discs used to seal milk bottle tops and spray-painted them black. Then I, otherwise known as "tail-end Charlie" in this operation, had the tedious job of sticking one disc over each bullet hole and noting next to it the color of the bullet that made it. Confound Dru's bright idea: there were a hundred and sixty of those damn-blasted little bits of card to wet with glue and position accurately—and all from the top of a high, wobbly ladder in a nasty, sea-laced wind. I began to dislike heights; but now, at least, Williams could record the whole target on film and show up the strikes for an avid posterity to ponder.

Back in our office and armed with a fine photo enlargement, I colored each individual bullet position with its own code. We could now see that the overall pattern was ideal and that the colored groups were in their right places. Just what the doctor ordered; we were elated. Would the pattern hold for firing in the air under combat conditions when the wings are under stress and perhaps deflected? We had to stretch our minds again to devise a way to find out.[7]

Eventually someone suggested a target hung from a free-flying balloon for the air test. I called Farnborough—the Royal Aircraft Establishment, or RAE—a civilian unit formed for basic research in aeronautics early in World War I. I knew there used to be a balloon section there and hoped it still existed. By good fortune the British scientist never throws anything away. It was still in existence and very much alive. They designed for us a lovely fifty-foot-square target with a black cross in the middle to aim at. It was to hang from a balloon equipped with a time fuse to let the gas out after the attack, returning it to earth with our results.

The RAE people came over and tested the apparatus prior to

the occasion: it worked faultlessly. The next day was beautifully warm and sunny. We laid the huge balloon canopy out across the airfield and pulled the target into place below the neck of the balloon. As hydrogen hissed out of the massed array of cylinders in the trailer, the canopy slowly inflated into a heaving, obscene mound. At last, like the Ugly Duckling, it rounded out into a silvery, glistening sphere; a thing of beauty, alive and anxious to go.

Dru was ready in the Hurricane, armed as before with colored bullets, twenty per gun. We let the fidgety, impatient balloon go and up it went. The offshore breeze quickly took it into the gunnery danger area over the sea to the east of Orfordness. Dru lined up the Hurricane and in a straight, steady attack pressed the tit just outside one hundred yards. All of the bullets were gone in under a second and he broke away.

A cinecamera mounted in the fighter recorded the precise wander of Dru's aim during the one-second firing run. Everything

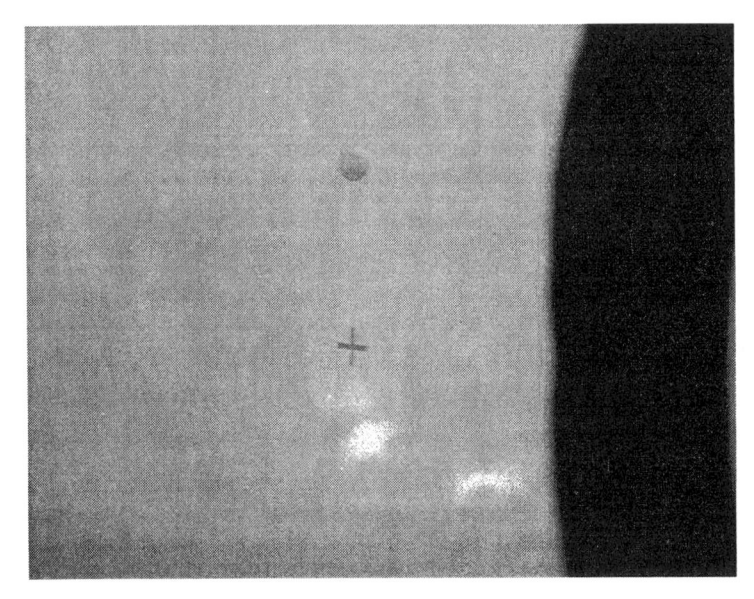

1939—Air target hung from free balloon for test firing new eight-gun fighter gun harmonization pattern.

1939—Blackburn ROC Naval two-seat day fighter. Ground test firing salvo from four .303-caliber gun turret.

1939—Marking bullet holes on "jump card" from ground firing tests of ROC four-gun turret at 200 yards. Orfordness gunnery ranges, Suffolk.

went off well. Dru flew around, waiting for the fuse to blow and return our baby to earth. But no! The balloon continued climbing slowly in a very determined way, moving out over the North Sea toward Germany. We certainly didn't want this vital bit of operational information to get into the hands of our probable but as-yet-undeclared enemy. Dru frantically returned to base.

"Get up there, Dixi," he yelled, "and shoot that damn thing down!"

The only airplane with guns already armed up was a Blackburn Roc,[8] undergoing trials of its four-gun turret. It was a naval single-engined fighter with an electric, power-operated turret behind the pilot. I manned the turret, loaded the four guns, gave the pilot a thumbs-up, and off we went.

The recalcitrant balloon sneaking away with our precious record was well out to sea when we caught up with it. Dru had by now alerted the air-sea rescue launch, and we could see it creaming out below us with the proverbial bone in its teeth. We made a slow run, passing close to the top of the big fat paunch of the balloon to test our tactics.

On the second pass I gave a long squirt from the turret guns into the top of the bulge. We came round again to see small flickers of fire, and suddenly the whole thing erupted into a flaming torch. As it fell rapidly toward the boat below, I wondered if there'd be any evidence worth retrieving. We'd have to do the whole blasted thing all over again. Luckily, when we got the target ashore and spread it out on the hangar floor, it was only partly burnt. We had a splendid jump-card from the sky.

From the cinecamera film record of the aim wander while firing we canceled out the wander of the bullet groups during the short burst. We compared the air results directly with those we got on the ground. They were virtually the same, proving that stresses of flight on the Hurricane did not affect the alignment of the gun battery. We could reproduce the boffins' magic harmonization in the air. Fighter Command was advised of the results, and all guns on the new eight-gun fighter were initially aligned to the pattern that gave the "best chance of not missing."

As the Battle of Britain hit its stride a whole year later, the new aces soon abandoned the slightly spread gun pattern and concentrated their guns on the same spot at very close range, with much more success in combat. Eventually they all did the same thing. However, I feel sure the calculated optimum slightly open alignment did improve the chances of success for some of the new, barely trained young pilots who at first needed all the gimmicks they could get just to stay alive. When they learned to press in close before firing and could hold a steady aim under the great pressure of combat, the need for this particular crutch was gone for them, too.

The early months of 1939 were crammed with diverse problems. War with Germany seemed well-nigh certain, but we were woefully unready. With so many equipment problems still

1939—Some of "A" Flight fighter aircraft on tarmac. Martlesham Heath, Suffolk.
| Fury | Demon | Fantome | Tiger Moth |
| K2082 | K3764 | L7045 | K4281 |

unresolved, we felt we lived on borrowed time and were thankful for any breathing spell. Beside the crying need to prove the fighter gun installations, gun turrets were just being fitted to heavy bombers; these presented brand new problems all of their own. In particular, some basic research was still needed for accurate firing of turret guns on the beam.

French Air Force scientists had already predicted the probable magnitude and direction of the deflection of a spinning bullet when fired at right angles to the airstream of a fast aircraft. They named it the "Cazeau effect" after the research establishment doing the work. Such an effect, if large enough and not allowed for, would seriously reduce accuracy of sighting turret guns firing anywhere off the direct line of flight. By April we had a Blenheim bomber equipped to do the crucial tests, and a special research team was formed to conduct it.[9] It took many flights, some even in the flat calm of night,[10] to get the final results. When they were examined, sure enough, there was the theoretical Cazeau effect. Bullets fired downward across the airstream of the bomber were noticeably deflected. We could now allow for it accurately in our turret gunsights.

Temperature patrol was a duty we looked forward to. Each day when flight tests were being made, the aircraft performance section needed a record of air temperatures at all levels up to thirty-two thousand feet to standardize performance figures. We were only too happy to provide a pilot as often as possible for this pleasant task.

Two veteran single-seat fighters were earmarked for making the routine flights, and both old warriors were still capable of giving the rider a good canter. The very nature of the exercises—not tasks by any means—meant that temperature readings weren't needed when the weather was foul. The jaunts were always made when the weather wore a smile and the jocund sky beckoned with a siren's song.

One of our vintage aircraft was a Gloster Gladiator bi-

64 DRUIDS' CIRCLE

1939—Gloster GAUNTLET single-seat day fighter. Precursor of the GLADIATOR fighter.

1939—Gloster GLADIATOR/K7064 single-seat fighter. Recorded air temperatures up to 32,000 feet in the climb. Also flight of ROC two-seat, four-gun turretted fighters.

plane[11]—powerful, with huge muscle from a Bristol Mercury air-cooled engine. Capacious behind the great mass of that unit, the cabin was comfortable and warm. She was a very gallant steeplechaser rising with gently ease to clear each hedge of cotton cloud. A rapid-climbing classic, she almost did the job on her own. A Belgian-built Fairey Fantôme was the other fighter earmarked for the job.[12] More of a tigress was she, powered by an Hispano-Suiza engine as sweet-running as a jeweled watch.

I soon got my name on the list to fly these outings. Before long our phone rang. "Your turn for the Fantôme," said Hetty Hyde, CO of the armament fighters. "Now watch her like a hawk when you come in to land. You'll never believe how she floats across the ground."

What a sweetheart that plane was to fly. Even with the archaic open cockpit, she was breathlessly quiet. The controls were sensitive and sure, and I relished every moment of the climb that was over all too soon. After taking the air temperatures at every thousand-foot level on the way up, I eased back on the power at the peak of the climb and leveled out. It still needed a good fistful of throttle to maintain altitude and float along the attenuated air. It was quieter now and reality, itself, seemed to be strung out, less than real. Up there the Fantôme became more wraithlike, flying with less sureness and not as much of the quiet authority of her performance at lower levels. I talked to her with encouragement and felt a gentle nudging from the control column; not in response to the long, barely felt, waves of turbulence but from the plane itself, I swear. A jungle cat patty-pawing me, kittenish for attention. I thought hard in order to yank reality back to this unreal dream world. Words I'd just spoken were gone forever, and the furtive action of my wild cat had passed. Only thought and the memory of it were real. A vivid picture filled my mind, fresh and immediate. As in a movie flashback, I remembered how an old college friend and I, while quaffing a tankard of Colne Spring Special ale in our local pub, had penned our exchange of transient thought on a beer coaster:

Speech is but frill and action furbelow,
Yet doth man judge his fellow man by these.
Thought, only, unexpressed, is nude reality.

"Otis, you old bastard, our point was just made," I said. Though ten years had passed, what we expressed that evening was as stark as when we put it down. Only thought is raw reality.

"Come on, pussycat, let's go down," I told her. I nosed around and dipped into the long slalom to the field, taking the air's temperature again at every thousand feet. Good doctors, we.

We approached the landing area, coming in low over the fence. Mindful of Hetty's warning, I held her off the ground, the wheels brushing the tops of the longer grasses—and held off, and held off; but the apparition refused to sit down. Simply refused. I'd never come across such a reluctant critter.

We floated over the airfield like the ghost she was named for until I decided I had to go round again and try once more. "You stubborn Belge," I thought out loud. "We can't stay up here all day, damn and blast ye." This time twenty knots slower, close to her stalling speed, I finally won out and got her down; but it still needed half the field to complete a three-pointer.

GLOBAL UPDATE
August–September 1939

On 11 August the Western powers send a mission to Moscow by invitation of the Soviet Union to resolve how the rampant forces of Germany were to be met, but it is too late. Germany outbids us in the public market we evidently are in, and signs a non-aggression pact with the petitioning Soviets on 19 August. Russia will remain neutral in any German-Polish conflict. Britain declines to be bribed at the last moment by an Aryan brotherly offer of no future threat to the British Empire if she abstains from any response to an attack on Poland: her prompt reaction is to convert her unilateral guarantee to Poland into a formal Anglo-Polish treaty of mutual assistance. Mussolini withdraws from any military participation with Germany, complaining he had made it clear he could not be ready until 1942.

When the RAF rearmed against the Nazi menace, radical redesign had to be made. It was easier to define the armament for a new fighter: though its primary role was defensive, to counter enemy offensive air attack, its arms were offensive, the more powerful and immediate the better. It was a bold, Elizabethan move in 1935 to call for eight guns for the radical fighters needed and only made possible by the ultrareliable U.S. Browning machine gun. It was an heroic gesture.

The design of a new strategic bomber was more difficult. There had never been gladiatorial contest between heavy bombers and defensive fighters to guide the limits or needs for bomber self-defense. Some said none was needed and the bomber should rely on speed and altitude to render the fighter impotent. Geoffrey de Havilland championed this view, but his was a lone voice; we had to wait for his private venture, the Mosquito unarmed bomber, to prove his prescience. No clear direction came from experience or intrepid lead from the ministry. Thus by timidity, defensive weaponry became the imposed choice for the new bombers. Aircraft makers designed their own gun emplacements, at first open to the breezes and then enclosed, though still hand-held. Power-operated gun turrets followed, some electric and others hydraulic, and were now in most of the latest aircraft. The ministry wanted to standardize, and we were all involved to this end.

The prototype of the Vickers Wellington bomber we saw at our secret test base in 1935 was first of the new breed of "heavies." It was built around a fascinating concept, the brainchild of Barnes Wallis, a brilliant inventor and practical engineer.[13] His experience with airships in the 1930s had led him to conceive the "geodetic" construction of the Wellington. The whole fuselage of the airplane was made up of two enormous aluminum "springs," one going around one way and the second wrapped in the opposite direction; where the springs crossed, they were riveted together. The finished structure then looked like a continuous giant lattice or basketwork, which was then covered with heavily painted linen fabric. This innovative design was capable of taking massive damage from enemy gunfire without collapsing and could readily be repaired.

Tests of advance power-operated turrets in the Wellington were well under way when I joined Dru.[14] The turrets were designed and built by Captain Archie Frazer-Nash, famous for his very successful chain-driven racing cars. Archie had survived a stellar career in the Royal Flying Corps in World War I. His turrets were driven by oil motors and were easy to operate and maintain. On the other hand, the electrical turret in the Roc, the Fleet Air Arm fighter that I had used to engage our willful balloon target, was much more difficult to look after. As Archie confided to me, quite unbiased or course, "You can see a damn leak in an oil system. It's much harder to see an electric leak!" We first checked the turrets on the ground for correct functioning of the guns and the ammo feeds, and to make sure the fire interrupters worked properly when the guns were pointing at some part of the aircraft such as the tail or the wings. "Silly to shoot yourself in the foot, so to speak," said Archie, watching the tests. We were then constantly in the air, rotating the turrets at all air speeds, checking the rates of movement. The speed of rotation and rate of elevation of the guns were determined by moving control handles shaped like little bicycle handlebars. The guns were fired in all positions. We checked that the belts of ammo continued to feed in freely when the bomber was thrown around in simulated evasion tactics and that the empty cartridge cases and belt links were all thrown clear.

Heating for the gun installations was very important. Guns won't fire if they are iced up; and that goes for the frigid gunners, too. It was a real problem to get enough heat back to the turret in the tail, the most isolated and far removed gun battery—where only the strongest stomach can survive the roughness of the turbulence, the frantic evasive maneuvers of the pilot, and the Arctic temperatures at altitude. That's where the term "tail-end Charlie" really comes from—applied with some teasing and not enough sympathy.

The other heavy bomber being refitted with gun turrets was the Whitley, made by Armstrong Whitworth.[15] 99(B) Squadron was the first to get this airplane which replaced the long-in-tooth Heyford. The Whitley's original defense was pitiful: one single gun in the nose and a two-gun rear turret. We were testing the important four-gun rear turret designed by Frazer-Nash. It would be the first of several "F-N" turrets to become standard among our heavies and destined to play a major part in their defense.

It was good to be able to get away that summer for even a few hours to walk in the heather surrounding our little house on a rise in the sandy heath. The area was properly known as Martlesham Heath. Ann was now three years old, a beguiling little blonde, chattering away as she skipped through the bushes. Suddenly she scared up a baby partridge that gave her the fright of her young life. "We'd better get you a doggie to play with and to guard you," I said.

A chap in the village had a litter of cocker spaniels, and without further ado, we set off to make a choice. Ann picked the reddest of them all. "Okay, dearie, now we need a name. What do you say?" As we drove home we all three made suggestions. Finally we agreed to call him Rufus the Red. Rufus for short. Getting the puppy for Ann was the best thing we could have done. She was ecstatic and devoted all her motherly love to the sloppy ball of fluff. But Rufus grew and grew. Soon he was taking his willing mistress for mini forays on the heath.

On one such outing his excellent breeding stood him in good

stead. He suddenly took off like a small red rocket, over a bush and into a thick clump of heavy gorse. The little devil came out with a baby partridge in his tender mouth. He took it to Ann with his tail nearly wagging himself in half. She ran to me for help and together we freed the terrified bird; Rufus gave up his prize with almost a small bow, backing away, his front legs spread wide, his eyes boring holes in me. "Ann, just look at the lovely colors of this baby bird, and it's much happier now."

She took Rufus back to the house so I could release the fledgling into the heath without making her retriever lose face.

Our latest tests at Farnborough were showing that small machine guns were really not heavy enough against modern aircraft construction and would be hopeless against armor plate which was certain to be installed before long. We ourselves were certainly working on some better protection.

In July of that anxious year we did start to test both the Hurricane and the Spitfire[16] with one 20 mm Hispano cannon slung just below each wing, dangling out in the open air. Our first concern was whether the recoil force would slow the airplane down too much. More importantly, would the recoil force the nose down and spoil a steady aim. Our fears were much exaggerated. In spite of the unbecoming way they were mounted the new cannon proved to be eminently usable.

GLOBAL UPDATE
Fall 1939

The German Me 109 tries out heavier armaments, too. By good fortune for us they are still having much trouble with their new Oerlikon cannon, and the thin wing of the fighter would always work against them. There is no indication as yet of any armor plate being installed. By late 1939 the Me 109E-3 model becomes the standard fighter and is in mass production; the Luftwaffe now has just over a thousand of them. We have about twenty-six fighter squadrons with a total of some four hundred modern eight-gun aircraft, most of them Hurricanes.

As a result of our success with the Hispano cannon in both the Hurricane and Spitfire, the manufacturers, with renewed confidence, now got down to the urgent job of installing the heavy armament within the wings and adding more cannon per aircraft.

It seemed that time was always at our heels, and we really did not know if we were well prepared or not. Then Germany invaded Poland on 1 September and cut the knot of our dilemma. Tomorrow would tell, putting an end to our uncertainty. We would slip into what could only be a black hole, and the nightmare of war would begin.

Part Two

Three

GLOBAL UPDATE
First days of September 1939

As Poland is being invaded and before our twenty-four hour ultimatum for a declaration of war on Germany expires, a dozen RAF medium and light bomber squadrons deploy in secrecy to airfields in western France. They are combat ready.

While our ultimatum runs out so do the lives of the Polish air force men and her gallant, obsolete cavalry. The world watches in horror.

By late afternoon that first day of war, most pilots reached

Boscombe and an advance party of ground people trundled in to put the aircraft properly to bed where we'd abandoned them.

We collected in the mess to hear the CO, who had just landed. "News is a bit grim," he began. "A French assistant air attaché returning by air from a weekend assignation in Le Touquet neglected to file a flight plan, causing a general air raid alarm for southeast England. Hell of a flap! Two Hurricane squadrons from different bases were scrambled with minimal orders. Sadly, in the confusion they took on each other, and several got shot down, some fatally. A complete balls-up."

The assembled pilots, incensed, began bitterly voicing their indignation. "Pipe down!" called the CO. "It's a terrible thing to have happen, but now we've work to do. Go check all blackouts in your quarters. Any cars coming in must have all lights fitted with slit masks—diagrams are on the board. Everybody's confined to camp tonight. Meet here 0830 tomorrow. Okay that's it."

The previous occupants had taken some halfhearted steps after the invasion of Poland two days ago. Now that we were in the war too, matters of minor import yesterday became vital. It was a new ball game. German warplanes similar to our own cherished aircraft now threatened and made us nakedly vulnerable. With no experience of this kind of confrontation—what was coming? The best we could do was hide our heads from easy discovery from the air.

With blackout chores done, we trickled back to turn on the latest BBC news. They reported the country to be calm, but a nervousness in the way they said it belied their affirmation. Advance units of the British Expeditionary Force (B.E.F.) had embarked, and two Hurricane[1] squadrons had flown off to France. We knew they were deployed around Reims—the BBC didn't say that—but the Germans certainly knew.

A news item from the U.S. told of an appeal from President Roosevelt to all European nations "to abstain from unrestricted air warfare against civilian populations or unfortified towns."

1939—Fairey BATTLE light day bombers. Part of Advanced Air Striking Force (AASF) deployed in France.

The BBC said Britain accepted this stricture, leaving naval forces in open waters as legitimate bombing targets. Leaflet raids on Germany were discussed, but they didn't really count. News we wanted to hear was what the hell the damned Germans were going to do. We didn't have the initiative yet. As Hitler was calling the tune we had to dance his jig.

Missing from the news was the state of the RAF strategic striking power—our raison d'être. We had about 400 light and medium bombers[2] and 450 twin-engine medium-heavy bombers;[3] but only half of the heavies were fully operational. The Germans had at this time 1,200 medium bombers[4] and about 300 dive bombers.[5] In spite of the numeric disparity, we didn't much fear their bombers. They were trained for army cooperation and their bomb loads and range of action were of little use for strategic purposes, as we understood the proper use of air power.

While we fled to the west that noon a single RAF Blenheim made a high recce twenty-five thousand feet above the German North Sea naval base at Wilhelmshaven. Heavy warships moving out to the sheltered Schillig Roads and leaving the confines of the town could now be attacked. The lone Blenheim scout tried to radio the vital news to the U.K., but his set was on the blink. He had to fly all the way home to give the okay for a scheduled live-bombing raid, already poised for takeoff clearance. It was too late and we lost all the first day of war to vent any aggression.

The only good news, of a negative sort, came from the Hurricanes at Reims. They had several brushes with Luftwaffe fighters, which they found had more speed than ours but only half the number of guns—which the Germans knew full well. The Hun had turned for home when threatened, whether from official edict or fear, we couldn't yet tell.

Not knowing so many things only made our "...confusion worse confounded." I could have used a worry bead to good effect. Best to doss down now and see what tomorrow would bring. The first day of war was over, and surprisingly, we were still alive.

"G'night, Dru."

"'Night, old boy."

I felt better the next morning after a good country breakfast. We all met again, and the CO testily told us to get out and do something useful. He had no formal orders for us yet.

Dammit, the bomber boys had work to do. I half envied them. A second check on the location of the German ships found them out in the Roads, but the weather had turned sour. Plans were changed hurriedly to make a low-level raid using bombs with time-delay fuses to be—as the CO said—"popped down the nearest funnel." Fifteen Blenheims took off and flew to the target at no more than a thousand feet. On arrival they descended and made dive attacks from five hundred feet.

As the first RAF raid of the war, it was an utter disaster. The ack-ack guns must have been fully alerted, for their fire was murderous. The leader of the first ten Blenheims took on the largest vessel, the battleship *Admiral Von Scheer*, and although several bombs landed on the deck, they bounced off into the water. Five of the flock coming in behind were shot down; on fire, one of them crashed into the cruiser *Emden* and set it ablaze—an unwitting precursor of the kamikaze "divine wind"— to spring up later in the Pacific. The other clutch of five bombers, from a different airfield and unable to find the target in the miserable weather, was forced to donate its bombs to Neptune before groping a way home. A terrible, devastating ordeal and not a very salutary lesson in strategic bombing.

On the second day, six Hamden bombers sent to attack ships off Wilhelmshaven were also turned back by weather most foul. Fourteen Wellington heavies (known affectionately as Wimpys) set out, but only one could find and bomb the target. The flak again was extremely heavy and two were shot down. After this debacle the Royal Navy (RN) and the RAF agreed to postpone further raids on naval bases. It was too costly, and at this point, not worth the risk of provoking unwelcome reprisals.

I set out to walk over to the gaggle of fighters that only yesterday in some different and remote place had been the focus of our test flying. They were now raggedly dispersed on the far side of our new field begging for some attention.

The long walk provided a good chance to think over the past nine months since I'd joined Dru. I recalled the exhilaration in testing new armaments and great satisfaction of solving ever present problems, correcting design errors, and conceiving new approaches. Ironically our frenetic program had been aimed not only at the possibility of war but also at its prevention. Now here we were, up to our necks in the real thing with our efforts halted in midstride when so much remained to be done. It had become my lifeblood and I was beginning to feel bloody-minded about

Hitler's rude interruption.

In spite of the new fact of war there was a real sense of peace still surrounding this place, overlooked in self-pity as I walked across the soft turf of the old plain. Here was a quiet spot to readjust to a world that seemed to have lost its foundation. I'd been daydreaming about a departed world. Let it stay that way—it was high time to move on.

When I reached the A Flight aircraft it was good to find Reggie Emson already there; he, too, must have come out to do his own thinking and regrouping. We agreed that some action would be a good idea, so we fired up our small communications airplane and flew south to Warmwell, a small fighter field near the coast, to reconnoiter a possible firing range. We chose Lyme Bay, much to the eventual chagrin of the local fishermen, to whom the war seemed even more remote than it did to us. Lyme Bay was southwest of Boscombe and a bit farther away from the enemy. Habitation was sparse, better for the safety of those beneath where our firings would strew metallic dross, and the experimental tests would be away from prying eyes. This lovely bay served us well for the next few dreadful years and on into the peace that eventually did return. We flew back to Boscombe feeling a lot better and with one problem nicely solved.

GLOBAL UPDATE
The opening days of war

The day war breaks out the electrifying signal "Winnie is back!" flashes throughout a fully mobilized British fleet when Winston Churchill is appointed first lord of Admiralty and given a seat on the War Cabinet. It bodes well for seafaring Britain. Sixty U-boats are already carefully deployed, and the large liner *Athenia* is torpedoed after noon on 3 September with heavy loss of life, including American citizens. Our aircraft carrier HMS *Courageous* is sunk bringing as yet unorganized sea traffic into the Channel. The RAF abstains from bombing attacks on inland military targets in Germany mainly at the behest of France, who fears reprisals on her own war industry. Paranoia prevents France from moving into Germany at the very moment all the Nazi forces, less than half the size of France's waiting armies, are fully engaged in the destruction of Poland. The magic opportunity slips by.

It was time to review the priorities of the test programs on our prewar list. Each branch at headquarters claimed top place. The order on our list jumped all over the place with each new turn of events and with the barrage of urgent signals falling round us from London. At least all seemed to agree that for our fighters, replacement of small-caliber machine guns by 20 mm cannon would take top priority; final testing and production of gun turrets would be number one for the bombers. Professor Melvil Jones (the "Prof."), our very favorite boffin, left Cambridge University to become a permanent fixture with us. Dru joined him and—in the main—left me to my own devices and to the more mundane gunnery testing. With Reggie Emson and Dru and a couple of Cambridge whiz kids—known as "wranglers" because they took the highest math honors there—the Prof. formed a super group to be the Gunnery Research Unit (GRU). What a constellation they made.

GRU wanted everyone involved in gunnery development to join a brainstorming session. They arranged a meeting at Farnborough in a few days time. It was a real pleasure to find Sir Henry Tizard chairing the meeting. "You know, I'm sure," whispered one of the veteran Farnborough boffins who was sitting next to me, "that when Sir Henry was a captain in the Royal Flying Corps at the end of the last war, he was the first experimental gunnery officer to be appointed in the RAF."

"Well I'm damned!" I whispered back.

There he sat in the old airship shed, chairing our meeting to determine development policy—more than twenty years after he originated the post of EGO that I now jealously held. This was the same sage who was rector of Imperial College when I

1939—Sir Henry Tizard. First experimental gunnery officer in the RAF (EGO) after its formation in 1918. Rector of Imperial College in the early 1930s. Now U.K. scientist-at-large.

took my degree there eight years ago and who had been so supportive of our gliding club. At that time I had no idea of his previous extensive flying involvement. I should have known better.

Our Farnborough conference was lengthy, but in the end our priorities jostled nicely into place under Sir Henry's touch. He summed up the discussion: "We must have your best thoughts, gentlemen, your best—all of you!" He bit off his words, fixing us with his characteristically piercing eye. "We're not completely ready for this show yet. We have a number of problems still to solve. We have no time for pedestrian solutions. Go away and think up some novel approaches. For our fighters: attack—for air superiority. For our bombers: defense—to get them through to strategic targets."

Sir Henry was much in evidence on the scientific, technical development scene throughout the war in both the U.K. and the U.S. He was a great inspiration to us all.

We left Farnborough late in the evening. When we reached Salisbury Plain once again, the sun was setting low over that hallowed ground. The tall megaliths at Stonehenge threw long shadows across our track as we swung into land, perhaps to remind us to look carefully to our heritage and guard it well.

And so we began to press on with our tests and invent some new devices, if we could, to confound our enemy. One such was a rear four-gun turret[6] of an advanced design that we wanted to fit in all heavies of the future. The Mark V Whitley—a much improved heavy bomber[7]—had just arrived equipped with the super turret. It was formidable and put new teeth into the venerable colossus. The runic writing was appearing on the wall. These much improved and dangerous bombers could hurt the enemy mortally if we could arm them effectively against enemy fighters and get them through to the target. We believed they would eventually destroy him.

I bummed a lift in an aircraft returning to Martlesham to pick up my Alvis and take care of Pat and Ann's move out of our bungalow. I'd arranged for them to stay with my parents in Princes Risborough, safely away from the east coast. Pat, with strict instructions from Ann that it had to be a brother, would be able to bear our second child in a bit more comfort. The worst job I had was telling Ann that she must give Rufus to the local gamekeeper for the duration because it would be awkward to take him along. The dear child was great about it all and handed the golden bundle over without too much fuss. We'd take off for Risboro right away because Pat was due any day. The transport people arranged to pack up and look after our chattels until we needed to have them moved.

I loaded the car feeling much relieved that the necessary arrangements were in train. After dropping off the girls, I took off in a cloud of dust to try to make Boscombe by nightfall and avoid the misery of blackout driving.

1939—My ALVIS 12/60 car becomes airfield taxi, fueled now on 85-octane petrol, at our new wartime base.

A week after the Farnboro conference, I was already at work in our Wellington turrets, making service tests of an innovative system for gun aiming, developed in a few frenzied days by the new GRU. This clever method used tracer ammo spotted at specially determined intervals in the gun belts and by a simple formula gave a method of estimating the "lead," or how far to aim ahead of the target. Tracer is not new by any means, but the GRU method was. It really worked and was simple. Simplicity is, after all, the essence of any good idea. It was a great privilege to be working alongside GRU at this crucial time and be able to collaborate with them, as on this occasion or in any minor way I could.

There was no time to correct all the deficiencies that were beginning to show up in our light bombers seeing action in France. The rear defense in the Battle was a dreadful anachronism. It consisted of a single, hand-held, magazine-fed machine gun mounted in a hole in the top of the fuselage. It was hopelessly futile. I got much help discussing the problem with GRU, mainly Dru.

"You're right, Dix. We must do something about it; it's cruel and unusual punishment—it's inhumane," he opined.

"Damn right," I agreed. "If the Battles just tossed out ticker tape or johnny paper at random, it would be more effective."

I went off and dreamed up a whimsical idea that caught my errant fancy. Why not lay a controlled, towed minefield astern of the bomber, a favorite area for fighters to come in.[8] I asked the Prof., "Why don't we use the towed-target gear we already have to carry four twenty-pound shrapnel bombs strung out one at a time on tow lines made up from a double electric cable. We can troll out to about a thousand feet—into the area where the enemy fighter is naturally drawn in the tail chase—as our 'fish' gets ready to fire we press the tit, and—bingo!"

The Prof., God bless him, allowed as how it might just work and said I should go ahead. In those crazy days, almost any idea was examined seriously and often put to the test. With official sanction, we now tried it out. The plane had a rack for four flag targets and long towing wires wound on spools with brakes to control their rotation. We removed the targets and stowed instead four twenty-pound practice bombs, each hung by its nose, just like a good fishing plug. After several abortive attempts to get the bombs to fall away cleanly and not foul the lines, I managed to drop one of them off and it began to fall rapidly away behind. I soon lost sight of it—on and on it went! I was braking hard at the spool, but it made no difference. The brake system evidently had a day off without giving notice. The little bomb pulled out all the wire from the spool and just kept on going.

Later, Pete Whitworth (a chum of mine and one of the pilots from A Flight) and I picked up our slow, communications aircraft and flew over the area where we had lost our bait, but it was hopeless. We couldn't find it.

Meanwhile, the pace of other things stepped up sharply, and the priority of the Dean Bomb, as it was now officially dubbed, fell off. The local wet nurse had too many other charges, and I'm afraid it died of malnutrition. *Nunc Dimittis.*

Dru called me up a few days later. "Have you heard the latest? The Battles are tearing up French telephone directories and unloading the scraps on the 109s as they come up on their tails. Scaring the bastards right out of their pants. By the way, when the Prof. got the news he said he wants you to read his palm. He thinks your prediction was pure E.S.P."

"Any time," I offered.

GLOBAL UPDATE
September 1939

Intelligence sources give the strength of the German ground forces and their disposition by the third week of September: for the destruction of Poland they are using fifty-eight divisions of their most experienced troops, blooded in the occupation of Austria, in the Sudetenland and in seizing Moravia and Slovak. The Nazis have mobilized as many more: forty-two divisions are disposed on the western front opposing the French and the rest are on duty in central Germany.

Intensive work is in progress strengthening the fortifications called the Siegfried Line, the Nazis' answer to the Maginot Line.

While we in the west were getting back into gear with our testing work, strangely undisturbed by the Führer, the teeth of the RAF were masticating lean game in this phony war. After withdrawing from the murderous attacks on warships our medium and heavy bombers took on the arduous task of dropping reams of leaflets—"bumph," as the aerial postmen called their mail—on German cities. Such futile penmanship used up precious fuel but served to indoctrinate the bombers in continental foul-weather flying and navigation over future target areas. The *Baedeker* bombing of major Nazi cities with dire written threats also served notice we could reach everywhere in their land. The raids also kept the Hun out of bed—he didn't know when the paper lion might roar.

Latrinograms from France began to bring bad news. The Battle was almost defenseless: its K gun fired slowly, often jammed and was drum-fed. In the fleeting kind of battle it was meant for, it was never there when needed. The drum ran out or the gun failed. It was a disgrace and hopelessly out of date.

To compound the Battle's difficulties, German fighters were discovering their soft underbellies and making mincemeat of the unfortunate bombers with no defensive armament beneath and no escort to protect them. The Battles struggled along on their own, gathering information and making recce runs up and down the Siegfried Line that stretched from Belgium to Switzerland. What they gathered was mostly sporadic small-arms fire from the ground. Attempting to hide their nakedness from the Me 109s, they now resorted to sorties at very low altitude and thereby collected even more attention from the obliging ack-ack gunners.

The Blenheims—in common with the Battles—had no protection beneath but when possible were given Hurricane escort for their now much deeper leaflet raids into Germany.

Dru had been playing about for some time with the idea of replacing the K gun with the new belt-fed Browning—the mainstay of our eight-gun fighters. Dru and Jimmie Martin had already devised special feed chutes from the new ammo boxes to the guns in the new fighters. We now tried the same chute to feed a belt from a fixed ammo box into a flexible, hand-held Browning on a swivel in the upper mount of a Battle. It worked so well it was introduced as an immediate modification to the bombers in the field.

A shadow factory[9] had already started a modification to put a long trapdoor in the floor of the Battle. A nonrigid gun was to be mounted at the forward edge of the trapdoor that opened down into the airstream; but old habits die hard and they chose the K gun for the job. I pounced on the chance to follow Dru's lead and worked out how the K could be ousted by a more suitable Browning in this under mounting as well. These significant improvements a little earlier on would have greatly extended the life expectancy of the Battles, but the whiskered veterans were put out to pasture before many of them could be given the better arms.

Charlie Dann, my opposite number in the bombing development field, was our experimental bombing officer (EBO). His office was next door in the old wooden army hut we appropriated when we came to Boscombe. Charles was also a senior wrangler at Cambridge and a real brain. His brilliance was frightening, but he was so modest withal, it wasn't a pain in the wrong place. We'd come to know each other well at Martlesham and both enjoyed a good verbal wrangle. He wasn't infected with the flying disease as badly as I, but he loved all the problems associated with the design and development of bombs and bombsights and getting his ironmongery to the right target.

Charles needed a place nearby where he could drop bombs of new shapes for trajectory tests. Since we touched down here he'd been hobnobbing with the custodians of the New Forest, a lovely wooded area thirty miles to the southeast. The very old ninety-thousand-acre hunting ground was made a royal preserve by William I (the Conqueror) in 1079, soon after he took over England. Deer abounded until removed in the mid 1800s, and though a public park now, the place is still administered by the "men in green," keepers for the reigning monarch. Charles found them to be most cooperative, and a large central area in the park was cleared and fenced for his bombing range. There were still many deer in the woods in spite of their supposed removal, and some were trapped inside the fence and would multiply out of control if left alone. The keepers would let him know what would have to be done about them. I was in his office when one of them called back. "Well I'm damned!" he said, "That was my pal from the New Forest."

"What the hell are you talking about?" I was curious to learn of the progress of his plans to seize that chunk of erstwhile royal land for his bombing tests.

"The little men in green will have to shut me down for at least two days every year to harvest a dozen deer or so—for the sake of the ruddy trees—they've just told me."

"Oh, come on! That's a lot of balls."

"That's what they said. Apparently the little buggers strip off the bark for their lunch, and it soon kills the trees. But they've invited me to join them for the deer shoot. 'Keep what you kill,' they told me. What else could I have done?"

"You could have bloody well got me an invitation too," I told him testily. I certainly should have been asked to share this obvious bribe.

"Oh, I don't know," he replied. "We'll just have to see about that." It was now up to me to look into this important matter more closely and determine my next gambit.

Later on Charles rushed over to me in the mess. "Hey! I've found a cottage in Middle Wallop only ten miles away. It's got two extra bedrooms and we could share it for a bit and save a lot of dough. What d' you think?"

"Sounds great!" I replied. "But do I go on that deer hunt?" I had him cold.

"Oh, all right, you blasted little thief!" was his reluctant reply.

I called Pat that evening and told her the news. I know it comforted her that there would soon be a place to settle with Ann and the newcomer. Pat was fond of Charles' wife, Anna, a very amusing Finn (good-looking, too), so it would all work out fine. Charles and I drove out the next day to see the cottage. It was delightful—a bit ancient, with a roof groaning under a heavy thatch, tiny windows, and just-passable plumbing. We had to take it before some other rapscallion got in first.

"Okay by me," I said.

"Great!" he replied, just as pleased as I was. I'll go and sign up right away."

We shared another concern: that it was our responsibility to make sure all the armament worked properly and could readily be used by the crew in the heat of battle. To us the aircraft was primarily a fighting machine. Too bad that this often seemed to be at variance with its performance. We were soon to become Dann and Dean, the twin *bêtes noires* of the poor aircraft designer and of our own performance testing section.

In the halcyon days just gone, aircraft performance testing tended to have priority over armament testing. Now armament was coming to be recognized as equally or perhaps more important. I had no compunctions about making myself unpleasant to secure early flying time for armament testing on the new prototypes, nor had Charles for his bombing trials. I also insisted on flying the new fighters myself, refusing to accept the opinion of the performance test pilots as to the "suitability of the aircraft as a gunnery platform." I invented this sonorous term—lovely, I thought—as an excuse to get my paws on as many new types of aircraft as possible. I had feisty opposition from some of the manufacturers' test pilots who considered me a dangerous nuisance, but I was in deadly earnest and eventually got my own rotten little way. Nor did I hesitate to call for aerodynamic changes or structural redesign in a prototype when I knew for sure they were needed for acceptable armament performance. It often made me a wee bit unpopular but soon led to the production of more than one prototype of a new aircraft. Then we each had one of our own to mess up.

Before long both Charles and I became interested in almost every experimental aircraft coming in for trial because even at this early stage, fighters were being considered for use as light bombers and heavy bombers for forward-firing roles. The fighters were tacitly my bailiwick, and Charles had to get in line. He was much more concerned with heavy bombers anyway: the problems of loading, carriage and release from the bomb bays and testing new bomb sights. When push came to shove, he usually had first crack at the prototypes of the heavies, and my turrets in them tended to come second. Sometimes I had to barge in on a test flight, and not needing to fire the guns, could try out the turrets for rotational and vertical movements, gunner's comfort, adequate view for firing, and a myriad of nonfiring requirements. When I wanted to make air-firing tests in the heavies, Charles usually wouldn't come along. He didn't like flying in the same besotted way I did. He said that he had better things to do than ride around in a metal box—generally cold—getting gassed by cordite fumes and deafened by gunfire. We exhibited less competition with the very latest four-engined heavy bombers beginning to arrive. They were of increasing importance to our cause, as the war was obviously settling in for a long drawn-out tussle. We knew we would have to give way to each other now and again to get them out to the field in a hurry. We knew something of the history of these huge machines but nothing about the magnitude of the technical problems in the offing.

The RAF decided to build four-engined heavy bombers in 1936. It's a mercy the German Air Ministry didn't do so as well. With such bombers in 1940, the Luftwaffe could have achieved air superiority over England and could well have undertaken invasion, impossible with only light day bombers and those specialized in dive bombing. As it was, our first four-engined bomber off the stocks was the Short Stirling.[10] It was ordered in 1938 and made its maiden flight in early 1939; but because of serious birth pangs, its first operational use was delayed until February 1941.

Unfortunately, the Stirling had flying-boat genes in its pedigree: long fore-and-aft girders used in its design so cramped the bomb bay that initially it could not carry bombs larger than five hundred pounds, and even after extensive modification, could never manage any larger than the two-thousand-pounders to come.

Two other super heavies had also been started, both to be powered by only two huge, experimental Rolls-Royce Vulture engines. This ambitious new engine was much more powerful than the superlative Merlin—then in wide use, notably in the Spitfire and Hurricane. We hoped that the performance of these really heavy twins would be equal to or better than that of the Stirling. Avro laid down their version, calling it the Manchester;[11] Handley-Page's design was known as the HP 56. Both of these colossi were ghastly failures. In 1938 a Manchester prototype crashed; it was full of woes. Only a few were built and sent to squadrons—even before service trials with us were completed—to be on ops at the same time as the first Stirlings. The fate of the Handley-Page HP 56 was swifter, and none was tested at all or used in anger.

Both super heavies were redesigned, now powered by four proven Merlins. The first to be born was the Halifax,[12] from Handley-Page, and using very revolutionary assembly methods, a high rate of production was immediately assured. Soon after the prototype Manchester had been found sadly wanting in the Boscombe trials, Avro moved into high gear to producer the incomparable Lancaster,[13] the amazing "Lanc" that first flew in February 1941. Because the bombing equipment and gun turrets had already been extensively tested in the black sheep Manchester, it was able to be on ops early in 1942.

GLOBAL UPDATE
June–September 1939

By the end of September the first blitzkrieg the world has ever suffered is over. Poland lies vanquished under the Nazi heel. Warsaw, the capital, is the last stronghold to fall after three weeks of gallant but quixotic defense.

Germany's brand new ally, Russia, moves in rapidly from the east to claim her secretly-agreed-to half of the crushed country, much to the mortification of the German führer. He had not intended to share any part, but the Bear, with equal cunning, now blocks him from the oil in Poland and checkmates his long-term aspirations for Rumanian oil and Ukrainian wheat.

Wing Commander Bilney, the armament technical officer (ATO) and our boss over in HQ block at Boscombe, dropped into my office first thing one morning about a fortnight after we got there. He tossed a pink file stamped "most secret" on my desk. "Dix, get over to Gloster's for a conference at 1600 hours on 19 September," he said, "Inspect and comment on the mockup of a new fighter—a very important fighter indeed. The agenda is in the file with all the poop you'll need and the players who'll be there. Get *au fait* with this stuff and let me have the file back before you go." He turned at the door. "And I'd like a report pronto. Have fun."

I read the spec sheet. The aircraft itself had a code name; the power units called for were two "Whittle Units." What the hell did that mean? That was all it said. The armament was terrific—couldn't be better—four 20 mm Hispano cannon in the fuselage with a hundred rounds of ammo per gun. Beautiful!

"Charles, what on earth is a 'Whittle Unit'?" I asked Dann as he shot past my door. He had a good ear to the ground and just might know. He came in and glanced at the file. "A Whittle Unit? Why, it's probably a bloody rocket!" he facetiously suggested—a pretty close guess as it turned out when we later came *vis-à-vis* the jet-propelled prototype, now called the Gloster Meteor.

On the day of the conference, Hinton, my new long suffering batman, woke me at 0630 hours with his usual cup of piping-hot tea, which was more like soup than tea since he always made it so strong and sweet. Hinton had been looking after me only since we settled at Boscombe. He came with the territory—the single officers' quarters I'd been put in—and he had quickly adapted to my strange hours and needs. He was a pearl of great price.

"Sorry, sir," he apologized. "It's a real stinkin' dye out there. Wished I could've done yer more proud!" As he drew back the regulation green curtains, I could see it was still almost dark. Spittles of rain were slipping down the window panes.

"Don't forget yer rynecoat, sir, an' yer gasmarsk. P'raps yer'd better sty at 'ome todye."

"I'll be okay, Hinton. Just say a nice word for me upstairs, there's a good chap."

Before going to Gloster's, I had an appointment an hour away to the northeast. I was going to land at RAF Station, Halton and take a car to Risboro, only five miles off, to see how Pat was faring. She needed every possible support at this time, and I had all day to get back to Gloster's airfield at Brockworth for the conference.

I drove the Alvis out to the flight line where a favorite Gloster Gladiator fighter was already warmed up and waiting, whickering discretely like an impatient mare. The weather boys said five hundred feet overcast all the way, improving slowly. That ought to be good enough to get through. The drizzle had stopped, so we took off and turned onto our first course which ran directly before the nasty little wind that was bringing in racing, low stratus clouds.

I kept the hood open for a better look-see and reached the hills near Newbury hoping there would be enough room under the muck to slip through. Suddenly I didn't like the look of a row of tall trees ahead. I eased her up gently and was immediately in the wispy, cotton wool mist. Damn! Double damn! I was forced to climb on up, blind, until at six thousand feet we broke out into the innocent, empty, sunlit world of early morning. Confound it; this is hopeless. Get back south and down into earth contact again. No hole to be seen, no break. I returned for fifteen minutes on a reciprocal course, to sink slowly back into the false, bewitching feather bed, to probe, to feel with my dangling undercart for the clearance below the clouds. With conspicuous relief, I broke out below the thinning scud, and the world was green again.

The level of the cloud had not lifted noticeably, and yet, was that a break? I flew back on my original heading for another ten or fifteen minutes, hoping to squeeze through now. "Idiot!" said my conscience, my damned nagging watchdog. Get down and wait for half an hour. I looked about and found a smooth, level pasture and set the lady down in the soft green grass. Switches off! How deserted, breathless, and wringing wet.

Over in the corner of the field a white gate opened and a small boy appeared, followed by a second even smaller. Then came a very old man. I walked over to meet them.

"Hello," I said, addressing all three at once.

"Why have you come down in our field?" asked the older boy. "Have you come to see us?"

I had to confess that I'd only really come down to wait for the rain to let up. "But I do hope you don't mind me using your field."

"Oh, no! Not at all!" said Timothy, who then politely introduced himself, his younger brother, Peter, and the old gardener, Williams. "Do come and have breakfast with us. We'd only just started when we heard you coming in to land."

It seemed like an excellent idea. "I'd love to," I said and dug my service cap out of the cockpit where I'd shoved it away.

Williams had offered to watch the aircraft, so I left him standing protectively by the wing tip. We left the field, a boy on each side of me, skipping through the grass and chattering like a couple of bluejays.

We walked two or three hundred yards down a narrow lane and came upon a lovely old stone house almost hidden in the trees. The front door stood ajar, just as the boys had left it in their haste. We were met by a gracious older lady, addressed by Timothy as "Gran'ma." She renewed Timothy's invitation, and we sat down around a large, polished table already set for breakfast with old silver and fine glass. "Coffee?" asked Mrs. Courtney.

The conversation switched between gusts of high-pitched questioning from the boys and heavy silences while they stole shy glances at me under cover of eating their butter-soaked toast. I learned, for my part, that they had arrived the week before, evacuated from London for the duration.

An hour passed very quickly, and I had to excuse myself. The weather was much better; and there was old Williams, still faithfully on guard. Though the brakes were on, we dragged a fallen bough in front of the wheels to hold the fighter back, set the switches to "on," and wound the heavy engine over by the hand cranks. It burst into life with a testy cough and a growl. I let her warm up while I said good-bye to my new friends. Williams and I tugged at the branch to get it free, letting the brakes hold her.

I climbed in and buckled the safety harness. Waving good-bye to the two solemn little faces and my thanks to Williams, I moved off to the downwind side of the meadow. As I banked over the rapidly diminishing little group, I had to smile at the fluttering handkerchief in Peter's hand. The horizon was clear ahead and before long I was on the ground at Halton, my first destination.

Pat was in great shape—though her rueful glance downward would deny that description—and in good cheer. We talked about the cottage in Middle Wallop, scarcely believing the name of the old village we would soon be part of. I thanked my parents for all their help and promised to call when I got back that evening. My brother David, a doctor practicing in Kings Lynn, Norfolk, had been called up immediately, since he was already in the Royal Navy Volunteer Reserve. He was down at the naval hospital in Haslar at the mouth of Portsmouth harbor. Mother wanted me to get him on the phone, too, when I got back and tell him to call her.

I drove the service car back to Halton to find my Gladiator still unfed. They had none of the high octane fuel my fine thoroughbred demanded, but surely there ought to be enough left in the tanks to get me there.

I had to pass over our house and had time for a couple of slow rolls and a loop, just like any unruly cadet wet behind the ears. After this unseemly bit of showing off I set a course west. The miles sped away, and the passage across England was almost made. All I had to do was nip over the Cotswold Hills to drop into Brockworth for the meeting. Once again, dammit, I found myself being squashed betwixt hill and cloud. With only fifteen minutes to go, I had to turn back and fly north a tad to where my chart showed a gap in the hills at Cheltenham. I had a good five hundred feet below so I was feeling pretty pleased with a neat bit of weather evasion until my engine interrupted with a loud bang, a falter, a short series of surges—and silence.

I instinctively eased back on the trim wheel to keep the nose up and let the speed bleed away. The hood was already pushed back, the better to see in the rotten visibility as I searched anxiously for a place to park. The area was moderately built up on the main road between Cheltenham and the airfield at Brockworth and there wasn't much empty space left.

Ah! There's a good patch if I can reach it. Looks big enough. Here goes! I pulled the flap lever right down. The aircraft began to sink steeply toward the edge of the field and the hedge came up with a mighty rush. With the ill-treated fighter brushing the hedgehop and sinking like a stone, I hauled back on the stick; I was much too slow.

We landed on three points all right, but heavy as hell. Crump! The port tire burst and the wheel jammed as we slid across the rain-soaked grass. The aircraft slewed around to the left in a sickening way. We came to rest with the starboard wing tucked under the far hedge—as though in shame to hide my miserable disgrace—like the unhappy ghost with his head tucked under his arm.

I climbed out feeling like the bloody fool I was. The house on the corner of my field had a phone; they told me the airfield was only a few miles down the road. When I left Boscombe that morning, I had no intention of trying to set some sort of record for two forced landings in one day. If the truth be known, I've kept pretty mum about it ever since...the full details, at least.

Mechanics from Gloster's were over very soon with a new wheel. It was a happy chance I'd chosen a Gladiator from their own stable to ride that day. The chaps also removed the pressure control capsule from the carburetor so that when I left I could "go through the gate" and get emergency power for take off. I was glad, because the field seemed to have shrunk since I dropped in. The gladiator flung into the air with hardly any run, like a stepplechaser going over the high hurdle at Beecher's Brook in the Grand National. I was at Gloster's in time for the conference trying to look cool and hold my tongue.

The mock-up of fighter "X" was very impressive. It was a twin-engined design and huge, as fighters go. There were no signs of propellers on the shapes outlining the two power units, but I managed to bite back any foolish questions. The four

Hispano 20 mm cannon were mounted within the fuselage, two on each side, one above the other, obviously not behind any propeller discs but that didn't prove there wouldn't be any. I noticed the tailplane and elevators were mounted at the top of the vertical fin. Was that in order to be out of prop wash? Or out of the way of what? It was an intriguing mystery.

All I'd learned so far about the big cannon and its idiosyncrasies was from tests made with it mounted completely outside the fuselage—out in the open below the wings of the Spit and the Hurricane. This minimal knowledge hardly justified any sage or constructive comment on this radical inboard mounting, but nobody else knew any better so I confined my pearls to advice on ease of servicing the guns and to the risk of possible damage from blast to the exit tunnels where the cannon barrels emerged. Heads wagged wisely in agreement, and duty was done. I strolled out to the tarmac with studied nonchalance and climbed into my patient and true Gladiator to fly the fifty-odd miles back home. The conference provided much food for thought and I now wanted to find out more about the unknown and mysterious propulsion units. As I flew along I thought of the nickname we gave to the old Siskin fighter—the two-seat trainer model. It had only a tiny lower mainplane and was boxy in shape; it was often called "the ugly whore" because in addition to its lack of grace, it had no visible means of support. Fighter "X" could not be called ugly, by any means; but virtuous or not, how was she going to support herself?

Behind the scenes thirteen years before war broke out, a string of events of great importance occurred that because of high secrecy was known to very few. My involvement began just after we got to Boscombe with that visit to Glosters, but I was kept in the dark for months before being given the whole story.

In 1926 a young cadet at the RAF College, Cranwell, conceived the idea of pushing an aircraft along by gas thrust from burning fuel, like that of a blow torch. His name was Frank Whittle. After graduating two years later, he served as an instructor in fighters, and then tested seaplanes. In his own time he pursued his dream and wrote papers upon papers to the Air Ministry, who constantly, if politely, turned him down. They did not forbid him to continue his efforts, however, and he doggedly persisted, eventually raising enough cash to set up a small company[14] to build a working engine. His first prototype ran in April of 1937. The ministry—completely taken aback—awarded him a contract for an experimental engine and then a second for an engine to fly a small research aircraft[15] to be built by Gloster that flew on 15 May 1941.

As Gloster pushed rapidly ahead, de Havilland was designing both a jet fighter and its engine.[16] A range of Whittle turbojets was also being developed by Rolls-Royce, by Rover, and by his own company. In addition, General H. H. Arnold, chief of staff of the U.S. Army Air Corps, imported a Whittle engine and drawings to the U.S. just after war broke out. He had Bell design a twin-jet fighter called the Airacomet, which flew in October 1942.

In the nature of things we knew nothing about similar German developments. While Frank Whittle was dogfighting with the Air House, Hans von Ohain was the first to design a turbojet engine in Germany. Heinkel built it for him, and it ran only a month later than Whittle's in 1937. A modified version powered the He 178 which flew as early as 17 August 1939, to be the first jet aircraft in the world. But like Whittle, Ohain evoked little official support in his work. It was left to Junkers and BMW to initiate design work on radically new axial-flow turbojet power plants. A mock-up of a twin-engined airplane was ordered from Messerschmitt by the German ministry in June 1939 to test these new engines. It was ready in March 1940—six months later than the mock-up of the Meteor—and was called the Me 262.[17] By a merciful turn of fate, the Germans only gave low priority to such vital forward steps in aircraft and engine developments. Although our own brass has been indifferent at first, we were doubly blessed that Whittle had an unquenchable dream and that he was able to stir our chiefs from their lethargy and believe his prescience.

My faithful Gladiator got me back to Boscombe to find another conference in the offing. Like the earlier one, I just made it as I walked into the mess anteroom. We were all nervous and I suppose a little frightened underneath it all because we didn't know what was going on. Where were the bloody Germans? Was this a war or wasn't it?

There was much important development equipment spread all over our rambling, wide-open field. We didn't have protective pens to house the scattered prototypes, and none seemed to be planned. Our contingent of the newly forming Air Force Regiment, trained to defend airfields, was so small it could hardly look after fifty yards of our perimeter round the clock. We were mortally vulnerable to a carefully planned sneak attack. Like any good housekeeper concerned about possible burglars, we made our own brave though amateurish plans. We drafted groups of our own people; everybody, including the cooks, was on a duty roster. We all pretended to be infantrymen trying to guess how foot soldiers might behave. We knew something about airplanes—and a few of us a bit about guns—but precious little about ground defense.

The next day the newly designated group commanders drove around the perimeter of the airfield in a truck and assessed the points of likely danger. There we set up command posts and built defenses. Our weapons were not much better than those of our Saxon ancestors against earlier invasions; even so, the last one that was successful took place in 1066.

At my assigned position I was luckier than others. I had access to and promptly commandeered the test rig of the advanced Frazer-Nash bomber tail-turret with four browning guns that we were trying to make standard for all new heavies. It was a fully operational rig with electrically driven hydraulic motors and boxes of a thousand rounds per gun. It commanded a fine, wide field of fire on the main tarmac in front of the hangars at the top of a hill that dropped away over the landing area to the south. We only manned the posts during the hours of darkness, figuring that surprise would be much more difficult by day. Also we had our testing duties to do in the daylight. We all did four-hour stints every other night.

Winter came early and cold with much more snow than usual, and the wind across Salisbury Plain blew hard. I took the late sitting when I could—from two to six A.M. That watch was promptly nicknamed the Ground Dawn Patrol. It made us feel a bit closer to our heroes of long-gone years, with their Camels and their Harry Tates rising at first light to meet the Hun in World War I.

I found a most agreeable companion nearby—Wing Commander David Waghorn. He had a small sandbag pillbox over by the petrol pumps and a couple of my armorers with rifles as crew. Stretching our legs, we met halfway and discussed, as young Napoleons will, our strategy for meeting the Prussian. David was a quiet man, "...he was a verray parfit gentil knight," doomed shortly to succumb in the lists of our daily test-flying tournament with the unknown.

As we watched the sun come up, shade by shade, we spoke of this absurd moment. How had we been so duped or so stupid or so craven as to be caught in this dangerous vacuum? And of the future—what of these peace overtures we were hearing about? Hitler was making quaint broadcasts that the Germans had never had any thoughts of war with the men of England, their brothers by race. And still nothing happened. We were left to wonder, gradually relaxing our vigil, lulled by inaction. At least we were ready for the events lurking around the corner, barely half a year away, that would try us more sorely.

Germany soon launched a widespread campaign laying

magnetic mines in the mouths of important British harbors which went on for several months. Many ships were sunk or damaged. The immediate counter was to degauss vessels plying the Channel and the RAF developed an idea for blowing up the nasty contrivances from the air. We watched in some trepidation the arrival of a Wimpy bomber with a huge horizontal circular magnetic coil mounted on top. A powerful current passing through the coil generated a strong magnetic field designed to trigger the fuses and destroy the mines. The aircraft flew at nought feet over the sea lanes and swept the barbaric inventions away. The idea worked, but not all of the aerial mine sweepers got away unscathed. It was very dicey. In November a couple of sample mines were retrieved from the mud off Shoeburyness in the Thames estuary by some brave naval armorers and from their dissection we were able to master the proper countermeasure by year's end.

1939—WELLINGTON bomber with fifty-foot diameter circular electro-magnetic ring for triggering Nazi magnetic mines in the Channel sea lanes by flying low over them.

GLOBAL UPDATE
December 1939

At this same time we discover a pocket battleship marauding in the south Atlantic, revealed by the trail of a couple of sunken merchantmen. Three British cruisers—each outgunned by the prey—ambush the *Graf Spee* off the mouth of the River Plate and hound her into Montevideo. With his time-limit for sanctuary about to expire Admiral Langsdorff sails out into the shallow river and blows the great ship up rather than face our three cruisers waiting off the mouth of the river, perhaps augmented now by overwhelming battleships.

As the bleak winter months drifted by, floes on a gelid river, the declaration of war seemed hardly genuine. The futile bumph raids went on at great cost and with no obvious gain. A story of a typical mission tells of a five-Whitley-bomber leaflet raid—or nonraid perhaps—since they fought the weather which was the wrong enemy and they carried bumph which was the wrong bombload for real persuasion, and on this raid the junk mail was not even delivered at all. Before long one of them was forced down from cruising altitude with so much ice-buildup all the crew bailed out, except for the poor bastard in the rear turret who didn't get the skipper's message. By some miracle the aircraft landed itself without a pilot and without giving the gunner so much as a scratch. A *Marie Celeste* of the air. With a cabin temperature of thirty degrees below and six inches of ice on the engine cowlings, the others flew on to Munich. One bomber caught fire and crashed on a hillside, and from yet another all the crew bailed out. Only two got home, badly shaken but safe. It was a winter of great discontent for Bomber Command. Flying these miserable raids with no heating, no heated clothing or deicing gear, conditions were well-nigh impossible. Relief came only when the incontinent winter laid down so much snow the airfields could not be cleared.

October 12, 1939—Prototype Westland WHIRLWIND L6845 twin engine single-seat day fighter. Four x 20 mm cannon starts firing trials. First with this armament.

Peter Goodearl Dean, my new son, decided to burst on the scene at the end of September. I flew down to congratulate his mother and examine the handsome new arrival. His bright red complexion, often referred to as "expensive-looking," was what his father probably should have had but for some unknown reason did not. Ann was not very anxious to share her new doll with me at first, though she soon agreed to let me take a peek if I kept it short. Two weeks later, we all drove down to Middle Wallop to take up residence with Charles and Anna. It was much fun and a happy relief. It kept us all a bit sane.

We received a revolutionary airplane in October. It was the Westland Whirlwind,[18] our first fighter to carry four 20 mm cannon mounted in a neat, compact package in the nose ahead of the pilot. It was a giant leap ahead from the pip-squeak caliber of World War I—a step we had espoused for ages. We needed the greater velocity, range, and hitting power of the cannon to overcome the tough construction of the newer aircraft and the heavy armor plate that latrinograms predicted.

The Whirlwind had two Rolls-Royce engines of new design, a smaller version of the splendid Merlin, with the delightful name of Peregrine. The two engines rotated in opposite directions to balance out propeller torque, making the aircraft safer during takeoff and more evenly maneuverable once in the air.[19]

First we had to find out how to fire the new multi-cannon installation on the ground. The stop butts already on the field were quite unsuitable. They were designed for practice firing of personal small arms and rifles only.

Less than a foot below the short, springy turf of Salisbury Plain lies solid chalk. I got my armorers to dig out a pit in the steep slope where I'd parked on my first arrival. We tried firing one of our small-caliber multi-machine gun installations into the newly exposed vertical chalk face and it worked very well, but when we fired the Whirlwind's four 20 mm cannon, the solid slugs bored through the chalk and came popping out of the turf above in a most aggressive manner. Then I tried a ten-foot-high square box of wooden railway sleepers, filled to the top with coarse gravel. The apparatus retained the 20 mm bullets safely until the sleepers, themselves, gave up the ghost, letting the gravel pour out of the huge hole punched in the wooden timbers by the highly concentrated stream of motivated metal. We might not have been too concerned, but some of the crews at the aircraft dispersal points half a mile behind started to complain of warm slugs falling in their midst, even though well-nigh spent on arrival. Much ado about practically nothing, we thought.

We were able to clear the Whirlwind cannon installation for ground firing with great dispatch. The mountings withstood the dreadful recoil load with all cannon firing at the same time, and nothing broke. Empty cases vomited downward from the guns passed cleanly through the ejection chutes leading through the bottom skin of the nose beneath.

The novel stark reality of live combat sharpened our understanding and we made the air tests even harsher. A new and essential test requirement was made for all fixed, forward-firing fighters: all guns must successfully fire all the ammunition in a single sustained burst of fire while the aircraft performs a complete slow-roll maneuver. Thus demon gravity is applied successively in all possible directions. The Whirlwind was the first fighter to face this ordeal.

With great élan I started air firing at medium heights. The recoil from the cannon fired in salvo felt like hitting a tree, and the noise and smoke enveloping the cockpit were fearsome. But all was satisfactory for low altitude functioning. Everything worked, even during the final slow-roll test. We were getting there! This magnificent battery would knock Jerry's pants off. At maximum altitude, alas, when firing in short bursts with pauses in between, the cannon soon jammed, one after another. I turned away from the Lyme Bay firing range, and headed back to Boscombe. As I flew along at a couple of thousand feet, two of the cannon let go suddenly on their own,[20] each firing a single round at no one in particular. Scared me to death.

We discovered nothing apparently wrong with the two headstrong guns, but the other two had misfed and were well and truly jammed. The guns and magazines were all soaking wet, giving us a clue to the mystery. Because the breeches of the Hispano cannon remain open between bursts of fire, blasts of minus-forty-degree air from the airstream are forced down the barrels into the gun mechanisms and magazines. At high altitude, the frigid air evidently froze water vapor from burnt gases into solid ice inside the guns and magazines, jamming them most effectively.

To stop this nonsense, I resorted to the simple expedient of fitting the protruding snouts of the cannon with French letters (large size). This turned out to be but a short-lived palliative working well for the first burst before the condoms ruptured but after that—back to square one. The pretty creature had to go back to the factory to have a hot-air system fitted. She returned for more tests six months later, and we were able to demonstrate that as soon as the cannon were kept warm, they worked perfectly at all altitudes. It was too bad the delay put the aircraft out of the running for large-scale production. A few squadrons were equipped and were very effective in action, even though the delicate overall design did not lend itself to easy servicing.

We were also bending our best efforts toward clearing powered gun turrets and other gun defenses for a covey of different light bombers that dropped in like migrating birds.[21] A Blenheim[22] with a two-Browning, power-operated turret was a welcome addition, even though it had teething troubles like most newly born.

A Lysander[23] flew in for trials of her rear defense system. It was the only plane the RAF had specifically conceived for an army coop role. It was a high wing parasol design, fitted with all the sky hooks imaginable. Wing slats and slots to give ultrahigh lift at very low speeds, enabling it to take off and land in very confined places. With a low stalling speed, the Lysander was earmarked for gun spotting and field reconnaissance, but it really found its *métier* later on in clandestine operations with the French resistance as a first-class, covert night delivery van. Many have kissed British soil after climbing out of a Lysander.

A Defiant[24] with a single 20 mm cannon in the turret was a surprise. It kept us busy for a while as an R & D item. We did extensive beam firing against a towed banner target with camera gun records for the Prof. He was able to further verify the Caseau effect, now with a larger caliber and higher muzzle velocity, but it was never a serious battle wagon.

The Stirling,[25] first of the new four-engine ultra-heavy bombers showed up with hydraulic turrets and bravely entered our lists. The turrets were all tried-and-true Frazer-Nash models and the testing routine was more of a check. We soon turned her loose for production and she was on ops within a year.

August 5, 1940—Boulton Paul DEFIANT K8310 with one 20 mm cannon in turret for beam firing tests in the air.

As winter relented her grip, the pace in the air flared up over the Champagne district in France. On 24 March, Hurricane squadrons grouped around Reims had their busiest and most successful day of the war. England didn't know about it at first because correspondents over there were having a little strike, but Charles Gardner, the doyen BBC observer, was able to send in an early report. He told of the exploits of 73 Squadron, famous since the first days of the Royal Flying Corps. In some four or five separate encounters with Dornier bombers and both Me 109s and the more heavily armed Me 110s, they shot down seven of the enemy that day, losing only one Hurricane in spite of being outnumbered by at least ten to one. One squadron member, who had gone under the nickname of "Cobber" in previous reports for security reasons, was now further identified as "a young New Zealand pilot." He was Flying Officer E. J. Kain, already wearing the Distinguished Flying Cross (DFC) and due for a second. Cobber shot down two Me 109s but was badly hit in the canopy with a cannon shell. On fire, he had to bail out and was almost shot on landing by an overzealous French officer. Things were hotting up and it was good practice for things soon to come.

GLOBAL UPDATE
May 1940

The worst fears of the German general staff are quieted when no ground attack by the Allies results from the Polish invasion. Troops we reserved for defense of Scandinavia are sent to bolster France. We are thus powerless to stem the Hun invasion of Denmark and Norway and our remaining men are withdrawn from there.

As usual without any warning Hitler launches a blitzkrieg attack through Luxembourg, Holland, and Belgium on 10 May, toward the borders of France.

Spring came to England in deceptive peace, but in France all innocence was to be stripped from the countryside once more as the Hun returned after only two score years to savage, loot and conquer yet again. His forces smashed through the neutral Low Countries completely outflanking the north end of the impregnable Maginot Line.

In England Chamberlain resigned and that magnificent old warrior, Winston Churchill, gladly took the helm to become our new prime minister and wartime leader.

The untried troops of our expeditionary force, acquitted themselves well. Not only did they hold their own in many places but they even had the audacity to make minor counterattacks; however the sheer weight of armor against them and the devastation of accurate dive bombing proved too much.

Our air force was not trained in an army coop role and had only small bombs to help but the well-nigh useless Battles were more than vindicated in an exhibition of great glory. two vital bridges over the Albert Canal near Maastricht had not been demolished by the Dutch as planned. They had to be bombed to prevent an immediate heavy German advance and two flights of Battles went on the suicide mission. Both bridges were destroyed, but only two airmen survived who were decorated in the field with DFCs. It was one of the epics in RAF history. The two leaders received posthumous Victoria Crosses for their extraordinary bravery, the war's first air awards of this supreme decoration.

The new blitzkrieg thundered and flashed through the French center—the hitherto believed impenetrable Ardennes. The Gallic military mind had vowed *Ils ne passeront pas* but the Boche achieved what all had sworn impossible. The French fell back muttering defeatist imprecations.

Our air bases were soon overrun; planes returning from combat often had to land at a new base to the west. The Battles suffered heavy losses by day and were forced to resort to night raids. Although ill-trained in this art, losses were much reduced and bombing accuracy remained adequate. But in three days, the Advanced Air Striking Force (A.A.S.F.) lost half their aircraft.

The German thrust swung north trapping the Belgian army, two French divisions and nine of the B.E.F. against the coast at Dunkirk. Britain faced the most disastrous loss in its history. About half a million irreplaceable men seemed doomed to capture. Now came the miracle of Dunkirk. Between 26 May and 4 June hundreds of all shapes and sizes of yachts, fishermen, tugs, lifeboats, pleasure boats—anything—dared the twenty-five miles of open sea and threat of the German Air Force to pluck the cornered men away in ones or twos, or as many as their often frail craft would carry, to ferry them to larger vessels waiting in deep water, or perhaps to take them all the way home. The RN performed prodigious feats under bombardment from any Hun who managed to get through the RAF fighter screen. Three hundred and forty thousand Allied troops were saved, and the Luftwaffe was powerless to stop their salvation. It cost the

1939—Boulton Paul DEFIANT two-seat fighter with four-Browning .303-caliber gun turret. Soon withdrawn from operations.

RAF nine hundred and fifty-nine aircraft in nine days of evacuation. German air losses were also heavy. Our outnumbered fighters took an average toll of four to one. The RAF had established its superiority over the Luftwaffe and was ready to exact the same toll again in the next few months.

Charles Garner tells how the Defiant came into its own. It had been withdrawn from ops, and few Germans had met one in combat. The aircraft resembled the Hurricane in general lines and could easily be mistaken for it. Some of the Hurricanes mixed Defiants into their formations and flew along, throttled-back, until attacked by Messerschmitts. The Germans clearly did not suspect the ruse and lined up behind and above for attack on yet another outnumbered collection of Hurricanes. As the Germans came into range, the Hurricanes pulled away, leaving the enemy to fly into a hail of bullets seeming to come from nowhere. The surprise worked. In two days the Defiants shot down thirty-eight Germans and must have sown something like panic among the pilots until the Hun cottoned on. The Defiants had won their Pyrrhic victory. Churchill said of the fighter pilots and airmen of Dunkirk: "May it not be that the course of civilization itself will be defended by the skill and vision of a few thousand of these men. Beside them the Knights of the Round Table and the Crusaders now fall back into a past, not only distant, but prosaic."

Not knowing the truth, the rescued troops naturally blamed the RAF for the bombs that fell on them and their ships at Dunkirk. Hinton, my old batman, told me of an encounter when he ran into a new crowd of very scruffy soldiers in his pub. The Army always called the Air Force "Bryl Cream boys," after the then-popular, greasy hair oil, said to have an irresistible attraction for all the female beauty in the vicinity. On the other hand, the RAF dubbed the Army "pongos" (but surely with no thought of the Borneo jungle). It was easier to see why our sailors were known to us as matelots—red pompons or not. As Hinton reached for his ale one of them challenged him: "Where the bloody hell were you last week, eh?" Then the rest turned on him and threw him out on the street. I told him why they thought we ratted on them, and didn't know of the huge losses the RAF bore in giving them any chance of escape. My little homily did no good. "Well, sir. One of those buggers got the beer I paid for."

The irony was I had to pretend to be a sort of pongo myself the very next day. With invasion imminent, we reinstated our airfield defense, but I didn't have half the enduring patience of a real pongo.

Four

In England spring was yielding to summer, but every day the news got bleaker. We were still licking our wounds from the conquest of France, and our troubles were far from over. Churchill promised us even more for good measure.

I was manning my guns one night and had the good fortune to capture an "enemy" as dawn broke. The strange twin-engined aircraft circled low with its wheels down, not attempting to make an attacking run, and landed properly into wind. I left my turret, which I had kept trained on him the while, and ran over with my revolver cocked. The plane had French markings. The pilot stopped, killing his engines as I flagged him down with my gun. "*Bon jour, Monsieur!*" he said, emerging from the hatch.

Three more of them came out to stand around with great grins on their dirty faces. We spoke some sort of French together, and I told him, *"Ce n'est pas la France ici."*

"Oh! Oui! Oui! Grâce à Dieu!" they said as one man, crossing themselves and muttering something about *"Le bon Dieu!* and *"les sales boches!"*

I drove them over to emergency quarters at the mess and an English breakfast, which they didn't seem to mind too much. That evening after they had a bath and a bit of shut-eye, we put on a celebration party. The language difference seemed to solve itself. We were kindred spirits; and for our part, we were glad they had escaped to remain on our side, very ready to get back on the job and have at the Hun again.

The capitaine and I cut off and exchanged our bottom tunic buttons—the ones normally hidden behind our belt buckles. I asked Hinton to sew them on in their new positions, putting the pilot partly in the RAF and me partly in *L'Armée de l'Aire Maritime.* I explained he was a French officer and on our side, and by affording him this help, he wasn't aiding and abetting an enemy. I wore mine until that particular tunic wore out and was thrown away. I'd forgotten about the button by then and was not just discarding our brief friendship as a short-lived entente cordiale. We'd had a good time; the amity we established and support we exchanged would never be lost. They were very welcome refugees from the common enemy, as were many more coming from all over Europe for weeks on end.

The two of us also had a more tangible exchange to show. I'd given the capitaine a new toothbrush and a pair of pajamas, so before leaving the following day to fly to an airfield designated for such migrants, he reached down, handing me their single rear-defense machine gun with an Alkan gunsight and a couple of full ammunition drums to go with it. *"Pour vous, monsieur,"* he said simply. *"Ma mitrailleuse, et—merci, merci beaucoup!"* I kept that piece of ironmongery just in case it might be necessary. As Mr. Churchill told us in our beleaguered isle:

"If and when they come, take one with you." I took the gun home, mounted it upstairs in the window over the front door, and promptly showed Pat how to use it. The full drums of ammo hung to hand on the wall beneath. We had a clear field of fire over the approaches to the house, and we were ready.

The rear turret in the Whitley Mark VI came back with a new servo feed system for the ammo belts, now stowed in long, open trays or tracks running forward along the walls of the fuselage. The idea was to move the weight of the ammo toward the center of gravity forward and also to permit a much-increased supply for the remote outpost of Empire in the tail. The system worked well under conditions of no stress, but in air turbulence and changing "g" loads the pull on the belts varied too much. By their very nature, guns ask for their meal in a most erratic manner: pull...stop...pull...stop. The servo motors could not cope with such capricious demands.

"You can't get there from here," said Dru as he had a passing look at the curious feeding troughs.

"Okay, let's do something about it," says I.

We went off into a corner and designed a small "recuperator" to be fitted to each gun to relieve the excessive loads on the belts and divorce guns from their servos.[1] The aircraft people made the device, put it into the system, and all was well.

In those days of increasing woe, I was very much cheered when in early June 1940, a heavy twin-engined fighter from Bristol's flew in. She was called Beaufighter,[2] probably because the design used many of the components of the Beaufort torpedo-bomber, whose turret we had already approved, and was now in production for Coastal Command. The "Beau" fighter was fitted with four Hispano 20 mm cannon mounted in the bottom of the fuselage, below the pilot. The cannon were accessible to the second member of the crew so stoppages could be readily cleared in the air and the cannon reloaded with full

Hubert W. Dean

1940—Prototype Bristol BEAUFIGHTER R2055. Four × 20 mm guns and nineteen-round drum feed was cleared June 1940. These two photos are of BEAUFIGHTER R2060 and first British-manufactured belt feeds. February 6, 1941.

1940—BEAUFIGHTER ground firing crew. Left to right: Mr. Green (Bristols), Flt Lt Lockie, Flt Lt Norman, Sdn Ldr Whitworth, and two aircraftmen.

ammunition drums when called for.

We noticed another good feature: access for mounting the guns in the aircraft or for adjusting their alignment to harmonize with the gunsight was via long hinged doors in the belly. That arrangement made life easier for the armorers. They could do their work with some protection from howling winds, the blistering sun in a tropical arena, or the nurturing, gentle rain of our homeland.

Again, as with the Whirlwind twin, we had to summon a crane from the transport section to hoist the heavy tail of our Goliath onto a trestle for ground firings. Recoil from our salvos was scarcely felt. The rugged Beau budged not an inch. We were ready to shoot up Lyme Bay.

We wasted no more time and began air testing this important battery of powerful, heavy guns to the ultimate—from low down up to maximum height, in steep turns, and in any attitude we dared impose on the huge fighter. It all worked out very well.

"A great job, Mr. Green!" I told the Bristol representative who had designed the armament and came to see the trials. In only two weeks we were able to clear the Beau for production and to drink a very happy tankard of bitter to celebrate with Green that evening in the mess.

It was ironic that while we were exulting in the introduction of our second four-cannon fighter, we cleared another but perhaps already outdated type of installation for production with equal dispatch. It was a Hurricane,[3] probably the last of that genre of fighter we produced—mounted with an unbelievable battery of twelve small-caliber Brownings. A real shotgun. But we were sure the gauge of shot was only suitable for pigeon. We didn't need any more fighters armed with BB pellets. The Hurricane needed desperately at least four 20 mm cannon. It was not certain that number could be installed in the wafer-thin wing of the beautiful Spit, but we could get two in at least.

The week before the Battle of Britain officially began, a delightful and very modest army gunnery officer appeared on our doorstep without warning. Captain Bill Adams had flown in from Paris, having escaped with some help from the French resistance. Under his arm was a vital piece of gun development hardware that he'd "liberated" from the R&D shops of the *Companie Chattelerault* in Paris. It was a new belt-feed mechanism for the Hispano cannon. What fabulous luck!

The Beau with the four magazine-fed cannon had not yet been ferried back to Bristol's, so we could use it to test the French feed mechanism. Bill Adams explained how the intriguing piece of French artistry worked.[4] "The gun recoil keeps the feed spring wound up," he told me. "Simple!" It took but a half hour ground firing to prove the single gun involved in this historic test. We were all impatient to get into the air to show off our exciting new piece of jewelry.

"Would you care to come with us?" I asked Captain Adams. "It won't be a very comfortable trip because we intend to put this baby through its paces, and we certainly won't be kind to it."

"You're damn right I want to! After I've come this far with it, what do you think?" he responded with some heat. My armorer, Corporal Tucker, begged to come along, too.

David Waghorn, my neighbor on the Dawn Ground Patrol, was going to fly the Beau for me. Henry Waghorn—his brother, I believe—flew with the RAF team in the International Schneider Trophy race at Calshot in England when Britain took it for the third time in succession and thus won it outright. That historic feat in 1929 was accomplished in a Supermarine S.6B seaplane—the forebear of the incomparable Spitfire.

I discussed with David the maneuvers I wanted him to do: some straight and level passes to start, then steep turns and dives with hard pull-outs to test the downward "g" load on the feed. Most importantly, I wanted some steep climbs immediately followed by hard push-overs, which would impose strong negative "g" forces.

"Okay," said David. "Let's go!"

We were in the air for over two hours. I was exhausted, and

I know Bill Adams was too, but I was more used to that sort of nonsense. David pushed the Beau's nose over, and I have never seen anyone so surprised as that gallant captain of gunners when he gently floated to the roof of the cabin. I was ready for it, strapped down close to the gun so that I could study the belt being drawn into the maw of that voracious dragon.

The feed mechanism behaved beautifully, with characteristic French femininity: flawless, satin-smooth, and insatiable. I don't know who was the more pleased, Bill Adams or I. He had liberated the continuous-feed mechanism—*alimentation continue* as written on the casing—from under the nose of Attila; but best of all, he had liberated us from the limitations of the nineteen-round spring-fed drum. We now had the means to arm our cannon fighters with enough belted ammunition to match the time they could stay in the air. Bill went away with a mile-wide grin to the Birmingham Small Arms Company to put it into large-scale production.

As chance would have it, a couple of days after that marvelous success with the French feed, a second Whirlwind fighter, almost a forgotten wallflower, arrived with a quite different automatic feed for its four cannon. It had been designed by Lewis Motley, a very bright industrial engineer, who turned up in the afternoon to watch the trials.

Lew's feed system was ingenious.[5] Each cannon now had a hundred rounds compared with the paltry nineteen in each initial drum. Unfortunately the system could not cope with the severe tests we now imposed on it. It would never do.

Lewis Motley had the opportunity to see the French design in action in the Beaufighter. As we walked away he said with doleful resignation, "Makes my mechanism look a bit like a dog's dinner, doesn't it?" But he took the defeat gracefully. Months of hard work down the drain in one fell swoop. Later on, Lew was of enormous help to me in designing and building other very important and interesting armament developments.

GLOBAL UPDATE
June–September 1940

Before Italy finally commits herself to war against France and Britain, Churchill appeals to Mussolini to stand by old ties of friendship existing for many generations, but does not succeed. Il Duce sticks by his treaty with Germany and prepares to issue a declaration of war when he is ready. He and Hitler agree the date is to be June 10. On that same day, President Roosevelt makes a critical broadcast in which he says: "...The hand that held the dagger has struck it into the back of its neighbor..."

Britain continues to bring into France reinforcements against the German onslaught through western French ports and urges the French people to stay in the fight somehow, somewhere—as guerrilla warfare from within or from a base in North Africa. The confused French government continues to press for the few remaining fighter squadrons in the U.K. to be sent over, even though it has already been decided to capitulate.

Russia picks the opportune moment to take over the three Baltic states and seizes control of Rumania on her other border.

The U.S. in an uplifting gesture of faith makes plans to sell reserves of weapons to rearm the stubborn British.

The Blitz in France was over just a few days after the last survivor was picked off the stained beaches at Dunkirk. Hitler harangued England for several weeks about making a separate peace to avoid further strife between two blood-related nations, a futile exercise on his part.

The saddest episode of our few weeks of active campaigning with France was the way it ended. We had absolutely no intention of halting the fight with Germany—for us there could be no terms or surrender. But in France there was a pervasive defeatist attitude among such as Pétain, Weygand, and the deceitful Laval.

President Reynauld wanted to move his government to Africa and continue fighting from there, but defeatists wished to seek terms for a cease-fire. Britain made a supreme offer to France on 14 June to form a solemn Anglo-French Union joining the two empires into one and to fight together to the end. It was too late, and a capitulation forced on France settled everything.

French warships in British ports came under British control, but at Mers-el-Kebir and Oran, Admiral Gensoul would not accept any of several alternatives for putting his fleet out of action. In a most distressing operation on 3 July, British Force H blew the badly needed ships out of the water. Only the *Strasburg* and seven cruisers from Algiers escaped to Toulon. World reaction was critical, but the underlying necessity for the dire decision was understood. Though Britain was about to be invaded, the move said clearly she was not on the brink of surrender. She feared nothing and would stop at nothing to destroy the Hun.

Churchill asked for about four hundred Luftwaffe pilots shot down by the RAF in France to be handed over, but the French dallied too long, and soon we had to shoot them down all over again in the Battle of Britain.

After a month of tempting Britain to give in, the führer announced he must now, with reluctance, copy Caesar. His staff strongly advised against any invasion plan until the opposing air force had been overcome, whereupon Goering undertook to remove the threat without delay. September 15 was set as the provisional date for an invasion, code-named *Seelöwe* (Sea Lion).

As the Luftwaffe regrouped for the coming mortal struggle for air supremacy over Britain, President Roosevelt approved the formation of the National Defense Research Committee in June. The wartime mobilization of science had the most profound influence on American technology of anything in the first half of the twentieth century. It particularly affected weapons development and underscored the paramount importance of science in national defense for scientists and military leaders alike. The eminent and well-liked Dr. Vannevar Bush was appointed chairman, and the new committee, with independent funding, had power to take technical initiative. Moreover, it was to report directly to the president. Its simple structure permitted action without red tape. An original division of the committee was "A" (armor and ordnance) under Dr. Richard C. Tolman with Dr. Charles Lauritsen as his deputy. Soon after, Dr. Bush paid us a visit and spent all day at Boscombe. It was a signal privilege to talk to this fascinating scientist. A British scientific mission headed by Sir Henry Tizard visited the U.S. in August 1940 and exchanged secret information on military subjects including radar, fire control, underwater detection, chemical warfare, explosives, and rockets.

The first phase of Goering's plan to achieve air supremacy over England called for closing the Channel to all shipping and softening up the defenses of the seaports needed for the invasion on the south coast. Simultaneously he wanted to draw RAF defensive fighters into battle so they would be destroyed by attrition. Thus, on 10 July 1940 the German Air Force was launched in strength with massive fighter escort, expecting to need only a short time to nullify the air defense. In spite of more than six weeks of engagements, the RAF was able to husband its strength and retain command of the air over Britain.

Goering tired of this protracted and apparently futile effort announced the start of Phase II—a full-scale attack against the British fighter defense system as a whole—to clear the way for invasion. A major assault he called *Adlerangriff* (Eagle Attack) would start 12 August. The Luftwaffe outnumbered the heavily depleted RAF and had the initiative. There should be no further problem with those tiresome flyers.

The day before *Adlertag* (Eagle Day), special units made

very successful raids on all the mysterious 350-foot-tall radar towers along the south coast of England; but the damage was patched up by the next day, and the German intercept service regretfully reported none of the stations had been put out of action. In any event, it probably didn't matter, they felt, since the RAF fighters seemed to be controlled by their own local stations, and the towers had nothing to do with their control system.

The Eagle Attack started in chaos we could not fathom. They completely misunderstood the RAF fighter-control organization. Our squadrons were thought to be as mobile as the German air fleets, and their intelligence about the allocation of airfields was hopelessly inaccurate. The target list was lengthy: ships, harbors, RAF units of all kinds, and factories producing anything to do with aircraft. Altogether a glorious muddle. Even their meteorology boys got the weather forecasts wrong. Forty-six German aircraft were lost that day to thirteen RAF fighters shot down; but there were also forty-seven more RAF airplanes destroyed on the ground and eleven Wimpy bombers were lost over Germany. A punishing day for both sides.

The strategies of the rival air forces were really very simple. The Germans had to destroy Fighter Command before undertaking the planned invasion. The RAF had to keep Fighter Command viable until bad weather precluded invasion.

The largest air battle of this phase was waged on 15 August, dubbed *der schwarze Donnerstag* (Black Thursday). Hun losses were seventy-six to the RAF's thirty-four. On 24 August all-out attacks began on every operational fighter field the Germans knew about. Over the next two weeks, Fighter Command was almost driven to its knees. A quarter of its thousand pilots were lost or seriously wounded. The only replacements were raw young pilots still in training. The fearful wind of desperation reached out even to us at Boscombe; we heard a whisper that those of us who were fighter pilots would very soon be called up.

On 24 August, by mistake it is now generally believed, the

Germans made a raid on central and east London, obviously non-military objectives. Churchill seized the opportunity to send eighty RAF bombers to Berlin the next day, the first time the German capital had been bombed in its long history.

The crux of the Battle of Britain was 15 September. Not realizing how badly our fighter organization had been mauled and how very nearly he had achieved air supremacy, Goering persuaded his master that indiscriminate, heavy daylight raids on the capital alone should now take the place of any further attempts to put Fighter Command out of action. He proclaimed that his new tactic would soon bring Britain down, and she would sue for peace. Hitler agreed and called off Sea Lion indefinitely. He would now be free to return east and complete his plans for an immediate assault on his Russian ally—a treachery he had been carrying foremost in mind for some time.

As the crucial battle intensified without mercy, early August brought us a day fighter for test that offered at last some

August 6, 1940—Prototype HURRICANE V7360. Four × 20 mm cannon with nineteen rounds per cannon drum feed mechanisms.

belated hope of overwhelming the enemy with a superior armament. It was the Hurricane we had been awaiting so long, with four Hispano cannon mounted within the wings.[6] We were ecstatic. The guns were fed from nineteen-round drums because the new French belt-feed was not yet available; but it was a huge step forward. The tests had top priority.

We ran into an immediate and serious problem when we started ground firings. The two outer guns were well behaved, but both inner guns jammed after only a few rounds because the large, spent cartridge cases couldn't get round a sharp bend in the ducts provided to let them out of the aircraft. The bend was necessary to get past a vital rib on which the wing strength depended. That was no excuse. The empty cases must be given free passage, or the guns couldn't work.

Our real trouble was that we didn't know exactly how the empties behaved as they came flying out of the gun. We needed to know the path they took and how they twisted and tumbled as they careered away if we were to tell the aircraft designers what pitfalls to avoid. We had to go back to school ourselves to be ready for the arguments we could see coming.

I went over to see Williams, the highly skilled photographer who had come with us from Martlesham, to seek his help. It was necessary to negotiate past a large chestnut horse tethered outside his office door. I struggled to remember what you say to placate such a threatening obstacle before I dared to try to get round it.

"Bill," I shouted to him, "what the hell is this bloody thing guarding your gate?"

"Oh! That's Pegasus, my petrolless steed. He's harmless. There's a war on, you know, and we have petrol rationing. He brings me here on a gallon of oats, which lasts for more than forty miles!"

I told Bill I wanted to study the way the empty cartridge cases came out of the new cannon to solve the problem plaguing us. He said he'd have to borrow the right camera from a pal of his at Farnborough. "We'll need at least a thousand frames a second to catch what you seem to want."

Three technicians arrived in a van with an impressive water-cooled cine-camera, and we got down to work. We fired a trestle-mounted cannon with nothing around the opening below the breech, where the empties shot out. We filmed the action from the side and from the rear. Next we built an ejection shute of clear, thick plastic sheet to fasten below the opening. We repeated the performance to find out in what way a chute interfered. Finally we did it all over again with the gun on its side, as it was in the Hurricane. The results were illuminating. We projected the film, one frame at a time, tracing each outline of the empty case on a piece of paper. There developed a perfect dynamic picture of its path, step by step, halted in increments of time showing every twist, turn, and bounce.[7] The plotted paths of the fleeing, jostling, empty cases proved there was no way they could navigate past the tight bend in the inner chute. A hole would have to be cut through the main structural rib on each side of the unlucky airplane for the chute to pass straight through. I hated thinking what a major modification it would be; I hated even more knowing who would have to tell Hawkers.

Thank heavens I had the camera records to back me up when I took off in that trusting Hurricane, it being blindly unaware of its upcoming major surgery. I flew the fighter up to the Hawker Brooklands factory, where I met for the first time Mr. Sidney Camm, their awe-inspiring chief designer. I recounted the difficulty we had and how to overcome it.

"Nonsense!" he shouted. "Bloody impossible!"

I showed him the tracings from the photos to prove why we needed large holes cut through his precious ribs.

"Just who the hell do you think you are?" he bellowed. "Coming into my factory and telling me how to design my bloody aircraft! Get out!"

I retired with the armament draftsman, and we pored over the immense blueprints of the troublesome wing area. When I showed him the camera results, too, he got the point. "Mr. Camm's quite right you know," said the loyal engineer. "Strengthening the ribs after hacking them about your way will add a lot of weight to the fighter. But I do agree with you. We've got to do it. Obviously, nothing can be allowed to interfere with the working of the guns."

Sidney Camm left his office and came up quietly behind us, leaning over our shoulders. "Okay. What are we all wasting time about? Let's get this bloody installation modified and out again for these clowns to retest! Ruining my bloody aircraft, that's what they're doing!"

Walking through the plant, I was glad to note some armor plate being fitted to the Hurricanes as well as self-sealing petrol tanks...none too soon.

George Bulman, Hawker's chief test pilot, quickly arranged a lift back to Boscombe for me. As we flew home, I was still in mild shock, wondering what the hell had hit me. Sidney Camm was something else, a real experience. One consoling thought crossed my mind: from our film plots we could now design an ideal ejection chute, small enough to minimize the entry of bitterly cold air from outside at altitude yet large enough to eliminate the bird's nest produced by mutual interference of the empty but far-from-spent cases. I eventually wrote a brief report on our moviemaking with technical details to circulate to aircraft designers.

A Spit arrived for test with one 20 mm cannon and two .303 machine guns in each wing.[8] The version was already in limited production but it was the first we had seen of it. A small number had been sent to squadrons engaged in the battle over Britain for operational trials, an opportunity thought to be too good to miss by the tactical pundits in the ministry. The unchecked equipment suffered the usual teething troubles and the pilots who fought with them came away with very mixed feelings. Later, when things had been put right the extra range of the cannon and their hitting power were more appreciated against the heavier armor plate being fitted by the Germans.

I was glad to land back at home base after some trials we ran over Lyme Bay from a fighter satellite field near Exeter. A Polish squadron scrambled from there all day against massive German raids against other airfields in southern England. It was hairy experience sharing the field with these wild Slavic pilots. Between sorties they parked all around the perimeter. Refueled and rearmed, they just took off from where they stood, pointing at the middle of the grassy field. They somehow missed colliding but it was bloody dangerous. I know some of their props must have been clipping grass, so quickly and abruptly did the Poles raise their undercarts—the sooner to get their gunsights laid on the Hun again.

Squadron Leader Peter Whitworth caught me on the phone as I opened the door to my office. Pete was senior pilot in the fighter flight and we always shared much of the flight testing in the progress. "Dix," he said, "we have to get cracking. We're to join Fighter Command tomorrow. They are down to their very last reserve of pilots, and any one who can fly a Spit or a Hurricane is being rounded up. We'll be given actual squadrons and airfields tomorrow."

I rushed home to pack a small grip for our departure at dawn. We returned to the mess to lower a couple of pints together, thinking it might be a while before we could do that again.

In the morning we were told to stand by until noon, then until evening. It was the same the next day; and in the end, the whole emergency was called off. Fighter Command managed to stave off the evil day by themselves. While we waited nervously in the wings, unneeded stand-ins, the curtain came down on the Battle of Britain, and our own lack of combat experience was never tested.

Sidney Camm meanwhile had all the stops out to produce effective fighting machines for us. Within a month, the ribs of the experimental Hurricane had been brutally operated on and sewn back together. We also successfully completed air firing tests of the model and cleared it for production.

Hawker proved again, in late September, that they really did have the wick turned up. They sent us a brand new Hurricane with four cannon now having the French belt feed (British version). It was more than a great step forward; it was a three-league giant's stride ahead. The plane now had five times more ammo aboard. Unfortunately, we could not foresee the technical problems lying in wait. After two months of agony, not much ecstasy, and a bad bout of bronchitis from working in the snow out on the wings of our Hurricane, I had the problem licked—just before it licked me.[9] At long last, the weapons worked as well as guns ever do. I was satisfied we could do no more. Unhappily the superior fire power was too late for the Battle of Britain, but it was certainly ready for a lot of useful work elsewhere in the many battles to come.

GLOBAL UPDATE
September–October 1940

In an action of fearsome portent and supreme faith, the U.S. delivers the first of fifty destroyers to escort British convoys in exchange for ninety-nine-year leases of naval and air bases in Newfoundland, Bermuda, and the British West Indies.

The Italians advance into Egypt from Libya and push the weak British forces back to Sidi Barrani, fifty miles into Egypt.

Victory of the RAF in the air over Britain prevents invasion by Germany, but others, like vultures awaiting a kill, know only that the U.K. suffers relentless bombing every night. The remains of an old empire will make good pickings.

Tokyo joins the Rome-Berlin Axis and makes strong threats against the British use of the Burma road to help China. Russia gives Germany massive aid in raw materials as her ante. Spain offers Gibraltar and U-boat bases to the Germans, but the price asked staggers even Hitler. Franco wants Morocco and all of Algeria from Oran to the western border.

The nadir in collaboration is reached when Laval almost succeeds in moving Marshal Pétain into the war against Britain; but Pétain sees through the ruse and fires the traitor. Britain is fearful of a rumored move of two French battleships to Toulon for completion but Pétain gives his word not to allow it. Roosevelt offers to buy them but Pétain cannot sell under the German/French armistice terms.

Daylight raids increased in intensity, but Fighter Command was better able to cope with the killing pace of battle. Airfields could now be kept serviceable, and more importantly, sector bases that controlled fighter deployment were left undisturbed. Thanks to the incredible energy and push of newspaper mogul Lord Beaverbrook, appointed by Churchill to be chief of a new Ministry of Aircraft Production, there was no longer a shortage of fighters. Pilots were still slow in coming, but the crisis was over.

Very heavy German bomber losses forced the Luftwaffe to turn to night raids, as we had to in France in the spring. This shift also made them safe from the guns of Fighter Command, who could not engage at night with any degree of success. We needed heavy night fighters of long endurance, with sufficient armament and capability of carrying the ponderous new airborne radar-detecting device with a second crewman to operate it. As the Beaufighter came off the stocks, this deficiency would be righted thanks to the brilliant foresight of Mr. Frise, Bristol's chief designer. His contribution was invaluable to our nighttime air defense. Our stars seemed well cast and our luck in good shape. We were squeaking by, outliving the follies of the twenties and the grave mistakes of political appeasement. If we could win the last battle, as is supposed to be the smart thing to do, we'd be okay.

London was burning as fiercely as it did in 1660 in the great

Fire. Most of the children had been moved out for safety, and the people who kept the great city working went to ground at night and survived. Historic Plymouth was torn asunder; Coventry lay ruined. It was not easy. To improve the shining hour, the Germans started dropping huge blast bombs weighing a thousand pounds or more. They hung from parachutes that opened near the ground and were fused to go off immediately on contact. The concussion was horrendous on city buildings, particularly dwellings, and these German engines of war quickly earned the apt sobriquet of "blockbuster" from the irritated cockneys.

As for our own strategic bombing efforts, all our heavies were raised for night operations and were better prepared for such work than the Germans. But the winter weather was merciless, and we needed improved blind-flying aids and help in finding our targets. We needed more heat in the cabins, electrically heated clothing for the crews, and deicing equipment for the aircraft.

In July 1940 we were struggling with the gun turrets in the first very heavy twin-engined bomber—the Avro Manchester. Because of the urgency attached to its clearance, we had to combine turret tests with initial performance trials.

With a servo-feed arrangement for the four-gun tail turret much like that of the latest Whitley, the Manchester had long ammo tracks laid all down the fuselage from four monstrous rolls of three thousand belted rounds per gun carried up forward close to the center of gravity.[10] Such weight could not possibly have been carried in the tail. We didn't need to retest gun functioning because it was already well proven. Air tests of rotational and vertical gun movements had us immediately baffled. The outer shape of the fuselage at the tail was quite different from earlier heavies: larger and more boxy. As we started to rotate the turret, we lost precise control during the first small angles of movement, a problem that disappeared at larger angles. Our pilot bellowed loud complaints as I fiddled about.

He said I was making the aircraft yaw all over the place—much worse than the minor disturbance created by the same turret in the Whitley some months before.

With a mock-up plan of the turret laid over a fuselage plan on my office floor, I found out why the turret was creating such strong sideways suction on the tail end of the fuselage.[11] Avros made several variations of airflow spoilers to cure the problem—the long and the short and the tall—as the old barroom song will tell. We tried them all. Some helped a bit; some made it worse. At last "faired deflectors" did the trick and we gave the turret an okay without further messing about.[12]

The Manchester left our hands shortly afterward, never to be seen again. Besides the expected teething troubles of a brand new engine design, there were apparently many other problems that we knew nothing about. The performance pilots confided to me she was a bitch to fly, with or without successful turret deflectors.

Although the Manchester design was scrapped, from its ashes rose a new and beautiful phoenix, with four well-tried Merlin engines and many of the unburned bones of the Manchester intact. The new bird was christened "Lancaster" and became the backbone of Bomber Command. It was the best of all the heavies. The Merlins had ample power to allow design modification time and again, to stretch its performance. In the end it carried tremendous bomb loads to any target we chose. The Lancaster increasingly became the dreaded scourge of the enemy for the duration of the war; it brought him much well-deserved grief.

Charlie Dann moved quickly to test new blast bombs, inspired by the German blockbuster, carrying a much higher percentage of explosive than our current standards—and weighing two thousand pounds each, for good measure. It was lucky we could order the steel cases for these beastly things from the U.S. where twenty-four-inch diameter oil pipe was now available for that purpose.

1917—First "Little Bertha" aerial high-capacity, light-case bomb. 1,650 pounds. At an aerodrome in France.

1940—Prototype high-capacity, light-case 2,000-pound "Blockbuster bomb." Boscombe Down, Wilts.

Not all of my gunnery tests involved fighter aircraft or bomber turrets. A novel opportunity came my way to lighten a gloomy day. David Waghorn appeared in my office demanding a cup of tea. He carried a small gun.

"This little rifle of mine doesn't seem to be working very well," he mentioned, after we'd properly discussed the weather. "Do you think one of you chaps could look at it for me?"

"My dear fellow," I replied, "for you, nothing but the very best! I'll fix it myself." He left it on my desk and took his leave.

The rifle was in two parts, which like a bayonet, were joined together with a quick half-twist. The bullets were of small caliber, but the little menace carried about twelve shells, pushed along by a spring in a long tube within the gunstock. It was designed to fire semiautomatically, one shot at a time, reloading itself as it fired. The trigger had to be released and pulled again for each shot. I found that a small part had broken off of a lever and been lost. The lever could easily be copied and replaced if only I knew what its original shape was. It was an interesting bit of detective work to figure it out and draw up something for the machine shop to work on. I designed a new lever that made the rifle fire all twelve shots in a burst, fully automatic if the trigger was pulled and not released. With a small modification, the same device would behave the way it was supposed to, making the rifle fire semiautomatically.

We had a very good tool-and-die man in the workshops, and I gave him drawings of both pieces that I wanted and left the rifle with him. Thomason enjoyed the little intrigue and soon brought the gun back with the fully automatic design fitted. The machinist and I repaired to the range and fired a few rounds. It worked like a charm.

"Thomason," I said, "you are an absolute craftsman! I'm glad you're on our side."

I gave Dave a tinkle. "Your rifle is ready for you to collect and the fee is a pint of bitter. Come and try it out on the butts." I really don't quite know what mischief got into me when we met at the range and I loaded the little beauty for him. "Be careful," I warned. "It's an experimental part. Aim low at the target, and hold on tight!" But my warning wasn't enough. David aimed and pulled the trigger. The little rifle burst into song, sounding like the tearing of a coarse piece of calico, and within a second was suddenly silent. All twelve shots had gone, the last one over the top of the twenty-foot bank of sand.

David's face was a sight to behold. Surprise, consternation, and a bit of anger. "What the hell!" was all he could say, but he quickly recovered. "Here, take the damn thing!" he said, thrusting the smoking barrel toward me. "I don't want this menace."

"Hey, don't point it at me!" I shouted. "Put it down!" David stalked off in high dudgeon, and I had no time to explain that I also had the semiautomatic version for him to try.

So that is how I came to own a neat little rifle, ideal for poaching, because each dismantled half could be put down a trousers leg and there be undetected. It could knock down a bird at fifty yards, as Pete Whitworth and I found out on one of our evening strolls around the edge of the airfield.

The results were even more satisfactory after the mess cook had done his stuff, to the envy of anyone who happened to sit down to lunch with us. "What kind of favoritism is this?" asked Reggie Emson in dismay as we enjoyed some rabbit stew.

I finally got to explain my rotten behavior to David, but he was no longer interested. "Keep the bloody thing," he said with a twinkle. "You're having much more fun with it than I would." I was really forgiven when we shared some of our poaching loot with him, a rather typical British compromise. My family as a matter of course came into some of the booty for an evening's indulgence, requiring a minimum of meat coupons.

GLOBAL UPDATE
December 1940–March 1941

When reinforcements arrive in Egypt, the British launch a surprise attack and break the Italian line. In six weeks they reach El Agheila, capturing 150,000 prisoners and their equipment. The Duce's army is in chaos. The British are able to detach a small contingent of troops to Ethiopia to help cleanse the area of the remaining Roman aggressors.

In February General Rommel and his Africa Korps are airlifted to bolster the Italian remnants and revive the conquest of Egypt.

The U.S. Congress passes the Lend-Lease Act in March, a statesmanlike and generous action in these times of peril. It is a life raft for Britain and for world democracy.

The British go to the aid of Greece after Mussolini invades from Albania. To save his partner, Hitler throws huge forces into Greece and Yugoslavia from Bulgaria and steamrollers all resistance. The Greeks ask the British to leave in order to save their country from destruction.

Admiral Cunningham's fleet intercepts an Italian armada heading east to help the Nazis in Greece. Off Cape Matapan three enemy cruisers are sunk and a battleship badly damaged; British naval supremacy in these waters is reaffirmed.

After boasting to his führer two months earlier that he would clear the skies over Britain necessary for Sea Lion, on September 6 Goering acknowledged defeat.

Hitler's reliable peasant wisdom told him the invasion could wait. Britain was helpless to threaten Europe and could now, as he so nicely put it, "be beaten into submission and her will destroyed" by unrelenting terror bombing across the country. He switched the Luftwaffe to massed, indiscriminate attacks on open cities and ports. The raids started in daylight because the German bombers were trained to operate in support of the army. They soon learned that the strategic use of bombers is safer and more certain of success in the dark of night. They had a good beam navigation device in the *Knickebein*[13] until we found out how to jam it. Then came the mysterious *X-Gerat* system,[14] much more sophisticated and harder to counter. As Britain was a global maritime power, many of the important targets on the Hun's shopping list were coastal or built around a large river estuary. Such cities are easily found at night without radio aids, especially when there is a moon and heavy clouds do not hide the reflected faces of the stars. Even on the darkest night, to the adapted eye there's a palpable difference between land and water. Aids are always needed when clouds roll in—the norm over Europe.

When the target was located, the German modus operandi—like ours—was first to bomb with high explosive to open up the buildings, then go in with incendiaries and follow up with more high explosive to spread the fires. It proved to be the most destructive method of bombing cities, with the bonus of providing blazing beacons for bombers yet to come.

As time went on, the RAF trained special crews equipped with ingenious target-finding aids to drop coded flares to mark aiming points for the approaching bombers and guide them in. For the Germans the *X-Gerat* system became the key to the obliteration of Coventry and other hard-to-find inland targets. We had no air defense to find and shoot down their bombers nor any system for countering the new beam. Our answer lay in the rapidly increasing production of the Beau heavy night fighter and the miniature radar airborne interceptor (AI). By May 1941 two hundred of these fighters were in service and became so effective the Germans were forced to give up mass attacks on Britain entirely.

We needed some sort of break to lift our spirits; it came in May. Our convoys were threatened by at least a dozen dangerous German capital ships. They lurked in ports from Trondheim to Brest and from time to time sallied forth to sink our merchantmen. We became aware of the secret sailing of the *Bismarck*, the newest and most powerful battleship in the world, and the eight-inch-gun cruiser *Prinz Eugen*. We had two battleships and a battle-cruiser poised at Scapa Flow to meet that very moment.

The German ships were sighted by cruisers patrolling north of Iceland. Our major ships in the Atlantic area, some eighteen in all, including at least two dozen destroyers, were given sailing orders to join battle. In an Herculean encounter the *Bismarck* was sunk. It was a major defeat for the German navy though we lost the battle-cruiser *Hood* and most of her fifteen hundred men.[15]

During the terrible blitz that went on every night from early September 1940 until May 1941 the royal family very often visited newly devastated sites by the next day. Their brave presence lent great support to the people in their hour of deep distress. Their Majesties' encouragement gave new heart to the stricken civilians with whom they so clearly identified. With the blitz inferno quenched, the royal family had a little time to get out of town and see how the other half was living. About this time after breakfast one day, the CO called a conference of the senior officers. "Gentlemen," he announced, "tomorrow, the king and queen will honor us with a visit. They will arrive in separate cars at 1230 hours. I will meet His Majesty outside and escort him in to the card room, where you'll all be assembled. The queen will then arrive and be brought in by her attendants.

"After a glass of sherry we will have lunch at 1330 hours, and you'll then leave for your various stations on the airfield. Be ready to explain to Their Majesties what we are doing here at the experimental establishment. There'll be no flying after lunch and when that's over, we'll all meet again for tea and be joined by the king's mother, Queen Mary."

He briefed us on protocol—how we should address Their

Majesties, seating arrangements for lunch, and subjects we might discuss.

We rushed over to the flights to arrange some sort of interesting exhibition for our visitors and made sure we each had a passably decent uniform ready. We pretended to be blasé about the whole thing but were secretly thrilled to the proverbial core at the prospect.

Thank God it was a nice day for the occasion. Everyone had done something to clean the place up. Looking smart and eager, we all seemed to turn up early in the mess to be in good time.

Right on schedule "a pinnacle from far away" came flying in, one of the mess batmen, bearing news that the queen was at the gates and heading our way. We pulled our ties straight for the last time and formed a reception line by the open door of the card room.

Her Majesty Queen Elizabeth came in. She didn't sweep in. There was no great fanfare. She walked graciously through the door and quietly greeted each one of us, saying, "Good morning to you."

"Where's the king?" I asked Eddie Dark, sotto voce.

"Dunno," he replied. "He should've been here first."

Firm footsteps down the hall presaged the arrival of His Majesty King George VI. The queen broke away from her conversation to hurry over as the door opened once again. "Darling, where have you been?" she asked with real concern in her voice. "You're late, you know."

"Yes, my dear," the king responded, "but we got held up at the level crossing; and with the war on, we all have to wait!"

We were then introduced to His Majesty, by the queen, herself, who affectionately made the rounds again with him.

Lunch was great. Nothing special, though a free glass of a nice claret was welcome, and the atmosphere was genteel but not stuffy. The king and queen went out of their way to put us at ease. Their entourage, distributed among us at table, was kind and fascinating to talk to.

The show took up most of the afternoon, and the king, in particular, was intensely interested in everything. He showed considerable knowledge of my side of things and stayed a long time chatting about air armament. A gentle man, obviously enjoying this relaxed duty to his people, to men who bore his standard and were granted his commission. It was a pleasure and a unique privilege.

We hurried back from the field to get there just ahead of the king's mother, who did sweep in most regally. I was somewhat in awe until she smiled disarmingly and bade, "A very good day to you all."

Tea was a little hectic. With the addition of Queen Mary's retinue it was indeed crowded. I was gingerly holding a cup in one hand, wondering how I could tuck into a thin brown bread cucumber sandwich with the other, when an aide I was talking to lowered his voice and leaned close to my ear.

"Why don't you take Queen Mary a slice of that cream cake over there. She simply loves cream cake!" So I put all my stuff down and went over to the table where the cakes were displayed. I proceeded to lift a goodly slice of the richest and creamiest onto a plate for Her Majesty, tickled by the little conspiracy.

At an opportune moment I carried it over and, excusing myself, asked Queen Mary if she would care for a little cake.

"How thoughtful of you, young man," she beamed. "How ever did you know. I just adore cream cake. How lovely. Thank you so much!" I could only grin, backing away in the prescribed manner, and go and retrieve my half-eaten sandwich. Queen Mary certainly had won my heart.

I was next to David Waghorn in the line as Their Majesties prepared to leave. When Queen Elizabeth said to him, "Good-bye, Wing Commander," he bowed slightly and quietly replied, "Good-bye, sir." It was hard to suppress a smile, but I managed to hold it until their party had gone outside. Those of us who had heard the lovely little gaffe just broke up and roared. David was teased about it for days and sometimes even addressed as "ma'am." Dear old David. Alas, not long after, he was killed in a crash.

GLOBAL UPDATE
April–May 1941

The Royal Navy rescues fifty thousand men from Greece in a second "Dunkirk," but without adequate air cover, embarkation can only be made in the hours of dark over a period of five nights. Half go to Crete to continue the fight there and the rest to Tobruk to face Rommel. The small Greek navy sails to Alexandria and joins the British fleet to continue the fight.

Unbeknownst to Hitler, Deputy Führer Rudolph Hess flies solo to Scotland in a Messerschmitt and parachutes down close to the Duke of Hamilton's estate. He believes the duke is a friend of Germany and can persuade the king to throw out the present government and negotiate a truce. This insane mission earns him imprisonment for the duration, and eventually for life.

Crete proves to be a temporary stop for the British evacuees from Greece because of a massive invasion by German paratroopers, though the Royal Navy prevents any amphibious landings. The British are forced to withdraw and are rescued once again by the navy, though losses are cruel.

With over a year of war under our belts, the well-defined and highly specialized roles of different types of aircraft were beginning to change. Fighters, conceived solely to destroy other aircraft in the air, had proved invaluable against ground targets in France, especially the few on field trials with four 20 mm cannons. We needed an agile fighter-cum-bomber unto the day we'd be back on the Continent, working closely with the army. We also needed fighters with a longer endurance for escorting bombers by day and similar heavier fighters for night defense at home.

In the long winter siege of 1940–41 the Blenheim, a light

bomber, was *faute de mieux* pressed into service as a night fighter for a short while, but it wasn't designed for the specific job of attacking other aircraft. It wasn't nimble enough nor were the controls sensitive enough for air-to-air combat, but the winds of change were building.

The chief designer of de Havilland's honored us with a visit so he could see for himself the state of the art in the armament testing world. "I think it's high time we got away from all the heavy defensive stuff in our bombers," he started off. "Since 1938 I've been preaching that we should go for the lightest, most powerfully engined airframe and rely only on speed and altitude for protection."

"Bish," and I dared call Bishop by his fond nickname, "what kind of load will such an airplane carry?"

"Well, I'm pretty far along with a design that has a useful payload of at least a thousand pounds and will have diverse applications," he replied.[16] "The first one is a long-range fighter for night use, with a bomber variant to follow right behind."

Charles Dann and I were able to make a few suggestions to which he listened with flattering attention. "Tell me about what you want in armament installations," said Bish. "I promise you we'll give you the best ever! What are you finding wrong in your tests so we'll know what to avoid?"

We began receiving many different types of aircraft with forward-firing armament for trial. In the past, most would not have been expected to perform in this role. Some were not good enough in terms of "aim-ability." The planes had minds of their own when we tried to hold a steady aim on a target and wandered all over the place. They lacked sufficient longitudinal stability for accurate fixed forward-firing armament, a basic requirement neither specified nor emphasized in their design. I discussed it with Dru, my old mentor, telling him I planned to install a camera gun in these mongrel types to record their aiming characteristics.

"Yes, you should," he said. "You'll need a record of just how well these bloody airplanes can be held on target. If you don't have valid proof the performance section won't believe you when you want something changed; and you certainly won't get the makers to do a damned thing about it without performance's blessing." Deep wisdom.

Willy, our photographer, fitted 16 mm cinecameras in the test aircraft aligned with the gunsight and hooked up to the firing button. We'd show the world our aim in black and white.

I chose a splendid, ready-made aiming point on the ground some five miles to the west of the airfield: it was Stonehenge. The ancient monument, about four thousand years old, served our needs perfectly. The two inner circles of megalithic stones, some more than twenty feet high, gave us a beautiful bulls-eye. The much older ditch running around the outside was three hundred feet across and photographed as a big oval. By measuring its width, we had the range to target; by comparing the height to the width of the oval, we had the angle of dive. As we projected the movie, we were able to assess just how well our aim held.

I'm sure the Bronze Age astronomers who founded this place couldn't have cared less what we did, nor would the Druids who later used Stonehenge as a temple have considered our dummy attacks sacrilegious. Hurtling down for the first time with my gunsight trained on the bluestone horseshoe of the inner sanctum, I did, however, take the precaution to murmur in propitiation the only Welsh-Druid words I knew: *Diolch yn fawr,* "Thank you very much." Just in case, of course. Thereafter, all airplanes carrying forward-firing weapons were so tested. With film evidence to back us up, we no longer relied solely on our superb intuition.

The de Havilland Mosquito fighter proved to be a truly outstanding aircraft.[17] The kind and generous visit that Bish had made six months before to discuss the armament really paid off. We on the gunnery side found the mosquito to be the easiest

1941—The ubiquitous MOSQUITO for close support with standard four × 20 mm cannon in bomb bay and four .303-caliber machine guns in nose and also four more 20 mm cannons in container beneath fuselage forward of bomb bay and four 3.5-inch rockets under each outer wing.

RAF Museum photograph.

1941—MOSQUITO W4052 and SPITFIRE W3237 ground cannon trials. TYPHOON R7579 and SPITFIRE P8134 stand behind awaiting their turn.

fighter to operate and rearm that we had yet encountered. It was even more convenient than the well-designed Beau. With the huge bomb bay doors open our armorers could work in comfort on the four 20 mm cannon, protected from rain or from the blistering hot sun of the desert. Because the Mossie was low-slung, even the shortest armorer could hoist into place the heavy cannon and the ammo belts. It was a dream. It flew as swiftly and as gracefully as a swallow. Moreover, everything functioned flawlessly and without any need for modification. This baby had been born, like Mozart, already grown up.

With this superb airplane cleared for production, I called up my boss. "How about a few days' leave, sir, if poss?" I begged. "We've been at it without a break for months."

"Sorry, old boy," came the firm reply. "Four more aircraft for you will be here any day now. You'll just have to wait." At least I tried. So—back to the grindstone.

In they came, over the perimeter fence, one after another in rapid succession: the Hawker Typhoon[18] with a huge, newly designed Sabre engine, the most massive single-seater we had ever seen; a large, American twin-engined Havoc II.[19] The third, believe it or not, was a colossal, four-engined bomber, the U.S. B-24 Liberator[20] destined for Coastal Command—its forward firing 20 mm cannons dedicated to attacking surfaced submarines. Within a month, "type hog" that I was, I had the pleasure of flying six new types of aircraft. That made up a bit for weary bones and a heap of stress.

GLOBAL UPDATE
May—June 1941

Roosevelt freezes all German assets in the U.S. and closes all consular and propaganda offices.

Britain's 1930 treaty with Iraq, stemming from the post World War I protectorate, gives full facilities for passage of forces in war. Though still neutral, Prime Minister Rashid Ali and three leading officers conspire against Britain and work with the Germans. The British bring additional brigades to the port of Basra to protect their rights and to safeguard a great air-assembly base being established for the U.S. The RAF responds to opposition from the Iraqi Air Force at the Habbaniya air base and wipes it out. Baghdad is occupied and the deposed Regent reinstated. Peace is restored by 1 June at small cost.

On June 22 Hitler invades Russia without warning, in spite of their mutual defense pact. The Red Army is rolled back at an appalling rate on a thousand mile front from the Black Sea to the Baltic; a blitzkrieg on a scale for Alexander the Great to envy.

General Sir Archibald Wavell is commander in chief during all the successful campaigns in North and East Africa and the peripheral actions in the Balkans and the Middle East, and needs a well earned relief. An exchange of command is made at the end of June with General Sir Claude Auchinleck, commander in chief India.

As if we weren't busy enough, an American single-seat fighter, the Airacobra,[21] was flown in by Col. George Price of the U.S. Army Air Corps for us to test. About the size of a Spitfire, it mounted a strange mixture of guns: one large 37 mm Colt cannon (short-barreled) mounted to fire through the hub of the propeller and four smaller-caliber machine guns installed in the nose.

The big cannon was intriguing, the largest we had come across in an aircraft. We hurriedly taxied her to the stop butts for firing. With a tricycle undercart, the Airacobra's tail was up in the air ready for us to slide a trestle underneath and tie her down. When we let fly with the cannon it was an impressive performance by any standards but so short-lived. The blasted thing, painfully reminiscent of our earlier trials and tribulations, only fired a few rounds before giving up the ghost.

With the nose cowling removed, we saw that we were back on familiar ground. There was a beautiful bird's nest of empty shell cases built up in the ejection chute leading from the gun to a hole cut in the side of the nose cowling. I decided we had to go back to the movies for help and called up Bill Williams to get his chums from Farnborough over with all their fancy camera gear. I also called up the American Embassy in London.

"May I speak to Colonel Reed?" I asked.

"One moment, please," came back the operator's beguiling American accent. I could tell she was good-looking and was about to ask her for a date when a male voice came on.

"Colonel Reed speaking."

"Froggie! This is Dixi Dean. We have an Airacobra with a sick 37 mm cannon installation. How soon can you come down and give us a hand?"

Froggie Reed was military attaché at the embassy and a good friend. We saw him quite often at our experimental establishment and he had *carte blanche* to all we were doing. Furthermore, he played a mean game of squash and always brought his racket. Fortunately, there were more of us than of him, so we could spread out the punishment; but I don't think he lost many games.

"See you tomorrow," he said.

George Price had to get back to Wright Field, the Army Air Corps test establishment in Ohio. "I'm really sorry, guys," he said. "I can't hang around any longer, but watch this baby when you get to fly her. She's a real hot ship!" We were to remember his words when Squadron Leader Bamber, one of our test pilots, was killed in the aircraft during a trial a little later on. The Airacobra's bite was venomous.

We unscrewed the massive securing bolts and got the cannon out with a crane. We fastened it down to a trestle at the butts and threw some heavy sandbags around the support. I spent some time examining the gun, trying to figure how it worked. It quickly took its revenge on me, as if to teach me not to tamper with a creature I hardly knew. The heavy breech block ran forward when I pressed a sensitive spot and seized the end of my thumb.

"Hang on!" shouted Corporal Tucker, quickly getting a crowbar to free me. As I look down at the thumb today, I can still see the scar where the doc was able to sew the end back on.

Froggie turned up on the morrow and we started to take our high speed movies. "I've asked the ordnance people in Washington to send out someone who knows the gun," he told us. "Rosie Taber is flying over right away. Can you put him up in the mess?"

Col. Rosie Taber lived up to his name—a cheerful, likable person, all smiles but no fool by a long shot. We examined the films together, and it was immediately obvious where the trouble lay. As the gun recoiled and the breech opened, an ejection lever shaped like the crooked finger of a witch came down smartly to strike the empty shell case near the rear end. Now nobody, and I suppose also nothing, likes to be smacked on the rear end. The point of impact was much too far back, half an inch behind the empty case's center of gravity. The case shot out of the long hole in the bottom of the gun, rear end first, and began to tumble backward, end over end.

Rosie, glancing at my bandaged thumb, took the gun apart for us, cleverly and without any self-inflicted wounds. "Got to know how to handle these bitches!" he said with a grin.

We looked at the drawings of the gun. "Why don't we make a longer ejection lever," suggested smart aleck Dean, "and try that?"

"Oh, good heavens no!" protested Rosie. "We can't do that without getting it approved by the ordnance committee back home in Washington. Really!"

"I didn't hear you," I whispered to myself.

I gave the ejection lever from the gun, and a sketch of the extension I wanted to Thomason in the workshops. I also borrowed Rosie's official drawings to study and somehow or other left them overnight with the machinist. Careless thing to do.

Thomason slipped the drawings back to me in the morning before coming over to the armory with a professionally blued piece of mechanism that exactly fitted into the cannon. Rosie, of course, washed his hands of the whole affair. He more or less had to in his position, and we understood.

We put the gun back together, and the cameras rolled again. The next set of high-speed shots showed the cases coming out flat, without any tumbling. Better still, with the gun back in the aircraft we found all nineteen rounds in the magazine fired without a stoppage—on the ground and in the air. Yoicks!

We'd solved the ever-patient Rosie's problem as well. "Look, Rosie," I offered, "I know I've been a pain in the backside, but let me write a memo suggesting that a longer ejector might get rid of the empties more cleanly...just maybe, of course." Rosie sent it off by courier to Washington, and faces were saved all round.

The gunnery trials on the Airacobra were over. We had the 37 mm cannon working well. The machine guns needed no help from us but I had to record wander-of-aim before writing it all up.

I took her up with a camera gun and attacked Stonehenge. I didn't like it much. The aircraft was unstable fore and aft, hunting up and down, dolphinlike, in the attack. Once you knew about it and took a little care, it was controllable. I made a note to recommend the aircraft be corrected on the production line. I must also tell how we found—as the weight of all the ammo forward was used up—she became tail-heavy, producing a condition as dangerous as a lee helm on the bounding main.

The plane unfortunately had other drawbacks, but I think what disturbed me most about the big but short-barreled cannon was its low muzzle velocity—far too low for armor penetration for close support ops and too low to give an effective tactical advantage in long-range air-to-air engagement. All in all, I felt I could not recommend it for RAF day-fighter use at that time, even though it was being offered on Lend-Lease.

"Dixi," said Pete, "don't be such an ungrateful bastard. You really shouldn't be looking a gift horse in the mouth!"

"But it's the teeth that matter, Pete!" I was obliged to say.

The Airacobras were not wasted by any means. We did use them in the RAF eventually in some arenas to excellent effect. In the meantime, they were largely diverted to our ally who had immediate use for them—the Soviet Air Force—the red devil with whom for some time we'd been supping with a long spoon.

GLOBAL UPDATE
March–June 1941

Rommel attacks Wavell's small army at El Agheila in March, and by June 1941 pushes him back to the Egyptian border, regaining all the port cities along the way except Tobruk.

Wavell was told to hole up in Fortress Tobruk, which is well protected and has an excellent harbor. The Desert Fox is too wily to bypass this thorn in his flesh—one he is unable to pull out. For a spell the desert war is halted.

The British Air Staff was urgently seeking means to give closer support to the Eighth Army's campaign. "Army Co-op" as we knew it before the war was mainly reconnaissance. The RAF beamed the cavalry and acted as spotters for the heavy artillery. The RAF's role *vis-a-vis* the army was growing into more active, close-support involvement, with German tanks as a prime target. However, the forward-firing weapons currently available to the RAF were simply not adequate against tanks. We had been somewhat preoccupied with the Battle of Britain.

Charles Dann gave a green light for the Hurricane to carry a couple of bombs[22] (one under each wing) weighing either 250 or 500 pounds each. It became our first aircraft for true close support. Put in action in the desert in November 1941, it revolutionized our land-battle tactics, but the guns were still much too light to destroy many of Rommel's heavier tanks.

For the time being, only bombs could knock out a tank, though they were not accurate enough when dropped from a safe height. Fighter-bombers could get in close and let go at low level, but the bombs became a menace to the bomber, itself. With the instinct of newborn whales, bombs have a nasty habit of keeping up with the mother aircraft as they slowly drop away. The bombs also had to be fused to go off on impact. If set with a time-delay, any near miss bounced past the target to "…waste its sweetness on the desert air." A steep turn immediately after bomb release was highly recommended to assure a safe and final parting.

Charles and I discussed the relative charms of using guns or bombs against tanks. "I realize we haven't got a big enough gun yet," I said, "but if I may coin a simile, bombing a tank at low level is like hanging on to a hand grenade too long."

"At least a bomb can do some damage," he argued. It was time to deliver my *coup de grâce*.

"Yes," I agreed, "but does the messenger have to be sacrificed so often? Human cannon balls are considered somewhat passé, you know." I think he found my argument difficult to refute.

Perhaps we should take a lesson from the Luftwaffe trained specifically for army support. We did not have an airplane designed for dive bombing, and we'd have to become proficient in that art. Should we look into modifying our fighter-bombers with dive brakes and pilot bombsights—and banshee sirens?

Five

In September 1941—a month after we wound up the Airacobra trials—my old and trusty Hurricane[1] came back armed with two unbelievable 40 mm Vickers cannons, one slung under each wing. Each carried fifteen rounds in a hopper. It was an awe-inspiring sight. I couldn't wait to get Charles Dann on the phone. "Can you spare a moment?" I asked. "There's a new installation on the tarmac I thought you ought to see."

I waited by the Hurricane for him to join me. "Good God!" he had the decency to say. "Poor Rommel!" I wondered.

The fearsome beast's ground trials started with the familiar tail-up-on-a-trestle scenario. I decided it would be prudent to begin with a single round from the port side Big Bertha only. I

RAF Museum photograph.

1941—Prototype HURRICANE Z2326. Two x 40 mm Vickers "S" cannon with fifteen rounds each. HE or AP ammo. first air fired at Boscombe 21 September 1941.

fired it by remote control, and was immediately deafened by the clap of thunder it made. As we watched the retaining sleepers at the target fly into splinters, a second crash brought our attention back to the aircraft. On firing, the Hurricane had slewed around from the recoil. The left wheel jumped clean over the chock; the tail slid off the trestle and fell heavily to the ground. "Oh damn!" I groaned. "Now I've wrecked the whole shebang!"

Luckily, Mr. Camm made the Hurricane strong enough to take heavy landings, and this was surely a heavy one. Careful overall inspection showed no damage, either from the cannon's recoil or from the carelessness of the chap in charge.

I made sure we had double ropes and larger wheel chocks for the next shot and fired both guns at once to balance the recoil in each wing. When the dust had settled, we found it was by and large a most satisfactory show. The aircraft bucked and groaned but took it all in stride. The cannons were also designed to fire automatically, but I daren't try it on the ground. The guns from

Vickers, sired by the machine guns that armed our fighters in World War I were behaving with professional efficiency. We could get on with air firing.

"That's it, chaps. That's enough," I called out. "Let's turn her around. Get her up again and level her in flying position. Line up pointing exactly at that target over there."

I climbed into the cockpit to align the gunsight, previously harmonized with the line-of-flight datum, on the black cross painted on our distant target. Corporal Tucker—my right-hand man—trained each gun on the cross, too. "Okay, sir, I'm on!" he shouted. I figured the shells would take about half a second to reach the target and during that time would drop five feet earthward. So I adjusted the gunsight down to aim at a point five feet below Tucker's black cross. We were ready to go.

I went into the flight office at dispersal to set up our first air firing test. My good friend, collaborator, and fellow poacher Peter Whitworth was at his desk. He bellowed to the flight sergeant to get the Hurricane readied and he turned back to me. "You go and have a bite of lunch, Dixi. I'll take her up for you," he volunteered. "Just tell me the program and I'll be off."

"Pete, you old dog," I responded, "in this rat race with a lot of unknowns, I have to do it myself. Sorry, but it's my job anyway. We all know you're an excellent airframe driver and all that stuff...that's not the point. As an armorer, I've got to stick my neck out first. Thanks anyway."

"Bloody nonsense!" he burst out. "That's absolute poppycock. You just want all the flaming kudos!"

"Maybe," I replied, "but I doubt it. I know I'd rather live with you if the first test works out than have to live without you if some stupid thing goes wrong with the armament that I could've fixed. I'll take bloody good care, really."

"Okay, laddie. You win."

As I climbed to ten thousand feet, a comfortable height to bail out if need be, I thought over our recent exchange of views. Pete was a real pal, and I understood just what he was saying. If put to the test, myself, was I the magician I claimed to be?

I pulled the hood open, dialed to fire both cannon in salvo, semiautomatic, and very gingerly pressed the tit. The Hurricane seemed to pause in flight as I heard a huge explosion. Before I could react, recoil pushed the nose down well below the horizon. It was awesome, yet we were still flying and the wings were still on! I'm sure I heard a little voice break in. Yes, it was Pete saying, "Piece o' cake!"

I was ready for it the next time. I pulled back on the stick immediately after firing, as one instinctively hauls on the tiller of a boat just as a gust blows up, and the nose stayed put on the horizon. "Piece o' cake," I echoed.

I tried an experiment. I fired five pairs in full automatic, and by anticipating the nose-down thrust each time a pair went off, I could haul the sight back onto the cloud I was aiming at on the horizon. It was great—it could be done.

I flew back to the airfield, absolutely ecstatic—so much so I couldn't do anything about it when the Hurricane did a victory roll over A Flight dispersal, all on its own. It must have drawn a disapproving frown from the flight commander, but fortunately I was too far away to see.

The cannon installation was working so well we immediately started an accuracy trial against a simulated tank. The armorers set up a canvas screen, ten feet high and twenty feet long, on the side of a hill and painted a life-size tank silhouette on it. With a high muzzle velocity of over 2,000 ft/sec we knew our accuracy would be spectacular and armor penetration satisfactory when we got to that test, too.

Pete and I now indulged in a running battle to get the best results. My first attempt produced only eight hits out of thirty; the next was better—sixteen in the black area. Pete's scores were much the same.

We drove over to see the target where our shot holes were marked and identified. "There's something wrong here," I said. "See this last set of yours? It's a beautiful tight group right in the middle of the target, but it's about five feet too high. Half of your shots on the canvas are over the top of the tank—and mine too. Look!"

Pete nodded his head. "Yes, the ruddy guns are accurate all right, but they're high all the time."

I got hold of the designer from Vickers, who was holding our hand during the trials. "No problem," he told us in the soothing bedside manner of a country G.P. "With large guns like these we often come across a phenomenon called 'gun jump.' Just allow for it in your sighting. You'll find it'll be very consistent."

"We're really in the big league now, Pete," I remarked. "Just like a bloody battleship." I still had a slightly uneasy feeling that the kind doctor was fobbing us off a bit.

I had the center dot of the reflector gunsight raised five feet (at four hundred yards), and we returned to our tournament. We both now raked in scores with all shots in the tank: a dead heat. But when we tried to get in two or more pairs of shots on the same run, it didn't work out as well.

We procured a Valentine tank and set it up on the range so we could attack from all angles. Head-on wasn't very effective; the heavy frontal armor baffled us. We could do crippling damage from the side—the tracks didn't like it a bit.

"Pete, we ought to talk to the Tank Corps boys to find out where they think they're most vulnerable and what evasive tactics they might use."

We were warmly welcomed by the horseless cavalry and had a very useful exchange of ideas. They even let us drive their hot, smelly, noisy dragons, the better to understand their problems. Driving a tank is pure purgatory. It's painful. It's hard to see ahead, and that's the only direction you can see anyway. Without warning, you find the damned thing rearing up and up and up, and then...wham...down over the rise with a shock that jolts every tooth and bone.

"Let's get back to civilized war, Pete," says I.

"Do come back and have another ride," invited the helpful

tank major, grinning slyly behind his big mustache as we took our leave.

We did learn a lot from that visit. All in all, we figured a flank attack was surely the most effective, even though the tank would probably be moving at speed across our bows, making the aim more difficult. It was much the largest area and the softest, where he'd have the hardest job spotting us. If we only damaged a track it would stop him, leaving him to be picked off later.

The diameter of the transparent orange dot at the center of the reflector sight covers one degree of angle. At four hundred yards (a good sighting range), one degree covers twenty feet—just about the length of a tank. I was constrained to make up a dreadful mnemonic for the squadron pilots to help them remember to press in close, at least within four hundred yards before firing and to give them a crude range finder. It ran: "If your pip fits, you'll get hits!" Corny as it was, Gp. Capt. Eddie Dark, our new ATO, evidently thought it good enough to include in our official report on the aircraft under the recommendations and operational aspects section.

The hefty cannon installation was so successful that we passed it for production in less than a fortnight. Only three weeks after firing it for the first time, I had orders to put on a special demonstration for the absolute top brass: the chief of Air Staff, the secretary of state for Air and the minister for Aircraft Production—no less. It was an SRO show. They were suitably impressed and as pleased—I hope—as we were.

Disaster struck soon after. My not-very-complimentary report on the Airacobra had by now reached the ears of the high-ups in the American Army Air Corps. They knew about the new Hurricane with the Big Berthas through their air attaché and asked us to put on a comparative trial of the Airacobra and the Hurricane against a real tank so they could see for themselves.

The American officers drove down from London and just before lunch came outside to watch us land. I touched down first in the Hurricane, taxied up to the tarmac, and got out to join the group. The pilot who was to demonstrate the Airacobra landed next and turned toward us. Suddenly, as the aircraft approached to some fifty yards away, it sank to the ground as though genuflecting to the crowd. We all ran to see what had happened. The young man's face was scarlet to behold. On the Airacobra there are two small switches side-by-side on the starboard side of the dashboard. One of them operates the flaps an the other, guess what? The undercart. The poor fellow had meant to raise his flaps after landing.

"Goddammit!" spluttered the senior U.S. general, "You SOBs did that on purpose to foul up the trial jut because you don't like the airplane! You know very well it's a good ship!"

"Come back again next week, General," said our CO. "Damn sorry about that. It really was an accident, you know. We'll fix up the Airacobra good as new and show you. Now come on in and have a nice glass of sherry. There's a good chap."

We were particularly careful the next time. Some things you can get away with only once. The generals were finally satisfied that the Colt 37 mm cannon was not man enough for a tank at any angle.

Our Hurricane became the Mark IID but did not reach service in North Africa for six months. By that time Rommel's armor included the dreaded Tiger tank. The Hurricane IID was a real menace to the Afrika Korps, but against the massive armor of the Tiger at least, she had tough sledding.

GLOBAL UPDATE
August–December 1941

Roosevelt and Churchill meet in secret at sea off Newfoundland in August and issue a statement of common war aims known as the "Atlantic Charter," a beacon of hope for the surviving civilized world.

The Nazi hordes are deep into Russia by September. Leningrad is completely encircled, starting a siege of over two years. Kiev is captured, capital of the Ukraine, one of the richest and most productive states of the Soviet Union.

"Once upon a time..." is how the story of aircraft rocket development in the RAF should begin. The way an overgrown firework matured in less than two years into a lethal and versatile weapon is truly a fairy tale. Its blossoming was as confused as the growth of a teenager, but its ultimate role and direction were as clear as a bell to true believers.

The first known rocket to be fired in anger was used in China in A.D. 1232 by Kung Fai Fu, but there is no authentic record of how it fared. Nearly seven hundred years and many wars later, Captain Albert Ball of the Royal Flying Corps lashed four small rockets in a fan to the interplane struts of his SE.5 fighter. He went on to attack German observation balloons with firery and satisfactory results. But U.K. officialdom viewed the rocket with scepticism and gave little encouragement to its development before World War II broke out. By 1939 the dreamers were still a frustrated fraternity.

Dr. R. H. Goddard, an American and the father of modern rocketry, was indeed a prophet without honor in his own land. Only in Germany was there any official advanced work in progress. Even there as a weapon, it was still somewhat of a Cinderella until after 1939. The Russians, in their blunt, ruthless approach, produced a good, simple, and terrifying artillery rocket in time to help stem the Nazi invasion along Napoleon's fateful route to Moscow.

In the U.K. a barrage weapon was being developed for some time before the outbreak of war. It was meant as a backup to the ack-ack batteries deployed for the defense of London and other cities when conditions precluded visual gun prediction, and radar for this purpose was still a gleam in Robert Watson-Watt's eye. It was a cheap rocket with an explosive warhead, capable of taking on aircraft at great heights. Woolwich Arsenal developed it under Alwyn Crowe, later dubbed knight and known (out of his hearing but with affection) as "Sir Carrion." His rockets were fired pell-mell into the nigth skies in great numbers with great enthusiasm but limited effect. The main damage they did was to the roofs of the city below, caused by empty rocket cases falling carelessly to earth.

In August 1941, Dr. Charles Lauritsen of Caltech paid us a visit to exchange technical information. An important subject on his list was rockets. Back in the U.S. his report elicited informal approval from Dr. Vannevar Bush to start a new rocket program at Pasedena, with Lauritsen as director of research. He wanted to establish production of a high-energy propellant, specifically the "double-base"[2] compositon Alwyn Crowe was using. Dr. Crowe sent him a batch of our rockets to play with.

The rocket has always held a magical fascination for the armorer. There is no recoil when it is fired, nor is a heavy breech needed to contain the explosion propelling the missile. Guns are an awful nuisance to hold onto when fired: a large gun has the kick of a healthy mule. As we, ourselves, now knew firing a large automatic cannon gives a small airplane on which it is mounted serious pause for thought. To neutralize the heavier tanks being deployed by the Germans, we needed bigger shells than it was possible to fire from any cannon our fighter-bombers could carry. It all began quietly with no great-to-do and little promise either. A fortnight after the 40 mm cannon show for the top brass, Eddie Dark sent me over to Farnborough. "Dixi, go over and take a look at a new rocket installation that's coming to us shortly. Sounds weird. You might have some ideas."

At Farnborough I taxied across to the armament hangar. An old Hurricane stood waiting patiently outside with the air of an overburdened ass. It sported what looked like a couple of bedsteads, one hanging from each wing. I met a boffin crawling out from under one of the beds. It was Carpenter, an old armament chum of mine. "Hi!" he said. "Here's the rocket setup we're getting ready for you. What d' you think?"

"Well, I don't really know," I temporized. "Does all this junk go with it?"

"Well yes, to begin with," he admitted.

October 25, 1941—Prototype HURRICANE L1760. Six × 25-pound warhead rockets with triangular tail fins and twelve-foot rail launchers. First air firing at Thorney Island.

"Okay, which is the bloody rocket?" I inquired, a bit uneasy and querulous about this ugly insult to the Hurricane.

"Here we are," he said, relieved to be on a safer subject. "They're known under the code name 'U.P.'[3]—unrotated projectile. This tube is the motor with a solid armor-piercing 'shot' from a twenty-five-pound gun on the front. The triangular fins at the back end are to stabilize it in flight, like an arrow."

"Good heavens! Back to the Battle of Hastings," I groaned.

"Certainly not," he said, obviously a mite miffed. "These are the same U.P.s being fired at aircraft over London. They're very powerful; they'll reach a bomber over thirty thousand feet up. From a plane the rockets will hit a target a quarter mile away in about a second and a half and will strike at over a thousand miles an hour. Bit better than an arrow, huh?"

"What sort of damage to a tank?" I asked, suitably humbled.

"Well, we don't know yet," he answered. "We're building a target of four-inch-thick tempered-steel armor plate, forty-feet by forty, for you to shoot at. We think you'll get through it."

"Wow!" I blurted, off guard and much impressed.

I had to complain about the awful air drag from the ghastly mess under the wings of the poor Hurricane. "It's made this way because we don't know what'll happen when you fire in the air," Carpenter patiently explained. "We had to put that heavy plate under the wing because the flames from the rocket exhaust are very hot and have a tremendous blast. We've got to have those rails to guide them because they start from rest, so to speak. It's the best we can do for now. Bear with us."

We arranged to have the first ground firing test from the southerly edge of the airfield on Thorney Island about five miles east of Portsmouth. We'd shoot out over the English Channel. "We'll be ready in a week," said Carpenter.

On 25 October 1941—a date I'll not forget—I collected the heavy-laden Hurricane[4] from Farnborough and flew south to Thorney in a jiffy. The scientists were waiting for me with high-speed cameras set up and all the needed ground equipment. "Up with the tail!" shouted someone, by now a cry like some operatic anvil chorus in my ears.

We fired a single rocket by remote control, more or less to see what would happen to the long-suffering airplane. It was a very impressive performance. I'd never seen such a large one fired before. My God! What a din! Rocket exhaust makes a devilish noise, a reverberating howl of anguish that seems to go on forever. Its flame reached back beyond the tail of the fighter. The missile seemed to hesitate before taking off like an express train, a white-hot star getting smaller and smaller in the distance until it was no more.

The quiet of that remote spot returned, and we came back to our senses. We went over to examine the Hurricane for damage, but nary a scratch. Neither the launching rails nor the blast plates were even warm.

"Would you like to fire one from the cockpit?" asked William Cook, senior chap from the Projectile Development

Establishment at Aberporth in Wales.

"Sure," I replied. "Always good to know how it all works before getting in the air." I climbed into the cockpit, leaving the sliding hood open. "Here we go!" I shouted and pressed the tit at the top of the control column. The second rocket roared away toward the English Channel. I'd not have known of its passage except for the noise, that brief sibilant thunder. I realized I was missing the violence and anger of the expected recoil from a weapon of this caliber. It didn't seem quite right.

"Don't go too high; we want to get a movie of the first U.P. fired in the air," Carpenter instructed me. "For posterity and all that." I agreed to fly over the cameras at two thousand feet, running south.

"Catch me if anything happens," I begged. In due course, flying with the hood open and my heart in my mouth, I fired the beast. It sped off, falling slowly away to the wind-flecked sea below. "Test the controls," said my guardian angel. "Okay? No smell? No fire aboard? Nothing? Incredible!"

A quick swing around, wheels down, flaps down, easy as we go. Back at the camera base, I cut the engine and hopped out. No sign of any damage. Just beautiful.

"These bloody rails wave around like a conductor's baton." I complained to Carpenter. "I can't see how we'll ever hit anything with all that wig-wagging going on out there."

"Let's wait and see," he suggested.

"I noticed a sunken coaster offshore," I said. "I'll go and have a shot at it with our next rocket."

Once more in the air, I made a brave attack on that already-fallen warrior sticking half out of the water, but when I hit the firing button, nothing happened. I eased out of the shallow dive half expecting a hangfire, a common little firework trick as I seemed to recall, but still nothing but a nasty hush. I aimed out to sea and tried again—same thing. On the ground, we found that the electrical pigtail had come unscrewed and fallen out of the back end of the rocket motor. No wonder it refused to play.

In the next pass at the stern of the rusty vessel, the rocket flew away like a bird, so smoothly did it leave it seemed a hit could do no harm. Neither the Hurricane nor I felt a thing. The rocket steamed ahead, dropping off sharply till it landed in the drink a hundred yards short.

"These damned things of yours, Bill," I told Cook, "don't behave like a respectable shell. They don't just drop off a wee bit down range—that's called gravity drop. Your toys have got what we shall now christen 'gravity droop' instead." I could see that Cookie was not amused. After all, it was his child.

"Can't we speed up the burning time?" I wondered, "to cut the flight time and reduce this fearful fall-away?"

"If you want to wait until next year, the answer is yes!" said Mr. Cook, a trifle stiffly. "Don't forget 'the best is the enemy of the good.' We have a damn good weapon right here, in full production."

"Touché!" I admitted readily. I knew when I was bested. I'd used the same argument myself, on occasion, with other scientists when they wanted to perfect something that was already good enough and was needed today and not tomorrow.

A few days later one of the Farnborough pilots pushed open my office door. "I've brought you the Hurricane with the rockets on. Carpenter's chaps have overhauled her after your escapade on Thorney Island. She's right as rain. I'll be off now. Good luck!" That was fast, I thought. I was mighty glad to get on with the trials of this formidable new weapon with such exciting potential. It could be just what we needed to tip the scales permanently against Rommel in Africa. The trouble was we might be too late; but until we made some practical trials, it wasn't at all certain we had a weapon at all. The most crucial test would be in mid-December against the armor plate target being built on a cliff southeast of Exeter.

The Hurricane carried three rockets under each wing. We'd fired singles in the air; it was time to fire some full salvos to find out if the aircraft could take it and the rockets would be kind enough to keep the fire in their bellies to themselves. It was reasonable to hope they wouldn't blow up in our faces—the antiaircraft pongos had fired enough of them by now. Over Lyme Bay with a buddy in another Hurricane to monitor the fun, I let off a barrage of six at once. We flew back to base to find all was well and we had nothing to fear.

Now we were ready to check the accuracy of our new toys and hunted for a safe place to fire them from the air. We found a sparsely inhabited area behind Ashley Walk and built a target of canvas sheeting to catch our shots. Our first joy turned to ashy dust. The results were very disappointing. The untamed rockets with minds of their own flew off down the range with careless abandon, almost totally ignoring our ten-by-twenty-foot target. Oh, indeed, we did hit it once or twice, and I was grateful for that modicum of cooperation.

"These blasted things aren't much good, are they?" said Pete Whitworth as he jumped down from the wing of the Hurricane after a futile attempt to score a single hit.

"Which way were you pointing?" I asked him innocently, earning a swift punch in the kidneys. "Let's fly down to Exeter and see how the armor target is coming along," I suggested to divert his wrath.

There on the cliffs we found a gargantuan structure rising. Two huge stanchions with cross girders surrounded by scaffolding had already taken shape. The half dozen workmen on the job were dwarfed by the immensity of their creation. They almost fell off as we made a low, steep circuit for a closer look-see. We saw about half the large squares of four-inch-thick armor plate were in position, secured to the framework.

"We certainly ought to be able to hit that thing," shouted Pete in my ear. "It's a hell of a lot bigger than any barn door!"

On 11 November 1941, a fortnight after the rocket's birth, my second son was born. His first appearance on the world stage was not as spectacular, but he held just as surely the same promise of a bright future. I was able to shove off for a day or two to see him and his mother settle down in our new house at Cholderton.

There was plenty of room for the newcomer. Three kids do not a rabble make. Anthony Michael Roger Dean fitted into the progression nicely: Ann was now five, and Pete was two. Ann's highly protective soul had matured to the point of being able to share her newest brother and not be overpossessive. She would be a wonderful baby-sitter one day. Pete took it all in stride; the logic of his philosophy carried the day. Suddenly his being the paté in the sandwich made things better all round for us.

My family had thoroughly enjoyed sharing the cottage in Middle Wallop with the Danns and bade them a sorrowful au'voir when we moved a few miles to the west—nearer to the airfield. We had half an acre of land to play with and soon had rows of vegetables on their way to our wartime pot. We tried our hand at chickens with the able help of a local farmer, and our egg supply was soon established. The only setback we suffered came from the newly developing skill of our neophyte egg collector. Ann appeared at the back door with two eggs nestling in her small cupped palms and her face heavy with concern. "I'm sorry, Mummy," she sighed. "One egg was very bad! It jumped right out of my hands." A small basket was introduced into the supply chain and the wastage reduced.

While Ann was collecting eggs, I should have been collecting, like any worthy and doting parent, some of her marvelous usages of our tongue. I'm still mindful of her response when reprimanded, mildly of course, for some infraction and being told to behave: "But I'm are being have," she said, and whatever it had been was immediately forgiven.

I was able to get home fairly regularly, interrupted only by overnight trips or trials conducted in remote places. Although we were at it for long hours at a stretch, the respite of time at home brought relief from the constant pressure. I couldn't help noticing the idiotic contrast in my own affairs. Personally I could not have been luckier and was the first to avow it. I spent almost all my time, naturally and properly, developing armament—a mission of destruction yet also one of preservation of our way of life. Now I had to get back to the camp and see what kind of care my other baby was receiving. No nurse truly trusts another, no matter how qualified.

I reported back to Eddie Dark. "You're just in time," he greeted me. "General Brett of the U.S. Army Air Corps, Air Marshall Linnell, and some other bigwigs want to come down and see these U.P.s of yours. I suggest we put on a show with a couple of attacks on the Valentine tank at Ashley Walk."

We had been firing the six rockets in three pairs, one from each wing, in moderate dives as steep as thirty degrees. To make the demonstration as impressive as possible, I decided we'd come in level at treetop height, passing almost over the heads of our guests. Just past them, Pete and I would fire all six rockets in a salvo. We were rapidly becoming showmen of the worst kind.

Waiting for the big day, we tried everything we could think of to make the rockets more accurate. We doubled the number of hangers along the body to keep the weapon straight as it flew off the rails. Farnborough thought it would help to double the size of the fins at the back end and ordered enough for testing. For a while, though, our exciting toy remained but a barrage weapon, a glorified shotgun with only half-a-dozen shot.

"In any event, Pete, if we can't hit the bastards at least we'll scare them to death!" I said, begging the question.

The demonstration went off with great aplomb. One rocket knocked a sprocket off the tank and sent the track flying, which was enough to show our baby off to advantage. The generals loved it. It was good to talk to Air Marshal "Black Jack" Linnell once more. I had not seen him since the days when I was under his stern command at Mildenhall in 1935. He was a marvelous leader, I could now recognize.

The happy result of the show was an immediate high

priority to get the rocket into service. Phones were jumping for the rest of the day. The chiefs wanted it just as soon as possible. "They want it," Eddie Dark told me, "more or less the way it is. Improve it, of course, but not now. You can do that later."

We were much gladdened. We already felt that in this weapon lay escape from the confines of the conventional gun. Here lay the only line of development to make possible an increase in close-support firepower for fighter-bombers.[5]

One call to Eddie that day wasn't so good, however. Thank heavens the generals had departed by this time. It appeared that one of our rockets, now fired in level flight, flew out beyond the confines of the range and set fire to some stacked wood in a timber mill, miles behind. The irate owner and local firemen managed to douse the blaze and rightly concluded that only we could be to blame.

"Please!" begged the bereft owner. "Could you fellows stop doing this sort of thing? It's becoming downright dangerous!" He was right, and we understood full well. We had just suffered

1942—HAVOC night fighter with six x .303-caliber upward firing guns destroyed with others by the only hit-and-run bombing raid on Boscombe airfield during the war.

a nasty little visitation ourselves from a stray hit-and-run German daylight raider out of the low clouds. He wiped out three of our experimental aircraft on the ground. The saw-miller had a point. It was getting to be a bit dangerous.

We were forced to find a new test range where we could fire in level flight and have a better measure of the accuracy of the shoots. I looked around the vicinity and found an excellent long, shallow valley leading west into the enormous army artillery range at Larkhill, ten miles to our northwest. The area was owned and worked by a farmer who lived at the mouth of the valley at Enford, just off the road leading north to Pewsey.

Eddie talked to the army. They had no objection but said we must coordinate with the farmer, who although actually within the limits of the danger area, did his farming when no gunnery was in progress. Pete and I called on him and drank tea in his cozy kitchen. We explained what was on our minds, and John Ludden was most obliging. We promised not to fire until we were well past his house and beyond the barns where his cattle were stabled. "And also, young man," he added, "we would very much like to have a couple of days closed down during the season when we can go shooting." John gave us a knowing wink as he showed us out. "And if you two would each like to bring along a gun and join us, by the way, you will be very welcome." He recognized a pair of wily poachers and knew how to buy off possible danger to his game. "I can promise you both a good day's sport."

"You have a deal," I said, noting that we had a pretty good bargain ourselves.

I thought a lot about possible targets. I wanted a vertical face at least twenty feet high and forty feet wide—four times the area of the largest target we had used to date. We needed to catch all the errant rockets, if possible, and by measuring their spread be able to detect any accuracy improvement after we changed anything. We couldn't use a large sheet of canvas. It would balloon out like a great spinnaker and be impossible to hang onto in any kind of wind. An image came to mind of fishermen's nets drying in the breeze on the sea wall down at Lyme Regis where we made our tests almost daily. The solution was simple: we'd get a large fishnet and stretch it between two poles at the west end of the valley.

The heat was really on, somewhat self-imposed, to be sure. Armor plate penetration trials were given the highest priority. A final conference at Farnborough on Christmas Day 1941 laid out the detail. Just after the holiday the team would meet at the Exeter airfield, our base for the trials.

All of the intricate machinery for such an undertaking was put into action. On a hunch, the day after the conference, I flew down to inspect the target for the last time. It was quite obvious there was no way in the world the last row of plates could be mounted in time, and the tournament would have to be rescheduled.

On the way back to Boscombe I landed at Warmwell for a bite to eat and to say hello to Ginger Lacey, the CO there. Ginger was an accomplished ace from the Battle of Britain days and had spent a while with us doing performance testing. A nice fellow. He was complaining to me about not being able to get into the air to continue giving the Luftwaffe the hell they richly deserved.

"These goddamned daylight hit-and-run raids really are a bloody nuisance," he bitched. "They come in below the radar, so we have no warning from sector to go after them. Flying so low, they do have a job finding us in time to get a good aim, but look at those confounded wireless masts over there! They're a perfect landmark for the bastards, and the bloody things are out of use, anyway!"

"Ginger, old pal, if those two towers just vanished overnight you could say 'lost to enemy action,' couldn't you? I need them badly."

"They're yours," said Ginger. "Come and get them. The sooner the better!" I'd just solved the problem of supports for my new fishnet target.

I headed back to Boscombe and to Eddie's office. He really

went all out for me. As usual, he was great. I'd hardly left the room before he was arranging a gang of men and someone who knew about wooden latticed masts to be on the road to Warmwell. They were ready to leave by tea time, aiming to return within two days. "Meet you out at Enford," I told the gallant leader as they left camp. "Call me from Farmer Ludden's place when you get in."

The two masts were ideal. With large pulleys mounted at the tops, we hoisted the twenty-foot sides of the target, making its bottom edge a good fifty feet above the valley floor. The corners of the net were hauled down by ropes and tied to the bases of the towers, producing a nice taut screen. I just couldn't wait to try it out. "Get ready for a shoot," I told Corporal Tucker.

In the air for a trial run, I fired a pair of rockets. When the net was lowered onto the grass, it was easy to see where they had passed through. A couple of ex-mariners I found in my crew quickly repaired the holes with proper sail needles and marlin spikes. We had it made.

We next sewed a big white cross in the center and threaded broad white tapes through the net vertically and horizontally at five-foot intervals, marking out a big grid. Using binoculars the ground crew could pinpoint each impact and immediately record it on paper without holding up attacking aircraft between passes. Happy day!

GLOBAL UPDATE
December 1941

After a two-hundred-year search for empire, Japan makes the same fatal miscalculations as Italy and Germany—that democracies will continue to allow the predications of dictator-led states. When Japan seizes French Indochina and Hainan Island, off Hong Kong, the U.S. says—enough. A total embargo is imposed and all Japanese assets in the U.S. are frozen. Negotiators go to Washington but during the talks war plans are being finalized. The Japanese fleet has already sailed. At dawn on 7 December without warning two heavy air attacks are launched on Pearl Harbor, destroying the bulk of the U.S. fleet and most of the planes on the ground. Fleet carriers are out on maneuvers and escape the odious action which has been planned since January of 1941.

Roosevelt declares war that day calling it "A date which will live in infamy!" Britain promptly declares war as well.

All the forces of the democracies in the world are now in the field against the satanic trio.

We hear the news as night falls on our opposite side of the world and experience the same shock as two years before when Chamberlain addressed us. Though inured to bad news, we empathize with our old ally going through that fatal moment from peace to total war. We cannot help feeling, too, an ineffable sense of relief that we are no longer completely alone and there is no more doubt of the final outcome.

Three days after Pearl Harbor, the British navy moves the battleship *Prince of Wales* and the heavy cruiser *Repulse* up the Malayan coast to the north. Acting on faulty intelligence they undertake the passage in spite of air cover not being available. Both warships are immediately attacked and sunk by Japanese bombers from the mainland.

A follow-up conference on the top-secret Gloster fighter was held in January 1942 to approve the status of its development. The plane was called Meteor and powered by jet propulsion, a brand new concept to most of us. When I asked a year ago, Charles Dann wasn't so far out guessing the engine might be a rocket. By now I could offer better advice about the armament. We had a wealth of practical experience with successful inboard-cannon mountings in several different aircraft, and I no longer had to don the garb of a phony pundit. The Meteor had the hallmarks of an outstanding aircraft.

I secretly thought our best hope for effective forward-firing lay in the rocket, but we had to improve its accuracy to give it a passable chance of hitting a tank at four hundred yard. The next step seemed to be larger stabilizing fins, and I waited anxiously for them to arrive from Farnborough.

Others worried about the problem too, but my approach derived from a pilot's point of view, expressed sometimes with a paucity of patience. Cookie told me they were trying to improve the way the propellant burned in the tube.[6] "We understand what you want," Cookie said, "and wish we had an easy answer. The only thing to do for the moment, a palliative at best, seems to be to constrain the rockets with long guide rails to the maximum possible speed before release."[7] Naturally, the boffins' approach to the problem and our own were biased, but each had merit. As we got to know each other better, we found much common ground and could both contribute something useful—cross-fertilization, sort of. There was little time to do much about it before the armor plate trials.

Three weeks into the new year, Eddie Dark came on the phone. "What are you waiting for, Dixi? The Exeter target is ready, and I do think it warrants your passing attention!"

Pete and I took off in high gear to pick up our emergency weekend bags. In less than the shake of a lamb's tail, we were on the field at Exeter, moments ahead of the people from Farnborough and PDE in Wales. There was a genial gathering that night in the pub where we stayed; it was a good opportunity to bounce our ideas back and forth.

"These bloody rails have to be changed!" I challenged for the umpteenth time between rounds of "lah-de-dah," a game in which I was forfeiting all my loose change to the more mentally agile boffins. What I really meant was that the rails should be dumped.

"Don't be so damned impatient." This from Carpenter. "Let's just see how it goes tomorrow."

We started first thing in the morning. A firing-point marker was set up on a line at right angles to the face of the armor target, four hundred yards away. The target looked absolutely enormous. How could we possibly miss it? But we did! We missed it all day. Pete and I took turns firing the six rockets in pairs as we passed over the marker a quarter mile away. We could easily have come closer and wanted to, but our scientific guides pointed out that the rocket took just over a second to burn out and attain maximum final speed for penetration. Unfortunately, launched at the speed of the Hurricane, it needed a quarter mile to do so.

By five o'clock that afternoon we were an unhappy group. Only one shot had clipped a plate near the target's edge and gone right through. It may have been a fluke, and we needed more than a single lucky shot to prove anything. It certainly would be a fluke if we ever managed to hit a small tank. The scientists left for the pub while we laid plans with the armorers and the ground crew for an early start on the morrow.

"Pete, we've nothing to lose," I confided out of earshot. "Let's shorten these bloody rails and cut off all the flexible, unsupported lengths up front. And for God's sake, don't tell old Carpenter. They won't see the aircraft until after tomorrow's shoot."

"Dixi, you can't do it. At least clear it with them first," Pete remonstrated.

"Since when have you developed cold feet, you old Afrikaner sheep farmer?"

With a sharp hacksaw I cut four or more feet off every rail, back to the main forward support. I would like to have cut off more, but the design wouldn't permit. In any event, the rest of the guides under the wings were nice and stiff and wouldn't throw the rockets off their stride. Trouble was—the rest of the rocket mounting still gave a lot of drag, cutting down the combat speed of the plane. We oiled our way back to the pub with expressions most bland.

That evening over a jug of good local ale, the truth leaked out. Alcohol, besides being the lubricant of social interaction, has a way of loosening the most firmly clamped jaws. Cookie and Carpenter descended on me, as one.

"What the devil do you think you're doing?" they shouted in unison. "You insufferable jockey pilots think you know it all! No wonder we have so much trouble."

"Calm down, Cookie," I beseeched. "Dear boy, we can always put the bits and pieces back on again. Right? let's try tomorrow and see if it's any better. Couldn't be any worse than today." Nevertheless, I had to buy drinks all round to pay for my crass indiscretion. I hoped it would prove worthwhile.

Next day firing resumed as soon as there was enough light to see. Both Pete and I managed to hit the target fair and square about six times. Our shots passed clean through the tough armor as though it were made of the local creamy Devonshire butter.

We had a field conference and decided to shift the marker for the firing point around to one side and attack at an oblique angle of about forty-five degrees. The target now looked only thirty feet wide instead of forty and was obviously more tricky to hit, but what mattered was that the shot had to penetrate six inches of steel if it did not merely ricochet off. We made a number of hits and most of them went clean through. The olive-shaped nose of the warhead was designed by clever gunners to bite into metal at acute strike angles. By midafternoon we had demolished the target. The huge plates lay all over the place with nasty, shiny purple wounds in them. The supporting stanchions were cut to pieces and had ignominiously collapsed. A satisfactory day's destruction.

Everyone agreed on the vital importance of tactical air support for our ground forces in Africa and that fighter-bombers were the best way to give it. The Hurricane IIC with four 20 mm cannon was proving to be great against lightly armored vehicles; and in a dive from the rear, it could set a medium tank afire with strikes through the engine louvers. It was clearly not man enough against any of Rommel's heavier tanks, and for the nonce the fighters had to use bombs on those toughies. The 40 mm cannon would change the picture considerably when we got them into the field.

1942—Prototype HURRICANE IID Z2326. Two × 40 mm Rolls-Royce "BH" cannon. Twelve rounds/gun. HE or AP ammo. First air fired at Boscombe 4 February 1942.

February 4, 1942—Prototype HURRICANE Z2326 being hand-loaded with first round, for first air firing test.

At the beginning of February my workhorse Hurricane[8] came back from the factory at Brooklands with two 40 mm huge-caliber guns made by Rolls-Royce instead of Vickers. A strange switch from making elegant cars, I thought—or aircraft engines, for that matter. Anything stamped "R-R" is bound to work perfectly and the trials went flawlessly. Ground firing tests of these jeweler's pieces went without a hitch. In the air the recoil force was no more and the accuracy the same as the Vickers version. The guns were quickly cleared for service, giving us a second string to our bow to augment our close-support arsenal. But now, after the fantastic success of the new rocket against the armor plate target it became more important than ever to improve its accuracy. It would then give us a matching weapon against the Tiger, where the 40 mm cannon was a doubtful competitor.

Good news—as well as bad—travels fast. When we got back to Boscombe, we learned the chiefs of staff of all three services wanted to see for themselves. An immediate show was laid on, and the cocky "Boscombe Down Players" were only too ready to stage it. Shoeburyness was chosen as the site. Here on the north bank of the Thames estuary, all British major weapons testing has been going on for generations. It has been the proving ground for the ancient and venerable Ordnance Board since the year dot when it was set up to advise on the sharpness of the king's arrows. Be that as it may, the board is like an armament high court, a joint services group of senior experts with members full time for a two-year stretch. They meet very formally once a week and issue proceedings, beautifully printed, like acta from any respectable parliament, even having an elegant printing press for publishing these documents. The proceedings give the stamp of approval and solemn advice on all items of ordnance which an individual service will ignore at its peril. I'd served on it once. I know.

The range was chosen mainly because it was much nearer to

London than ours at Boscombe. Besides, a trial or demonstration at Shoeburyness lends considerable authority to the exercise. To the south of the range, out on the beach where the first magnetic mines were found two years ago, we called for a big canvas target with a black tank silhouette painted on it. A grandstand with steps, railings, seats, and a gay, fluttering canopy—for all the world like a jousting tournament pavilion—was set up on the dunes a few hundred yards back from the shore north of the target. By the time all this was ready, we'd assembled three Hurricanes, each equipped to fire six rockets. The aircraft would attack one at a time and each fire all its rockets in salvo.

On 18 February Pete Whitworth, Micky Bell-Syer, and I left Boscombe and flew east, a gaggle of geese in easy vee, headed for Rochford airfield, close to the proving ground. The weather got worse as we curved around the north of London and reached a point about ten miles north of the field. To the south where we had a mind to go, it was pea soup—pure, unadulterated, bloody pea soup.

I spied a railway line running down to the coast, and my chart showed it passing close to our destination. I split up the vee and got down on the deck so the others could play follow-my-leader along the "iron compass" under the fog. We plopped down one after another onto the airfield, to our own relief and the surprise of the local people. The seagulls had more sense: they'd all been grounded.

We had a day's grace before the show, which was just as well, since the fog from the ancient river still blanketed our world. Julius Caesar was right: the island was hardly worth keeping.

The next morning we were due over the range at 1100 hours, and the weather kept us below a thousand feet. Our initial entry into the lists was in a tight arrow around a small headland just west of the target area. Constrained to a hedge-hopping approach, we arrived largely unnoticed.

I heard afterward that as the minute hand of the large range clock in the pavilion with which we were synchronized crept up to 1100 hours and no aircraft had shown up, a very senior army officer remarked, in jest I feel sure, "And so the Air Force is late again!" just as we flashed into view from behind the headland a couple of seconds early. They hadn't even heard our coming. It certainly helped the drama we were at pains to create. Over their heads we split into a spectacular floral burst, and we came round one after another to beat up the canvas tank.

After we completed the attacks, made at close range to ensure the most hits, the brass walked out to inspect the tattered tank. I know for sure that each service chief began to dream up how and how soon this exciting and surprising weapon could be brought into his own arsenal.

GLOBAL UPDATE
Early 1941–late 1942

U-boats give Britain great concern posing a mounting threat to vital supply arteries across the ocean. Particularly in a large area in the middle of the Atlantic where the defense system against them is weak or missing altogether. Long-range aircraft similar to the German Condor are needed to cover the vulnerable expanse. Bomber Command is ordered to transfer some heavies to Coastal Command, but even the best they have to give have not the necessary endurance. Fortunately, Coastal Command receives a gift from the gods, a number of U.S. B-24s, or Liberator bombers. One of the maritime modifications the British make is to install forward-firing 20 mm cannon to engage U-boats on the surface. The Liberator has the range required to reach submarines lurking in the unprotected hole in the middle of the ocean.

The air battle over Britain was fought by our fighters; over Germany it was fought by our bombers. The struggles in the two arenas were of an entirely different nature, as though fought by two different species of antagonists. Fighters made swift, burning flights through the upper daylight skies over their own home, in full view of their kin. Their battle was won in three months. The bombers droned on in slow, tortuous struggles through dark and icy nights, waiting a turn on the altar of Mars, wreaking damage on industry and sadly, on historic, irreplaceable buildings beneath. Their fight lasted for over five years and only during the last half did it have any important military effect; and the battle was never completely won.

There came a critical low point in the fortunes of Bomber Command in late 1941. It was the second time the value of strategic bombing came into serious question—was the basic doctrine of an independent air force with a primary mission of long range strategic bombing a valid one? Early in the war when determined daylight raids on Germany began, the aircraft loss rate ran about eight percent, unacceptably high for the damage inflicted. The bombers were forced to turn from daylight attacks and seek the protection of darkness for survival. Though trained before the war for night ops, they were found to be ill-equipped for that duty, and their efficacy came under critical review.

Bomber squadrons battled on for a year against impossible odds. No escort was possible at night, and there was no reliable electronic aid to show the way to the target or help locate it on arrival. Station-keeping lights couldn't be used over enemy territory ruling out formation flying by night. It was everyone for himself, with no support from the dozens of other bombers milling around all trying to find the same target in the blackout. The dull, pervasive fears of engine failure, of icing, and worst, of collision with a friend were ever present. Most crews in their doomed pilgrimages had seen a midair collision—that sudden flash as fuel tanks ruptured, the flaming fall sometimes ending in a hideous ball of fire as undropped bombs exploded. The first ones to arrive on target were lucky. After bomb release they were free to turn away from the terror stream, change height and course, to gain a chance of a winning ticket home. Those still to come often bombed the flashes from the first release whether accurate or not. Deep raids could only be made in the long night hours of autumn and winter when the weather over Europe including their U.K. bases was execrable. German flak improved relentlessly and night fighters rose to pick them off or lie in wait for their uncertain return. The bomber boys began to lose confidence, and their will to succeed burned low.

As an ill-founded gesture of strength, an all-out effort was made on Berlin in early November 1941 with almost a hundred aircraft. Despite a late forecast of thick cloud and icing over the routes to the target, the foolhardy raid took place. One bomber group objected before takeoff and was sent to another target where better weather prevailed. They met with some success and little harm to themselves. From Berlin only scattered bombing results were reported. Aircraft losses were over twenty-one percent. it was the last major raid on the capital for over a year. The repercussions of this disastrous raid almost spelled the demise of Bomber Command in its present role. The War Cabinet halted the strategic offensive until a decision could be made on the future employment of the command. The ban remained in force for more than three months. The command might well have been reduced in size and relegated to a more tactical mission. Beating Germany would then have required a murderous land campaign after a costly invasion.

Bomber Command was in a "slough of Despond" waiting for the War Cabinet's decision when the first officers of the newly formed Eighth Air Force of the U.S. Army Corps arrived in Britain. Under General Ira C. Eaker, the command was promptly set up in quarters vacated by a well-known Ivy League girls school in High Wycombe, a country town also hosting Bomber Command headquarters. There's a tale both true and entertaining about the first military occupants of Wycombe Abbey's deserted dorms. They found notices on the bedroom walls saying: "If a mistress is needed in the night, please ring the bell." Edgar Allen Poe would have been proud of the nocturnal tintinnabulations.

These early arrivals, so soon after the disaster at Pearl, were warmly welcomed by the command. It looked forward to a close integration in a joint assault on the Hun if and when it returned to strategic ops.[9]

The Eighth came reared on the same basic doctrine as the RAF but believed the strategic effort should be made by day to be effective. They trained with the highly secret Norden bombsight which made possible strikes within a few hundred yards but needed a long, straight and level approach. Their bombers were heavily armed with power turrets carrying guns of almost twice the caliber we had with bullets of five times the weight. They planned their raids, flying close, massive formations relying on a dense crossfire pattern for defense against fighter attack. For safety from ack-ack they were to fly very high. Added to our attacks by night, such tactics would subject Germany to round-the-clock bombardment.

After much debate Churchill and the War Cabinet agreed to a continuance of Bomber Command in a strategic role thanks in large measure to the efforts of Sir Charles Portal, chief of the Air Staff. The decision also permitted the bombing of aircraft plants and other crucial targets even if located in densely built up areas because it was impossible to pinpoint those small industrial targets.

In February 1942 Air Chief Marshal Sir Arthur Harris became the leader of Bomber Command. All he was given to carry out the new directive was a total of five hundred and fifty bombers, no more than were operational a year before. Heavy losses and diversion of aircraft and crews to other commands had kept their numbers down.

On the plus side, all four-engine bombers coming off production carried heavier bomb loads, and effective electronic navigation devices were beginning to appear. A change in tactical procedure cut down losses. They concentrated on bombing fewer targets, and limited the time spent over the target areas. Bomb loads had more incendiaries, used mainly after roofing was blown off with blockbusters. Then, HE bombs collapsed walls into the streets, blocking the passage of fire equipment. The fire factor was thus exploited, doing more damage and overwhelming the firemen with devastating effect. "It is easier to burn a city down," said the new commander in chief, "than to blow it up." That oracle was fearfully demonstrated later on by the ghastly fire storm that incinerated Hamburg on 24 July 1943. Sir Charles Portal's rescue of the command from near annihilation had the firm backing of the prime minister. It was justified many times over.

Four thousand heavy bombers were needed to stage overwhelming strategic bombing. Bomber Command was already using—many said squandering—a third of our industrial capacity yet was only able to field a quarter of the estimated numbers of aircraft and crews necessary for the job. Probably heavy bombing would not shatter civilian morale. It had neither done so in Britain nor seemed likely to in Germany. There was tacit recognition that it alone would not do the trick; it was a necessary evil and was not, as some were saying, just a luxury for the Air Marshals.

Delivery of aircraft to the U.S. Eighth built up during 1942 until in August the first raid was made on the Continent with twelve B-17s against the railroad yards at Rouen in northern France. The raid was successful and without loss. Unhappily the good fortune did not last for long. The German fighters appeared in larger numbers and overwhelmed the bomber defenses in raids into Germany. Long-range fighters were needed but were not yet available for escort. The RAF gave Spitfire protection to the limit of their short range, both going in and meeting raids coming out, but the Eighth was on its own for the most dangerous part of the missions. Losses from German fighters and flak began to mount to hideous figures.

While the Eighth lacked long-range fighters we needed our new ultra heavy bombers with their superior performance to carry more bombs farther and fly faster and higher—for their better safety by night—to continue the obliteration of German industry, in all parts of the continent.

At last the interminable gestation of our big bombers was over. The Halifax came to us early in March 1942, soon followed by the Lancaster. All turrets were standard Frazer-Nash designs. Our tests were soon done—the problems minimal. A new trial we made with each giant was front-gun attacks against ground targets. We dived at various angles on primeval Druids' circle, with movie cameras running. Both bombers were very docile in this extreme form of attack, but the Lanc was superior in maneuvering control.

"Go do your worst," we bade as we launched them. "Good luck to you and those who come to fly you, too."

Charles Dann sent the bombers a new toy as well. He'd passed the latest eight-thousand-pound blockbuster for service, a powerful addition to our strategic arsenal. "I must tell you, Dix, that's not all," he confided, lowering his voice. "I'm trying out a fascinating gadget with Barnes Wallis for knocking down dams." He went on to describe a backward-rolling round bomb that skipped along the surface of the water after being dropped at very low altitude. "It will reach the dam wall, roll down the inner face and burst about fifty feet under water. The last problem we haven't solved is how to measure the exact dropping height when we're over the water at night. Sixty feet up ain't much," he said.

A few days later he kicked my door open. "I have it!" he yelled with a cry to rival Archimedes, "We'll button two small searchlights under the Lanc's wing tips and cant them in to meet sixty feet below. The navigator can make sure the puddles of light stay as one, and Bob's your uncle!"

"Can't you make it a bit more complicated?" I asked. "That's just too delightfully simple—it's liable to work." About a year later we found it did.

GLOBAL UPDATE
January–May 1942

A Declaration of United Nations is signed on 1 January 1942 by twenty-six countries, forming a massive coalition against the Axis powers.

The Japanese take over Manila as General MacArthur retires to the Bataan Peninsula. The Netherlands East Indies fall. A month later the British surrender Singapore. The defeat of an Allied fleet in the Java Sea precedes the surrender of Java itself. The British evacuate Rangoon. General Wainwright surrenders Bataan and makes a brief stand on Corregidor. All the Philippines fall twenty days later. A dreadful recitation of woe.

A silver lining glints briefly on 18 April when Col. Jimmy Doolittle flies sixteen B-25 light bombers from the deck of the carrier *Hornet*, six hundred and twenty miles off Japan, to bomb Tokyo and other cities. His daring raid uplifts the hearts of the groggy Allies and shakes up the Japanese beyond belief.

Japan attempts to isolate Australia. Tulagi in the lower Solomons and Port Moresby on Papua are the objectives. A task force under Admiral Fletcher, the *Yorktown* and *Lexington* with support from Allied cruisers and destroyers, engages Japanese fleets twice its size in the Battle of the Coral Sea. Both sides suffer serious losses. Although the Japanese sink more tonnage, including the *Lady Lex*, the Allies win the battle because the enemy loses the use of two heavy flattops for two important months. No Japanese warship ever dares come so far south again.

From the U.S. in early March 1942 came a well-bred airplane for trial. It was a day fighter, one of the first American P-51 Mustangs.[10] Built by North American Aviation of California to British specs and funded by the British Government, the order was placed in mid-April 1940, a month before the German blitzkrieg into France started. It was stipulated that because of the serious war situation in the U.K., a prototype must be completed within 120 days; it was ready in 117, but without an engine. The first ones coming off the production line in November 1941, initially with the low-altitude-rated Allison engine, were unfortunately not suitable for a high-altitude fighter role and RAF interest in the plane had lessened. The armament worked well, and four .50-caliber Brownings were impressive; but we were committed to the much larger 20 mm cannon which the P-51 mounted later. But from the start it was one of the best fighters of its day.

There was to be a large show of air-to-ground firepower at Imber, an abandoned village on the vast army range near Larkhill fifteen miles northwest of Boscombe. Tanks and other motorized vehicles were set out in the target area with a complement of dummy troops parked in elaborate array. In the early afternoon several squadrons made their attacks, but with the hazy weather, lack of rehearsal time, and confusion between the real troops and the dummies, a dreadful tragedy occurred: a confused fighter pilot attacked the spectators instead of the target, severely wounding many or killing them outright.

In spite of the debacle, I had to put on a similar show for Winston Churchill three days later at the same site. He wanted to see the 40 mm cannon against tanks. I made reconnaissance flights over the area two days in a row and a mock attack on the target the day before, to be very sure of things. Just before show time, I flew out to Imber and pinpointed the target tanks. Nearby, Mr. Churchill and his cortege were assembled with important members of every service who had to be there, if not to watch, then surely to be seen. It was immediately apparent that the two groups—the dummies and the live—did look dangerously alike from the air. Knowing the scene well by now, I could make a safe and reasonably impressive attack on the tanks. By good fortune they were old models and already well beaten up. Any new damage inflicted by the 40 mm guns was hard to identify, but the PM liked it. Sparks flew off the stricken warriors in abundance and the purpose of the exercise was achieved.

Six

"How would you like a trip to Ireland, Dixi?" Eddie Dark popped his head around my door. I gave him a cup of my precious tea and asked what the big joke was all about. "No joke, old boy," he said. "Plans are under way for building landing barges and tank landing craft LC(T), for amphibious landings. They're protégés of Churchill's. We have to find out how vulnerable they'll be to cannon fire. You and Pete get off tomorrow, at 1400." He told me the fighters and ammo to include in the trial.[1]

I met Pete out at dispersal. "Ready to go?" he asked.
"Okay, old lad." I replied. "You lead, but don't hurry; my

radio's a bit sick, and my old Hurricane with the 40 mms is a bit slower."

Within the hour we landed at Sealand Airfield near Chester, 250 miles north, to refuel and check weather over Erin. We still had over 300 miles to go northwest, more than half of it over the Irish Sea. It was a bit hazy, and the lowering sun in our eyes didn't help; but the air was pleasantly smooth. Pete was ahead to starboard. I guess we were both dozing a bit, at least I was, thinking about the interesting trials coming up. I suddenly realized Pete was drawing inexorably ahead, getting smaller and smaller as I watched.

"Hey!" I shouted, to no avail. "For God's sake don't leave me!" But I had no means of calling him. I was running at eighty percent power to keep up and didn't want to goose it any more or I'd run out of oomph.

I needed clearer visibility down and to the side. The Isle of Man should be in sight about now, ten miles or so away. Woof! As I pulled back the hood my chart fluttered up from my lap and blew away on the wind. Damn! Damn! Damn! Now I had no chart, no radio, and no leader.

"Relax," I said bravely to my faithful steed and to myself, "We can't very well miss Ireland, right?" It was an uncomfortable and lonely change in the erstwhile tranquillity of our little world. Pete was now out of sight and out of mind, too.

The only thing to do was point straight ahead, along the course of about 310 degrees we'd been holding for the past half hour. That much I'd noted. My first flying instructor told me so many moons ago (strangely, his name was Flight Lieutenant Moon), "Always keep your eye on your compass, and keep a field in mind where you can land—one with a big house alongside so you can stay the night!" He didn't say what to do over the drink where I now hung, but there was still the compass to watch over me.

I looked carefully but didn't see hide nor hair of the Isle of Man. Must have passed it in a daydream. It wasn't too long before I espied ahead the mountains of Morne sloping down to the sea.

I hadn't memorized the flight track in detail and so found myself subconsciously pressing in a whisper of right rudder. I mustn't fly to the south of Lough Foyle, the big inlet running down to Londonderry from the north, or I'd finish up over Donegal west of the border where neutrality is vigorously protected, if only by word of mouth.

Here we are! I breathed. Coming below the nose was a huge stretch of water, at least ten miles across, running north and south. But it's too soon; that must be the pride of Belfast, Lough Neagh. Was it? I pushed on for another ten long minutes before realizing the hills below must be the Sperrin Mountains. There, mercy be, is the River Foyle and the field right ahead waiting for me. In we go now—at last. Switches off.

An airman ran over and pulled down the retracting step. "Where's the other Hurricane?" I shouted to him, as I unbuckled the harness. "He should have been in fifteen minutes ago."

"You're the only one today, sir."

"Where are we?"

"Limavady, sir."

"Where the hell is Eglington, then?"

"Oh! About fifteen miles south. Down the coast, sir."

"Okay thanks. Stand clear! Contact!" My battery took the load, and my sweetheart started right up.

There was still plenty of light, and I had no qualms about finding our base now. Quickly airborne, a circle to the left staying low, eyes peeled for Eglington. Wait a jiff, I thought, my helper's idea of fifteen miles is pretty cockeyed. I'm on top of an airfield south of Limavady almost before coming back to cruising. Couldn't have been more than five miles away. Never mind, better make sure. In we go. I taxied over to a parked Spitfire and waited with the engine running, determined not to be fooled again. A crewman ran over and climbed up onto the wing.

"Tell me, is this Eglington?" I yelled to him.

"No sir, Ballykelly. Eglington's just down the coast."

I felt as though I was caught at the bottom of Finnean's rainbow, and seek as I might, would never find my pot of gold. Pyrites, maybe, the gold of fools. A few minutes later, I found airfield number three and also Pete Whitworth, lying in the grass with his eyes closed.

"What kept you?" he asked, with insincere concern.

A complete, steel landing barge had been moored on the east shore of the estuary, and alongside it a thirty-foot section of a landing craft (tank).[2] The targets were afloat for a couple of hours at full tide, but when the tide ran out both were left high and dry, accessible for checking the damage we intended to inflict. On the opposite bank only five miles away lay the wee town of Muff in "neutral" territory.

"Do you suppose they have any charts of Ireland in the Air House?" Pete asked with his practiced, innocent air. "Why are we doing trials with secret weapons in full view of a country lousy with Nazi spies?"

"Search me!" I answered. "Maybe they'll realize we're getting set for invasion and be scared to death wondering when we're coming. Seems crazy!" To this day I'm still puzzled why that venue was chosen. There were plenty of alternative places in England.

We had twenty-four hours to wait until the team of scientists arrived. "This might be a good opportunity to get our act together," I suggested to Pete. We took to the air and made dummy attacks on the vessels lying in the water, making sure we didn't infringe the neutral airspace five miles to the west. We were not seeking an international incident.

On the next two mornings Pete and I each made three live attacks against both targets while the tide was in. We spent the afternoons out on the beach examining the damage. Close scrutiny showed that none of the shots for either the 20 mm or the 40 mm guns penetrated the barge or the LC(T) below the water line. While not expected to sink either type of vessel, solid

May 15, 1942—Center section of tank landing (ship) target for air trials with 20 mm and 40 mm cannon.

May 15, 1942—Steel landing barge target for air trials with 20 mm and 40 mm cannon.

steel 20 mm shot did penetrate above the water line and rattle around inside. The high explosive 40 mm shells burst against the walls, making holes one to two feet across and blowing nasty fragments of steel inside—to the dismay, no doubt, of anyone within. Both were dangerous to fragile machinery and personnel, but we did need a larger caliber weapon. A rocket?

We packed up to leave but got no cooperation from the damned weather. The forecast for the next day was little better. Pete borrowed a shotgun to help pass the time, and we strolled off down the drying beach, putting up with the reek of low tide.

"How about a little duck for dinner?" Pete lifted the gun and felled a bird off to our left. We went over and picked it up. It was a shell duck, one I'd never tried before and never will again. It turned out to be the most fishy nonfish I've ever eaten. It tasted foul, and I had to leave most of mine, which only served a miserable poacher right. After that nondinner, a couple of RAF fighter boys operating from Eglington lent us civvies, and we all drove over the border to a local pub.

"Would ye lake a drap of foin Liffey watter?" asked the pub keeper. What could I say but "Sure!" It turned out to be delicious Guiness stout, straight from the barrel: black as treacle; smooth as cream.

The natives were very friendly and saw nothing fey about their idea of neutrality. They knew perfectly well who we were yet gave us a real welcome. Two young Irishmen we were drinking with told how they helped a Hudson aircraft from Coastal Command that had to land on the beach for lack of fuel. They filled him up from their own cars and told the pilot, "Get the hell out of here before we remember what we're doing!" We knew their petrol rationing was much stiffer than ours. They're absolutely mad; delightfully so.

It was a bit hard to reconcile their generous action with an attitude that permitted Luftwaffe bombers to fly in from France, proceed up the backbone of Ireland, and go on to attack our cities on the northwest coast of England and Scotland. Or succor

German U-boats on the west coast of bonny Eireann. Strange.

What's more, they were happy to sell, for a decent price at that, a pair of fine Irish smoked hams to take back to England. Very strange...or maybe it seemed that way to us because we Limeys really don't understand the Irish.

The weather cleared up enough for us to get under way, and this time our Wellington bomber with good navigational aids would lead us Hurricanes directly back to Boscombe. Pete and I tucked in close to the bomber's tail, stealing a glance downward now and then to check our passage. I had a new chart and kept my hood closed. The last clear glimpse I had below was in passing over the Isle of Anglesey (all these bloody Isles!) and on into Wales. We ran into flitting clouds and I shoved my starboard wing tip in as close to the bomber as I dared. I was almost touching the rear turret as it got darker and darker, but I couldn't hold it. Our blimpy host disappeared in a dense patch of cloud, and I had to break gently away. I'd lost him for good.

I was at 7,000 feet, approximately on a southeast course, now flying blind. The only problem—I was nearing Snowdon, at 3,500 feet, the highest mountain in Wales. Brecon Beacons, topping 2,900 feet, lay in wait eighty miles farther on. So I had a bit of clearance to play with.

I let my height bleed off slowly, hoping to get out of the murk: six-five...six thou...five-five...five thou...At four thou I began to see the mountains "as through a glass darkly" but they were too close for comfort. Damned if I wanted to play hide-and-seek with them. I couldn't even pronounce their lispy Welsh names. Another well-drummed-in lesson from instructor Moon reminded me: "Always avoid a cloud with a hard kernel!"

My tanks were still half full, or only half empty, depending on one's point of view; but it seemed prudent to get down on the ground and find out the weather at Boscombe while I still had visual contact. Tucking my tail between my legs, I veered off to port, away from the overt threat of the Beacons, and sensed the ground falling away. Now flying to the east, I was soon over much more hospitable terrain. And then, just over there, was a nice airfield with a welcome sign hung out. I immediately took up the tacit invitation to come in. It proved to be Honeybourne. The weather report was not too promising, but Hurricane and I wanted to be in our own stable for the night, so we pressed on. Indeed, we did have to perch once again, briefly, at Pershore. It was that bad.

Come early evening we were home. Once again Pete had beaten us by a short head because he was obliged to make only one precautionary landing. Afrikaners are tough; it must be the biltong they munch instead of chewing gum. "Damn your eyes, Pete!" I swore. But next time I made a vow to pick the faster steeplechaser.

GLOBAL UPDATE
June 1942

A month after its first naval setback in the Coral Sea, Japan attacks the U.S. base at Midway. It wants the tiny islands as a springboard for the conquest of Hawaii, a little over a thousand miles to the east. A diversionary landing force sails north to seize the two Aleutian islands of Attu and Kiska, and a large carrier force is to attack Dutch Harbor, seven hundred miles east of Kiska. The main carrier strike force nears Midway from the northwest on 4 June under Admiral Yamamoto, he who led the treacherous attacks on Pearl six months before. Unfortunately for him, he doesn't know his Naval Code has been cracked, and two U.S. task forces with three large carriers await him off the small Midway islands. In a fierce four-day battle, Japan suffers her worst naval defeat since 1592,[3] and the losses sustained affect her throughout the war. The threat to Hawaii is removed, and the Japanese are forced to confine future efforts to the Solomons and New Guinea. The victory at the Battle of Midway is the turning point in the Pacific, indeed, in the whole war, and effectively shatters Nipponese dreams of empire.

It took two squadrons of Spits to force the bastard down, to make him land in Wales—finally out of petrol—but not before he shot down two of ours. The Hun landed his brand new Focke-Wulf, Fw190A intact at Pembrey on the coast just south of Carmarthen.[4] It was mid-June 1942, and although the exceptional German day fighter had been in operations over France for some months, it was the first to be captured intact. What a prize.

I flew over to take a good look at her armament. There she lay, still sitting a hundred yards from the watch office where the pilot had stopped. The duty pilot described how he'd watched the strange bird come in low over the field, heckled by a veritable swarm of angry Spitfires, land, and taxi toward the buildings. He'd run over to challenge him with his .38 revolver.

"Pourquoi you landez ici?" he asked the pilot.

The Hun was indignant and shouted, "Eesy? Nein! Focke-Wulf vehr deeficult landen!"

The duty pilot warned me not to tamper with the cockpit hood because the pilot indicated that the aircraft would blow up if it were opened. It seemed like a sensible self-destruct measure to guard the secrets of a brand new type of plane. I examined the guns as best I could from the outside and with more care still when I saw at least two of the four 20 mm cannon had jammed after only a few rounds. A heavy thump might easily free a hang-up and fire off a round across my bows. I was delighted to note however, that the enemy seemed as beset with stoppage problems as we had been. Most of the rest of the ammunition seemed to be expended, including all from the two smaller guns in the fuselage. I steered well clear of the closed hood, ominous, glinting in the sunlight as though alive and daring me to touch it.

I took a van to the officers mess, where I met the German, now under house arrest with the orderly officer. He had a little English, and with my pidgin German, we conversed—sort of. I asked if his 20 mm cannon jammed very often. That didn't seem to phase him; he really wanted to talk about tactical maneuvers, aircraft performance, and so on. From the anteroom window he'd seen me arrive in a Spit and was being bloody nosy about how it handled and climbed. I cut him off abruptly and went back to my own interrogation. I suggested it was certainly an advantage to have a large number of cannon. He began to posture and bray that he'd just come from a *gruppe* with Me 109s, having only a quarter the number of cannon in the Fw 190. "*Eine Kanone*—enough for me!" he bit off, arms akimbo. That he downed two Spits in the recent scrap tended to bear him out, but he was an arrogant S.O.B., and I soon escaped his insufferable line of bull—after I solved the mystery of the canopy's explosive device. It was designed to help the pilot jettison his hood if he had to bail out, in extremis. At high speed it was impossible to open by hand. We were fooled for a brief moment and certainly lost face providing the cocky kraut prisoner with a chuckle at our expense.

The Focke-Wulf so impressed the Air Ministry they wrote a spec for a similar fighter. Hawker jumped on the ball and came up with a proposal for a plane they called Fury, but they already had a superior fighter built round a massive new engine in the final stages of a painful, protracted gestation. Within only a few months this Typhoon would prove to be more than a match.

GLOBAL UPDATE
July 1942

The news from North Africa is grim. Rommel retakes Tobruk in June after six months of fighting his way back east, more than four hundred miles from El Ageila. Tobruk is the most important supply port in the campaign area and a bastion of strength. For this outstanding feat Rommel is made field marshal. By July he is deep in Egypt but trapped in the Alamein bottleneck only sixty miles from Alexandria. Like the hot, dry *fohn* coming down from the Atlas mountains, we feel him breathing down our necks.

Fighter Command didn't like the restricted view over the nose in the heavier fighters caused by the great bulk of the powerful engines. The squadron pilots, bless their wits, again outdesigned the Farnborough boffins as they did once before when they fitted the first rear view mirrors to their aircraft—a boon and often a salvation—in the Battle of Britain to reveal a "Hun in the Sun" creeping up behind. They now designed and fitted a couple of mirrors that allowed them to see through the engine of a Spitfire with a much larger Merlin engine. Their "perimirror" embodied the basic elements of a periscope. The trick, as learned Confucius would say, "was all done by mirrors."[5] The device was much like those used by the unfortunates in the third row of a crowd trying to watch a royal procession. They sent the new Spit installation for our look-see. I'd just started to test out the ingenious idea when a Typhoon fighter also blew in with a factory version of the same periscope built in. Word evidently had traveled fast and been acted on as quickly by Sidney Camm at Hawker's.

At the same time also came Jimmie Bright to relieve me and take over my job as EGO. Eddie Dark had warned me it was about time to be moving on. "You've had the best experimental flying job in the Air Force for long enough, you old devil!" he told me. "You just can't hog it any longer."

Squadron Leader James Bright, D.F.C., survived the Battle of Britain and had the scalps of six confirmed Nazis on his belt. Jimmie knocked quietly on the door of my office and waited. I looked up to see a great big smile on a face that Charles Dann said later resembled a "good-looking David Niven."

"Come in, old boy," I said, getting to my feet. "Come on in." We talked. We talked immediately and for a long time. There was no hedging or pussyfooting. Jimmie was for real, exploding enthusiasm. We had a good time getting to know each other, and it was great to meet this ball of fire. We drove over to A Flight and met Pete and then went to try out the perimirror in the Spit. Taking turns in a second fighter, we acted as a target for each other. We also tried it in attacks on ground targets at low level, completely *ventre à terre*.

Back in the office, Corporal Tucker had put in another desk for Jimmie. We analyzed the quality of the perimirror, agreeing it was a very useful piece of equipment, especially helpful in low attacks, giving confidence with the extraordinary, apparent view through the nose. It is so easy to hit a tree just below your nose when you can't see it. The size of the mirrors did not seem to be optimal, so Jimmie asked if he could make a cockpit mock-up to play about with.

"Sure. Thought you'd never ask," I said, all poker faced.

He immediately got to work with a pair of sharp scissors and some of the large sheets of Bristol board we used for our jump cards and proceeded to fill the remains of our office space with a full-sized model of the front part of a fighter cockpit and cowling. He then mounted two large mirrors in the appropriate positions. While he sat on a stool where the pilot would be, he had me mark out on the mirrors the largest areas we could use for the periscope without blocking the pilots view. Our report approving the device to the Air House on behalf of Fighter Command included design guidelines for any other cockpit configuration to get the optimum view based on Jimmie's little research. He was born to this kind of job; his new coat would be a perfect fit.

The summer months of 1942 proved to be particularly busy and it was good to have his extra hand. It also gave me a chance to fly over to Whitchurch to see my younger brother, Pip, who was flying as a navigator with Imperial Airways. He quit Oxford before graduating to enlist. The idiot. They were flying unarmed Whitley bombers across the Bay of Biscay, staging at Gibraltar, and on to Malta with stores for the besieged fortress. Pip told me with a look of supreme disgust on his face how he had by chance discovered what was in one of the packing cases. It had opened up enroute, disclosing it was full of razor blades. He confessed to a feeling of sudden futility, risking so much for such a cargo. I tried to remind him that what he'd seen was only a small part of the load, and anyway, the British always shave and dress for dinner—anywhere! Part of the deal.

James and I flew as one in the flood of trials coming in. We needed a special gunsight installed for us at Hatfield. "Come on," I called to him. "Let's fly over and meet the boys at de Havilland's." Pete rustled up a couple of Hurricanes for us. "Better stay a bit close until we get there. They say the air's a bit murky." We taxied out, turning together, and took off from our huge grass field. After we'd settled down on course, I glanced back to port to see where Jimmie was and then more slowly turned my head back again, now touching the controls with thistle-down fingers. Jimmie's starboard wing tip, I swear, was stuck firmly in the RAF roundel painted on my fuselage, right by my elbow. Gingerly, I turned my head again and waved that happy, grinning face away. Please, my gesture said, I'm too old for this kind of thing. Go on, move out ten feet at least—twenty'd be better. What a fighter boy! Scaring the bloody wits out of me. At Hatfield we wandered around while the new sight was being installed and talked some more.

We landed back at Boscombe to see another Hurricane taxiing in ahead to A Flight. I saw it was a dear old friend now fitted with a "low-attack wing." It was a pleasure to introduce Jimmie to our first super close-support aircraft, the Hurricane Mark IV,[6] soon to become the "Hurri-bomber" to the squadrons.

August found us flying around the clock. We also had to put on a demonstration for General Echols of the U.S. Army Air Corps. We really didn't have time, but it gave us much pleasure and another chance to advertise our wanton waif. Firing eight rockets in salvo for the general's benefit at the start made a first-class show, and we were able to combine some of our business with a little P.R. for our R.P. (rocket projectiles).

• • •

A batch of long-awaited, sixty-pound warheads, designed for attacking ships, turned up for fuse testing. The gallant fighter shrugged off the three hundred extra pounds of two more rockets and heavier warheads without noticeable complaint, and I decided to combine trials for both the new low-attack wing and the fuses. We selected a range for live-explosive air firing that was due south on the coast at Chesil Bank, five miles west of Weymouth. Jimmie and I aviated down to Warmwell, our base for the trials.

While I opened the ball, Jimmie flew alongside to pick up the procedure. He then took over the attack, and I flew wing for him. It was enlightening to watch a rocket launch from so close by. Jimmie made some very neat, precise attacks, but the damned rockets were still a problem. Not even James could improve the basic inaccuracies of our unruly fireworks. The explosions at the target were muted because the HE charge had been cut to a minimum. We were only interested in the functioning of the impact fuses at this time and not the destructive power of the heads.

The real shame was that an extensive swannery was here long before we were. The birds inhabited the marshy waters at the head of the West Fleet, a deep, narrow inlet running between the land and the Chesil Bank. It seemed cruel to disturb them with our hideous din. Strangely, after a couple of days' firing, they settled down and accepted this penalty of war with very good grace. For our part, we appreciated such understanding and did our best to steer clear of their nests.

As if to disturb our concentration on matters more important, four strangers unexpectedly arrived at Boscombe. They were all captured Luftwaffe aircraft: a Messerschmitt Me 109 E; an Me 110; a Junkers 88; and a Heinkel 111 bomber. Jimmie and I were avid to get our hands on them.

We took turns flying the Me 109[7] and our Spit against each other. Flying the 109, I couldn't challenge James, but I could get away by a hard push-over into a dive. We landed and swapped planes. I'm glad the guns in his German fighter were not loaded, or I would have become another notch on his fuselage. He let me go unexpectedly and swooped in to land. I followed close behind and saw him get out, black with oil. His tunic was ruined by hydraulic fluid from a burst pipe. I taxied over to where he'd parked and jumped out. "Better you than me, old boy," I said, somewhat callously. "Attila's revenge, d'you suppose?" We turned our attention back to the rest of this interesting migrant circus.

I noticed that in all of the enemy aircraft there was a distinctive, unpleasant smell—stink I should really say to please grammarian Samuel Johnson. Unclean, I thought at first, quite unlike the college friends I'd known and visited in Bavaria before this bloody war. Sniffing around the cockpit of the Ju 88 to locate the ponk, I soon realized the awful odor came from the ersatz rubber they'd used. Our sanctions were working for once.

Flying enemy airplanes helped us get our perspective in place. We felt secure again about our own air armory. These were no master-race designs. Though somewhat long in the fang, they were nevertheless specimens of what we were up against; and were far less awesome in the flesh than in our fearful imagination.

I thought the Heinkel 111 bomber was a complete abortion.[8] It had half a ton of armor to carry around and was probably best suited for transport duties; as a bomber it was hardly second rate.

The Me 110, a twin-engined, long-range fighter, was pleasant to fly.[9] It wasn't as nimble as the 109 or as fast, but it had a heavy forward armament and sufficient range for long distance escort. Better than its reputation but, in all, not much to write home about. Its potential danger to us was as a night fighter lying in wait for our heavies during deep raids on the German homeland.

The Ju 88 I liked.[10] A powerful, husky, medium bomber we had already learned to respect, she handled with authority. Having a first-hand look at these aircraft was an interesting and enlightening experience.

August 16, 1942—German captured JUNKERS 88 light bomber No. HM509. We also flew an ME 109 E3B No. DG200; a HEINKEL 111 No. AW177 and an ME 110 No. AX722.

GLOBAL UPDATE
August–November 1942

The Japanese make a move in the Solomons, creating a threat to Australian supply lines. On 7 August U.S. Marines land in the north of Guadalcanal meeting little resistance; but fierce fighting occurs in some small islands to the north collectively called Florida Island.

The Japanese strike back, rushing more men in from their base at Rabaul. Heavy ships bombard the Marines dug in around a partially built airfield. Two days after the landing, four Allied cruisers are sunk, and another, part of a support convoy is badly damaged. The carrier *Hornet* is sunk and *Enterprise* put out of action, but retribution is extracted in mid-November when two Japanese battleships, two destroyers, and eleven overladen troopships are sunk in a naval action to become known as the Battle of Guadalcanal.

American ground forces go on the offensive and stay that way, keeping the Japanese in a defensive posture thereafter.

News from North Africa captured our attention. On 13 August 1942 Churchill sent Lt. Gen. Bernard Montgomery to take command of the Eighth Army. "Destroy Rommel!" he told him. Gen. W. Gott had been named for the job; alas, his aircraft was shot down on the way, and he was killed.

Monty soon made his presence known. He was an austere man, a fanatic for training, and a strict disciplinarian. He was supremely self-confident and some said a little vain, but these attributes are often ascribed to successful soldiers of high rank. Leaders of men need some element of the actor in their mien and an air of absolute confidence that may not necessarily be there. Monty went to some pains to show himself to his new command. He understood the uncertainties of the rank and file; he wanted them to know his rules and what he expected them to do. He came at an opportune time: the Eighth was dispirited after the long retreat and confused by repeated reversals over the past eighteen months. It had won and lost the same pieces of desert too many times. Monty announced that this nonsense was now over. The coming battles would be on his terms. He would choose where and when battle would be joined, and he would win. He would not move until he was ready and could be sure of the outcome. He went down among the men in corduroy pants and an old gray sweater wearing a rakish Australian hat with turned up side and massive brim—to the delight of the Aussies. It was shortly swapped for a jaunty black beret, resplendent with no less than two regimental badges, to be more practical for climbing into tanks.

He was a breath of fresh air for the overtired "Desert Rats" who had never won a decisive victory. They'd lost eighty thousand of their pals and had nothing to show for it.

Monty's first engagement was to be in the nature of a prologue to the main play. He planned to entice Rommel to attack at Alam Halfa where he, Monty, would call the tune; the Eighth would win this time, he told them, and come to little harm. So thorough was he that he staged a complete dress rehearsal before the real battle on 1 September. It was essential to the plot that Rommel make the attack, and so it went. Monty set up four hundred tanks, ordered to stand pat while the Fox was induced to make frontal attacks on this armor block, a testudo on which he blunted his spear. He dared not slip around the block of tanks and move east, thus exposing a vulnerable rear to the massive enemy. Now stalled, his forces were pounded from all angles especially by the Desert Air Force, now well integrated into the overall plan and well versed in the close-support role. The Hurricanes, all with four 20 mm cannon and carrying bombs or armed with two 40 mm cannon, acquitted themselves well, and heavy bombers attacked in strength behind Rommel's lines to destroy his supplies and petrol at Tobruk. Monty broke off the battle at his choosing and allowed a badly hurt Rommel to withdraw. The battle had run its copybook course and the tide had turned. Monty went to his tent to hone his plan for a battle to defeat Rommel once and for all with overpowering armor and air power—at El Alamein.

The first Beaufighter with eight rockets installed flew in for test on 6 September 1942.[11] She had four of them mounted under reach wing, outboard of the engine. I flew her to Thorney Island to the same spot where a year ago we'd launched the first-ever aircraft rocket weapon.

All went well with the ground trials, and I was anxious to start air firing. The Beau was destined for Coastal Command, and they needed it badly. In my paranoia about dispersion I had to be sure the rockets were truly aligned. Performance testing section couldn't tell me. They'd had no chance, they averred, to check the true flight line with the latest rocket configuration because I'd bitched so much about getting the armament tests done first. I'd have to wait for their results, they said. Touché.

September 9, 1942—Prototype BEAUFIGHTER EL329 with eight × 3.5-inch rockets. Sqn Ldr Bright died in a crash, test flying this aircraft on 24 Sept 1942.

Wait I could not. I painted a long white six-inch-deep stripe all down the fuselage of the Beau, parallel to the expected line of flight at normal operational speed—as worked out by the plant. I now coerced the help of Bill Williams, our expert movie camera man, my old pal-cum-conspirator in such nefarious affairs.

I warned performance section to keep their heads down for half an hour and proceeded to fly the Beau, level and low past the hangars at the top of the hill. I flew at various attack speeds, finishing at three hundred mph at the end of a shallow dive. Bill sat on the hangar roof filming the passes. From his projected pictures at each different speed, we compared the horizontal flight path of the Beau with the line along the fuselage. In no case was it parallel to our white line—hardly surprising with all the added rocketry gear hanging outside. We could, however, now line up the rockets with the actual slipstream at our attack speed and know they'd take off accurately without being deflected from the straight and narrow path—of proper behavior. A step in the right direction.

We tried her out on the Chesil Bank range, firing some of the HE rounds being used in the fuse impact tests. We noted the Beau was a little more accurate than the Hurricane, but it could have come from the greater stability of the heavy fighter. We'd have to confirm our tentative judgment, but in my heart I knew we needed a much more dramatic improvement—something quite radical.

I resolved to measure the flight paths of all forward-firing aircraft in future and not rely on the aircraft makers data. I also went back and checked the Hurricane IID[12] with two 40 mms and found it flew two degrees nose down at battle speed, which accounted for the famous "gun jump" we experienced. With this new nugget of oracular lore we made appropriate adjustments on the rocket Hurricanes in our stable, hoping for some small improvement in accuracy.

I'd become good friends with Jimmie Martin, designer of the elegant ammo boxes in the new fighters—we got on well together. I saw him often after we moved to Boscombe. He was always available to give incisive help with my constant technical posers, and he would make up bits of intricate ironmongery I needed. Jimmie was a brilliant aeronautical designer and a skilled machinist. Wonderfully rebellious and very Irish, he couldn't abide bureaucracy or the tyranny of officialdom. He had a factory near a small landing field at Denham on the western fringe of London.

I was thinking about Jimmie and of going up to see him on the matter of obedient rockets when the phone rang. I was pleased to hear his voice but devastated to hear his dreadful news: Captain Baker, RFC, his partner and old, old friend, had just been killed in a test flight of the Martin-Baker prototype fighter.[13] "Oh, no, Jimmie." I could hardly speak. "I'll be there right away." I took off for Denham and met him waiting at the

1942—Prototype Martin-Baker single-seat fighter. Final fatal test flight when Capt Baker was killed.

strip. It was an awful blow and really broke him up.

We walked round the lonely grass field together in the depths of woe, glad of the silence. He turned to me and said he had to go...things to arrange. No, he didn't need any help, thanks. "No more than you've just given me, laddie." He got in his car, and I waited till he was out of sight before starting up my Spit. Dear God! What an ill-starred day.

The Beaufighter was a bit of a monster. Once the tail was off the ground during take-off, it developed an incipient swing, which if not immediately checked, could easily develop into a full-blown ground loop. We lost quite a few inexperienced squadron pilots from this vicious propensity, but she was a good, stable gun platform, excellent for testing rocket accuracy.

We returned to the Enford net target to record just how good or bad she really was, but something in the air was dogging our footsteps. The electrics packed up and put her out of commission for several days—trying my patience severely. When she came back on line with a clean bill of health, I made a careful attack, with Jimmie Bright and Carpenter from Farnborough aboard. I tried hard to make the runs smooth and accurate to demonstrate the correct procedure for Jimmie to use in our comparative dispersion trials.

Pete Whitworth and I went over to watch the last attack of the afternoon, which Jimmie was to fly, and I also wanted to look at the day's records. We were gathered behind the farm when Jimmie appeared low over our heads, making a steady, precise dry run at the target. He wheeled around and came back down the valley, letting fly as he passed right over us. I have to say these bloody rockets are impressive from so close beneath, and worse at the receiving end, I'm sure. James made four runs, firing a pair of rockets on each pass, then pulled up and away in a mighty, vertical turn, with typical Jimmie flair.

As the ground crew began recording the shot holes, I could see that we were getting better. We left them to mend their nets for the next day's catch and drove back down the valley to Boscombe. We made good progress that day, and everything had gone well for a change. As we emerged onto the Amesbury road into the more open country, we saw ahead a nasty, black column of smoke billowing up with flashes of dull red from below.

"Bloody hell!" shouted Pete, "that's an aircraft, for sure. Who is it?"

My Alvis car flew like the thoroughbred she was along the country road as the awful column rose higher and higher, drifting toward us. Five miles down the road we reached Bulford and could see the source of the fire over in the army camp. We sped past a stunned sentry. But it was all over. Three fire engines had doused the inferno. The stench was awful, and a greasy fog hung in the air like a pall. We pushed our way through and could see from the remains of a burned out Bristol Hercules engine that it was, indeed, a Beaufighter. It was Jimmie.

"Dear God!"

I'd picked up the pieces before. Like the ocean, the air is a cruel, unforgiving mistress, a thought we try not to brood on but certainly try never to forget.

What had gone wrong? James was a superb pilot. Over half a dozen Me 109s that never came back bore final witness to his skill. He'd flown Blenheims for over a year, also Bristol-built and with some of the characteristics of the Beau. It wasn't possible.

I really don't remember getting Jimmie's things together, packing them up, cleaning out his desk. Eddie Dark phoned me the next day. "He wanted his ashes to be spread over the airfield. Will you do it?"

"Of course," I said.

I noticed a small, plain pine box on Eddie's desk. He pushed it over to me. "We collected what we could."

Pete answered the phone. He wanted to know why I needed the Hudson at that late hour. When I told him, he said he'd like to fly it himself.

"Of course," I said once again.

I put the little wooden box on the metal walkway running up the middle of the cabin and went to sit in the navigator's seat alongside Pete as he took the Lockheed into the air.

"Go up to about five or six thou, old boy," I suggested, "and fly over the field into the west. I think Jimmie might find that an amusing heading."

I slipped back into the cabin and made my way aft to the under gun position. I beckoned Corporal Tucker, who had asked to come along, to help me get the gun out of its mounting. Winding the crank to lower the hinged door seemed to take forever. As the door pressed into the slipstream, the outer air splashed in.

"Pass me the box." I gestured to Tucker, who had by this time pried the lid off with a screwdriver. I grabbed it by the open edge and felt the gritty ash within. "Hi, Jimmie!" I whispered, more depressed than ever. "Not far to go now." I leaned down through the open chute and pushed the little box out into the slipstream. As I turned it upside-down, the grayish ash spumed out, most of it gone on the wind; but I have to say that an awful lot blew back into my face, into my eyes, back into the cabin.

"You old bastard! You still want to fly with us, don't you?" I said aloud. I brushed some ash from the door out onto the wind and figured that was about it. Jimmie stayed with us and flew in that Lockheed Hudson as long as its wings did bosom the air. Those who flew her after she left us didn't know how honored there were to have him still aboard.

Driving up Beacon Hill that evening on my way home, I looked down into the valley of Bulford. Over the place where Jimmie crashed, lay a heavy mist, like a fitting shroud for a brave warrior. I blinked away the start of some rather unbrave tears. Startlingly clear came the words of Callimachus:

> They told me, Heraclitus, they told me you were dead;
> They brought me bitter news to hear and bitter tears to shed.
> I wept, as I remembered, how often you and I
> Had tired the sun with talking and sent him down the sky.
> And now that thou art lying, my dear old Carian guest,
> A handful of gray ashes...

The hardest part came the next day when I flew Jimmie's and my favorite Hurricane up to Denham, to see Monica Bright. As I greeted her, there was very little I could manage to say. We just hugged each other. All I could do in the end was turn and leave her to wait for the baby Jimmie would never see.

GLOBAL UPDATE
July—September 1942

Sevastopol, the main Russian stronghold on the Black Sea, falls after a month-long siege.

The deepest penetration into Russia in hundreds of years is made by a German advance guard of a third of a million men to the areas to the north and south of Stalingrad. After a furious bombardment that reduces most of the city to ruin, the Nazi Sixth Army under General von Paulus moves in to take the city by storm; but the advance pauses for weeks for no very good reason. The Russians quietly and mostly by night reinforce the remains of the city against expected further attack.

Hitler says he will strangle us at sea. Allied Atlantic convoys including those with diverted Lend-Lease material and from our own manufacture on the Arctic route to Murmansk, come under the heaviest attack of the war. Nineteen forty-two shows a huge expansion of U-boats at sea from 90 to 196, and sinkings exceed shipbuilding capacity for the first time. Over seven hundred thousand tons in one month alone are sunk including those off the east coast of America and in the Caribbean.

Newly at war with Germany, the U.S. Has not had time to raise sufficient forces to protect the vast traffic in her own waters. In March of 1942 Churchill sends the U.S. Navy twenty-four of the best equipped British antisub trawlers and ten corvettes with trained crews to help out.

German capital ships are a constant threat to our convoys. After incessant bombing at Brest the battleship-cruisers *Gneisenau* and *Scharnhorst* with the cruiser *Prinz Eugen* escape and flee through the Channel to Kiel on 12 February. Both battleships hit mines on the way; *Scharnhorst* is out for six months; *Gneisenau* never appears again and *Eugen* is badly hurt.

The presence of German capital vessels at Trondheim severely interrupt Arctic convoys. The battleship *Tirpitz*, the heavy cruiser *Hipper,* and the cruiser *Scheer* force us to keep a task force available to prevent them making forays to the north.

At the end of March a small force of 250 commandos under Commander Ryder, R.N., and Colonel Newman, Essex Regiment, sailed from Falmouth to carry out a particularly audacious raid on the important dry dock at St. Nazaire, five miles up the estuary of the Loire. It was the only one on the Atlantic coast large enough to take the *Tirpitz*. One of the traded U.S. destroyers, with three tons of explosive in her bows, was driven into the dock gates and sunk. The charge did not explode until the next day when a large party of German technicians and officers was inspecting the wreck. The lock was out of action for the rest of the war. Thus in all possible ways did we attack the weapons the Nazi navy was hurling against the vital convoys from our great ally.

Major warships covering the lurking surface raiders could ill be spared to escort convoys. The first sign of real improvement came when we sent naval support groups which included the first mini-aircraft carriers into areas outside the range of land-based airplanes. Their mission: seek and destroy U-boats. Seaborne air support was vital, functioning as the eyes of the operation. Air recce could both detect subs and force them to stay below. It all started with HMS *Audacity* and the six Swordfish aircraft bravely operating from her flight deck. She was eventually sunk by a U-boat while escorting a convoy out of Gib, but half a dozen such carriers were to be in service by the end of 1942.

The North African buildup for a final assault on Rommel's Afrika Korps proceeded relentlessly during September and October 1942. The arrival of five hundred new American Grant and Sherman tanks at the port of Cairo gave us a two-to-one advantage in armor and there were two fresh divisions from the U.K., desert trained to a fine pitch. Artillery numbered more than a thousand pieces. We had over twelve hundred aircraft, including those from Malta, operating in direct support against the German sea and land supply routes. Monty wanted to be absolutely ready; he wanted to attack as the moon waxed full on 24 October. The operation called for great secrecy and involved a huge effort at deception. Intense pressure was brought to bear on Monty to begin the battle in the last week of September. Churchill wanted it to dovetail with Operation Torch, the invasion of the west end of North Africa, and with certain Russian offensives. But Monty was obdurate; he even let it be known that if it must start a month earlier than he planned, someone else would have to lead the show. He got his way.

Supported by heavy air bombardment, the guns opened up on the night of 23 October. The infantry advanced over a wide front and two armored divisions followed. They made deep inroads but mines eventually delayed further progress. Rommel, recalled from a German hospital for the crisis and still a sick man, moved all his armor toward the threat on his left and made repeated, head-on counterattacks in the old style, very unlike the thrust-and-parry he preferred. The RAF moved in with heavy and medium bombers, and fighters with permanent 20 mm cannon and underwing 40 mm cannon or bombs. They were able to crush the German initiative before it was completely organized. It was the last time Rommel would try to take the offensive. A breakthrough was made in the center and though Hitler forbade any retreat nothing could stop our advance. After twelve days Rommel was in full rout and was only saved from complete annihilation by a providential twenty-four hour tropical downpour. Lt. Gen. Bernard Montgomery was knighted and made full general following this great battle, and in the words of Winston Churchill: "Before Alamein we never had a victory. After Alamein we never had a defeat."

I missed Jimmie Bright a lot. I really hadn't known him all that long, yet he was such a good companion it felt like a lifetime. A Typhoon[14] with a lightened rudder returned from Hawker to keep me company and get my mind back where it belonged. Some time before I'd complained about the lateral control of the huge new fighter. Diving at the Druids' circle I found the directional stability much improved, and filming bore me out. It was good to have the problem corrected because factory production was getting into high gear. We badly needed her to counter the Fw 190.

I learned on 1 October that the ill-fated month of September hadn't quite finished with me. Eddie Dark walked over to my office to tell me that my younger brother, Philip, had just been killed at Gibraltar. "Why don't you go to Whitchurch and get the story from them direct," he offered with a quiet smile.

I flew over to Imperial Airways HQ at Whitchurch airfield right away. It appeared that Pip's Whitley bomber, bound for Malta, landed at Gib after dark for fuel. The bomber swung as it touched down on the long, single strip and sideswiped the nose of a resident Spit parked by the overcrowded runway. Minor damage to their tail section was repaired overnight. At dawn they taxied out and were cleared for takeoff, but the Whitley never left the ground. It roared down the length of the extended runway and plunged straight into the harbor, where it still lay, five fathoms down. None of the crew escaped.

Whatever could come next?...Bake...Jimmie...now Pip. It did seem that once again, as at Flodden's gory field "...the flowers of the forest are a'wede away."

I had to see my parents and sought Eddie's permission. "Get going," he bade me. "You hardly need my okay today, of all days." That's the kind of guy he was.

Dad let me in. He'd been in charge of the Royal Engineers in Cherbourg in the last show; he knew the form, so we could talk together without getting all screwed up. "Mother hasn't taken it very well," he finally told me. "She's still in bed, and the doc has her quieted down. Don't be surprised if she doesn't know you. Go up and see her now, and then we'll have some lunch." By the time I could get another day off a few weeks later, mother had been moved to a quiet home nearby where they could care for her special needs. Her heart was broken, and her sweet mind had lost all belief. She never came back to us.

Eddie called me up to come and join a conference for planning trials of a Swordfish with our rockets.[15] The Swordfish was famous. A large, old-fashioned-looking biplane designed by the Fairey Aviation Company as a shipborne torpedo-bomber, it had almost entirely eliminated the Italian fleet at Taranto in November of 1940. It was still doing sterling service out of Malta against Nazi convoys taking supplies to Rommel and now became the teeth of the new escort carriers. Because this gem looked as though it had been put together with chewing gum and twine it gained a favorite nickname—Stringbag. Absolutely no reflection on her great gallantry intended.

"You're kidding, sir," I expostulated. "A Swordfish? An old Stringbag?"

"Yes, indeed," he said. "There's one waiting for you on the tarmac. And watch your damned sarcasm when you get over here. I have a couple of nautics from the Admiralty waiting to meet you." I shot over to Eddie's office and was introduced to our guests. "Commander Jackson, Naval Ordnance, and Commander Moultrie, Naval Air Staff...Dixi Dean, our gunnery guru." John Moultrie and Jacko looked at me a bit sideways, and I wondered if they could have heard my unguarded reaction to Eddie's announcement over the pipe. It was only my guilt. Both of these first-class chaps would become excellent friends of mine during the trials and beyond.

I smiled to myself as a quick memory flitting across my mind of an ill-timed loop performed over Malta by a Stringbag flown by my old chum, Scotty Pryde, probably after some minor victory. Poised briefly upside down on the top of the loop, the navigator's drawer in the open rear cockpit slipped out. From it flew the secret signal code manual, tearing to pieces, descending like a small, unseasonable snow shower on the beleaguered isle beneath. Pages fell all over Malta and on the beaches and into the sea. Scotty's whole squadron fanned out to scour the rocky terrain and collect the valuable pages, but they never did find them all. The local naval and air forces had to change their code books in a hurry, and Scotty lost a year's seniority with equal expedition.

Eddie broke into my irreverent thoughts. "The Navy's got a very high priority to clear the Swordfish installation. The overall plan is to use high explosive warheads against shipping, including subs on the surface. Oh! Their Lordships of the Admiralty want a firing demonstration three weeks from today, no later!"

I wasted no time. The old lady and I flew to Thorney Island, our rocket spawning ground, for the initial ground firings, which went off sounding like the 1812 Overture.

In the demonstration for Their Battleships, we planned to

1942—Prototype SWORDFISH DK 424 with eight × 25-pound rockets was first test fired from Thorney Island. This is a later model, landing on a carrier.

1944—Arming a SWORDFISH of 834 squadron with rockets aboard HMS Battler *in the Indian Ocean.*

attack a submarine outline cut through the sod into the chalk on the downs nearby. We practiced firing in forty-five-degree dives, but barely half the rockets hit within the outline. "Don't worry, Dix," comforted Pete. "One hit will be enough!"

The day dawned bright and clear, thank goodness, and it was a great outing. The admirals loved it, even though I missed completely with the first full salvo. A second, steeper dive produced fifty percent hits: all rejoiced and the bo's'n piped.

After that rather premature show of strength, we got down to more serious business. The Stringbag was much slower than earlier fire-breathers but the accuracy was okay. Most important was proof that the frail but gutsy Stringbag seemed in no danger of going up in smoke from the Chinese brand of fiery arrows. I wonder if there was an ancient kinship, with genes of some old oriental kite built into her fabric.

The Navy's prime need was for aerial rockets to use against surfaced or near-surfaced submarines. They were the weapons of choice to round out the concept of escort carriers.

Although the explosive head seemed at first to be the right warhead[16] for U-boats, we decided to try out the solid-steel head against the center section of an actual submarine, firing from the Swordfish in vertical dives. The target was readied and moored, floating at periscope depth offshore from Pendine Sands in south Wales. At low tide the sub lay on the bottom and was completely exposed, so flat is the beach and so far does the tide go out. Pendine Sands! What memories that name conjures up: Malcomb Campbell, later knighted for his exploits, driving his superb racing cars to such record speeds.

We would operate from the Pembrey Airfield ten miles to the east, the same field where the Focke-Wulf 190 had been constrained to land earlier that summer.

We started on a miserable November day with rain on its breath. I dived as steeply as I dared, but the clouds building low over the target made it impossible to get into a vertical dive and pull out in time after firing. The Farnborough boys assiduously took high-speed movies from the shore at right angles to the line of attack. As the morning wore on, the weather got worse and worse, so we packed up for lunch. Then, with the tide in full retreat, we all tramped out to inspect the damage. The boffins carefully recorded all the shots that had penetrated the pressure hull going in and coming out.

"You know, I don't understand how so many shots went through the boat," I ventured. "I saw a number of rockets fall short in the last few dives, but I don't see where they went into the sand in front of the target." John Moultrie made an interesting comment. "I saw some of the shallow ones come out again, still burning after going two or three hundred feet underwater." It was extraordinary. "Yes," he went on, "they came out climbing at an angle of twenty or thirty degrees!"

That evening we compared the films of the attacks with the actual record of the shots that hit the sub. There were more holes in the target than there should have been. From John's observations and the absence of ricochets off the sandy bottom, we could only conclude that the rockets were being deflected upward slightly on striking the water's surface, then proceeding underwater on an upward curving path and never reaching the bottom at all. The boffins agreed with Jacko that the ogive-shaped nose of the solid shot would impose a powerful upward force on it at impact forcing the rocket to curve upward underwater thereafter. It would account for all the extra shots that penetrated, even though—initially—they'd fallen short.

We'd made a marvelous accidental discovery. Being forced by the clouds to make shallower dives than intended (about twenty degrees as recorded on our film) we stumbled on the ideal dive angle for attack. The boffins added icing to the cake: "Attack the U-boat on the beam, aim at the bow, and the rockets will impact at the conning tower," they said. "Splay—or spread—the rockets up and down a bit to give a vertical stick to lay across their damn back. You can do it by adjusting the launchers up and down a tad from one to the next across the bank of four," they added. Their suggestion appealed to the nautics who were used to the gospel of straddling—or bracketing—the target.

"Beautiful!" said John Moultrie. "Impossible to miss!"

By chance a Coastal Command Hudson flew in to Pembrey the next morning. The aircraft had just arrived at Boscombe equipped to fire eight rockets, so Eddie had sent it over for us to look at. We were confident enough by now to include her in the trials that day. She was a little more hair-raising in the dives than the more docile Stringbag, but we hit the sub with more than half the rockets. Almost like the real thing and highly satisfactory. I wanted to claim an operational quarter-kill, at least, but the target was one of ours.

Our tests at Pendine Sands did enough damage to sink a whole wolf pack of U-boats. The Swordfish seemed to dance her way home to Boscombe in sheer happiness.

Coastal would be pleased and would want the rockets as soon as could be. The heavy twin was not as facile as the

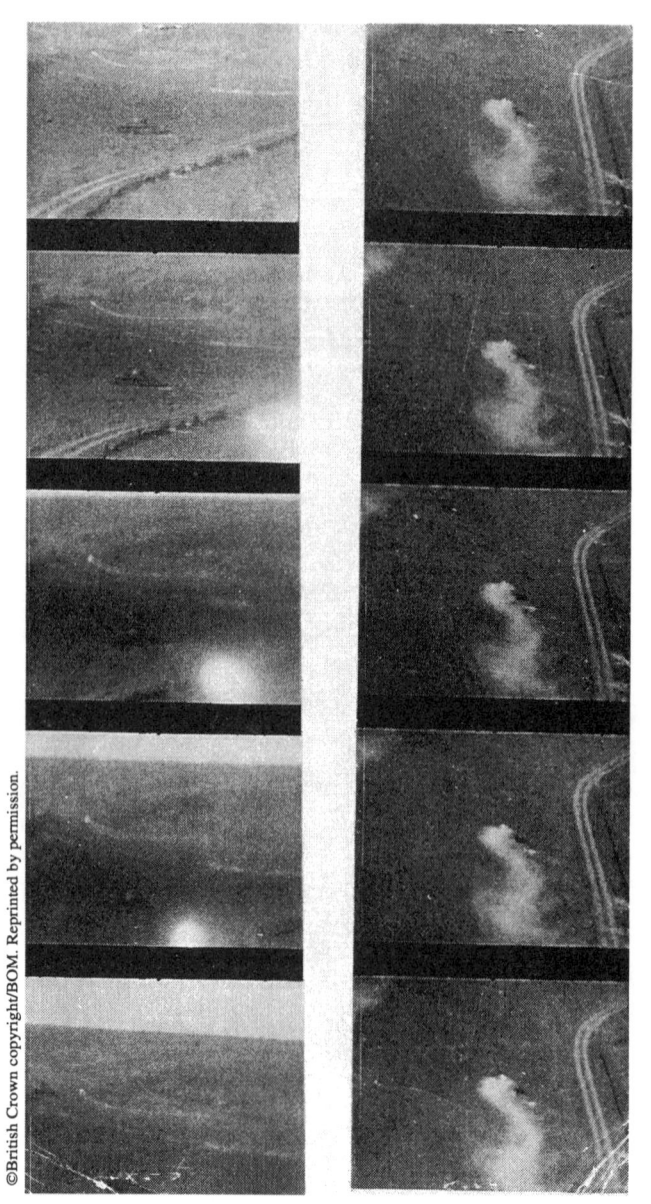

October 15, 1942—MATILDA tank attacked with rockets with 25-pound AP warheads from HURRICANE. One shot went through turret skirt and set tank on fire.

Swordfish in making twenty-degree dive attacks, but it was practical. We telexed approval of the installation to the Air House, followed by details of our fantastic discovery of how to sink subs with fireworks. For once we needed the spread of the rockets, but controlled accuracy would be a more elegant way to achieve the required naval bracketing.

We had to settle the confusion about the proper choice of warhead. We'd fired a few solid-shot heads at the odd tank but never with devastating effect. Even a direct hit was not spectacular, at most knocking off a track. I decided we should keep on until we had a hit with the armor-piercing shot that should, if it were the correct design of head, be lethal. An improved Hurricane gave better success. One hit I made on the Matilda penetrated just below the turret and set it on fire. Evidently the shot became red hot in passing through the steel and ignited the oily rags that always seem to collect inside a tank. It was a flamer—a wreck. However, the odds were heavily against such a lucky shot. We had to better our chances.

Latrinograms arrived to the effect that our gunners in North Africa, short of armor-piercing shot normally used for tanks, had resorted to using howitzers instead. The big guns lob light-case, high-explosive shells not intended for penetration. To their surprise and delight they found that a hit almost anywhere on a tank would lift the whole turret right off its bearing ring and concuss the crew within.

I discussed an idea with Pete. "You might just be right, old cock," he said. "Our HE head is very much like a howitzer shell."

"Okay," I told him. "Go and have a crack at another tank with some fully live HE's, and get a direct hit."

I had to told the phone well away from my ear. "I knocked the bloody turret right off!" he exulted. "It sailed into the air like a flaming bird!"

So the incredible came to pass. Two rocket heads, each

designed for a specific purpose, had changed roles almost completely.[17] It was an unbelievable switch.

GLOBAL UPDATE
November 1942

Thousands on both sides die in besieged Stalingrad in house-to-house fighting. Russian armor reaches the city and Gen. von Weitersheim pleads for a withdrawal. He is relieved of his command for his pains. Two weeks later Gen. K. Rokossovsky attacks with his tank army overcoming two Rumanian armies protecting von Paulus's rear. As severe winter sets in, Hitler takes charge of the battle. A relief force he allows to move up is wiped out. The German Sixth Army is now surrounded.

A special corps of soldiery had developed for a unique mission. The concept arose because of the growing need for small cadres of men to handle special projects, generally in a hurry, free of normal procedural regulations. They underwent a high degree of training and discipline for their unorthodox tasks. They learned new arts of war: unarmed combat, lone survival techniques and secret penetration of hostile situations. They studied methods of amphibious landing and spawned other tactics such as landing behind the front by parachute and massive glider. The establishment opposed such radical thinking, saying the job could be done by any bright regular soldier, and it would ruin good discipline to pick out a few for what was seen as privileged duty. It took a long time to overcome such a spurious argument but with help from the very top the new breed was allowed to grow.

In the European theater the first experience of amphibious warfare on a large scale was gained by a force of Canadian, American, and British commandos under Lord Louis Mountbatten, commander in chief, Combined Ops. Select troops trained for a novel kind of warfare in a number of forays of different strength on the coasts of Norway and France and in the Mediterranean. For example, in November 1941, a small band of these unusual warriors landed behind the German lines in Lybia, to attack Rommel's HQ. The general was not at home, but in the daring raid he lost a number of his top officers, and we also picked up a lot of valuable information. Commando losses were small.

In the Pacific arena, American forces were the first of the Allies to be involved in full-scale amphibious landings when the Marines went ashore on the island of Guadalcanal, 7 August 1942. It was the first in a long series of island-hopping operations there that went on for the rest of the war.

Twelve days after the Guadalcanal landings, the Commandos (as they now became known) in Europe made their first large-scale seaborne strike against the Germans. Ten thousand strong, they landed around the port of Dieppe on the French coast. In their nine-hour stay on the continent, a third of the force was lost. Thousands of very brave, highly trained special-services men perished, and the RAF lost ninety-eight aircraft for ninety-one of the Luftwaffe and two hundred probables. Also one British destroyer. It was a dress rehearsal for a major invasion of North Africa and for later landings in France as a prelude to the long march on Berlin intended for late 1943 or 1944. They took a nasty blood bath at Dieppe, but the lessons learned were of great value and were carefully studied by General Eisenhower, newly named commanding general of the Allied Forces, Operation Torch.

Dr. Charlie Lauritsen's group at Caltech was going great guns, if one can so describe the progress of the inspired, capable group producing rockets for the U.S. Navy. Their first operational weapon was the Mousetrap 7.2-inch antisubmarine rocket (ASR). It was based on the British Hedgehog, which worked like an inverted mortar to throw out a killing pattern of depth charge, but using small rockets to eject the charges. The Navy

1944—Dr. Charles C. Lauritsen, head of Caltech rocket program. Pasadena, California.

ordered it mounted in all sub chasers over a hundred feet long, making it the first substantial U.S. installation of tactical rockets. Deliveries started within three months, the first of a series of records for speedy production set by Caltech.

In June 1942, Dr. Lauritsen and Rear Admiral Wilson Brown, the new commander, Amphibious Forces of the Pacific, together devised specifications for barrage rockets with a range of a thousand to twelve hundred yards to be fired from landing craft approaching shore. They were to continue bombardment after the fleet had to lift its barrage supporting the landing. Once again, the team outstripped reality and on 25 August staged a successful demonstration of the new weapon system at Solomons, Maryland.[18]

We often noticed in the U.K. that successful trials of such toys bring widespread and unreasonable demands for immediate delivery. As could have been expected, BuOrd asked for fifty launchers and three thousand 4.5-inch spin-stabilized rockets and fuses to be delivered to the Atlantic fleet within thirty days. It must have been hectic, but they came through with the last of the rockets in time to meet the impossible deadline. This heroic feat made it possible to use them in Operation Torch: the maiden flights of the barrage rockets contributed greatly to the successful landings at Casablanca. Over a million and a half of them were made and used in every major landing in all theaters. The rocket was aptly dubbed, "Old Faithful."

GLOBAL UPDATE
8 November 1942

The invasion of North Africa begins at dawn 8 November 1942, less than a year after Pearl Harbor. About eighty thousand Allied troops sail from England through the U-boat-infested Bay of Biscay and the bottleneck of Gibraltar Straits—the Americans to Oran, the British to Algiers. Unbelievably, at both ports the Torch armadas evade detection until the last minute. Thirty-five thousand more U.S. troops leave the U.S. to make landfall at the same time. There is resistance from the Vichy-controlled French at all landings. British destroyers try to seize both Algerian harbors, and although sunk by shore batteries, they both landed assault troops effectively.

By a strange turn of fate, France's Admiral Darlan remains in Algiers, delayed by his son's sickness. The Vichy admiral, hating the British—the bitter gall of Toulon still in his craw—fiercely opposes their landing in North Africa. However, the adroit politician wisely swallows his Gallic pride, and soon orders all opposition to cease. Four days later it was all over.

On Salisbury Plain that morning a new briskness in the air presaged an early fall. John Ludden phoned to arrange the promised big-game safari at Enford. "I hope you haven't forgotten about it, young man," he said. "We're looking forward to having you and Commander Whitworth over, too. Just bring your 12-bores, we've got plenty of cartridges." I asked if Charles Dann could come too. "No need to ask," he said. "You name the day."

After an early breakfast we fired up the Alvis and headed for the rocket range. When we got to the big barn past John Ludden's house, a large dray awaited us with square bales of fresh scented hay piled down the middle to cushion our backs. Several of John's local pals had already gathered, and we stood around chatting until the party was complete. Off we went, with John on a tractor tugging the dray up the hill behind our net target, lying across the ground, resting for the day.

At the top of the rise we turned to run along the brow and drop off the guns in position every twenty-five yards or so for the first drive. When everyone was sheltered behind whatever cover there was, John gave the word for the beaters to advance. We waited in the keen air, unable to move about to keep warm, immobilized by the protocol of the hunt, and anxious not to be caught napping when the birds at last came over. The call of a startled cock brought all guns up, and the beat of a dozen wings aflutter filled the silence. Bang—left! Bang—right! The thump of a pheasant on the turf; a cry of "Fetch!"

The drive brought over a goodly bag; Pete and I each dropped a bird or two while Charles got an unwary hare. After the flurry died down and the game was retrieved, we calmed the dogs and got back on the dray to move on to the next stand. After a couple more drives we moved down over the hill where John had his root crops and found a lot of partridge. They came up whirring, for all the world like a mass of overgrown humming birds, rocketing up vertically as they spied us, a maneuver very final for many of them. We walked the fields for a while until noon had passed, raising a red fox at one point. John cautioned us not to shoot it. "Best leave it alone," he said with a grimace. "We'd not be too popular with the Marlborough Hunt, even though I know that little bugger likes my chickens. Why don't we meet back at the barn and see what the missus has rustled up for us. I'll go and pick up the cart."

Mrs. Ludden and some neighbors had laid out a trestle table with a checkered cloth and a bunch of wild flowers in the center. It was great. A big ham to carve, loaves of still-warm bread, and a cask of beer already spigoted waiting to yield its foaming nectar. John arrived with the bag laid out on the dray, and with a vengeance we fell to on his wife's most unwartime viands. He kept us there until the cask ran dry. As we left at last he pressed a brace of fat birds on us. "My compliments to the ladies at home," he said with a broad grin.

Three months had already slipped away since Jimmie Bright bought it. Pete and I sat sipping so-called tea in his office at dispersal. I'd tried to instill the rudiments of tea making into this likable Afrikaner but had finally given up. "Don't look now," I said, "but I'm beginning to think they've forgotten to post me away, after all. And I don't want them reminded, okay?"

"Perhaps they just don't think you're worth replacing."
"You bastard!"
And so we promptly forgot all about it, too.

Seven

At first blush it seemed our two warheads, each designed for a specific purpose, had changed roles. The AP solid head had been considered right for tanks and the HE light case design for ships. But neither was a first-class weapon for small targets such as tanks—our rocket was not accurate enough. By good fortune we discovered the amazing upward curving underwater path taken by the AP head rocket after entering the water in a twenty-degree dive. When we make a flank dive attack on a U-boat her full length becomes the target and by deliberately aiming short all rockets fall in the area between us and the sub. These two factors virtually enlarge the target and exponentially improve the chance of a kill. It is a special, fortunate case.

To make the rocket HE warhead suitable for small targets we must increase the size of the head to the *size of a bomb*, effectively increasing the lethal area of the target. A rocket propelled bomb is to be preferred to one that must be delivered to the doorstep. The fighter-bomber can launch it a quarter mile from the angry panzer and never come close to the HE burst.

I looked closely at some of Charles Dann's toys. The general purpose bombs (GP) were ideal for adaptation. The body was very strong to withstand impact and without the rear half—which was a removable stabilizing cone—there was a nice flat area at the back of the bomb body, a perfect place to button on several of our rocket tails. I decided to cut my teeth on our 250-pound bomb that weighted 200 pounds, without the rear cone. Now one rocket motor gives our 60-pound warhead a velocity of 1,000 mph, so four would be adequate to propel the small bomb—of four times the weight—at the same speed.

My genius in the workshops quickly made me a matching plate with four threaded bosses on it, nested together to secure four motors in a small, neat fasces.[1] He clipped the plate on the back of the bomb and we left for the Enford range. I fired it from an upward tilted tubular launcher and it took off like a scalded, purposeful cat, with quite a meow—seeming to know where it was going. The Hurri-bomber with a couple of these rocket-bombs was now equivalent to a ten-inch field gun—with a two-shell salvo.

We wrote an official report on the unscheduled trial and included some impressive shots of our baby in flight as captured by the redoubtable Williams. The first rocket-bomb weighed about 350 pounds. We took the liberty of including drawings of a similar rocket-bomb we were constructing, double the size and with about twice the propelling oomph. The monster weighed nearly 700 pounds.[2]

From these modest beginnings came—in due course—a specially designed 1,000-pound rocket with a set of official specifications. Code named "Uncle Tom," it arrived in time for some limited operational use in the Pacific theater.

Worry, worry! I'd never be happy until we could fully benefit from our spectacular rocket weapon—denied us because of its inaccuracy. Worst of all, being an arrow, it was forever under the hypnotic influence of the local airstream when loosed off; also the current design of propelling charge often made it veer off at the last moment because of uneven burning. Nothing could alter the inverse pattern of speed to target where a rocket takes off at zero velocity relative to the airplane, building to a maximum at burnout. This is the opposite of a gun shell whose speed is maximum out of the barrel, slowly diminishing on the way to its victim.

A rocket takes more than twice as long to get to the target as a well-behaved gun shell and falls five times as far toward mother earth—a lot harder for a pilot to allow for the drop.

Stiff launching rails helped a little to educate the rockets on the path we wanted them to take in life,[3] and we were forced to use them for U-boat attacks to produce the vertical spread. Otherwise I said they should go. The concept of no rails at all got the quaint name of "zero-length launchers"—a rose by any name.

To bypass the launcher problem I wanted to vent the exhaust gases around the front of the tube and let the high-speed stream be a "curtain" to protect the rocket body from any extraneous, off-line windage.[4] I gave Thomason drawings to make a prototype. I couldn't avoid showing it to the wizards in Wales: I had to. Though skeptical, they were at least decent enough to fire the model on the test stand in their witch's kitchen at Aberporth. Thrust was the same as from the normal rear-end venturi, so I did get that bit right. It didn't blow up—another bit right. But try as I might, I couldn't whip up any enthusiasm for my quintessential idea. We were listening to different drummers. I still regret not trying it in the air. I had no time to make any more myself or plead further with the experts, but I knew damned well it would give us a more accurate missile, unaffected by the vagaries of the slipstream and whose mountings would cause a lot less drag. Parental love-wishes no doubt.

I thought we could moderate the changes in direction caused by the unevenness of final burning of the propellant by giving the rocket a slow spin. Lew Motley made me two launching tubes with spiral steel guides all the way down the inside to prove the point in principle.[5] He dropped off the finished tubes at Jimmie's factory to be mounted below the wings of my Hurricane—Jimmie was in on this skullduggery, too. My "rifled" rocket tubes were in place on our return from a pleasant plowman's lunch at the local pub. "Now be sure and let me know how they work," said my puckish friend as I tried to thank him adequately for his conspiratorial aid.

We fired a quiver of the rockets with clipped tail feathers from Motley's tubes. Measured on our net target, they proved to be twice as accurate as our unrotated rockets, but it would be impossible to use tubular launchers like these hung outside the aircraft in the breeze. I used them only to prove the efficacy of putting on a slow spin.

A call came in from Farnborough. News of my fell deed was out. "I thought you were anti-rails and heavy-drag launchers," scolded Carpenter. "Whatever next?" The boffins pulled my leg mercilessly when they heard about it, but I hoped they noted that slow rotation markedly improved accuracy. Canting the fins and firing the rockets from support pylons might have done the trick, too, but we didn't try it. Today, using unimpaired hindsight, it does look like a good idea.

Gravity drop is like the common cold. It is ubiquitous, it is common, and no cure has yet been found. The only way I could see to stay the rocket's fall in space was to give it a pair of wings and teach it to fly straight and level.[6] We'll all need to sprout a pair eventually, anyway.

I told Jimmie that slow spin greatly improved rocket accuracy. He was delighted, and I was glad to hear the Irish laughter back in his voice. We often shared our triumphs and disasters and tried—as said the soldier's bard—to "treat those two impostors just the same." Jimmie said, "There has to be a better way than with those fancy tubes, moind you. Come on up and let's talk." After lunch and swapping some slow-spin ideas, he led me into the factory.

"I want to show you a gadget of mine," he said as we came upon a strange contraption in the center aisle. It was a pilot's seat with a parachute in place, attached to a couple of girders going up to the roof of the hangar.

"Set yourself down in it, my buoy," bade Jimmie. "Now, jest get comfortable. Go on, straap yourself in toight!" His brogue became more pronounced but held no hint of Gaelic deception.

I did as he told me. He reached over to a box set with dials and pressed a button. Though still sitting in the seat, the next moment I was up in the roof looking down at Jimmie's wicked, impish smile.

"Hold on!" he shouted. "I'll bring you back down." Still laughing, he wound a large crank that lowered the seat and its very surprised passenger to the floor.

"Did you feel anything, now?" he asked with a twinkle. "Last week I shot the vice chief of Air Staff up there, and I'm afraid I hurt his back a bit. I think I got the charge right today. You're Number 2. Maybe those prahstitutes at the Air Ministry will listen to me now!"

I was fine and not hurt a bit. It all happened so fast I really don't remember the upward ride. Now I knew why Jimmie cadged the cordite from me. I'd been salvaging the propellant grains for him for some time from 20 mm shell cases damaged in gun jams. I suppose one could repeat that old cliché with an accuracy of a high order: it was my turn to be hoist with mine own petard.

Jimmie's apparatus was the prototype—nay, even earlier—the first experimental model of the Martin-Baker ejection seat, the first device to jettison the pilot out of his aircraft on demand. It was destined to be standard equipment in high-speed jets well into the future and in many air forces.

Many pilots had died because they couldn't open the hood at high speed. Early Spits had that problem as I had good cause to remember on a flight to North Coates airfield, where I'd taught air bombardiers in 1937, and the damp sea air still lingered in my bones. We lost many bombing days to the sea rack "...all ragged and brown," blowing in from the steppes beyond the North Sea.

A Coastal Command squadron recently equipped with Beaufighters had started rocket attacks against shipping. I was anxious to learn about their doings, so on the third of February 1943, I left Boscombe late that morning in my hoary old Spit, delayed by the usual tail-of-the-winter weather. The low rain clouds at North Coates were lifting, they said, but when I got to the Lincoln Wolds, low hills twenty miles short, the tops were in cloud. I figured I could make a gentle hurdle over them and drop out again ten minutes later, but it was not to be; I couldn't find a break and was too scared to go any lower in the soup. I had to climb to a safe height and—in the traditional escape maneuver when caught flat-footed in "visual flight conditions gone bad" in Britain—turn back on a reverse heading then in fifteen minutes fumble for the cloud base at a thousand feet where you'd just come from. Didn't always work.

It was damn cold, and the Spit had no heat. The whole of the inside of the cockpit canopy and windshield rapidly became misted over. No heavy icing around, I hoped. I still don't know exactly what happened, because I decided to climb out on top to warm up in the sun and evade any icing problems. The clouds were incredibly deep but not all that dark. I became disoriented, the instruments flew all over the place. I tried to steady down by leaving her alone with hands and feet off. Height was winding down from the ten thousand level, faster and faster. I took back the controls and eased back on the stick but the speed, already way up, just increased. I tried to roll her out but it made no difference that I could tell, I'm ashamed to admit it—I panicked. We were going to buy it and there was no time left.

I tried to open the hood to abandon ship but heave as I might the bloody thing wouldn't budge—we were going too fast. The only thing I hadn't tried was pushing the stick forward; something told me to do so—now!

I put both hands on the top of the spade-grip and shoved as hard as I could. Boy! I came out of the seat and hit my head hard against the canopy top. All kinds of dirt, mud, bits of rag flew up in front of me, and like a cork from a Moët bottle, the Spit and I shot out of the bottom of the cloud layer, upside down (as they say in the tallest of tales), with port wing well down and going like the proverbial bat out of hell.

God! I was scared, with my heart pounding louder than the tortured Merlin up front. I rolled her level and said an honest, grateful prayer. I came to an airfield immediately, another plea answered. It was Wittering that I'd passed over only fifteen short minutes earlier, going east. It all happened so quickly, so unbelievably, so unexpectedly. What a bloody stupid way to get bumped. Two hours later, chastened and well fed, Spit and I moved on with the clouds now broken but still unconquered.

At North Coates the boys were having a ball with the rockets. "Best thing we've had for ages," they said, "but get us those HE heads soon." They restored a shattered confidence, and I flew home with head raised back up again.

In response to early difficulties reported with the first Spits, Jimmie had made a mechanical release for the hood, worked by a little chain for all the world like a miniature water closet pull. It was fitted to all Spits later than the one that almost made me have kittens. I recalled that the Fw 190 in Wales treated the hood's aerodynamic lockjaw at high speed in a more forceful manner—explosively and simply. Like Jimmie's ejector.

A number of pilots were also killed or badly hurt by hitting the tail even if able to bail out. Jimmie designed his "people cannon" to solve all ejection problems: recalcitrant sliding hoods, interfering tail units, and even impending prangs at low altitude, because the pilot left with his brolly and all, to be expelled well above the airplane. Jimmie was eventually awarded a well-deserved knighthood for this vital, far-reaching invention.

Over Christmas and into 1943 we were busy testing a new rocket warhead, adapted by the boffins from an existing thirty-pound incendiary bomb as a backup for the sixty-pound HE head. Our trials proved the new weapon to be most effective and devastating. The head passed intact through a one-inch-thick steel plate to ignite reliably behind and produce an unquenchable, long-burning ball of fire. It was a valuable weapon in its own right.

The sixty-pounders began to avalanche off the production line at Woolwich Arsenal, and the first batches had to be checked. We set up base at Pendine Sands and to save time used the beach as a landing strip. The whole area had been covered with nasty steel posts intended to prevent landings of Attilian hordes. Most posts below high water mark had been removed so by landing just above the tide we could ignore the remaining menaces. It was a thrill to side-slip in over the beetling cliffs, and like Canute nine hundred years ago, dare the waves to stay back as we claimed the wet sand for our own. The time-delay fuses worked just as they should—no prematures and accurate delayed bursts fifteen feet behind the one-inch plate. After three days we were well pleased and cleared the production-line for service use. We packed up to fly home, to buckle down, and face the tedium of writing a report that inevitably follows the joy of air trials. Fun always exacts a duty.

No sooner had I taxied into dispersal at Boscombe than Eddie summoned me to his presence. "Forget your Chinese crackers for a while, laddie," he said, "and get ready to prove our old reliables again. We're to test the 40 mm cannon against railway locomotives with steam up. An invasion of the Continent is planned, and our Hurri-bombers must be ready to help halt rail traffic prior to the landings."

"But!—"

"No buts," he interrupted. "We have to hit the engine every time. It's a very small target, and your noisy toys are not accurate enough yet. Now go and find out if the 40 mms are man enough."

The trial was to be at Shoeburyness range in February. Micky Bell-Syer and I got cracking and took off for Rochford airfield. "Break!" I shouted, waving to Micky, and we opened up our massed formation of two. The weather was just as bad over the seaside town of Southend as a year ago when we staged the first big rocket show for all the chiefs of staff. Once again we groped our way into the airfield, tails between our legs.

The results were not conclusive. Although we hit the engine

February 25, 1943—Trials with 40 mm cannon against European style of railway locomotive using AP and HE shell in preparation for invastion of the continent. (Wg Cdr Dean, Pilot; Gp Capt Baker-Carr, Min of Air Prod.· Sdn Ldr Bell-Syer, Pilot)

every time, only a few of the strikes did enough damage to inflict lasting hurt on the tough old Clydesdales. Areas vulnerable to the 40 mm shells were limited, as was our ammo supply for the big guns. "We must make the rockets more accurate, that's all," I pontificated to Micky as we walked away from inspecting the damage. "We need more clout for these Puffin' Billies."

GLOBAL UPDATE
January–May 1943

Roosevelt and Churchill meet at Casablanca to decide Allied strategy and the next area for invasion. They issue terms for unconditional surrender by all Axis forces.

Surrounded before Stalingrad, the German Sixth Army surrenders and the day after being promoted field marshal, General von Paulus is captured.

In North Africa the tide of war has turned. In full retreat, Rommel seizes all remaining transport for German troops only, stranding 30,000 Italian allies, for them an inadvertently merciful betrayal. He escapes by the coastal road, only slipping past the British by the lucky advent of a severe tropical storm. The Desert Rats are at his heels for three months picking off straggling tanks, vehicles and thousands of men who fall exhausted by the wayside. He loses 60,000 men, 500 tanks, and 1,000 guns. At the Mareth Line a hundred miles into Tunisia, Rommel pauses to regroup and integrate a large force fresh from Germany. Now some 200,000 strong, he attacks Kasserine Pass to the west against untried U.S. troops from the Torch landings, throwing them back fifty miles, but Allied reinforcements come to foil a breakthrough. The British Eighth Army arrives from Egypt and joins Torch forces to defeat Rommel in the Cape Bon peninsula. The Germans and remaining Italians, 275,000 strong, surrender. It signals the end of fighting in North Africa. It is May 12, 1943.

During 1942, only by strategic bombing could we physically engage the heart of the enemy and hurt him. We locked horns with the German Navy from the day war broke out and we suffered more harm from U-boats than the Luftwaffe had ever been able to do. The Wehrmacht was off on a skiing holiday in Russia and could do us no harm. Harris's task was to destroy the German war industry by aerial bombardment. If this meant hurting civilians or hitting domestic buildings, so be it. It became a serious bone of strife during his first year of command that the ruthless treatment of German cities was not a civilized way to make war.

Bombing people and their houses, per se, will not bring down a determined nation. We knew this from our own taste of the medicine. It is necessary to destroy their means of waging war. Harris's campaign was not for revenge, though such a motive was impugned by military radicals. Targets within the command's directive were raided, and the bombers did the best they could.

It was not the second front our ally, Stalin, kept demanding—but the bombardment forced the retention of a huge force in the Vaterland for ack-ack guns, night fighters, and massive fire brigades and air raid defenses. Bombing interrupted production, at first, but the Hun proved a master of dispersal, concealment, and protection. Underground facilities continued to turn out war products of all kinds. The Germans had hordes of slave labor for vast construction and manufacturing needs.

Our crews kept doggedly on, night after night, in spite of months of heavy losses, rarely less than five percent. The equipment was never perfect, in many ways inadequate for navigation or accurate bombing of precise targets.

GLOBAL UPDATE
March 1943

German subs are having murderous success in the Atlantic; new tactics being used by wolf packs are devastating and the Nazi boat commanders display their arrogance the more. They are bringing their satanic piranhas back on the surface for part of the home leg, daring our Coastal boys to make depth charge attacks which need nice low-level runs over them in the face of powerful ack-ack guns mounted on their foredecks. Clearing the Strait of Gibraltar by night, they run at full speed on the surface to French ports. Perhaps our new rockets will improve their execrable manners; the Hudsons there will soon be able to try.

Eddie caught up with me on the tarmac with an urgent signal ordering me to leave right away for North Africa to show some Coastal Command squadrons how to use rockets to attack U-boats. "That's what you told me you'd like to do," he said with a very straight face. I could only grin back—he had me there.

"I'd like to join you." It was John Moultrie on the horn, just having heard the news. "But I have to prepare the first Swordfish squadron with rockets, to sail with HMS *Archer*, a new pocket aircraft carrier. She's off with an escort group to the mid-Atlantic; I imagine we'll sink a sub before you're even operational in North Africa."

"Them's foightin' woids, me boy! Worth a case of bubbly, at least!" I challenged.

"You're on," said John.

We loaded a Lancaster with rocket guide rails, blast plates, and a multitude of boxes of armor-piercing rockets and stuffed her full of fuel. We took off soon after midnight heading for "…a beaker full of the warm South." As we scurried across a storm-embroiled Bay of Biscay, I slept soundly in the aisle on a pile of rocket boxes, weary from all the preparations.

A squadron Hudson was waiting at Gibraltar and carried me, my armorer, and a lot of our stores along the ancient North African shore. We fetched up, dusty and hot, at Blida airfield, an old French air force base in the foothills of the Atlas mountains.

A message from Air Force HQ in Algiers was waiting for me. The deputy commander in chief wanted to see me, pronto.

"Hell! I haven't a decent uniform," I complained to the squadron CO, Wing Commander Spotswood. "Don't worry, old chap," said Denis. "Tedder's very relaxed and will most likely be in battle dress himself."

Denis drove me in his staff car to Algiers, twenty miles to the north. Within the marble halls of the requisitioned Georges Cinq hotel in the hills behind the city, we were ushered in to the office of the commander of Allied Air Forces in the Mediterranean. Air Chief Marshal Tedder sat on the corner of his desk and wanted to know all about "these funny rockets." He listened, very quiet, sucking away on his neat, long-stemmed pipe. "Just let me know what you need: an inland area for firing practice; sea targets? Whatever. And for God's sake, get a move on! We really need those things."

I set up a training course for squadrons 500 (Denis's) and 608 (Wing Commander Grece, CO), informal and simple but

1943—Coastal HUDSON with eight × rockets for sinking U-boats. 500(C) Squadron aircraft at Blida, North Africa.

DRUIDS' CIRCLE

with a tough passing standard. The first day: briefings for complete aircrews of both squadrons as available from ops. All had to suffer a pep talk on how we stumbled on a super method of sinking the bastards, why it worked, and why they must follow the attack drill exactly: to dive on the boat abeam at twenty degrees; to aim at the bow; to fire at four hundred yards; and *not* to follow the rockets into the drink. Simple!

The station master, Gp. Capt. W. V. "Struggie" Strugnell, Military Cross and bar from Royal Flying Corps days in World War I, had his own personal Hurricane. It was abandoned at Blida as a write-off until he had a couple of smart technicians work on the deserted fighter and glue her Icarian wings back on. She bore the proud letter "V" at her waist, surely a mark of victory to come. The boss man trustingly lent me this valiant Boadicea to recce for a spot to practice our U-boat attacks.

I painted a huge circle, like the outer ditch at Stonehenge, in whitewash on a broad, dried-up river bed as a target. A range

1943—Photo of target circle shows perfect range and angle of dive for ideal U-boat rocket attack. 500(C) Squadron aircraft at Blida, North Africa.

mark at four hundred yards showed when to fire. Exercises began as soon as crews passed "Rocket 1"—the intro lecture. They started installing launchers on aircraft grounded for periodic maintenance or battle damage repair, but even with top priority for my conversion, operations came first. It took a neat bit of juggling and many futile arguments to get all crews through Rocket 1 and into their aircraft for Rocket 2—dummy photo attacks on the "Druids' Halo," as the crews called the whitewash circle. At first I had to schedule crews to make a Halo attack at the end of a mission while they were still airborne before being allowed to land for their well-earned rest. But they didn't seem to mind too much; they were very excited about the weaponry and joined in the practices with zest. It was not surprising that they all overestimated how steeply they were diving. A dive of twenty degrees in a Hudson seems well-nigh vertical, when you're not used to it. We installed a camera that was activated by the firing button, and analyzed the pics for

1943—Live rocket firing against sea target. Algiers.

steepness of dive and range of firing. The best and the worst were displayed on the notice board in the crew room for one and all to see; this nastiness proved a great incentive. Last came Rocket 3—air firing at sea.

I next arranged for the Navy to tow a sea target at fifteen knots down the coast out of sight from Algiers. The air crews let fly one or two of our precious supply of rockets at the elusive, moving drogue. They were then cleared for ops.

They let me go on the first operational sortie out toward Minorca. We flew and we flew. From looking and looking, my eyes ended up like a Peke's with goiter, but nothing of import was there to see. Much like any other fishing trip, I thought.

The crew on the second sortie the next day had better luck. They found a surfaced sub creaming along for the isle of Majorca. The Hun was taken completely by surprise because the approach was not a depth charge attack he'd normally expect. He didn't have time to man the large antiaircraft gun on the foredeck. It was a classic rocket attack, executed to perfection; within five minutes the U-boat sank, its bows reared to seventy degrees. The epic feat took place on 22 April 1943.

The pilot had a disagreeable final task to complete. The new weapon and method of attack were so secret and so deadly to the scourge that threatened our very existence, secrecy must be kept at all costs. There were to be no survivors to tell the tale until the German navy knew all about it.

There was quite a party in the mess that evening. As a new boy, I had to sign my name on the ceiling. The pyramid of French bamboo café chairs erected on the foundation of a rickety table was decidedly unstable and swayed like a Pisan tower. The tropical, stone-flagged mess room had a ceiling fifteen-feet high, and there was no magic carpet to soften a crash landing. The "X" that I proposed to make would not suffice. "Sign in full!" they chanted in relentless unison.

After dinner a few of us drove up into the mountains to a delightful Arab village with the appropriate name of Bouzeria.

Hubert W. Dean

1943—First U-boat kill in the Mediterranean with rockets 22 April. She sank in six minutes with all hands.

1943—Enlargement of first U-boat sinking, bows 70° up.

Sitting in the dusk round a tiled fountain, we quaffed cool white wine pressed in some local Cistercian *Trappe,* and relaxed as the heat of the day slipped out of the paving and was gone. Here we found our missing Arabian carpet, to enchant but not intoxicate.

At the flight line the next morning, half a dozen figures were crawling all over one of the Hudson's wings. "What's up?" I asked.

"Your blooming rocket gear is buckling the upper wing. That's what's up! Here, next to the engine," the flight sergeant grumbled, hastening to add, "sir." I climbed up alongside him, and sure enough, the upper magnesium skin between fuselage and engine had a series of distinct, deep wrinkles—a very furrowed brow. The flight sergeant had a right to be upset. These birds were his personal charges. Damage from combat was okay but from some half-baked excrescence buttoned under his wings, oh, no!

"Any more like this?" I asked him.

"Yes, sir," said Brough. "This is the third."

No easy explanation came to mind. "It's beyond us here," I said. "I'll fly the worst one back to the U.K. and let them find out what's wrong." I was sure it couldn't be from the rocket installation, well outboard the wrinkled area—on the other side of the engine to boot. We had too much happy experience with other installations for this sturdy Lockheed product to cry foul on us, but the boys needed a rebuttal more official than mine; I'd not try to fob them off with any sort of placebo; we'd visit a real doctor.

I left that afternoon with four other pilots prepared to ride with me in an albatross with a broken wing—anything to get off on a couple of weeks leave, particularly to the U.K. Twelve hours later, we were safe on home ground at Boscombe.

We were supposed to land at Port Reath in Cornwall to clear Customs, but my lame story of a damaged test aircraft returning for a post mortem and with only a limited number of landings left convinced the excise men. They waved us on by radio. In this slightly sneaky manner we could unload bottles of Algerian wine and boxes of oranges away from eagle eyes. I believe our loot tasted the better for it. In England we needed the little lift.

Eastleigh airfield was the home of Supermarine, where the Spit was born. The company now also had responsibility for looking after the Hudsons in use by the RAF. As soon as I woke the next day I took them the Hudson with the puzzled brow and left her for a "physical."

It was vital to get the African squadrons back in the air. As a backup, I decided to investigate the problem at Boscombe as well, using the original Hudson we'd already tested. I planned to reproduce the conditions of the actual rocket attack and watch the upper wing surface. The aircraft was loaded to 19,000 pounds, with eight rockets. I performed the dive attacks, but no wrinkles appeared; so the rocket installation, per se, wasn't the culprit. We now fitted a "g" meter to measure the amount of downward force in the pullout from the twenty-degree dive. Mr. Cook from performance mounted a movie-camera aimed at the area in question, and we loaded the willing camel to 21,500 pounds, the maximum allowed under any condition. I eased her gently off the grass.

At a respectable height, I made several simulated attacks and gradually increased the severity of the load on the wings during dive recovery. Finally, with just over three "g" force showing on the guage, Cook shouted above the noise, "That's it! We have wrinkles. Ease off! Ease off!"

We circled to burn off fuel and lighten the load before going in to land. The problem was solved. The squadron boys were being too ham-handed pulling out of their dives and would have to cool their ardor. I sent a signal to Denis at Blida to that effect, adding that lovely remnant of the British Raj in Injah, "Softly, softly catchee monkey!"

I knew the chap at the Air House who handled disposition

of American aircraft. He gave me another Hudson to replace the one I'd brought back. The overseas wallahs at Lyneham made me do an endurance test of over two hours to prove I could stretch the gas to reach Gib, though I'd just brought one back. We took off early from Port Reath the next morning, too early for decency, making a wide swing outside the Scillies to keep clear of the Lufftwaffe's Condor nests around Brest in Brittany. It was a crisp mid-May morn out over the Atlantic well out of sight of the enemy French coast. I jockeyed the aircraft "up on the step"[7] and she droned along happy as a sated seagull. Four hours later we fetched land at Cap Finisterre and felt more secure from attack. We broke out the coffee and sandwiches; they taste so much better aloft, and I'll never know why.

The Hudson was flying beautifully, the engines purring with contentment. I should have left well alone and wasn't trying to show off, but I noticed the port engine was feeling a tad cold so tapped the louver control switch a couple of times. To my horror the louvers controlling the opening for taking in cold air kept on closing until they were shut tight. No amount of cussing or fiddling with that blasted little switch made any difference. The gills stayed shut. I throttled the engine back as far as possible but the cylinder-head temp rose steadily to the limit. I had to switch off the engine. We crabbed on, maintaining our height without great difficulty with so much fuel used up, but gone was the heady joy of passage.

We had less than an hour to go, but it was all over water. I hugged the Spanish shore past Cadiz, hoping the king of Spain had forgotten that Drake singed his royal beard there in 1587. That was Cape Trafalgar we just passed, where Nelson died on Hardy's arm. We cleared the narrows and the brooding Rock lay right ahead. For permission to approach and land, I was supposed to flash the letters of the day on the Aldis lamp and fly round the Rock at a thousand feet to be identified. I conveyed my dilemma to control on the summit. "Only one engine," I flashed. "Request immediate landing." No answer. "I think it's one of the monkeys," said the jester beside me.

"Cut it out, you buffoon. We're in trouble," I told him. "We are not amused!"

I got the okay and dropped in over the harbor to the west of the only landing strip. I don't like single engine landings in a twin: you only have one spin at the wheel. We began to reduce speed a hundred feet up when a bloody Spit slipped in beneath us to land on the spot where I'd staked my claim. He kept rolling, thank God, to the far end where he turned off abruptly—not to get out of our way I'm sure—he never even knew we were there. Bloody clot!

Before I left the next day with the Hudson's gills breathing freely again, I visited the engineer officer and asked about the crash of a Whitley at the end of September last year. "I wasn't here then, sir, but I'll look it up for you." I called him from the watch office as we got ready to take off. "It seems there was some question about the elevator controls being reversed during repairs," he told me, "but because it was in the sea water so long, the matter wasn't pursued."

"Good God!" I exploded. "You don't really know what happened, do you?" He didn't answer, so I hung up. I was much distressed, but in wartime life has a different value. I'd never find out, and I couldn't ever tell the rest of the family what I suspected. Dear Pip, rest you quietly in the shadow of the Rock.

Blida was waiting for us three hours later. I explained to the two squadron COs how the pilots were overstressing the wings in the pullout; ops had already been resumed after my cable, but there'd been no more sightings. Had word leaked out?

I could stay no longer and got a lift back to England. There I learned that a Swordfish from *Hornet* had sunk a U-boat in the Atlantic on the day before we did from Blida. The Swordfish flapped around in happy circles after dealing the dastardly blow. A Martlet fighter from the carrier proceeded to eliminate the U-boat crew, as ordered. Screamed the Swordfish pilot, "Hey! Wait a bit, we want some survivors!"

252   DRUIDS' CIRCLE

"How many?" came the laconic Drakelike reply.

Thus I lost a well-nigh certain bet with John Moultrie, but the nice guy never did press for payment; and I, being me, just plain forgot. Not quite. Though a day late getting the first kill ever, we were officially operational on the day the *Hornet* stung fatally, so I guess I had a good case to argue. A draw?

In due course the rockets proved to be the most effective weapon available against submarines on the surface or at periscope depth. Our little baby—all growed up!

GLOBAL UPDATE
March–July 1943

General MacArthur begins the long march back to Manila; his forces, spearheaded by Australian infantry, are soon joined by U.S. troops landing at Buna. Large reinforcements of Japanese arrive on 2 March in eight transports and eight destroyers—but

1943—Coastal Command WELLINGTON with rockets for U-boats.

1943—Coastal Command LIBERATOR with rockets for U-boats.

are intercepted. All transports and half the escort are sunk in the Battle of the Bismarck Sea.

Admiral Nimitz begins his painful way back to the west, retaking—in leapfrog routine—dozens of small island groups from the Japanese. He relieves Attu and Kiska in May.

Another prong of attack is taken by Admiral Halsey who leads the U.S. Marines north after Guadalcanal to the Russel Islands, Rendova and—in July—New Georgia.

The next step in the Allies strategic plan in Europe is to take Italy out of the war. As a stepping stone, Sicily is invaded on 10 July and conquered in just over five weeks. Mussolini resigns as premier on 25 July to be replaced by Marshal Badoglio.

With the defeat of von Paulus' Sixth Army, three hundred thousand are captured or slain. Before this disaster the Germans have already lost over a million and a half men. As the Russians pursue the Nazis back to Prussia, they grow ever stronger and inflict mounting losses, but it cannot be blitzkrieg in reverse. The Red army is fighting over its own devastated, scorched earth and unable to live off the land. Wisely it does not outstrip its supplies. The end is a foregone conclusion, though, and only a matter of time.

The Red leader continued to fire off a constant barrage of querulous pleas for the Allies to open a second front in Europe to relieve the enormous pressure on his armies engaged with the bulk of the Wehrmacht on the eastern front. It was useless to keep pointing out to the Bear that we were holding masses of skilled men in thrall guarding the German homeland against our continuing bomber raids or to mention the heavy losses we endured shipping supplies to him via the Atlantic lifeline, in aid of which he offered nothing. The complaints on both sides were valid; we shared a powerful common foe who had almost overcome each of us in turn. We offered a sop in the form of sixty Hurricane IVs, with four 20 mm cannon in the wings and two 40 mm cannon beneath, for close support. They were delivered April 1943 and must have been of help. At Boscombe we never heard how they fared—but then, a sop is not a second front.

For both the newly formed U.S. Eighth Air Force in Britain and RAF Bomber Command, 1942 was a year of preparation. Rearming with new aircraft: the Eighth with B-17, Fortress and B-26, Liberator; the RAF with the three types of four-engine heavies. The RAF planes all had technical problems, particularly the Lancaster with a wing tip snag needing several months to cure and holding up four squadrons. The Americans—escorted by British fighters—only bombed one German target but had worked up to a fine pitch with the relatively small maximum effort they could field daily, hitting pinpoint targets in France. They had twenty thousand men at airfields all over East Anglia and some five hundred planes, but their results did not overly impress Washington. General Eaker flew to Casablanca in January of 1943 for a luncheon with Winston Churchill. Only by an impassioned appeal was Eaker able to persuade him to support continued efforts by the Eighth to build an effective, massive daylight bombing force. Otherwise the Eighth faced the same fate Bomber Command so narrowly avoided at the end of 1941.

The RAF developed a navigational device known as "Gee,"[8] which improved accuracy considerably at ranges within "line of sight" or about two hundred miles at twenty-five thousand feet bombing altitude. The secret of the device was soon discovered and jammed. A more secure and accurate version quickly appeared named "Oboe," first tried in raids against Lubeck and Rostock, large estuary ports on the Baltic coast. Both attacks were so accurate and concentrated that the two cities were laid waste. The raids were led by master bombers with the new aids, who planted markers on the target. Thus was born the Path Finder Force (PFF) to lead our bombers for the rest of the war.

We developed another important electronic device which we found out later was also in the minds of the German scientists. Code-named "Window," it used a vast number of short strips of foil cut to the exact length of the radar wavelength used to detect our bombers. Sown in the air behind one bomber, the strips would make the image on radar scopes appear to be that of a large formation. But we did daren't use it for fear of inciting German retaliation using the same device. A ridiculous, unwarranted fear because Luftwaffe bombers were completely preoccupied with covering the retreat of German armies in Russia.

With more accurate bombing possible, Harris gave the green light to active development of specialized bombs designed by the wizard Barnes Wallis. We already knew of the rolling bomb for dams; others were to include "earthquake bombs," the first weighing ten thousand pounds, and known as

"Tallboy"; followed by "Grand Slam," to weigh an astounding twenty thousand pounds.

Dr. Lauritsen's dynamo team started work on a forward-firing aircraft rocket in June 1943 under the guidance of Dr. William A. Fowler, assistant director of research. They successfully produced an extrudable, solventless powder much the same as our double-base propellant. It was quite unlike the powder used in the 4.5-inch air-air rocket developed by the Army for the Air Corps with which he had little sympathy. An Army rocket took to the air on 6 July 1942 at Aberdeen, the first U.S. rocket fired from a plane in flight. The Navy air tested the Army rocket in early 1943 and decided a higher velocity was needed. Blowups began to occur, and the solvent ballistite fell under deep suspicion. Thanks to our operational successes in the Atlantic and the Mediterranean, the U.S. Navy put full emphasis on the U.K. design approach for their first model.

To obtain a proven weapon with the least delay, the first Caltech design was as near a copy of the British as possible. It had a similar 3.5-inch motor with a solid 25-pound warhead and was called 3.5-inch AR. A second HE warhead was adapted from a 5-inch existing U.S. shell with a new fuse and called the 5-inch AR. Naval air firing began July 14, Lieutenant Commander Tom Pollock firing a British round from each wing of a TBF-1 (Avenger) at Goldstone Lake. A month later, a full load of the Caltech-built model was fired with complete success. A wonderful achievement.

Lewis motley took our thinking about rocket rotation a step or two further. He brought me some beautifully detailed drawings of a small "spin rocket," as he called it, for air-to-air use. It had several small venturis evenly spaced in a circle around the base instead of the single one we were used to. The smaller exhausts were angled at ten degrees from the fore-and-aft axis so that the jets would make the rocket spin around that axis as well as propel it to the target. For the rocket body Lew specified beryllium, a somewhat rare metal having only one-sixth the weight of steel. Later on, by agreeing to a compromise on aluminum for the body—three times as heavy as beryllium—and filling the spinners with a suitable propellant, we were able to fire our elegant babies with great success and astonishing accuracy. I was to learn we were a bit late on this one; before long the Germans began using small spinner rockets against Allied bomber formations over Germany.

GLOBAL UPDATE
May—September 1943

While the Allies are busy conquering Sicily, the fascist regime in Italy collapses, resulting in general chaos in the country. Mussolini is detained by the Italians and at the end of August is moved to a place of higher security in the mountains near Rome. In the meantime an unconditional Italian surrender is negotiated and signed in Sicily on 3 September.

Before dawn that day the British Eighth army crosses the straits of Messina to invade the mainland. A few days later Allied landings begin in the Salerno area, but a shortage of heavy landing craft severely limits the armor that can go in. The RN took six thousand First Airborne British commandos aboard warships in grand Tudor style for want of more normal troop transportation to capture the vast main harbor of Taranto.

After dark, the bulk of the Italian fleet sails from Genoa and Spezia, where they had run for shelter. Bound for Malta, they face a hazardous passage to the west of Sardinia where the flagship *Roma* is sunk, and the battleship *Italia* badly damaged. The British ships *Warspite* and *Valiant* escort the rest of the fleet to Valetta and Admiral Cunningham signals the Admiralty: "The Italian battle fleet now lies at anchor under the guns of the fortress of Malta."

> Germany reacts to the invasion immediately. Nazi paratroopers kidnap Mussolini from his hiding and fly him to Munich. The Germans set up a rump government around the erstwhile premier at Como in opposition to that of the reinstated King Victor Emmanuel and Marshal Badoglio at Brindisi. The Como group is an obvious front to divide the confused loyalties of the population. The Nazis also occupied the area north of Rome, including airfields we had planned to take with airborne troops.

In February, after the Casablanca conference, a directive was issued to the Allied bomber commands in the U.K. making their primary task the destruction of the German military, industrial, and economic system, and the complete undermining of the morale of her people.

Germany overcame our heavy and repeated bombing attacks by wide dispersal and burial of her industry using hordes of foreign labor to do so; she also replaced most of the loss in raw materials readily from conquered lands. But we learned from intelligence sources the Nazi leaders were becoming increasingly alarmed and were being forced onto the defensive in the air. They were concentrating aircraft production on fighters rather than bombers. It was an important turning point for the Allies, the beginning of achieving air supremacy over the Luftwaffe in Germany.

The power of Bomber Command increased threefold by overall rearming with four-engine planes. The average bombload rose from twenty-eight hundred pounds per aircraft to seventy-five hundred. The precision of the Path Finder Force (PFF) fitted with the very latest electronic aids put the power where it was meant to be, and from the design genius of Barnes Wallis came new weapons to make the surgery more specialized and the results more terrifying. The command fought what came to be known as the Battle of the Ruhr, waged in cruel intensity from March to July of 1943. It began with a PFF-led raid on Essen, the steel center, with about four hundred heavies, and the city was severely damaged for the first time in the war. As a result, the ack-ack defenses of the Rhur were doubled and one hundred thousand more men allocated for repair duties.

Allied losses were heavy by day and by night. By day the enemy fighters had an easier task to find and visually engage the bombers but blistering crossfire from disciplined, close formations of U.S., bombers made normal attacks from the beam or astern very costly, forcing the Hun to seek some alternative.

Nazi fighters started to bomb the massive formations from four thousand feet above, flying on the same course, using time-delay fragmentation bombs. They could fly over the bombers at their leisure, out of range of the 50-caliber turrets. It was wickedly effective. The Eighth would have to be given fighter escort to survive, but our Spits couldn't help because they couldn't reach targets deep in Germany. Long-range escorts were needed urgently. P-38s would be available before long, and eventually the superior P-51 was promised to ease the bombers' agony.

General Eaker realized he must first defeat the German fighter force before he could carry out the Casablanca directive, which the chiefs amended in June to give first priority to attacking the German fighter forces and their aircraft industry.

The RAF offered to help the Eighth Air Force with some upward-firing rockets to counter the overhead Luftwaffe bombing. The rocket development people already had in production a small high-performance rocket that could be fitted with an explosive head designed to burst at the pesky fighters' height and tickle them up quite effectively.[9]

An upper turret of a B-17 would be modified at the Prestwick depot in Scotland,[10] where most of the incoming aircraft on the ferry route from the U.S. arrived. Four steel launching tubes were to be mounted almost vertically for the point-blank shots.

On 16 May the RAF elite 617 Squadron using only sixteen of the latest Lancasters, made a very special raid on the colossal

Mohne and Eder dams that supplied the whole of the Rhur area with water and power. They trained for months with Wallis Barnes' rotating skip-bombs,[11] and both dams were destroyed. Wing Commander Guy Gibson, their gallant CO, remained with his squadron throughout, directing the raid. The damage was far-reaching and severe, but half the bombers were lost. Gibson was given the Victoria Cross for this incredible feat.

Continuing the latest policy of concentrating the bomber force, the British shifted focus and made four very heavy attacks on the major port of Hamburg from 24 July to 3 August. Led by the PFF and using H_2S radar mapping, they were very accurate. In Churchill's words the raids "…caused grater destruction than had ever been suffered by so large a city in so short a time. In the second attack there arose a fire tornado which raged through the city with a terrifying howl and defied all human defenses." Speer, architect of Germany's massive war production, said if similar attacks had been made against six other major cities in quick succession, production would have broken down. On those dreadful nights we decided to use the antiradar foil (window) for the first time against which neither ack-ack guns nor night fighters could operate. This happy condition prevailed for some months and bomber losses fell dramatically until the Hun found a way to see through the window.

Reports of German long-range rocket and pilotless aircraft R & D continued to reach our intelligence people over the many months since the fall of 1939. The situation was reviewed in the spring of 1943, and heavy air recce revealed details of both kinds of aerial threat in advanced stages of readiness, with London as the most probable target. In June Hitler inspected the Peenemunde research base and envisioned here a new hope of blocking the invasion he knew was in the wind. He gave the work the highest priority. Zero-hour for an all-out rocket/ unmanned plane campaign was set for 20 October 1943 and he called for thirty thousand rockets to be ready. We found out also that very long-range guns were in the works for deployment about the same time with suspicious heavy constructions on the French coast to house them. On the night of 17 August, bomber Command sent 571 heavies to attack the experimental base from medium altitude—for better accuracy. Several diversionary raids were made at the same time. They deliberately bombed in moonlight because the target was hard to find, but unfortunately the light made the raiders easy to spot on their way home; German night fighters had recovered from the deceit of the spoof raids and forty bombers perished.

The results justified the cruel losses. All manufacturing drawings were burnt, the main plant was badly damaged, and widespread dispersal initiated immediately. Research was moved to Poland, out of our range but within earshot of our faithful Polish agents. They gave us excellent feedback on the development of such a menace to our good health.

One year to the day after the Eighth made their first raid on the continent with a maximum effort of twelve B-17s, they mounted an assault of three hundred and sixty planes. Half to Schweinfurt to hit the ball-bearing plants—the rest to Regensburg where many Me 109 fighters were made. Still without escort, the missions were suicidal; but the crews held rigid discipline, and the ones who made it to the target dropped with precision. The Regensburg group turned south after bombing and crossed the Alps at the Brenner Pass, to find a haven in North African with eleven hours of pure, unadulterated hell behind them. Out of the hundred and thirty planes that took off to destroy the Messerschmitt factory, twenty-four were lost: a fearsome, dreadful percentage.

Gunnery trials at Boscombe were now relatively routine and no new installations were in sight. My staff could easily handle anything in that area, and so I'd been temporarily put on the staff of the rocket development branch at the Ministry of

Supply in London to be immediately available for air testing the many rocket developments in the offing.

We visited Prestwick to inspect progress on the B-17 rocket turret in early July and found the work well under way; everyone was flat out to get it to the squadrons fast. Hawker modified my warrior Hurricane with a five-inch-diameter chimney stack mounted vertically behind the cockpit, passing right through the fuselage and canted forward at about four degrees as in the B-17 turret. Without delay we must test the rockets for functioning, flight accuracy, and reliability under operational conditions at cruising altitudes. The overall job we code-named "Sunflower," and the little rocket, of course, became the "Sunflower Seed."

I flew the Hurricane to Pendine Sands and parked on the beach. We didn't bother to lift the tail, but ran a cable up to the high water mark, pressed the tit and fired the first Sunflower Seed just as she sat. It was a real crumph! The very short burning time of the rocket sounded almost like an explosion, and the little missile was on its way. Flames poured from the bottom of the launching tube, spewing across the sand. The unhappy airplane was momentarily enveloped in flame and smoke—almost on fire—but it was soon over and the acrid fumes cleared and blew out to sea.

"Good God," I complained to Cookie, "you've converted our poor Hurricane into an old steam engine! Like Stevenson's *Rocket*. An apposite name, but how very heartless of you."

"All in a good cause, old boy," replied Cookie, obviously with no vestige of soul.

We examined the blast plate covering the fuselage top behind the cockpit around the base of the grotesque chimney pot. There was no sign of damage; all seemed to bode well for the first air shot. A message to Santa in the shape of a rocket was stuffed up the chimney and held by retaining levers. The sliding hood had been taken off because the chimney stopped it from opening. I preferred it off, anyway; it made it easier to get out in a hurry. I climbed to a couple of thousand feet and flew along parallel to the shore so they could get a good photo. I felt quite a bump as the rocket lit up, and a hell of a draught blew in like an invading wraith.

I landed on the firm sand and taxied over to the group of scientists. "Switches off," I yelled. "All off!" As I jumped from the wing root and lifted my goggles, I could see they were all clustered round the tail in some agitation.

Cookie was coming forward. "What happened?" he asked.

"Nothing, as far as I know," I told him. "Why?" And then I saw that all of the top and all of the starboard side of the fabric covering of the fuselage had torn away from just behind the edge of the blast plate and was draped back across the horizontal stabilizer and out beyond.

"Lucky this 'towed target' didn't get caught up in your elevators, Dix," said Cookie, looking a bit tense.

"You know, I thought it was suddenly a bit draughty," I had to confess. "Well I'm damned!"

The mishap brought the trials to a halt and I'd lost my horse to get back to London. I returned ignominiously by road—very *infra dignitatem.*

London was now blessedly free from the nightly scourge. The last time I'd slept there was in May of 1941, toward the tail end of the heavy raids. It was a night I'll not easily forget. We had a conference on a bomber turret that went on far too long at the Frazer-Nash factory. It was so late Archie invited me to stay the night at his house in Kingston. We retired after an excellent dinner and a superlative glass of brandy, and the next thing I knew was Archie shaking me out of a deep sleep. "Are you okay, Dixi?" he was shouting. By the light of his shrouded flashlight I saw the bedroom blackout curtains hanging disheveled and torn. There was glass all over the bed.

"Yes, of course. What's up?" I asked, blearily.

"We've just had a bomb in the front garden," he said, "fifty feet from where you're lying. The main blast must've gone up over the roof. Thank God you're all right, old chap!" Archie never did fill in the crater. He said he'd make a rock garden and fish pond out of it as a memento.

In Wales the Hurricane was soon repaired, and a dent found in the blast plate was hammered out; she was raring to go. I ferried her due north over the mountains, to the little airfield near Aberporth. Here, five miles northeast of Cardigan, was the secret rocket Projectile Development Establishment (PDE), perched on the rocky cliffs, face-to-face with the neutral though mildly hostile Irish coast.

The rocket scientists had a dozen Sunflower Seeds ready, all frozen to minus ten degrees Celcius to represent the conditions in the B-17 at altitude. The warheads were smoke-filled with live delayed-action bursting fuses.

I made level runs at full speed past the cameras, a hundred feet up, heading east for Ireland, fifty miles away. The results were outstanding. All twelve of the rockets burst three to four thousand feet above the Hurricane and directly overhead. Although the blast plate did get pushed in somewhat, there was no more rending of the fuselage's cloak.

We spent a cheery night at the Ship Inn, the tiny, very Welsh pub in Aberporth village. The little harbor lay quiet below us; the war on a different planet. We made final tests a month later with live, high-explosive shells. At twenty-eight thousand feet, two of us fired them in turn—the other in a second Hurricane to time each burst with a stop watch, looking for about five seconds delay. Everything worked like a dream.

I went home for a weekend and found a call waiting from Charles Dann. "Hey," he greeted me when I got him. "We have a date with the gamekeepers in the New Forest. Can you come over tomorrow?"

"Sure, that's great." I said. "Thanks awfully." We were in for another local treat, much like the delightful day we had at John Ludden's recently. Charles kept the promise made to me when his bombing range first opened. He invited Pete and asked John Ludden as well, which was nice of him.

Once into the padlocked enclosure, we met at the deserted head keeper's cottage. One of the chaps gave us each a pocketful of buckshot cartridges and drove us to neat, unobtrusive blinds cunningly fashioned in the undergrowth. The men-in-green, our hosts, were to act as beaters, and we settled down to hold our breath and display a vast store of impatience.

"Sssh!" suddenly a hiss from Charles, our devoted sponsor. A faint crackle of twigs—and there stood an elegant creature, dappled in sunshine, aquiver with fear. The shotguns bayed, and the stag fell before us. It was too close a slaughter to be anything but gruesome. The first drive culled the number needed to preserve the forest and the keepers called it a day. I would not have minded so much shooting the deer at long range with a high-powered rifle on some open, heathered moor, maybe; but this encounter was at disagreeably close quarters.

"Don't be such a bloody prude, Dixi," said Charles as I told him how I felt. "You didn't mind getting the birds at Ludden's place the other day and you and Pete are always bringing in a hare or a rabbit from around the airfield. You're the best-known poachers in Wiltshire."

"That's different," I nitpicked.

But I didn't protest when the keepers had finished preparing the game for us to take home and hung a pair of antlers over the front bumper of Charles's car. Nor was there any objection when Anna Dann cooked a haunch of the venison, Finnish-style. She wrapped the whole thing in seasoned dough and buried it in the frosty ground a foot below the surface. Later she dug it up and broke away the hardened dough, which took with it any malodor from the deer. It was ready for her secret recipe from Lapland and had a wondrous taste. What a great party it was!

Then a call from our U.S. Air Corps pals:

"Our B-17 with a Sunflower growin' in the upper greenhouse is in bloom. Let's go before it turns into a wallflower." It was our impatient pilot who'd leave without us if we dallied. We drove out to Bovingdon, a U.S. base twenty miles north of London, and there sat our Fortress with the four-stack upper turret, meek and mild as could be.

"Come on, fellahs, let's get goin'," enthused Lieutenant Matske, our captain for the trip to Wales. I think he came from some Southern state in the U.S., but we were able to understand him well enough. We climbed up the ladder into the bomber and settled down for a pleasant hour-and-a-half trip to Pembrey. The B-17 is a quiet, comfortable ride—if you're not being shot at.

The acceptance trials were run the next day,[12] 23 September, and the turret passed for operational use. Alackaday! Though the tricky development had been conceived and completed in less than three months, we were too late. The wily Hun decided to try more effective measures and the fighters were now attacking head-on, boring through the formations at combined closing speeds of well over six hundred knots. They had a supreme advantage of surprise and gave the B-17 gunners minimal time to respond.

So the Sunflower bloomed in vain. Two hundred years before, Thomas Gray said it well: "...Full many a flower is born to blush unseen..."

GLOBAL UPDATE
October–December 1943

The Nazis shell Rome and occupy it in September. Soon after, the U.S. Fifth Army captures Naples, and on 13 October the Royal Italian Government declares war on Germany.

Now on a nonstop offensive, U.S. troops in the Pacific make landings on Bougainville, the largest northernmost of the Solomon Islands on 1 November. Admiral Nimitz captures "impregnable" Tarawa in the Gilberts in four days of bloody fighting.

The Red Army establishes air superiority and advances

steadily on the whole front from Moscow to the Black Sea. In the center the Soviet army surges forward to recapture Kiev.

Roosevelt and Churchill meet with Stalin late in November at Teheran in Turkey. There is consensus that the U.S. and British invade the European continent in early summer of 1944. General Eisenhower is brought back from command of the Italian front to be supreme commander of the Allied Expeditionary Force to mount the invasion. Stalin voluntarily announces that the Soviet Union will declare war on Japan the moment Germany is defeated.

North Atlantic convoys to Murmansk resume in November and tempt a foray by the German battle-cruiser *Scharnhorst* from Alten Fjord in Norway. A small British fleet with Admiral Frazer flying his flag in the battleship *Duke of York* engages and sinks the German.

Back in London, I found my temporary detachment as test pilot to the rocket development branch had been converted to a permanent posting. My Boscombe days were over, and I had hardly felt their passing—almost five years, the longest posting of my career, and the best. However, the change made little difference to what I did. The rocket was the new boy on the block and had priority. I was flattered to be in at the source of the new planning and still do all the air testing.

I shared an office in Thames House, overlooking the river, but spent most of my time shuttling between Hendon, where we had a few communication aircraft, Hawker's factory field (where my Hurricane was now hangared), and our rocket test sites at Pendine and Aberporth.

The sixty-pound HE warhead had improved, and there were new fuses which I checked on our steel plate targets at various angles of impact. As we wound up the trials at Pendine, a truck arrived from Aberporth and drove down onto the sands. On board was the first redesigned 750-pound rocket made at

Aberporth, to be ground launched. It was the same hybrid bomb-body/multiple-tail rocket I made, but to equalize the gas pressure in all the motors, it had a common plenum chamber at the point where the seven rocket tails screwed in.[13] With overweening parental pride, I watched the ugly duckling take off on a flight which was, to me, the flight of a swan. It was a roaring success. I returned to London in a warm glow.

There was a call from the Admiralty. "Dixi, this is Jacko. A load of U.S. Navy rockets has arrived. They're on their way to Aberporth for initial ground testing. We'd be much obliged if you'd fire a few for us in the air to see how they perform and get some pictures." Commander Jackson had told me some time before about the progress of aircraft rocket work at Caltech and was amazed they had been able to send us some so soon. It was less than three months since Cmdr. Tom Pollock fired the first of these 3.5-inch AR in the air above the California Desert.

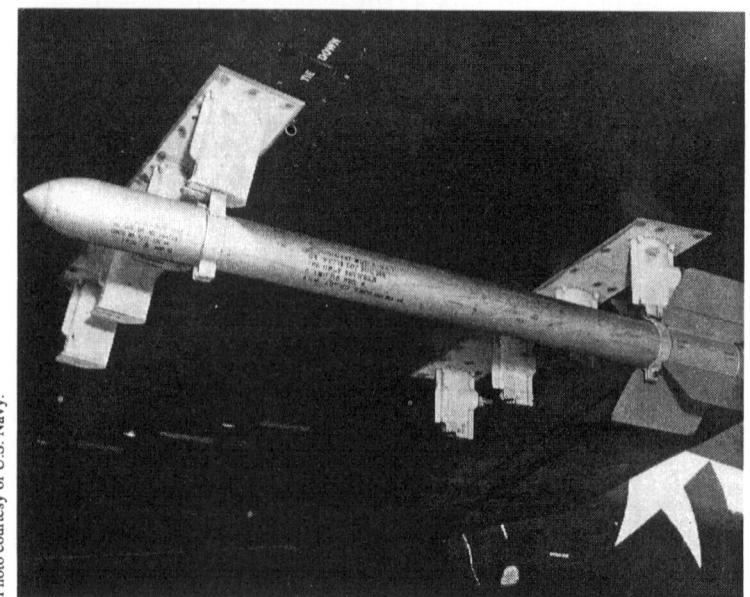

1943—U.S. Caltech 3.5-inch AR rocket as fired by Wg Cdr Dean at Projectile Devt. Est. Aberporth, Wales.

"No problem, Jacko," I told him. "When?"

We made a date and he agreed to book rooms at the Ship. I picked up the Hurricane and set out to enjoy a gentle jaunt across England, wishing for yesterday's sun—today was 10/10 overcast. How changeable the English sky can be, how fickle; then I recalled it was already late fall, and we'd used up our two days of summer.

It would be an hour to my old stamping ground at Boscombe, a good place to top up fuel before flying over the rocky bits on the last leg across southern Wales. I left my plane at the pumps and dropped in on the met boys. Though I already felt a bit of a stranger, they made me very much at home again, to the point of rudely advising that only a bloody fool like the Dean they knew would press on with the weather kicking up as it was.

I had to lay over for two days. Two days of low, hurrying cloud and a forgotten sun. I had a little time at home, and that took some of the angst away, but at last a glint of light in the sky made a half-hearted promise, and we took off in the early afternoon of the second day into November—impatient and a mite cross. Maybe I should have waited longer. Of course I should. Over Cardiff the frowning cloud enforced some low flying and dictated a track hugging the coast all the way round to my goal at Aberporth—a hundred and fifty miles of intimate beach combing. It was impossible to clear the Black Mountains near Brecon on a direct route. We skirted past Swansea, skimming the roiling surf off Pendine Sands. If I have to, I thought, I can always come back here and park on my well-known beach. On we went, across the Bay of St. Bride. The steep, rugged cliffs at St. David's Head bothered me. Early night scud was coming in fast from the Atlantic like the torn breath of an avenging Fury. From the level of the cliff top I spied an airfield of some import. "That's for us!" I told my indomitable erne.

When I reached the tarmac an unhappy aircraftsman in foul-weather gear appeared out of the now-driving rain to signal us to a hangar. He closed the massive doors, and you'd hardly have known it was piping up such a storm outside.

"Get me the orderly officer, will you?" I called down to the airman and jumped off the wing root to await the duty dog.

"Flying Officer Knowles, sir," announced the rain-drenched figure who came through the little postern cut in the main hangar door.

"This stuff on the Hurricane is secret," I told Knowles, a bit pompously. "I need a guard posted, and no one is to come near it. Who's your CO?"

"Group Captain Drew, sir," he said, "He's back in his quarters by now." I thanked him and picked up the wall phone.

"Dixi, for God's sake! What the hell are you doing here in this forsaken spot? I thought I heard an aircraft but couldn't be sure in this storm. Come right on over. I'll send my car."

I spent the night with the CO and his amusing wife, Bey, and talked and talked of the time we served together flying ancient Handley-Page Heyford bombers at Mildenhall some ten years before. We'd almost forgotten each other's existence. It was a delightful evening bathed in nauseating nostalgia.

By the next morning the wrack had blown away inland; and we were on the ground at Aberporth before nine o'clock. The rocket boffins, warned by St. David's watch office, soon arrived in a van full of spanking-new U.S. Navy rockets. We loaded the Hurricane with as many as she would take. Everything fitted perfectly. The Caltech people had made an excellent copy from our design. The weapons looked very professional and formidable. They proved to be completely interchangeable with ours on the launchers. Great for standardization of equipment between close Allies.

Three full loads fired over the recorders on the cliffs above Aberporth village proved the projectiles to be without fault. I noticed these rockets were more agile than ours and seemed faster, making them more accurate. "Three cheers for the Yankee Doodles!" I yelled on the passing Welsh wind.

The films we looked at later showed the American 3.5-inch

AR rockets had 200 ft/sec more legs than our own slowpokes, which were older and naturally less spry than their younger kinsmen. This day to remember was the 3rd of November, 1943. It could perhaps more properly have been the "fifth of November, a day to remember and never be forgot"—with a nod to the shade of Guy Fawkes, infamous in 1605.

Eight

In the winter of 1943 Bomber Command began the Battle of Berlin, continuing without remorse well into 1944. The miserable weather saved the city from the concentrated destruction of Hamburg. Pervasive cloud cover prevented visual marking by the Path Finder Force, and the radar blind-bombing device (H_2S) was impotent without a stretch of water to give clear contrast with adjacent land. The docks and seacoast at Hamburg provided ideal conditions for good radar pictures, and the city suffered for it. Continuous overcast prevented effective daylight recce photography and until March 1944 we didn't know how successful the battle had been. Sixteen major attacks wrought great destruction, but none were as concentrated or severe as those on Hamburg.

I was ever conscious of the outrageous gravity drop of our rockets, and I know I must have bored our scientists witless with my complaints. Blessed with much practice, I could now estimate range to target well enough to make a stab at the right allowance for the precipitous drop toward mother earth. A trajectory less downbeat would be of tremendous help under operational conditions during which the pilot's job must be made as simple and foolproof as possible. It's much easier to eliminate gross error at the source before going into battle than to cope with it in the face of an unsympathetic foe.

It is fundamentally impossible to give a rocket a trajectory as flat as a cannon shell's.[1] To my mind, something had to be done about it. I thought back to a crazy dream I'd promised to follow up: now was the time. I would try to make the damned things fly and thereby do what they were meant to do—hit the bloody target.

I discovered that a well-known toy manufacture called Lines Brothers had been busy making small pilotless drones on which our ack-ack gunners could vent their spleen and improve their aim.[2]

I had a chat with the design people at the factory, then got Cookie to send a few of the small two-inch Sunflower Seed rockets to the Lines factory for initial tests. The chaps there were great. They were intrigued with the problem and promised a solution. They made me some elegant little wings, mounted on a sort of girdle, that could be slipped over the rocket bodies and secured at the center of gravity.[3] The wings were designed to develop enough lift to support the initial weight of the rocket.

When we launched a few of the dainty birds, the results were surely a mixed bag in any day's hunt. Mostly they rolled gently around on their long axes and veered off at a tangent, soon to dive into the grasses of the meadow. But a couple did perform surprisingly well and justified the effort. Still more design cunning was required; some way had to be found to iron out the slight differences in overall lift between the two wings in each pair.[4] We needed a smarter inertial reference system to include all the independent and changing forces working mostly against each other.

To start with, what could be better than a simple gyroscope to act as a nonpartisan referee? I called Sperry and posed the problem. They wanted to bypass the small rocket I'd used and start design work on the standard 3.5-inch weapon. I agreed with that bold approach because it would give us a real weapon sooner. Lines Bros. could make the wings for the full-scale models.

Before I had time to pursue this fascinating new line of development, I was summoned to the Air House. Air Vice Marshal Pidcock glanced at me with a twinkle in his eye. "How would you like to go to America, Dixi?" he asked.

"On a visit, sir?"

"Oh, no, old chap," he added, "a posting to Washington."

They gave me some time off to get ready. I was sad about leaving my brood behind. When I mentioned it to the boss he asked me if I knew there was a war on. Space by air or sea was at a premium, and greenbacks (dollars, he explained) were in short supply. Fortunately my kids didn't realize how long I might be gone, so for ten days we pretended there wasn't a war on at all. We did things that would be fun to look back on, like picking a bowl of mushrooms from the rich hotbed behind the garage. We borrowed a couple of old horses from the farm next door and rode out across the frozen fields. The big guy I had, called "No-name" because no one ever gave him one, was feeling his oats in the crisp air. When a piece of captive paper in a hedgerow fluttered, he threw me. He got home okay but left me to limp back alone. I was sore, but not at him. Of course, I readily forgave the old rascal. Such memories to hold.

I left for Washington on 12 January to be chief of development (armament) at the British Air Commission. I was thrilled to the very core.

It was my first train ride for several years. The old railway station was smelly and seedy with war neglect. It was dark in the quasi-blackout, and people were bumping into each other in their mindless haste.

My orders merely said report to the embarkation officer. I found the harassed chap in a cubbyhole by the gate and learned we were to sail on the French liner *Louis Pasteur*, leaving that night. He enjoined me to silence about the time of sailing and also that we'd be unescorted. Yes, he'd take care of seeing my baggage aboard.

The guards checked my pass as I went up the gangplank and on to find the allotted cabin. The *Pasteur* had obviously seen some hard service. She hadn't been used as a passenger ship since her launching and was crammed with multistage bunks in the upper-deck cabins and hammocks below for troop transport. I was in time to grab an upper berth, a temporary structure built from pipe scaffolding that swayed in the breeze. Now there are pros and cons about uppers and lowers. An upper is poised in the stale night air, which only gets more fetid as the graveyard watch drags by. On the other hand, a lower is always in danger of disturbance from an upper occupant with a call of nature in the small hours. Hammocks are infinitely superior, but it seems that only troops in steerage merit them. I glanced around and saw there would be at least a dozen of us cheek by jowl in this stateroom made for two. Oh well. What the hell.

A familiar stocky figure hove into view. "Sammy!" I bellowed, "I don't believe it—that I should be so lucky. What the devil are you doing here?" It was Sammy Wroath, now resplendent in a group captain's uniform—as indeed was I. He was on his way to an appointment as our chief test pilot at Wright-Patterson Field in Ohio, the equivalent then of Boscombe and Farnborough rolled into one. Sammy was CO of the fighter flight in performance testing section at Boscombe. We'd had a few brushes along the way when I barged in, insisting I must test all new fighters for suitability as gun platforms before they got into the rigmarole of performance testing. We'd reached a sort of compromise: I got my flying time; he got my sincere thanks. Sammy was a good scout, and we became firm friends over the years.

"Let's go and find a drink," Sammy suggested after he had dumped his night bag on a bunk.

"Great idea!" I agreed, with ill-concealed alacrity.

"Where's the bar?" asked Sammy, hailing a passing orderly.

"No bar on this ship, sir," answered the NCO. "She's dry on account of the damn Yanks."

"Oh, no!" groaned Sammy. "It can't be." I suggested we go ashore again and find a nearby pub. We had four or five hours before sailing, but easier said than done. The guards on the gangplank wouldn't let us off. Fortunately, a ship's officer chanced by, and we appealed to him—beyond earshot of the dutiful present-day followers of Horatius Cocles. "We're not trying to pull rank, old boy," I said, "but could you escort us to the nearest hostelry and join us in a farewell noggin to the Jolly Old U.K.?"

"The real problem is security," he replied. "We're sailing at dark—keep that mum—and I've got to be back in an hour's time. But come on, let's not waste any more valuable drinking time."

We quaffed a couple of pints of the local bitter and brought back half a dozen bottles each in our greatcoat pockets, taking care not to let our new pal and savior see them, or the sentries.

He took us back past the guards and said he'd look for us on passage to see if there was anything we might need. Nice guy, but somehow we never did see him again.

Next day there was nothing to see but the bleak, gray-green

Atlantic. We had cleared Ireland in the dark, running at full speed with lights out. The French ship creaked and groaned in the mounting seas. I prayed their stress calculations had been accurate, albeit in metric.

"Looks like a nasty cold front," said Sammy. "Let's go and find a weather map." We wandered around and found all access to the control sections of the ship was cordonned off. We were just passengers on this voyage—or cattle, more likely. Our presence was neither required nor welcome in the chart house, the signals cabin, and especially not on the bridge.

We chose the second sitting for meals. The mess hall—or wardroom I suppose—was set up in a help-yourself sort of affair. We got in a queue and took what was ladled onto our plates. Stewards were unnecessary luxuries on this slave ship. While the first lunch sitting was tucking away, we sat on Sammy's bunk and sipped a bottle of our precious and now very limited cache of beer. Sammy reached up to unscrew the shiny brass porthole above him and then caught himself. "That would be stupid," he said. "We can't throw empties overboard; a bloody U-boat could easily track us that way!" He was right. Bottles have been used for messages at sea since bottles were first blown. We didn't need to signal the Hun or have our "dead men" tell their empty tales.

By the second day we were plunging through a full storm. Fiddles were attached to the mess tables to catch errant dishes, and attendance at meals dropped markedly. By staying on deck we not only kept our sea legs in shape but also kept our meals where they belonged.

Things were getting desperate by the third day. Our beer was long gone. Most of the ship's company was laid low, and we were bored to the very bone. The storm did, however, have its silver lining. We were wandering around in the long, empty passageways and came across another Groupy we hadn't met before. He turned out to be officer-in-charge-of-troops. He had a cabin to himself, a sanctum sanctorum beyond the locked bulkhead. After a brief exchange of pleasantries he invited us to join him there.

"Would you care for a glass of sherry?" he asked, once the cabin door had closed. "We're supposed to be a dry ship, but this is only cooking sherry, so I'm sure it's not against regulations." We were saved, and the rest of the voyage was soon behind us. As the storm spent itself astern we made landfall at Halifax, Nova Scotia, and disembarked in the middle of the night.

It dawned on us as we stepped ashore that we had forgotten all about the danger from U-boat packs. We'd been saved by the gigantic winter storm that escorted us all the way across, hiding our presence in its huge turmoil.

"An excellent start!" said Sammy as we headed out on our exciting adventure.

Part Three

Nine

We left the baggage chores to the RAF men at Halifax and took our first civilian airliner ever, a DC-3 of Eastern, southbound for the U.S. of A. Our first encounter with a heretofore unknown species aboard was overwhelming. "Would you care for something to drink, perhaps a cup of tea?" asked a glamorous apparition. We accepted a cocktail in lieu from the charming air hostess and knew we had found our Shangri-la—until we stepped out to meet a frigid welcome from a snowy bleak Boston, of tea tax infamy.

We'd been told to go to the University Club, as their guests, until our train left at midnight. Our uniforms attracted an older member, who came over. "I'm Joe Hayes," he said. "My son joined the Air Corps, and I'd like to say hello to you fellows." We had a quiet drink together, and Mr. Hayes asked if we would have dinner before boarding our sleeper to Washington leaving from South Station. "We'd love to!" we said.

We had a wonderful evening. After England's blackout, the bright city lights seemed overwhelming. Everyone was so well dressed and obviously enjoying life. At the Copley Plaza Hotel, the "Copious Pleasure," Joe called it, we sat on the slowly turning carousel and marveled the more. Joe told us about his boy. "Crazy about planes since he was a sprout." But we sensed a deep fear under the pride of his telling.

"Whether Chip goes east or to the Pacific when he's finished basic doesn't matter," I said to offer comfort. "He'll be in a cleaner war upstairs. The army fights at closer, dirtier quarters. Send him our best."

"I'll put you on the train at Back Bay." Joe offered. "That will give us time for a final drink." He could not have been kinder, and this surely had to be the lost Utopia.

Too excited to turn in right away, we explored the train. Like any foreigner, I opened the window to lean out and see the lights of the Boston suburbs rushing by and for my trouble got a large, black smut in my eye. I cursed at the use of soft coal in the trains here and found myself caught in the throes of a hasty, impulsive judgment of this new world. The conductor came by and with great tact told me it was unwise to open the windows at all. Besides being dangerous, it upset the air conditioning. I shut my fat mouth as he shut the window.

We moved on to the club car. What a great invention. Seated in luxurious surroundings, we ordered a nightcap we certainly did not need and marveled yet again at this incredible place. "What a country," said Sammy, taking a sip, "What a lush, plentiful, wasteful paradise!"

"There's so much so easily available that it's hard not to waste," I opined. "We'd do exactly the same."

"Not if you were a New England Puritan," added Sammy,

fresh from our first day's education.

I was facing the problem of getting into my "upper"—shades of the abused *Louis Pasteur*—when the courteous black attendant came quietly down the aisle with a little ladder. "Allow me, sir," he said. "Please press the bell if you need any help at all."

I found how hard it is to undress in a cell, seven feet by three by three, lay one's clothes out neatly in a net hammock, get into bed without falling out into the passageway below, all the while avoid generating cramps in both thighs and neck at the same time.

As sleep fought an unequal battle with the great joy of discovery, I lay thinking how different things were and yet how much the same. There was electricity in the air. A strong freedom, but an insecurity, too. What an exhilarating country and how completely exhausting. I loved it.

The train was mounted on softer springs than the one I took to Liverpool—"Children dear, was it yesterday?" as the Forsaken Merman pled—it swayed alarmingly. Though seductively pleasant, it was much too hot.

"Damn waste!" was my parting shot at this Brave New World.

GLOBAL UPDATE
January 1944

We detect the first of a series of launchings of very large German rockets about mid-January, but accuracy is not yet their strong suit. They land all over the place, and by good fortune one finishes up on the bank of the river Bug without exploding. It is expeditiously rolled into the river by our Polish friends until the hue and cry dies down. Several months later but before any of the monsters fall on Britain, an RAF plane lands secretly to pick up one of the Polish engineers who liberated the renegade missile and brings him back to England together with most of the vital parts

284   DRUIDS' CIRCLE

1944—V-1 at test site in Germany. Prototype fitted with cockpit for initial manned test flight.

1944—V-1 cockpit with a paucity of instruments. Hanna Reich was one of the test pilots who flew it.

1944—Operational V-1 at test site in Germany.

of the rocket and much technical data.

Another type of robot missile—a flying bomb—is expected to land on London first with April as the start of the onslaught. We detect construction of what could be launching sites for such robots in at least fifty places on the French coast in the Pas de Calais and as many more to the west up to Cherbourg. Each is a ramp pointing toward London with a strange kink at the bottom (probably for loading), looking like a giant ski. They become prime targets for Allied bombing attacks.

A defensive system against the flying bombs is set up starting with a heavy balloon barrage across the southeast suburbs of the city with a thick ack-ack gun belt adjacent outside. Fighter aircraft will be free to engage earlier in the robot flight path anywhere up to the guns. Mr. Churchill begs President Roosevelt to send electronic gun predictors and supplies of new radio proximity fuses for the gunners.

We drew into Washington, D.C., at 8:00 A.M. and lay in a siding until we should deign to get up. We had until 10:00 to leave the train. "Excuse me, sir, but there's a British gentleman to see you." The attendant was gently shaking my curtain.

"Be right up," I told him. "Give me five."

Shortly thereafter, we emerged into the palatial, magnificent Union Station, and there stood a smart Group Captain patiently waiting for us. It was Ted Hopkins, whose place I was taking. I told him how civil it was of him to meet us so early in the morning and apologized for our rude tardiness.

"Timing's different here, old boy," said Ted. "We all get going a couple of hours earlier than in the U.K. and knock off that much earlier. Makes sense in this subtropical clime."

I looked through the taxi entrance at the raw, wintry weather outside and withheld comment.

"I brought my car," Ted went on. "With gas rationing, cabs are scarce. Oh! By the way, gas is petrol," he explained. "You'll need a bit of help with the lingo, but the natives are quite friendly. It's a wild town until you learn the ropes."

The gentle snow was settling, melting on the black roadway. It made the morning bleak and cold, but the blast from his car's heater soon had the inside like a furnace.

Sammy and I were entranced by the wide, wide boulevards. We swished down Massachusetts Avenue at a frightening speed and were soon disgorged at the Old Dupont Building. Here the British Air Commission was housed in a lovely building, once a private home. We pushed open the heavy glazed door guarded by a handsome grille and stepped into the lofty marble entrance hall. It was splendid but quietly so.

While Ted parked his car we were quickly brought back to earth by the personnel staff who properly but with the studied aloofness of old timers, welcomed us to the commission. We obviously didn't yet know the proper deportment in this foreign land—and it was foreign, after all—in spite of a common language and hosts who were our closest allies. They quickly instructed us in the general scope of our duties, the clearances and permissions we would need. All very impressive and unquestionably necessary, but a crashing bore. An atmosphere of freedom surrounds those at the forefront of development and Sammy and I had both been in it too long to be much intimidated by rigid protocol. "Yes, sir! Yes, sir! Three bags full!"

Ted rejoined us. We hadn't run across each other before but I liked him off the bat. He was an impressively tall, handsome chap with the inbred demeanor of a career diplomat. He looked a bit like Anthony Eden and would be quite an act to follow. He took me round to meet the staff and bear their critical approval, five of them in all, and our charming group of Canadian secretaries that gladdened the scene.

He and I left for a private lunch so he could freely give me all the gory details of the job. I was delighted to find he had served at Martlesham Heath as experimental gunnery officer before Dru, and it made our changing of the guard the more facile. The Air Commission in Washington started as a branch of the original British Purchasing Commission very early in the war—well before Pearl. We placed a notable order in April 1940 for the building of the North American NA-73 fighter for RAF use, to become the Mustang P-51 I tested at Boscombe.

The Air Commission's job was far ranging and involved close liaison with all U.S. military services that flew and suppliers who furnished material. My new job as chief of development (Armt) covered all aircraft weapons and their means of being aimed and delivered. There were no holds barred except for the atom bomb, which obviously no outsiders knew anything about. We did learn after Hiroshima that several prominent British and Canadians were on General Grove's Manhattan Project throughout. In other matters we not only swapped secret information on all the latest developments but gave each other free samples of prototype hardware. "We fly together," Ted said, "and fight together. Our differences become assets—as you've seen in the round-the-clock bombing of

Germany—the Eighth by day, Bomber Command by night."

He warned me of the politics of air power among the services. "Much the same as in the U.K." He added with a lopsided grin.

After lunch Ted dropped me off at the house of an elderly couple who would rent me a room. "You settle in now, old boy. See you in the morning about 8:30." My digs were on Newark Street just off Connecticut Avenue, a handy half mile from the office. I welcomed the freshness of my room and felt at home right away.

The next morning I strolled down to the main drag and looked for the drug store where my landlady said I could get breakfast. "Breakfast in a drug store?" I queried. "I shall want more than a couple of aspirins." But there it was, and once inside I soon discovered the crowded snack counter and greedily read the menu printed in large letters on the wall. No rationing here. Eggs in plenty, bacon, sausages and—look at that—tomato juice!

"What'll ya hev?" asked the man in the apron.

"Tomahtoe juice, scrambled eggs and tea, please." I ordered.

"D'ya hear that?" said the man addressing the crowd, drawing them all in with a broad sweep of his arm. "Tamartoe duce. Wow!"

The row of heads turned and gazed at me in amused curiosity so I pointed to the wall and said, "That, please."

"Oh, you mean tamayta jewce!" he corrected.

A man got up to leave and gave me his seat. "Joe's okay," he said. "Don't let him get to you." My gaffe was soon forgotten, and the eggs were delicious.

Ted took me over the river to the newly commissioned Pentagon to meet our Air Corps and Army Ordnance opposite numbers. I felt Washington was much like Paris, perhaps a little self-conscious about it with almost a surfeit of beautiful buildings, one after another. The parks, the lungs of this lovely city, were gorgeous.

We came back to the old military buildings on Constitution Avenue, the Navy Bureau of Aeronautics (BuAer) and the Bureau of Ordnance (BuOrd). I wrote down a hundred names to remember but only succeeded in creating an indecipherable mess. "Don't worry, Dix," Ted encouraged me. "You'll soon sort them out. Wait till we start visiting the arsenals and test bases out of town; then you'll have a real worry. There are a zillion more chaps you have to meet."

Not long after this whirlwind indoctrination, Ted warned me of a meeting the next day. "Dress in your Number Ones," he told me. "We attend the Ordnance Committee meeting in the Pentagon at 9:30 A.M. and it's verree formal indeed." That morning we sat on a long dais right in with the brass and immediately to the left of the President. Much honored were we. It was even higher church than our own Ordnance Board—hard to achieve.

Ted had to leave. He was urgently wanted back on the war front, so I was left on my own. Not quite; the staff had very discretely kept our ship of state on course. It was time to call my own first staff meeting and find out how well our faces would fit. I could see they were a good bunch—professional, keen. Had some begun to acquire a faint American accent? I wondered. Going native? But that was silly and unkind. It was a very sensible blending in with the scenery. Good chameleon camouflage. My inner self quietly reminded me: "Look how your Limey accent reddened your own face the other day—just like a real love apple, you pitiful fraud."

"Tell me, Alek," I asked our senior member, "how our duties are split up." Wing Commander Fletcher expounded on the division of labor among the staff and a definition of our communication network with the U.K. "But in the field we often cover each others subjects for economy of effort," he told me.

"This country is so enormous it would be impossible otherwise with so few people."

They really don't need me too much, I thought. They're handling the nuts and bolts of the business most deftly. I'd been too long involved with those very details and the time had come to let go. I must get out and paint with a broader brush now.

I soon became aware of some bitter rivalries in Washington between the military services, and even between the branches of the same service, as Ted had warned me. The people I met first in the Navy, of course, were the aviators—the "brown shoe" boys. We already had many bonds inherent in our shared profession. Within BuOrd it was a little trickier because it overlapped the armament needs of both ships and aircraft, but there was much common ground with these officers as well.

The same thing was true for the Army. The Air Corps was still a bit of a stepchild for armament supply and had to fight to get proper recognition. I found myself acting as unofficial liaison between navy and army factions. It was a little uncomfortable at first until I realized both sides wanted this pipeline and welcomed the idea of swapping ideas this way. Pride of authorship got lost in the process, and dissension could easily be attributed to the views of the intermediary, without loss of face. A messenger with built-in insurance so to speak.

My secretary, Connie poked her pretty face round the door. "A Mr. McLellan to see you, sir. Are you free?" I glanced at his card. "Yes, indeed," I said. "I've been sort of expecting this visit. Pleas bring him in."

The chaps in BuAer had mentioned Steve McLellan when we'd talked about sights for aiming rockets. They'd promised to have him call me when next in town.

Steve McLellan came in, with a smile that filled the room. He'd been a flyer in the Marine Corps which explained why he almost broke my hand as we greeted. He'd been withdrawn from active duty to head a new laboratory and factory on Long

Island, New York, to conceive and manufacture new sighting methods for aircraft weaponry for the Navy. The facility centered around a Monsieur Robert Alkan, famous French gunsight designer who escaped from Valenton, near Paris, to continue his personal war against the Nazis. On his way through England to the U.S. he'd given careful details of his factory location and landmarks so that when the time was opportune it could be taken out completely. He had requested his workers be warned of the impending raid through the underground. His wishes were observed, and in due course the plant was destroyed.

"Steve!" I said when he had told me this moving story, "I feel I already know this great genius." So I told him about the name ALKAN stamped on the gunsight fitted to the machine gun I was given by the escaping French aviator in 1940, "to pay for a pair of pajamas and a toothbrush," as the capitaine had said.

We spent the best part of the day talking about the difficulty of aiming our aerial weapons. Steve hadn't yet come across our new rockets. He promised to help with the two main bugaboos we had in aiming them. "Gravity droop, Steve—my nickname for what is gravity drop for a shell—and the problem of angle of attack." I told him, "Think on these things."

I agreed to visit his plant, Specialties, Inc., as soon as I'd caught my breath.

GLOBAL UPDATE
January 1944

Eisenhower returns to the U.K. to make preparations for the invasion of France taking his top commanders, Air Chief Marshal Tedder and Generals Bradley and Montgomery. The Italian campaign takes second place. General Wilson, the new commander in chief, successfully crosses Kesselring's winter line on the Garagliano on 17 January but the attack soon peters out. A corps of fifty thousand U.S. and British troops land at Anzio, well behind the German lines, but have too few heavy landing craft to

DRUIDS' CIRCLE

bring in enough tanks to exploit the surprise move. The Anzio expedition is in a defensive posture for many months. The breakthrough south is stalled by the terrain round Cassino.

Everywhere I went the war was being taken very seriously. Stars hung in many windows, telling with pride of family members gone to serve their country—or the Allied cause—as many now were saying. Some special stars said their members would not be coming back. The grim atmosphere was the same as I'd just left behind, though by now the tide of battle had turned in Europe and in the Pacific, too, bringing a sense of solid optimism. Americans were suffering now with the British across the world. The huge effort in the Far East was borne by U.S. men and arms supported by the bulk of original battle veterans from Australia and New Zealand. Americans were also fighting and dying in Africa as well. A comradeship-in-arms had been forged in many joint ventures that overcame early suspicions of each others' basic intentions and objectives. This surge of strength did my heart good and quelled any possible doubt of the ultimate conclusion to the mortal grip with evil we were in together.

I began to find in this wonderful, vast country a multitude of discrete centers of research activity sponsored by a highly specialized branch of one service or another. The network was complicated, often overlapping. Careful observance of protocol was needed to avoid treading on wrong toes. I visited so many in such a short time that confusion almost reigned supreme. I went to Dahlgren, Aberdeen and Edgewood arsenals, to powder factories, to various laboratories, and last but by no means least, to the illustrious Bureau of Standards.

It was with growing pleasure and self-confidence in this plethora of seething development that I began to encounter so many examples of complete cooperation between ourselves in Britain and the myriad research facilities in the U.S. For example, the Bureau of Standards had a proximity fuse designed at

Farnborough. The ingenious device used a tiny radar set to fire at a chosen distance from the target. It was sent over and put in production in no time flat and greatly increased the effectiveness of all kinds of Allied weapons, from bombs to shells.

At BuAer I was delighted to find that the Farnborough Gyroscopic Gun Sight (GGS) for aircraft guns had been adopted by the Navy with almost no change. The mechanism was an elegant solution to the awkward problem of solving correct layoff for firing aircraft guns against a crossing target where the *lead* must be in two directions at once—vertically and laterally. Farnborough—Gold bless 'em—had simplified the problem and sort of distilled off the inherent difficulties. Those boys were very good at making projects out of problems. The gyroscope is the classic tool for measuring change, and in this case, instead of using one for each direction of lead, they used one gyro to measure both vectors. The solution was achieved by cunningly tilting the single gyro both forward and sideways through forty-five degrees. The measurements for deflection against this single cockeyed datum were accurate enough for the important part of the battle scenario and inaccurate only where it didn't matter. A beautiful concept.

I knew the Navy had duplicated our aircraft rocket, having fired some U.S.-made samples at Aberporth a couple of months ago. The Navy rocketeers told me that I really had to get out to the West Coast without delay to swap fibs with the people at Caltech who were doing all the Navy rocket work. They would set it up for me.

Back from the Navy Bureaus, I told Stan Curtis, one of my civilian scientists, about the planned visit. "You must call in at Wright Field," he told me in no uncertain terms. "It's on the way, and I know the Air Corps will be really peed off if you ignore them. They're a great bunch, you'll find."

"Okay, Stan," I replied, "glad you called me on this one." I also told this wise old bird to be sure to keep on doing so. "Don't be shy," I said, "I need your skilled feedback in this land of supreme competition to save my nervous scalp. Go ahead and set it up right for me."

And so with only two weeks of official Washington under my belt, I set off to discover America. The odyssey started ignominiously enough with a train trip to Dayton, Ohio. Wartime flights by commercial airlines were grossly overcrowded. Only by pulling priority could a seat be obtained at all. By the grace of our quasi-diplomatic status, we stood a better chance of getting a flight than most, but with such short notice I had to take a train for the first leg.

I settled down in the coach, grateful for the sudden peace and studied the program Stan had laid on. The dirty dog! I'd missed where he'd sandwiched in a few days with the Army at Dugway Proving Ground in Utah. His footnotes told of their extensive work on incendiary bombs and also of the chemical warfare R & D we were working on together. He was diplomatically pushing me into line. He knew I had to see the Army, as

1944—Colonel Harry Donicht. In charge of experimental gunnery and rocketry for the Army Air Corps at Wright/Patterson Field, Dayton, Ohio.

well, on my first swing around the country.

I arrived at Wright Field and was met at the gates by Colonel Harry Donicht. "Group Captain Dean? I'm glad to meet you at last; I've heard a bit about you and welcome you to Wright."

Harry was a veteran pilot involved with all new armament developments for the Army Air Corps. As it turned out, we were very much opposite numbers in our respective air forces. Harry was a staccato, dynamic chap holding some very strong views. We circled each other as warily as a couple of dogs while he told me how the tests he had underway were progressing. Procedures here were much different from those in the U.K. Requirements for aircraft and equipment were differently formulated; the technical jargon was strange and seemed less forcibly stated than we were used to. I began to see how tough it must have been for the Air Corps to develop much of an individuality or have a voice strong enough in Washington to command funds for the proper development of a strategic air force. The RAF had been separate since April of 1918, and it had made all the difference.

At the end of World War I there was a lone voice in the Air Corps wilderness—that of Brig. Gen. William Lendrum Mitchell who commanded the U.S. air forces. After the armistice he was made director of military aviation in the U.S. Army and argued vociferously for a large, independent air force similar to the RAF. To support his case of the overwhelming power of the bomber, he persuaded the Navy to let him attack the *Ostfriesland,* the "unsinkable" German dreadnought, then in American hands. In July 1921 Mitchell's airplanes sank the battleship with bombs exploding close below the waterline, but the U.S. naval chiefs said it would not have been possible if the ship were manned and fighting back. Mitchell's outspokenness as an officer upset the Army die-hards, and the Navy was mortally offended by his belittling pugnacity; both joined in condemning the courageous patriot. He was given an unfair court martial that resulted in his dismissal in disgrace. His prophetic voice went far too long unheeded.

I had harshly criticized some of the Air Corps planes I'd flown in tests. In ignorance and with unfair arrogance I said some seemed designed more to carry suitcases for weekend jaunts than to carry ammunition. I was particularly scathing about the provision of ashtrays in the cockpits. "How self-indulgent and sloppy" was my lofty pronouncement, overlooking that Sir Walter Raleigh was an Englishman and probably the one heavily promoting the habit of the noxious weed making us the ones really to blame.

"Harry, you must have read some of my reports from Boscombe about your airplanes. I think I was unduly rude and I'm sorry. Forgive?"

"Yes, of course," he said somewhat ruefully. "Some of what you said is true, but we've learned a lot since. After we got in the war, thank God we've had almost unlimited funds to fix the damage of neglect. Too bad you didn't know of our true plight."

"Yep!" I confessed. "We were much luckier. We've been on semiactive duty all during the peace years between the two wars." I regaled him with yarns of life in the RAF when, under the British postwar mandate, we had the job of maintaining law and order in Iraq and protecting the oil pipelines across the country to the Mediterranean—and when we also might see service in Egypt, Palestine, or India. "This all gave us an operational edge, Harry, during the peace years. Even so, we were really ill-prepared when war knocked firmly on our door in 1939." And so the walls of Jericho came down. We talked out our misunderstandings and exposed our very common aims. I know we were not the only ones in our two services so engaged, by a long chalk.

We got onto rockets. Harry was intrigued with first-hand news of our operations against shipping in the Channel and particularly against U-boats on the surface. I agreed with his choice of a short rocket burning time, but the tubby 4.5-inch brute,[1] conceived in the main by the U.S. Army gun people, seemed to lack the benefits inherent in a rocket. The propellant was burned out in less than a quarter second. It was more like firing a shell from a gun rather than the smooth and gentle "whoosh" of a rocket. The short blast meant a much higher pressure in the rocket motor case, which had to be stronger and heavier to contain it—militating against the highest possible velocity at burn out. The real objection I had was that their design was neither fish nor fowl. It was too small—only one third of our weight—to use against tough ground targets or ships and much too heavy for air-to-air use where more of a shotgun type of rocket is appropriate.

We both felt the rocket was the future weapon for aircraft, but we talked of guns as well. Neither of us thought much of the "super cannons" mounted in the large twin-engined planes: the Mosquito and the B-25 Mitchell. Waste of time, we agreed; it made better sense to develop a multiple-barrel 30 mm gun to give the essential shotgun result for air-to-air. Ground targets were more effectively taken on with rockets—the bigger, the better. Thus spake the two young pundits.

It was late in the day when we quit, but we had only just started to talk. We repaired to my room in the hotel downtown, and continued our debate until the small hours of the next day.

GLOBAL UPDATE
February 1944

The campaign in the Solomons is virtually over, though severe fighting continues in Bougainville. Such positions still in enemy hands are bypassed to be neutralized later on. After heavy air attacks on Rabaul fail, General MacArthur leapfrogs this tough Japanese base, and captures Manus Island in the Admiralty group five hundred miles east. It is to be his base for sustaining the advance on the Philippines.

Getting to Salt Lake City from Wright Field involved a short flight to the windy city of Chicago the next evening, followed by an eight-hour layover and a flight leaving at 4:00 A.M. Better than a train I thought until the hard bench I had stretched out on informed me otherwise. I learned an old saw from a fellow exhausted strandee: "If you've time to spare, go by air." I felt very ragged at the edges when day struggled to establish dominance as we fled from the sun. We were now halfway across Nebraska, crossing great plains that stretched out for ever and a week.

"And where are you from, sir?"

I turned my head to see a charming stewardess holding out a tray. "Oh!...England!" I mouthed still half-asleep.

"I'd love to go there," she said, "but I think I'm stuck with these commercial flights."

"Why don't you learn to fly and ferry some bombers over?"

"Maybe I'll try just that. Will you have breakfast now?"

After a pleasant snack it was indeed a new day. The ground pushed up to meet us as we crossed the foothills of Wyoming, and the plains changed to mountains. The map which my kind angel found for me showed ranges with romantic names like Medicine Bow and Laramie. I could almost reach out and touch their peaks.

The lushness of the prairie had given way to the harsh barrier of the Rockies. I revered the courage of the early pioneers, pushing westward through this inhospitable terrain. What I'd read could not begin to convey the stark reality of those treks. I looked down and lived with those stalwarts. There was so much in this great country to see and savor. My flight of fancy was soon cut short as we skimmed by the last ten-thousand-foot tooth of the Wasatch range and dropped in to land five thousand feet below in the capital city of the Mormons.

An Army car took me out to Dugway Proving Ground, far across miles of nothingness—only salt flats, scrub, desolation.

The immensity of the place was hard for a Brit to believe. Plenty of room to construct complete target villages for trials of incendiary bombs—one in the style of a German town and another in Japanese—or measure the concentration in a floating cloud of utter evil. Developments in this branch of armament had been well integrated between us from the start. My hosts laid on tests of some RAF incendiary cluster bombs made up of dozens of hexagon section magnesium sticks nested together in one single, wicked five-hundred-pound bomb. A fire they started in the Japanese town was hard to extinguish. I wondered if they allow smoking indoors in Tokyo.

We aired some of the latest thoughts on bacterial warfare—the inhumane experiments we both knew had to be done in view of the advanced German work. It would be crass stupidity to be unready.

There was so much to see and absorb at this overwhelming facility that I knew I'd have to come back.

For the last leg to Burbank, California. I squeezed on to a Western Airlines flight. The skipper was a genial Southerner with an accent as heavy as molasses. Soon after takeoff he came back to chat with us and seeing my uniform, invited me up to the cockpit. He shut the connecting door and insisted I take the controls. "You know, I haven't flown one of these babies before," I confessed to him.

"This here Dakota—DC-3 is one of the sweetest planes in the air today," said the captain. "Jest you go ahead. I'll take over to land. My boss might happen to be watchin'." She was a dream to fly, and a fine birthday present from Western Air to me on that 9th of February morning. The friendly pilot was lucky to get the yoke back at all—let alone to get to land his own ship.

In spite of the heavy haze ("smog"—our hostess informed me), Los Angeles did look intriguing as we circled into Burbank.

I called Caltech from the terminal. "Take a cab and join us for lunch," they told me. Thus started what was to become a happy association with a delightful group of people *sans pareil.* The nicest I have come across.

Dr. Charles C. Lauritsen studied under Dr. Neils Bohr in

Denmark and designed the Kellogg Radiation Laboratory at Caltech. He had shelved his basic research in physics to run a land, sea, and air rocket ordnance program primarily for the U.S. Navy, but also for the Army and the Air Corps. Lauritsen had assembled a galaxy of supernovae on his team. All learned doctors, but less like learned doctors than any academicians I'd ever met. Erudite to be sure—Nobel men all over the lot—they were witty and kind and just great fun to be with. "I'm Charlie," he said, and introducing his assistant director of research added, "Meet Willy. Doctor Fowler's my right-hand man."

It was fascinating to hear first hand the story of their aircraft rocket program. The Caltech group had no preconceived ideas and looked only for subtle simplicity and reliable effectiveness. They could not support the Army's approach that blithely ignored any previous work that had been done. Charlie launched into other projects in their massive agenda but we'd barely scratched the surface when it was suddenly time to call it a day.

"See you tomorrow," said Charlie as we broke up. "Then you can tell us your story. Eight-thirty okay?"

Showering for bed, exhausted but still keyed up, the events of this delightful conclave still flashed across my mind like a kaleidoscope. I felt a great exultation being with this group of free spirits; my own rebellious thinking discreetly echoed the tone of their whole approach. It was abundantly clear now why Fred Hovde, head of Section III of NRDC in Washington, had urged me to get out to Pasadena just as fast as possible—barely three weeks after coming down the gangplank at Halifax. I was glad no more time had been lost.

We met again early the next day, and most of the prime movers in the Caltech team had come along. "Listen, how would you like to visit our new rocket range?" asked Charlie Lauritsen. Without waiting for an answer, he turned to Doctor Anderson, "Carl, why don't you fly out with Dixi tomorrow. We'll have a cookout when you get back."

1944—Dr. William A. Fowler, assistant director of research, Caltech rocket program.

Carl turned to me, raised an eyebrow as if to say "Okay by you?" and held out his hand. "Hi!" He said.

I went back to the beginning and tried to tell them of our whole experience with the 3-inch UP (unrotated projectile) now released from the secrecy of that code name and called 3-inch RP. I told the saga of launch rails and my judicious use of a hacksaw (until there were none), forward venturis, and the fishnet target to record dispersion. Carl Anderson liked the net target idea as his main concerns were launchers and ballistics. We were agreed that rail launchers must go and at the same time more work was needed on the effect of aircraft angle of attack on accuracy.[2]

I recounted the fairy story of the discovery of the underwater travel of our rocket and the emergence of a standard operational attack for sinking U-boats on the surface.

"Yes," said Charlie, "We got wind of that and owe you one. We got a U-boat in the Atlantic only a month ago with our version of the same rocket!"

"Great!" says I, "Guess we all agree the rocket is the best weapon against U-boats on or near the surface."

Charlie showed me the records of underwater firing tests of the 3.5-inch AR, their copy of our rocket. The upward-curving trajectories bore out our own work which was comforting. "It's too bad we can't use the upward-curving path to get more hits with our new 5-inch HVAR in maritime action," said Carl, "We had to change the curved ogive nose which gives an upward blow to the front on impact (and hence the curved path). It breaks the head off the aluminum motor. Our new shape is a double cone and the rocket goes straight after impact and when underwater."

"Tell us more about that big one of yours," said Charlie. We got a good giggle out of the birth of the Gargantuan rocket made up from bits and pieces in our backyard at Boscombe.

"The Ministry of Supply has now taken us seriously about that little escapade," I told them. "They've laid on development

Late 1943—First forward-firing U.S. rockets used at sea: preparing 3.5-inch AR on carrier USS Mission Bay *in the Atlantic for surfaced U-boat attacks. First kill in this theater 11 January 1944.*

1944—Loading of 3.5-inch aircraft rockets on TBF Avengers on Mission Bay. *Massive expansion of the 3.5-inch rocket program was a factor in the establishment of the Naval Ordnance Test Station (NOTS).*

of a brand new thousand-pounder with a single rocket motor, code named 'Uncle Tom,' but knowing our shortage of development resources, it'll be a long time in the womb."

I told of the pleasure I had firing the Caltech 3.5-inch ARs[3] in the U.K. "They flew beautifully!" I enthused, "They really did." Then they let me in on their new 5-inch HVAR (High Velocity Aircraft Rocket)[4] now well underway and a great improvement on the 3.5-inch firstborn.

It was a wonderful exchange of ideas. When I broached the subject of stability and the design of spinners, I was taken aback by the enormous progress made at Caltech. I told them of my tests at slow rotation which made our arrows go twice as straight and about Lew Motley's pretty 60 mm spinners for air-to-air.

They quickly told me, in turn, that they had a 5-inch spinner, twice our caliber in service use. What else could I say but, "I looks toward you, and I likewise bows!" with the reverence that this announcement deserved. This was the 5-inch HVSR (High Velocity Spinner Rocket) built for surface-to-surface barrage that I heard of after the Torch landings. I hoped it might have great potential for air use.

It was a long day—a great day; for me, one of the greatest. I had encountered kindred souls, and that evening, having drinks with Willy at his house, I found I had also met with bosom pals.

Early next morning Carl Anderson met me at a navy Cessna ready to take off for Inyokern. It took an hour to get there. Up abruptly over the San Gabriel Mountains with "Old Baldy" peaking to over ten thousand feet to starboard. Then dropping down to the sprawling desert, heading for ill-fated and well-named Death Valley. It was hot already, but at least dry. The wind was kicking up little sand devils.

"This is Commander Pollock," said Carl, introducing me to the rugged aviator there to meet us. "Tom is CO of the Naval Ordnance Development Unit here."

Conditions were still rather primitive. Tom Pollock had

1943—Cmdr Thomas F. Pollock, NOTS test pilot and head of Aviation Ordnance Development Unit 1.

only arrived a month before, but had already worked wonders in the bleak, dusty desert. The location was ideal for rocket testing: miles and miles of flat shimmering, primeval space; scrawny cacti here and there; no habitation to hinder live firing.

Tom had a few test planes there and a handful of men to maintain them. We drove around, and I got the general lie of the land. We compared notes about the difficulties inherent in finding enough room for our tests. I know Tom was sympathetic with our claustrophobia back in England.

Tom had done all the initial trials himself. "I feel it's up to me to make these first firings," he said, "rather than one of my other pilots. It's my job."

"Shake!" I agreed. "That's what I insisted on at home. We have to take the first risks." And then lowering my voice I added, "Can't have these young whippersnappers getting all the kudos, can we?"

The day soon passed. "Come again soon, Dixi," said Tom.

"We'll wind up one of these old tigers for you next time, and you can try out the firing range."

"Love to," I told him as we climbed back into the Cessna. Dr. Jack McMorris, the warhead design man, joined us for the ride back. We tried to chat, but the little airplane managed to monopolize the conversation. I deeply regret I missed that talk. Jack was killed in an air crash very soon after.

We all went over to Charlie's house and proceeded to get on the right side of a good scotch and soda. I'd learned by this time that one didn't just ask for a whisky and soda in order to conjure up a scotch.

"I'm convinced," said Charlie as he turned over a steak on the coals, "that we should start development here and now on a really big rocket. I think we may have more funds available to produce this weapon quickly. Willy, let's get a detailed proposal ready with facts and figures to get this on high priority."

"To hell with Kelly!" said Willy. "The huge success these crazy Limeys had with their monstrous mongrel surely gives us all the ammunition we need to justify the development."

"But listen," he laughed, "we couldn't possibly call it Uncle Tom here. We must think of something else. How about Tiny Tim or something like that?"

Tom Lauritsen joined us—Charlie's son. "What kind of a blast problem did you have?" he asked.

"Well, none really," I answered, "After all, we've fired complete salvos of eight rockets hundreds of time without any grief, and here we stuck only seven tails on the back of the 500-pound bomb body." We all drank to that.

I found out a bit later, as we further relaxed, that these chaps had learned the silly games we played when school was out. They had learned well from dear old Cookie and others from our rocket development group in England to play such difficult games as "lah-de-dah" much better than I did. A number of dimes passed the wrong way a number of times. Fortunately, I just happened to have my well-worn liars dice in my pocket—

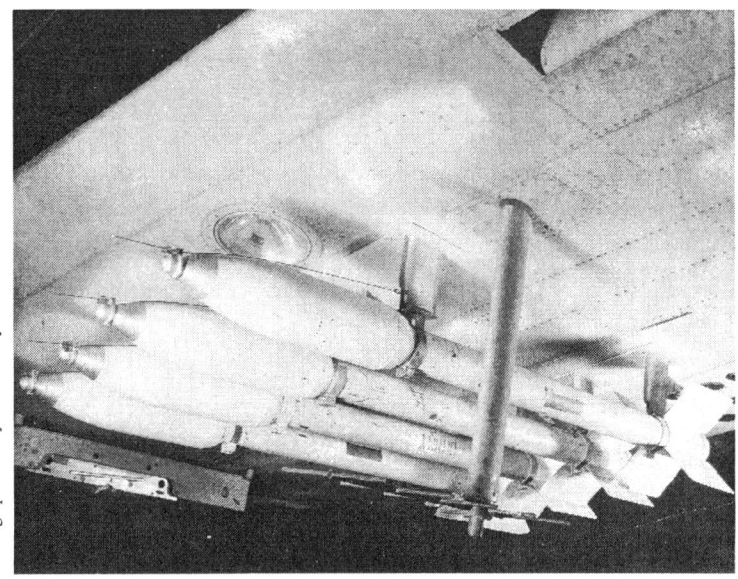

February 15, 1944—First five-inch AR rocket used in combat was by Marine Corps TBF (Avenger) Squadron VMTB-134. Comanding Officer: Maj. Allen C. Robertson.

February 15, 1944—TBF attacks in five-plane shipping strike at Karavia Bay near Rabaul on New Britain Island.

no, they were not loaded—and did manage to recover part of my lunch money.

It was really too late when we turned in. These Caltech fellows play as hard as they work, and that's hard. Tomorrow was Saturday, but we were still at war and it made no difference.

GLOBAL UPDATE
February 1944

Red armies enter Estonia and Latvia, once part of the Russian empire before World War I, with an eye on Baltic ports.

With Tarawa subdued, Admiral Spruance turns his attention north to the Marshall Islands. In amphibious operations on the greatest scale yet in this theater, Roi-Namur and Kwajalein are taken by U.S. Marines.

The Caltech five-inch AR aircraft rocket is used with spectacular success in the Marshal Islands from the carrier USS *Manila Bay*. Admiral Nimitz, commander in chief Pacific, orders procurement of one hundred thousand rounds per month. Truk, the main Japanese naval and air force base a thousand miles west of the Marshals is bombed by aircraft and shelled by the fleet and is no longer of use to the enemy. Hideki Tojo, chief of the Japanese Army General Staff, becomes military dictator.

I called Charlie to give my inadequate thanks. "Don't take so long to come and see us," was his characteristic reply.

It was difficult to book air passage. In the end I spent thirty hours on the ground cooling my heels in between twenty-four in the air on five different airlines. I covered five hundred more miles than a crow would fly—a half-witted one at that. There had to be a better way.

A pile of summonses waited impatiently on my desk and one was from Steve McLellan. I reached him at Specialties.

"You're a hard one to get a hold of," came Steve's voice, "I've been trying to find you for over a week. Can you come up and talk about the rocket sight we discussed the other day? Next Friday?—Good. Please stay the weekend with us."

And so a couple of days later by train to New York and on to discover the Long Island Railroad and Glen Cove. Nice name, I thought. Steve drove us through the pleasant countryside to his plant at an unbelievable address...Skunk's Misery Lane.

"This is Monsieur Robert Alkan," said Steve as we met the famous French gunsight designer at his drawing board.

"I acquired one of your gunsights," I told Alkan, "When a French Navy Air Force airplane escaped after Dunkirk in 1940 and landed at our field."

"Oh!" he replied, "Zat would be an auld design." We moved on to talk about newer, automatic sights, and I mentioned the British GGS—Gyroscopic Gun Sight—now in use in the RAF and duplicated by the U.S. Navy. "I see it, yes," said the Frenchman. "*Classique!* Really a beautiful concept. A new idea, and also one of much interest! Ze best kind of idea."

We discussed new sights for rocket firing which would allow for gravity "droop" and also for our new-found nuisance—changing angle of attack. The latter had been ignored in gun sighting before, but when I told him my little story of the 40 mm cannon "gun jump" explanation invented on the spot to explain our problem when no one knew any better, Robert Alkan was very much amused.

"It is a factor too large to be ignored any more, particularly with your new rockets," he said decisively. "We will examine the matter here, won't we Steve?"

"That will leave only gravity droop and angle of dive," I interposed. "The first we can get by measuring the range; the second is easy."

"*Oui,*" said Monsieur Alkan. "This we can do."

It was an intriguing visit and held great promise for improving the use of our rockets in the field. We drove back through the heavily wooded lanes to Steve's place in Glen Cove. We had a good time together and talked flying till the wee hours.

A visit to BuAer and BuOrd on my return cemented thinking on the development of a special, rather simple rocket sight for use against stationary or slow-moving surface targets. We didn't yet need an air-to-air rocket sight for large deflections—no suitable rocket was yet available to us. The Navy agreed to give us an F6F (Hellcat) fighter for testing the sight when it was ready for trial. In the meantime, they invited me to the Naval Aviation Test Center at Patuxent River, an hour's trip southeast of Washington, to fly an F6F before the tests began. I was impressed by the cooperative spirit shown at all levels to get the job done.

I got a ride on the daily shuttle from Anacostia, and was soon on the ground at the pleasant neck of land at the mouth of the Pax River. The wide peninsula jutted to the east into Chesapeake Bay, some ten miles wide here. It was a perfect situation. After we'd had a bite of lunch together, they pushed out an F6F for me to fly around for an hour or so, to get the feel of the airplane. It was a delight to fly and ideal for making our rocket sight trials later on.

Brian Hatfield showed me a brief from the U.K. telling us that after a disastrous raid by the Eighth Air Force in mid-October 1943 on Schweinfurt—when sixty bombers out of 291 were lost—they suspended offensive raids deep into Germany until sufficient first-class long-range fighters were available for escort.

A combined devastating attack had just been made 28 February 1944 on the same ball-bearing factories by 266 U.S. bombers by day without loss, followed by 734 RAF bombers that night. Subsequent recce showed that, unfortunately, the industry moved out without detection after the October raid. But at least the U.S. strategic bombers were back on unrestricted ops in Europe.

No sooner back in Washington flying my desk than Harry Donicht was on the pipe from Wright Field. "Where the hell have you been?" he bellowed. "Don't you ever come home?"

"What's cooking?" I asked him.

"I'm due in Orlando, Florida around March 20. I want to fire some of our new rockets in the air. Can you come down for a day or so?"

"Sure. Sounds terrific." I said. "I'll be there."

I asked Connie to earmark time and lay on transport. "Let me book you on the Florida Coastal Railroad," she suggested. "It's an experience you'll enjoy. You should slow down a bit, anyway, and that'll force you to. This American high-octane life can burn you out fast!" Dear Connie. A great gal and a great pal.

So I clickety-clicked my way south. The train ride was a wonderful luxury—the best part of a day spent in old-world comfort. "Southern comfort," as the proud and smiling attendant told me, obviously an old-timer with the line.

I savored my first stay on an air force base in Bachelor Officer Quarter (BOQ). Harry took me bowling and I was soundly trounced. "Sir Francis Drake would have frowned on my performance," I told Harry, "I'm used to a fine grass green; this wood's too fast."

"Who's Drake, anyway?" said Harry. "Don't make excuses."

Harry gave me the chance to fly a new type—a Thunderbolt, P-47. The fighter had a tube launcher hung under each wing to fire the new Air Corps 4.5-inch rocket. Over the ranges I lined up the target and gently pulled the trigger on the stick. I must say those two rockets left like a pair of squeezed orange pips. I didn't feel them go, see them go, or detect their landfall, but I sure heard one hell of a bang. I looked up the tubes after landing, and the rockets weren't there.

"Your babies take off in a flash, Harry, the way decent rockets should," I commented as he came up, "but you can't go to war with these drainpipe launchers."

"I know that, old cock. We'll do it differently later. The tubes aren't there for accuracy, but to protect us from premature motor burst to start with." he patiently explained, accepting my abject apology with grace.

As we walked back from the flight line, he turned to me. "We've requisitioned some land on the west coast of Delaware Bay just east of Dover Air Force Base for a rocket range. I'm going over in a couple of weeks, can you join us? We'll look it over and plan where everything has to go." I accepted with obvious pleasure.

GLOBAL UPDATE
March 1944

Pacific island-hopping continues. New Zealand troops under Admiral Halsey take Emirau Island in the Mussau group, an important base to sever the Japanese grip on the Solomons.

On 3 April, Lieutenant Colonel Donald Diehl and I left in a vintage B-18 bomber, now relegated to communications duties, and flew the two hundred miles to the east in short order. It was a great compliment to be in on the initial planning of the rocket firing ranges at Dover.

"We certainly aren't short of space," said Harry, "but we do have an anxious population below when we blast off, and we can't afford any setback from the threat of a Congressional inquiry."

We motored up the shoreline, bleak and uninhabited, ideal for Harry's nefarious affairs. Open water, more than twenty-five clear miles of it. Couldn't be better. It was still frosty, and a mean breeze coming in from Delaware Bay stole our breath, reminding me of England.

The next day we took off for an extended reconnaissance. We tested the approach and run that would be made at each of the different ranges, checking to be sure more than one could be used at the same time. Harry was well satisfied with the site. He wanted to do most of the rocket work here but other Air Corps armament ranges also were looking for a piece of the action. He'd not get it all. "An important factor is having a place to train operational pilots. Dover has political aspects, too," he added, "It's very handy to Washington!"

We stayed the night at the base and chewed the rag to pieces. Don flew me back next day to the fleshpots of the capital. It had been a busy few days, but very much my cup of tea—or should I now say, cup of coffee—in deference to Boston.

I jumped on a waiting bus one evening headed up Connecticut Avenue, meaning to alight at Newark Street where I lodged. I dropped my fare into the gaping maw of the machine. The bus moved off at great speed, soon reaching Newark. I indicated I wanted to get off.

"No stops," said the driver.

"But this is my street!" I protested.

"Express only," he bit off. "Next stop Chevy Chase."

"Where the devil is that?" I asked querulously.

"Three miles."

"Oh, come on!" I pleaded. "Let me get off, please! I didn't know this was express only!" I felt trapped and helpless and such a bloody fool.

"Do stop for him," spoke up a small, ancient lady with one or two small murmurs to back her up.

"Oh, all right!" he grumbled after hurtling on for another few minutes, "but it's against the rules." he pulled sharply to the curb, almost standing the bus and all its passengers on their noses. He opened the doors halfway back in the bus, but I was jammed up front amid the standing passengers, trying to keep my feet and struggle toward the exit at the same time. I made heavy weather and reluctant yardage, pushing and squeezing my way through. He could have let me out at the front, but that would have been a double no-no.

"Hurry up!" shouted my tormentor, almost managing to catch the flying skirt of my long RAF greatcoat in the pincers of the closing doors.

I looked up in time to wave my grateful thanks to the smiling little old lady watching this whole farce. She waved back as if to say, "We won, after all, didn't we?"

What a stupid thing to do, I thought, as I waited for a cab to take me back down Connecticut Avenue—to get so caught in the roilment of petty bureaucracy like that. I really must do my homework a bit better. But this sort of calculated tyranny was to be found in most places. Look at France, *par exemple,* or any other place where you haven't bothered to learn the ropes.

I hoped I was beginning to understand these people a little more. Foreigners by definition, but not strangers. Sharing our blood and culture, but grown to be a more open breed. Our common democratic freedom was based on the same basic laws, the laws of civilization for free men, ironically sprung from the ancient laws of the disciplined and ruthless Romans—tempered by the laws of the Greek city-states. Yet I felt a pervading difference stemming from the conditions of rapid growth in this rich and wild country. The laws back in England were much the same but seemed to be more commonly accepted as rules of behavior engendered by close living and concomitant mutual consideration.

The same laws here seemed writ more for protection against a primitive social intrusion, the depredations of the untamed pioneer, not lawless but barely law-abiding. Many pioneers had not yet gone west, I decided. In great wisdom, as my cab pulled in to pick me up, I concluded my self-imposed history lesson with the thought that any pioneer worth his salt, here or anywhere else, does need space to draw a decent breath.

The two passengers already in the cab moved over to give me room. Fortunately, wartime regulations required cabs to double or triple-up to conserve fuel. It was a very good idea and made getting a taxi easier to achieve and more interesting to endure. My companions were from Detroit and represented one of the large auto companies. They were having a hard time satisfying the army with a prototype truck just coming off the stocks.

"Goddamn committees in the Pentagon," said one. "Enough to drive you up a wall."

"Probably easier than getting an aircraft through," I interposed.

"I doubt it," said the other. "This truck has to work under every condition. All conditions, no excuses. I do have some sympathy with the soldiers, though," he added. "Those poor bastards do have to go through some pretty rugged situations, and their lives depend on this babe not letting them down."

"I wish we could talk some more," I said, opening the door as we drew up to my digs. "Good luck with your lorry—truck I mean."

The brief encounter with the engineers from Detroit made me think again about the problems of moving from inception of an idea for a military requirement to the finished field equipment. In spite of the evidently more relaxed approach in this country, there were still committees to circumvent and the protocol of developmental procedure to be obliquely observed. Perhaps democracy required it. Only in a dictatorship could one ride roughshod over the behavioral pattern of any commonweal.

I wondered how such differences between our two similar countries affected the way things got done here. What were the channels through which effective communications were made? How were the inevitable roadblocks overcome?

I tried to understand better the great difference in the overall approach to rocket development between the U.S. Navy and the Army Air Corps. In a new country its not a bad idea, I'd found, to try and understand the language. Here the language was the same, so I had to go a bit deeper.

A lot of it stemmed from the very different roles of the two services in peacetime. Navies of any country, with colonies or not, are always at sea on active duty, patrolling the oceans. They naturally sense the winds of strife, worldwide, and are first to become actively involved. No wonder U.S. Navy flyers knew early on of our successful experiments with a well-tried weapon (albeit designed for mass ack-ack use) now a formidable arrow for Icarus.

What was it that I found so exciting and exhilarating about this enormous country? Maybe I had come into a new Elizabethan age of the West. Sparked by rebellious action in the late eighteenth century, these people had the smell of freedom in their nostrils and expanded with a new adventurous spirit, as did the people in old England in the years of the first Elizabeth not too long after Runnymede. The world as known at that time had been won. Now, it was the West that, in proper context, had just been won.

What could I think but: "*Plus ça change, plus c'est la même chose.*" And so to bed.

Cabs and buses must have been on the cusp of my moon phase. Funny things seemed to be happening when I rode a bus or a cab. I arrived at the Palace of Railroads—Union Station—in Washington one evening at the same time as an old friend who was visiting from England. We shared a ride into town.

Scott-Hall was a very senior scientist then on the staff at Farnborough. Scottie and I began catching up on our recent doings. I'd known him a long time and always enjoyed his company. Our driver, an older man, handsome and well dressed, turned and said, "Welcome, gentlemen. Where can I take you?" Our conversation quickly became three sided, and our personal reminiscences had to wait.

The driver told us he owned a small farm over the river in Virginia that he had worked with success and a great deal of fun for a number of years. "More of a hobby, really," he admitted. Now, with the war on he'd bought a cab and plied the city most days as an independent. "My war work!"

"Not long ago," he told us, "my wife and I came over into the city for dinner. We went to the Mayflower, and of course I put on a black tie. As we came out of the house my wife didn't want to walk any father than she had to in her evening shoes, and with the cab right outside the door, we decided to take it instead of the Buick."

It all sounded a bit far fetched, but he was very convincing and his cultured accent supported the tale. Besides, I was beginning to get used to some of the startling ways of these delightfully surprising people. "Yes, do go on," said Scottie for both of us. "What happened then?"

"Well, as we left after an excellent dinner party and got in the cab, another couple emerged and hailed me. I waited and they slipped in. As we got under way the lady in the back could contain herself no longer. Obviously noticing my wife's décolleté gown and my dinner jacket, she said, 'But you're all dressed up!' 'Oh, yes,' I said, 'we always dress after six.' When we dropped them off soon after, the lady was still shaking her head. My wife made me turn off the For Hire sign at once."

"Well I'm damned!" said Scottie, as we too arrived at our destination.

I had a spate of reports to make, so writing them up provided a good excuse to hide away. "No phone calls or visitors, please, Connie. I'm serious," I begged.

Alec Fletcher helped to improve my cover at noon. "Let's go to Stouffer's," he said. "It's easy to hide there." Thus I met my first cafeteria, right across from the swanky Mayflower Hotel and only a step down Connecticut Avenue from our office. It was quiet in its anonymity but provided really superior dishes. Delightful because we could choose just what we wanted and at our own speed. What a great idea. Here, away from our desks and insistent phones, we could relax and discuss our problems in some degree of peace, and without any waitresses or waiters to shoo us away when we'd finished eating but still had more to say or write.

Alec had interesting news of Mosquito fighter-bombers of the specialized No. 617 Squadron, now fitted with H_2S, and able to mark very specific targets by night and in foul weather. Markers were being placed where the bombers could see them: bright ones below ground mist; airborne above 10/10 cloud. No. 617 Squadron's training took into account the weather conditions in the Far East, where they would move to when Germany fell, as part of the new "Tiger Force"—the RAF's bombing force planned for that theater.

Stan Curtis showed me a cable from home. "The director of armament development plans to come over," he explained, "to talk about changing the explosive used over here to a new Minol formula for filling bombs being made for the RAF. He'd like to visit the A. O. Smith Corporation in Milwaukee, particularly, because they are making blockbuster bomb cases for us. I'll start the planning, okay?"

"Sounds good, Stan," I told him. "Let me know when you need me, but give me some notice, there's a good chap." I depended on these busy, capable people—Stan, Alec, Brian Hatfield, and all the others in my crew. I know I gave them problems being away so much and not always fitting into their pet plans, but in the end I hope I didn't disappoint them too much. I overheard Connie say something one day about a "will-o'-the-wisp" but never let on I'd heard. Of course, it may not have been me she meant.

We returned from that first of many meetings at our Stouffer's office to our official one on the upper floor of the elegant, erstwhile Dupont mansion. Here I had a little dressing room off a large master bedroom. The staff occupied the huge bedroom, and the Canadian secretaries were down the hall.

Farther along the same hall were the signals and navigational boys. This was the same split as at home. The navigators and the armorers were two separate branches of technical specialists, but there was already a move afoot to bring these groups much closer together. Indeed, the latest latrinogram said they were to be joined. Perish forbid! It made sense though. Technical development, moving so rapidly ahead in these frenetic times, already seriously overlapped our carefully guarded separate domains. Navigators were using radar, and radar was now the armorer's primary aid for bomb aiming and night fighting.

I had already made my number briefly with these chaps. Air Commodore N. Buckle was in charge, and a most genial fellow was he. His chief sidekick was Wing Commander E. E. Vielle. I resolved to get to know them better.

GLOBAL UPDATE
April 1944

As the Allied invasion of Europe nears, heavy bombers of the U.S. and the U.K. are switched to preinvasion targets: railways, ammo depots, explosives factories, radars, and coastal batteries. No. 627 Squadron marks the targets with Lancasters dropping massive flare carpets. Mosquitoes dive-bomb to deck level with Red Spot Flares (RSF) for the main force to bomb. Marking accuracy is within twenty-five yards.

In London General Charles de Gaulle is made head of the Provisional French Government.

The German battleship *Tirpitz*, disabled in 1943 by RN mini-subs, is sufficiently repaired to refit at a Baltic port but she is attacked with heavy bombs from the RN carriers *Victorious* and *Furious* and by the RAF operating from North Russia. Immobilized once more, she is moved to Tromsö Fjord, Norway.

Tubby Vielle showed up shortly after I got back from my Dover junket. "Dixi, how would you like to come down to Florida to see some radio-guided bombs being dropped? We're also going to try out a new British blind-landing aid that might amuse you."

"That'll be great!" I replied. "Wunderbar. How do we go?"

"First class, of course," said Tubby. "In the Beech. Don't tell me you haven't used one of them yet. We have permanent use of a couple of Twin Beechcraft C-45 aircraft and crews, courtesy of the Air Corps at Bolling Field. You didn't know?"

"Hell's bloody bells!" I blurted out. "I've been here two months, and this is the first I've heard tell of this wondrous, generous accommodation. I'm glad someone told me—finally."

The 19th of April came on winged heels, sped by my impatience. The air commode (sic), Tubby, and I took an early taxi from DuPont Circle over to the base. it was my first visit to Bolling, though I'd flown from Anacostia, the navy field right alongside.

Bolling was a busy place. By the time we'd paid obeisance to the met prophets and walked out to the neat, shiny C-45, there was already a mass of air traffic. It was not even 9:00 A.M.

Indoctrination to the joys of a private air line was a great thrill. As soon as the wheels came up, our very willing crew chief, Corporal Dedeere, brought paper cups of excellent coffee and a few doughnuts, and then, smart fellow, retired for a well-earned nap in the capacious cabin.

The two navigational experts were also professional flyers. They got the best radio music on the dial for our delectation, besides steering our orgy barge with consummate skill toward Lower Egypt. They showed me the cunning involved in getting out of the Washington maelstrom and onto the aerial "beams" beyond. These early navigational devices were laid out all over the U.S. in a vast grid from airport to airport and places in between.

All that seemed needed was the right aerial map, a magnifying glass to read the vital, minuscule print thereon, and a knowledge of how to tune the little radios to the frequency of the next beam station—by cranks in the roof almost impossible to reach. Every minute the friendly beacon pushed out its identity in Morse code, begging to be recognized. It was a neat, simple system. Alas, when most needed, as in a nasty storm full of electrical nonsense, the beams were readily seduced from the straight and narrow and acted like the false signals sent by Cornish "wreckers" hid on the treacherous cliffs behind a driving gale.

We were flying high above tobacco country. It was cool and relaxing at this altitude, and up on the step, we were making good time, close to 195 miles per hour. We'd gas up halfway at Charleston, being a bit shy of making it in one hop to Orlando.

"Look, Dixi," indicated Tubby, "there's one of the radio beam stations down there. Those four lattice towers in a square near the Raleigh airport. Got it?"

Such stations transmitted a beam along each arm of the grid intersecting at that point. When riding a beam correctly, going toward it or away, we heard a single, continuous tone in the earphones. If we drifted off to one side the tone slowly changed to a series of letters in Morse code—*A's* on one side or *N's* on the other—as shown on the chart. Every minute the insistent ego intruded.

We had an auto pilot, known as "George" to all airframe drivers. Not only did George relieve the monotony of long flights but he took over in murky weather. We could always blame the gadget if by mistake we—it—ran into the hard core of a cloud.

Ten

Orlando, city of a thousand lakes, lay below us aglint in the late sun. Tubby turned George off and began to let down on a slow slide through mounting cumulus clouds. He laid the tail down on the runway with gently sureness and pushed open the side window. After the languid spring we had left up north, the air felt uncomfortably warm and humid. We shed neckties and rolled up our sleeves in a very unmilitary mode as we left Dedeere to bed down the Beechcraft.

Along with the scientist in charge of the experiments, we went aloft the next day in a four-engined Liberator B-26 to witness the dropping of an AZON guided bomb. This thousand-pounder was fitted with radio guidance to control surfaces in the tail, but its flight could only be controlled left or right, half the battle, at least.

It was the first time I'd seen a real guided weapon in action. To me it was an ominous portent of the way all our weaponry was going. AZON was certainly a step or two beyond the stumbling beginnings of the antigravitational wings and stabilizing gyro I'd started with on our rockets at home. It was a step toward matching the nastiness of the German scientists at Peenemunde. In guided weapons propelled by rockets lay the military future. We could ignore this trend to our own ultimate peril.

That afternoon we left for Boca Raton, halfway down the east coast of Florida and a playground of the very rich. The Air Corps car that collected us from the little airport turned into an imposing avenue of royal palms, and we soon arrived at the Boca Raton Club, a beautiful building fashioned in a picturesque Spanish style that was a real delight. It was designed by rebel architect Addison Mizner, a man before his time. He brought the sensible peasant style of spacious simplicity to the mangrove thickets of the "Rat's Mouth," as the original Spanish discoverers named the place.

We were enchanted by the tiles—on the floors, in the walls, around the windows. The rooms were cool and restful after the blaze outside. We luxuriated in the place that yielded its role as elegant winter watering spot to become wartime quarters for air force officers. Ole!

Awake early, we three set out in swimming shorts over an old wooden bridge crossing the Intracoastal Waterway to the beach beyond. The Atlantic was laid out as far as the eye could see, blue, green, and tropical aqua against the golden sand.

No more than ankle deep in the bathtub-hot water we realized others were there first. It was chock-a-block with jellyfish, layer upon layer. They were so many that the small waves were damped and unable to break. We made do with a cold shower back at the Club. "One must arise early," quoth

Tubby, "to be about before the medusa."

"The new system we're going to test," said our leader at breakfast, "is from the U.K. It's called Ground Controlled Approach (GCA). We'll make a wide approach to the field, and the people on the ground, completely hidden in a hut, will pick us up on radar. They'll take over control and talk us right down. Come on! Finish up, and let's go!"

The system was uncanny. We were a long way out, downwind from the runway, when the ground technicians came in with breezy authority.

"Okay. We have you bright and clear. Turn left...*turn left*...lose height...you're too high...hold it...go right a hair." Crisply and accurately we were directed down the electronic funnel until the ground gave us back our own. We did it several times.

We left Boca by 3:00 P.M. that afternoon, but a quickly developing cold front gave us pause. "We'll go into Florence," said the air commodore on the intercom. "I don't like what's ahead. Let's get a proper weather reading for the rest of the way."

The Delphics were optimistic. "This is passing through rapidly. Give it an hour or two and it'll be gone." The storm must have heard the voice of Florence and swept on through, leaving but ragged remnants of its anger. We took off in the dark but had no trouble finding the blinking red lights on the smokestacks across the way from Bolling field. An interesting trip and very instructive. More important, I'd joined our private air line.

GLOBAL UPDATE
April 1944

General MacArthur makes a four-hundred-mile amphibious leap bypassing fifty thousand Japanese at Wewak and takes Aitape and Hollandia well up the north coast of New Guinea on 22 April. Three hundred and eighty enemy airplanes are found destroyed.

> Mussolini is discredited and caught, clad in a German greatcoat and helmet, trying to escape toward the Swiss frontier. He and his mistress are shot and hung upside down in public view on 25 April.
> 627 Squadron marks the Schweinfurt target by day for the Eighth Air Force on 26 April. Two nights later the Pathfinder squadron pinpoints the Kjelle Aircraft Factory in Oslo for the RAF in the first "dive-bombing" marking operations with very few civilian casualties.

Washington was a lot more complicated and more intensely political than London. Men lobbied for a myriad of different reasons, all day and for much of the night. It was the most important—and amusing—game in town.

With so many things having to be done in a hurry, all at once, and all with partisan priorities being sought and fought for, it is surprising how much was actually accomplished. In addition, 1944 was an election year, war or no war, adding competition of yet another kind.

When I had to call in at one of the many cocktail parties being thrown by an aircraft manufacturer or a gun maker or a general, I stopped at the local drug store to drink a large glass of rich milk as my predecessor had wisely advised. "Particularly watch out with the Russians around," Ted warned me. "They make every drink a challenge. When you hear *Pieta dad na*, run for your life. It is a simple toast which requires you to drink it to the bottom. They're great chaps but a real menace when the liquor is broken out."

Much business was done at these gatherings and though we had to make the rounds, it was not always an unmitigated bore. At one such affair I ran into a chap I hadn't seen for donkey's years. At first I couldn't put a name to the animated face of the British Tank Corps colonel who came into view. "You don't remember me, do you? I'm Moolenaar," said the face.

"Of course I do," I fibbed. It was the unfamiliar uniform he now wore that put me off. "What on earth are you doing here?" I quickly added.

"Oh, I'm buying tanks in Detroit for the Horse Guards," he replied. "Have to come up to Washington, though, to try and get some of Monty's pet ideas put in. They aren't too popular with the U.S. Army procurement fellows at the plant!" He was the same chap who had been my father's super ad agent in London and who I met first in 1930 when at the Imperial College of Science in So. Kensington. I'd just been elected—very democratically in my unfortunate absence—to be editor of the college magazine, known as the *Phoenix* because it rose in newborn splendor with each new editor. When I took over, with unavailing cries of protest, it was a double-page mimeographed rag, hardly worth the johnnypaper it was on. I started to collect some material for the next issue and showed it to my father for advice.

"Talk to Moolenaar," he advised me.

Moolenaar joined me for lunch at the College Union and wanted to see back issues—as far back as possible. We dug out some that had been among the first off the press in 1886. The editor was H. G. Wells, who started the journal as the *Science Schools Magazine*, and wrote the whole first edition single-handedly—as he was at pains to point out in his maiden editorial.

"I have an idea," my Fleet Street ball of fire said. "Get your material ready for us, give us all rights to the advertising, and we'll have a thousand copies printed free by the best printers. We need about twenty-four pages of ads on thin paper, and you can have thirty-six pages on thick paper in the center, plus one halftone."

I called the editorial board together with Moolenaar waiting in the wings, almost like the villain poised for his entry cue. The board was astonished, wondering where the catch lay hid. It was a difficult job to convince them we had nothing to lose and everything to gain. The scheme worked. Waterlow and Sons,

Ltd., the printer of British bank notes, duly produced and delivered the free copies to us, and we had a ball. The first edition was sold out quickly at a sixpence a copy, netting an ungrateful board a bag of gold sovereigns—for nothing except obstruction on their part.

I am still awed at how easy it was to do. The magazine was elegant, being designed and put together by Fleet Street pros. My father also taught me a lesson in how to get hard things done in short order and how to assume an appropriate humility performing an impossible conjuring trick.

Colonel Moolenaar and I moved over to a sideboard to demolish a plate of excellent hors d'oeuvres. "Do you remember a little trip you made for me to Vienna, Dixi?" he asked in bland innocence.

"Of course," I nodded, "how could I ever forget coming through German customs, with your 'liberated loot' and my heart firmly stuck in my mouth on that crazy little mission of mercy?"

I never saw him again. He was off to Detroit the next afternoon, and I had a couple of urgent things to do myself in the morning. Our lines still wait to meet again, wherever parallel lines do meet.

Fred Hovde called to say the first Tiny Tim thousand-pound rocket was ready to be fired on the ground at Inyokern. Would I like to attend. "You bet I would, Fred. Many thanks!" said I with a wide grin.

"You'd better not waste any time then," he told me.

Long-suffering Connie put me on a rhumb line to L.A., touching down at 7:00 P.M. on 27 April, but when I got to Caltech the boys told me I was too late for the first launch. The bird had flown.

"Damn and blast!" I moaned.

"Don't worry so much," Charlie said, "there'll be another one soon."

"But not the very first one," said a certain spoiled brat not easily comforted.

Willy Fowler, I discovered, had gone to war. "He's with the fleet in the Pacific," Tom Lauritsen informed me, "to help to introduce our aircraft rockets. He'll be gone a month or two." That would remove the principal threat among the liar's dice aficionados, but I'd miss his cheery person till he got back.

They brought me up to date. The first Tiny Tim had been well-launched from a fifteen-foot ground launcher and behaved perfectly. Because of the severe blast from the igniter, it was essential to displace the rocket from the airplane before firing, and several approaches were being tried.

At the auspicious first firing of the new five-inch HVAR rocket, Duane Mack, one of the spectators, had loudly burst out, "Holy Moses!" Somehow or other this seemed an appropriate name for this beauty, and so it would now be called.

The first HVAR rocket was air fired on 30 March with great success. Incredible progress but very predictable.

Flying east across North America has to be uphill. It seems to take longer, though the prevailing winds are from behind. It took forever to get to Eglin, the new Air Corps test base in Florida. A brief look at the beautiful city of New Orleans made the agony bearable. It's so delightfully French it should be called *La Nouvelle Orleans*. Only slow boats seemed to ply out of this gentle, forgotten, cotton-picking part of the world, but I reached Eglin at long last and breathed an audible sigh of relief.

The base reminded me of Boscombe Down, at least the armament testing part of Boscombe, but it was much larger than one would believe possible, acres and acres of space. Many of the bitter lessons we learned at Boscombe had been put to good use by some of the chaps who visited us in England earlier on. The ranges were handy, well laid out, and altogether very workmanlike.

Again I was thrilled to the core by the great surge of energy that was so apparent across this brave new world. I loved it, and it constantly nourished my somewhat flabby spirit, dulled by the privations of Britain through five long, weary and until recently, lonesome years of war.

As planned, I joined up with the team already there from our air commission in Washington. Although primarily an armament meeting, operational aspects were discussed as a matter of course. We talked of our strategic mission, of the equipment needed to accomplish that task—aircraft and weaponry treated as a single entity. It was an ecumenic gathering of a number of different services, different air forces, and of interests more diverse. The good thing was how many were in general agreement. Active service and field experience brought new wisdom and empathy for other specialists. Parochial differences were disappearing. I could feel the soft winds rising, favoring the birth of a common military service—soon.

We left after lunch. By leaning out the fuel mixture to the limit and breathing in deeply to make ourselves as light as possible, we were able to make the trip in one hop without a pit stop. I was allowed to fly the C-45 quite a bit and now felt ready to do a trip all on my lonesome.

GLOBAL UPDATE
May 1944

On 9 May the Soviets recapture their Black Sea naval base at Sevastopol. On 11 May, General Alexander delivers a successful attack, assembled in secrecy, around Cassino. He holds back a breakout from Anzio until the U.S. VI Corps joins them on the 18th. By the 25th the Germans are in full retreat toward Rome which the Allies take, undamaged, ten days later.

General Eisenhower calls for Bomber Command to destroy a heavy gun battery at St. Martin de Varreville dominating Utah Beach—a U.S. landing area in Overlord to relieve the U.S. Airborne from the task in the coming invasion. During the night of 28 May, No. 627 Pathfinder Mosquito Squadron mark the emplacement precisely from four hundred feet up and sixty-four special Lancasters—each with one Tallboy twelve-thousand-pound armor-piercing (earthquake) bomb—obliterate it from high altitude.

A nice surprise awaited in Washington. It was an invitation to go off to school for a week—to a university, no less. Members of the corps of foreign military officers were invited to attend a minicourse at one or other of the more senior universities in the country. Twenty spots had been allotted, and I was lucky to get one. "How did all this happen?" I asked Connie as she gave me the program and plans for getting there.

"Don't you remember?" she asked, "I thought Brian Hatfield told you he went to Yale last year and had a great time...even learned something too, he swore. You said you'd like to go on one."

"Oh, did I? Well, well."

A dozen of us, all Allied military types, gathered on the stately grounds of the Princeton campus and were given rooms for our stay. They were the standard dormitory accommodations and took me back fifteen years in mind. Such rooms are not much different in any country, apparently, a little sparse, almost monkish, styled for midnight oil. On the other hand, the grounds were lush with wide well-tended lawns laced with pleasant, winding paths to nurture quiet thought.

Because the time was so limited, our course would be confined to American History.

"I know what's crossing your minds," said our lecturer. "You might think we can easily get through the whole of American History in half a day, but it's an old joke—so save your breath to cool your porridge, as they used to say in the old Scottish village where I grew up.

"What we'll try and tell you is an old, old story about discovery and conquest and even exploitation that may not be entirely unfamiliar to you. There are episodes in the histories of all nations in which little pride can be taken. Consider your own countries, if you will, and then take pride, with us, as we examine the parallel developments that have given us all the kind of democracy we now share."

Together we stepped through some of the pages behind the blossoming of the largest union of democratic peoples under one nation at any time in history. We marveled at our ignorance, at knowing so little. The United States has struggled for many years to hide from the evils from which most of its citizens have fled. In so doing, much of its history has largely been lost to the general ken of the old world.

Now, with a gentle shove from the affairs of 1917, followed by the insistence of the predatory Axis powers, this country was being forced to turn back and become a part of the rest of the world. An unwilling, gentle giant, more than a little annoyed by being woken from private dreams and the pursuit of very personal happiness.

This important episode in our sojourn in the New World was much more than a mere history lesson. There were so many happy, interesting comparisons to be drawn, none of which seemed odious. We could see more clearly our common heritage. We could now dream with more assurance of a feasible common destiny.

The week flew by. We glimpsed, briefly, Albert Einstein hurrying along a shaded path with hidden purpose. We talked with scholars in all branches of the arts and sciences until at last we were all seated at a farewell dinner in the faculty house ready to be sent on our way back to the real—but unreal—world. I sat next to Dr. George Gallup and learned much about the statistics of opinion. The good doctor, in turn, seemed interested to hear how we had used statistics and probability to help solve the otherwise intractable problem of concentrating firepower of multiple guns, widely spread out in the aircraft, for aerial combat. I still boast of being a Princeton grad.

• • •

Stan Curtis looked in. "Air Commodore Huskinson and his wife arrive next week," he announced. "They'll be staying at the Hay Adams." He passed me a copy of the program for their visit.

"Nice work, Stan," I told him. "I could use your help." Stan was part of the great full-time civil service behind the scenes in the RAF and had much humdrum business to perform without much of the glamour to bask in. I asked him along because he deserved to be in at the kill, so to speak, when we met with the top brass and the fate of pet joint projects—on which he had labored long—might be decided.

I'd served under Pat Huskinson briefly in 1937. He commanded the Air Observers School where I tried to teach raw NCOs how to drop bombs on a hapless, imaginary enemy. Pat was one of the first of the new breed of specialist armament officers. Pilots themselves, they were the experts whose job it was to develop, introduce, and control the weapons of the air.

At the beginning of the war, Pat was appointed director of armament development in the Ministry of Aircraft Production. Naturally, he lived in London right through the worst of the blitz. His keen interest in weapons, new and fearful, resulted in a dreadful accident, which Herr Albert Speer could never have foreseen. The Luftwaffe had just started using "block busters" with parachutes attached. The wretched bombs floated down to burst at rooftop level and by sheer, almighty blast easily flatten a couple of streets at a clip.

Pat wanted to see one of these monsters coming down with his own eyes. "We'll need to build some of the bloody things ourselves," he said. "A little tit for tat."

He did see one, and it was the last thing he ever saw. The explosion blew in the huge plate glass window of his flat on the second floor and laid Pat flat on his back, blinded in both eyes. After extensive but unsuccessful surgery, Pat returned undaunted to his office in the ministry. His gallant wife, Mollie, read the technical reports to him, carefully and with patience, and Pat Huskinson continued to direct and make his decisions.

I met them at their hotel on arrival and we had a nice glass of sherry together. Mollie had been allowed to come as Pat's secretary, but she was far more than that. Even more than just his "alter eyes," she was a constant filter against unpleasant things, an unobtrusive guard and guide. It was hard to realize at first that Pat was blind because a watchful Mollie fended off any potential trouble or embarrassment.

At dinner that evening, I was intrigued to see the clever way she organized his plate. The meat was cut up and placed south (toward him). Salt was laid to the east, mustard to the west, potatoes north, and so on. It was very impressive, and touching.

We retired to their suite for a nightcap. "I have a meeting laid on for you in the morning, sir," I said, "so I'll be on my way. I know you are both tired by the trip from New York. Let me pick you up downstairs at nine o'clock."

Pat, in his best bib and tucker, and sporting Hollywood dark glasses, was all ready when I came in to collect him. Mollie was there, too, but declined to come to the specially convened Ordnance Committee meeting in the Pentagon.

Pat wouldn't let me take his arm. He was fiercely independent asking only for instruction as to navigational hazards such as steps, turns, or hidden reefs. He had mastered the delicate art of the white cane, and his hearing was as acute as any Alsatian's.

Walking down the cool passages of the concrete labyrinth presented no problems at all. We went unnoticed by the officers hurrying past, except perhaps an occasional glance of sympathy. People did move aside to make Pat's progress easier but their maneuvers were discrete and humane.

The guard in front of the conference room came to attention and inspected our passes. Behind him the door swung open, and the president of the committee came out.

"That's okay, Barton. I'll vouch for these gentlemen," he said, and turning to Pat, "Welcome to Washington, Air Commodore. Hello, Dean, good to see you again. Come in, we'll be ready to start in a minute.

He led us to the long table on the raised dais and seated us on his right. The members who'd been standing around chatting took their places, their aides laden with impressive files and documents, and the buzz of conversation quickly died away.

The general rapped the table and launched into a generous welcome to Pat. "Gentlemen, the decision we must make today is a matter of the utmost importance to our friends in the U.K. and to us as well. We are honored by a distinguished visitor from the RAF to tell us about it. It is my great pleasure to introduce Air Commodore Huskinson, director of armament development."

Pat sat up straight and directed his pitch-black glasses around the room. "It's so very good to see you all today," he began, and though causing some minor puzzlement, his laconic witticism was not entirely lost. He got right down to the story of the development of the new Minol explosive and all its ups and downs and finally told of the great breakthrough. "We have found that adding ten percent aluminium powder—I'm sorry, Dean here has told me I must say *aluminum*—to our regular filling gives between fifty and one hundred percent increase in blast. But that brings its own problems because the fine metal powder is, itself, highly explosive. It was like the story of flour dust in old windmills that often and without warning, dispatched the millers prematurely to a place where the mills grind even finer. I'm glad to say we have now licked the danger of filling bombs with Minol and can recommend it with full assurance. I hope you will consent to use it in the bombs you're loading for us and feel sure you'll want to do the same for your own munitions as well. We have a technical team ready to come over to brief your chaps if you agree."

There ensued a lively, open discussion until the president rapped on the table and said he'd heard enough. The committee recommended to the chiefs of staff the immediate use of Minol. This vital, important decision was made possible by the persuasive tongue of our blind leader and the intelligent ear of the Ordnance Committee. Minol quickly became standard for bombs destined for the U.K., and soon after for all of us.

It was time to take Pat out to Milwaukee to see the huge four-thousand-pound blast-bomb cases being manufactured there by the A. O. Smith Corporation. They were Pat's answer to the parachute bomb that stole his sight. It was his bid—redoubled—in spades.

The first bomb case had been delivered from the U.S. to the filling factory near London a couple of years before, around Christmas time. Its arrival is still remembered fondly by all lucky enough to be there. When the fastening screws around the closure plates were removed, the astonished and grateful crew found the case filled to the brim with all manner of delightful foods and delicacies not seen by them for years. Needless to say, the contents were not sent on to Herr Hitler. We had a little more appropriate filling for his fiery belly.

I was glad to have checked out in the airplane of our private air line. I called Bolling and booked one for the morning of May 26. Mollie loved the idea of going out to Wisconsin this way. "Much better than any other," she said with a grin. "Pat will love it. When are we going?"

"Tomorrow," I said, returning her smile.

Stan Curtis and I collected the Huskinsons from the Hay Adams and we were soon cleared by weather and flight control. The local weather was marginal for our visual clearance as we soon found out. Thank Heavens we had "George" to take over and climb the Beech with confident, mechanical skill up through the banks of cloud that appeared from nowhere.

At seven or eight thousand feet the sun reigned supreme, and the white world was ours alone. Mollie, in the right-hand seat, just beamed. "I do wish Pat could see all this," she shouted across to me. "He does miss flying himself, you know. More than anything else in the world."

"I know," I called back. "I really do know. Flying has been his whole life. Mine, too." I could understand his great emptiness.

We refueled at Wright Field as the weather finally relented and cleared up. The leg from Dayton to Milwaukee was an invigorating experience with the last hundred miles or so over Lake Michigan adding spice to our miniadventure. The sun was lowering in the west, and small pieces of it were captured by the waves below—the water was filled with a myriad of stars twinkling from within. As we lost height to prepare for landing, the sun slipped below the horizon, dragging the rest of the day with it. We sank into the gathering pool of darkness to settle down, ourselves, into Mitchell Field on the southern edge of Milwaukee, almost within the city walls.

It must have been an aviator who scotched a very common belief held by most earthlings. He said that darkness does not fall: quite the contrary; it rises. As the sun sinks Lethewards, the hollows of the earth are the first to fill with darkness. It does indeed rise, up from the ground until even the loftiest mountain peaks are swallowed up, the last to go.

A call came to the hotel as we washed up. Mrs. Furrer, wife of the president of the A. O. Smith Corporation asked to speak to Mrs. Huskinson. Were we too tired to come over after dinner for a nightcap? "Nothing could be more agreeable," Mollie told her without consulting anyone else.

"Oh, that's just wonderful," said Mrs. Furrer. "We'll send Jennings over to pick you up at eight fifteen. Don't dress up."

We missed the last instruction, too. Mollie evidently didn't think it important enough to mention to us. Or there could have been another reason, because she proceeded to put on the evening gown that she just happened to have with her.

A wonderful, gracious evening followed. The Furrers had had some friends in for dinner: the George Downings and the Lloyd Raymond Smiths and a couple more. Their lovely house was in Fox Point, a fashionable neighborhood ten miles or so to the north on the shore of Lake Michigan.

We were ushered in to find the party just rising from dinner and coming into the very spacious living room—in this house it had to be a drawing room. Three or four strings and a young lady at a grand piano were assembled in an alcove. They were making the horrible discordant scrapings always necessary when a quartet girds for chamber music action. They were in evening clothes. Mollie had been right. Everybody was dressed. Pat and I were in uniform, so that was all right too. Stan looked just fine.

It was quite formal but not oppressively so. Delicate gold chairs were set out for us to dare to sit in. Drinks came round, and then gently and without fanfare, a Mozart concerto floated out to haunt the air.

We could sit and listen or stroll to the back of the large room to chat with some of the others. It was so very well done. No command performance at all and yet a rendition of great skill and beauty. It went by too quickly, but I still sense every nuance of that lovely evening.

The fact that the next day was Saturday made no difference. There was a war on, and all factories were working round the clock every day of the week.

Rudolph Furrer's office was on the top floor of the large main building at the entrance of the A. O. Smith plant. We sipped a cup of fragrant coffee as Rudie told us about the early problems of fabricating the huge bomb cases. They used ordinary oil-well pipe for the first two thousand-pound version, but when we upped the horror to twice the size, they needed larger pipe. Rudie was delighted with Pat's story of the discovery of the Christmas presents from his shop crew to the explosives arsenal in the U.K. I think it was news to him, but I'm not sure.

"Production is now in full swing and they're rolling off the line. Come and see," said Rudie, pointing out of the window at the roadway below.

"Go and have a look for me, Dixi," said Pat. "I'm not much good at that sort of thing."

Sure enough, Mollie and I could see several largish trailers being pulled along by a motor tug slowing down to take the sharp corner below. Each was loaded with half a dozen bomb cases ready to be shipped out.

"Pat," I said, "it should please your heart to see. They really are coming off the line in scads."

Ten or fifteen minutes later, Stan crooked his finger at me surreptitiously from the window. I drifted over to his side and followed his glance. There went still another little train of bomb cases taking the bend.

"They can't be the same trailers," I whispered to him, "though they do look like them. Rudie wouldn't do that just to cheer us up." I realized Stan was being mischievous and very successfully pulling my leg.

The tour of the factory blew all such demeaning ideas from our minds. The colossal effort it represented was heartening in the extreme. Hitler just didn't know what soon would hit him.

We had the Furrers over to the hotel for dinner that night, and they brought with them an invitation to a cookout lunch with the Downings for Sunday. I had become a little more aware of the absolute reality of "American hospitality," but to Mollie and Pat it was overwhelming. We swam in George and Lois Downing's pool, quaffed their drinks, ate hamburgers too many, and then lay out in chairs to enjoy the slightly bleak sunshine of late May. The show of warm welcome was so spontaneous and genuine that it certainly was not just a formal business affair. It did us all a power of good. The Lloyd Raymond Smiths had us all to dinner on our last evening to round out the unrehearsed program.

We took off for the return to Washington having promised to see them all again as soon as we possibly could. Not empty promises by any means but, rather, fond wishes we almost knew would never be granted.

Pat went to Walter Reed Hospital to find out if the remedial work done in New York had made any difference. In sadness they said all hope was gone; he'd never see again.

Preparations for the Allied invasion of France were picking up in a rapid crescendo. Few knew it was to be on the Normandy beaches. A deception of vast proportions was perpetrated in the Pas de Calais region and with General George Patton evident in command, confirmed the anticipation of the Hun. The north of France was now a railroad desert, transportation a nightmare. The night before the launching of the armada from a dozen British ports, defenses all along the north coast of France were heavily bombed. In particular the menacing batteries remaining at La Pernelle and St. Pierre Dumont had to be silenced. With the help of expert low-level marking, Tallboy bombs completely destroyed them.

On 6 June 1944, thousands of ships approached the Normandy beaches and the largest amphibious invasion in history was underway.

Nipped in the bud was a threat from the imminent passage of German heavy tanks through the Saumur tunnel, 125 miles south of the beachhead. 627 Squadron marked the hillside above the tunnel, and twenty-five Lancs with Tallboys, pierced the ninety feet of soil above the tracks, collapsing the tunnel as if by earthquake. It was not reopened for years—an appropriate tomb for tanks.

RAF Typhoons, the massive Hawker replacements for the gallant Hurricanes, came into their own during the invasion. Fitted with eight rockets, they were superb for close support in the field. They had been strafing for weeks, clearing the arena and on June 10 at Avranches, only fifty miles behind the beaches they had a field day. They destroyed 137 tanks of all sizes.

At last on 15 June the Germans had an operational V-1 flying bomb, and it made passage to Britain. It did no harm, but others soon to come hurt us badly.

GLOBAL UPDATE
June 1944

Admiral Nimitz attacks in the Marianas in the Pacific on June 15. With Admiral Spruance commanding a fleet of over five hundred ships, landings are made against very heavy opposition on the small island of Saipan. Two battalions of American troops trap 3,500 Japanese in the northern sector but during the night the enemy erupts in a desperate suicidal advance south. American losses are over a thousand, but the Japanese death toll is about six thousand. Before the island is fully cleaned out a month later, casualties will be three times as great for the U.S. and four times for the enemy.

At the same time in an all-out effort to remove a mortal threat to Japanese sea power, Admiral Azawa seeks the huge U.S., Task Force 58 under Admiral Marc Mitscher that is covering the invasion. U.S. planes, almost a thousand strong in the most powerful carrier armada ever, make mincemeat of the enemy. Twenty-nine of Mitscher's airplanes are lost to over 300 Japanese. The *Taiho* the largest and newest Japanese carrier is sunk on her maiden voyage in this, the Battle of the Philippine Sea.

The first B-29 bomber raid is made on Japan on 15 June.

With much surprise and even more pleasure I received an invitation to join the Caltech rocketeers on a bellicose mission to Europe leaving on 26 June. They were offering timely help to Britain, under siege anew, to combat the V-1 flying bomb launching sites on the French coast.

The beachhead in Normandy had been consolidated, but no breakthrough had yet been possible. In spite of constant bombing of the concrete "ski-sites"—as the launching devices had been christened—the frightening and dangerous weapons continued to arrive in increasing numbers inflicting indiscriminate damage on residential London. People had not yet become used to the spooky, pilotless aircraft and were still mighty scared of them.

The launchers were small and well hidden from the air, making them extremely hard to hit. They had been bombed and strafed for over six months, since they had first been detected, but frenzied construction continued and they were now in full blast.

Just at that time came the generous offer to supply an Army Air Corps squadron in England with the brand new U.S. Navy five-inch rocket to help knock out those damnable, satanic weapon launchers. Caltech had moved into high gear.

A goodly supply of rockets was being hurriedly assembled in California. Zero-length launchers, suitable for the Thunderbolt P-47 aircraft, were being turned out at flank speed and all other logistic needs being collected to equip a fighter-bomber squadron, as yet unaware, on the other side of the world. Charlie Lauritsen and Carl Anderson turned up in Washington to tie up the loose ends.

"I don't know what we'll do about you, Dix," Charlie pondered. "I suppose we'll have to go through that unique ritual of having the Air Corps 'cut orders' to make you legally part of an Air Corps squadron. Now, who can I get to do that for us?" It was a rhetorical question. Charlie had the ear of anyone he needed. He soon returned from a quick foray to the Pentagon, waving some papers in the air—orders in quintuplicate—or more.

"Where's Willy Fowler?" I asked Carl.

"Oh, Willy's at home, minding the store with Tom Lauritsen and getting the follow-up rockets organized," he told me. "He's just back from the Pacific. Now it's my turn to tip our new arrows with venom and gauge their worth. By the way, he sends you his best." Carl also filled me in on some important hot news: the first Tiny Tim[1] had been successfully air-launched a couple of days ago from a TBF Avenger, using a displacement launcher. Great news it was. I was sorry to miss the first air firing but we had a splendiferous crowd of brass from the U.K. to watch it— Lord Cherwell, chief scientific advisor to Winston Churchill, led the mission. I know it helped the cause of our own Uncle Tom development.

342　　　　　　　　　　　DRUIDS' CIRCLE

Late 1944—11.75-inch "Tiny Tim" rocket.

July 1944—Distinguished visitors watch "Tiny Tim" air firing from TBF. From left: Dr. W. A. Fowler; Capt S. E. Burroughs Jr.; Cmdr D. B. Young; Lord Cherwell, scientific advisor to Winston Churchill; Lt Col E. Boulton-King, British Army Staff; and Dr. E. L. Ellis.

Several colossal transport aircraft, C-54s from Air Transport Command, were waiting at Andrews. As soon as the first one was loaded with rocket stores, Charlie, Carl, and I barreled over to the base and climbed aboard. We were joined by Lieutenant Colonel Hornsby from Eglin and Paul Reichert from Wright, who were new to me. The other C-54s would follow as they finished loading.

We took off on our great safari at 6:00 P.M. on that memorable 26 June, two short weeks after the first V-1 was launched against London.

England seemed awfully crowded—troops in tents everywhere, trucks and tanks in every field and other odd place, all waiting for the breakthrough; all waiting to go to France.

We reported to U.S. Headquarters at Bushey Park and found out the unit we were to rearm was No. 513 Fighter Squadron, 406th Group of the Ninth Air Force. They awaited us at No. 417 advanced landing field at Ashford in Kent. Appropriately enough, the field lay halfway along the direct path of the V-1s on their track to London.

After we'd made the right noises in the right places, we repaired to the large marquee that served as the officers' club. Charlie, as befitted our leader, bought drinks all round for our team. Suddenly he cocked his head on one side and yelled, "Hey! Listen!" We heard a faint buzz that could only be one thing. Others also heard and began to crowd out of the tent, but Charlie was first. This he had come to see. Over the horizon to the southeast, a tiny, hurrying aircraft appeared, black and ominous as hell.

"Just look at that!" shouted Charlie in great glee. As we watched intently there was a falter, a splutter and then—dead silence. The monster quietly tucked its nose down into a steep dive from about three hundred feet.

"Down! Down!" shouted someone, frantically.

We threw ourselves to the ground, drinks flying in every direction, trying to flatten our profiles to nothing and hide our emu-heads in the sand.

Silence, a long one, then an almighty boom caroom, making us hunch down even more. All except for our dear doctor, who was now on his feet watching the debris still rising beyond the trees, still clutching his unspilled drink.

Not much jetsam fell near us. A protecting house in between had fended off the worst of the blast and rubbish. "Come on," shouted Charlie, "let's go see what we can find. I'd love to get one of those rocket engines."

By the time we found the bomb crater, air raid wardens had already taken over and cordonned it off. The Gothic gift had landed farther away than we thought, but it was certainly close enough for me. There was nothing left from which we could learn much, and the warden terriers wouldn't let us touch anything, anyway.

"Damn," said Charlie.

We had landed in a dream world. Chaos and confusion abounded wherever we went. Everyone seemed to know the script, but we'd not even been briefed. Everyone else rushed around us with arcane purpose, swirling in a semiorchestrated maelstrom. In the vast invasion plan we counted for nothing. Not being part of the original arrangement, we had to devise our own scenario and mostly write our own orders. Carl would have to organize the movement of the rocket stores, the aircraft launchers, the wiring cable harnesses, and a dozen other bits of equipment to arm the P-47 fighters with our precious rockets. We needed trucks, we needed bodies, we needed special tools, and mostly we needed time.

I went off to my own people to earmark a firing range we'd need for some limited live air training. I thought of the ranges at my old air armament school at Eastchurch on the Isle of Sheppey in the Thames estuary off Chatham. Barely twenty miles from Ashford, it would be ideal. Arrangements were quickly made for us to use them in about ten days time. We couldn't be ready before then.

Charlie Lauritsen had disappeared to hobnob with old scientist pals from the past up at Cambridge, at my old college and even in military headquarters. His was the job of a doyen diplomat to ease our difficulties before they became serious problems.

I'd been looking forward to my next visit with a certain smug self-satisfaction. I "borrowed" a complete set of the zero-length P-47 rocket launchers, enough parts to carry one rocket, and hied me over to the rocket development group in the Ministry, where I planted them firmly on the desk of the head man.

"There!" I said, exuding evil.

I didn't really get away with my nastiness, however. They all proceeded to congratulate me. "Yes, we've decided after much thought," they told me, "that this is really the best way to launch rockets, after all. Rails are dead!"

It took the wind right out of my sails. Worst of all, they impounded the launcher kit to have it copied at Farnborough. Carl Anderson wasn't going to be very happy because we were so short of them for the squadron at Ashford, and I had promised to bring the parts back. It served me right. It was a perfect case of the biter bit. I still wonder, though, how the obdurate mind of beaurocracy had been changed when I wasn't looking.

Hornsby commandeered a staff car, and the three of us took off east through the lovely, bucolic Kentish countryside. We found the landing strip by dint of a few inquiries as we approached the town. "It's just down the road," said the chap we asked—a master of the non sequitur, "you can't miss it. It's well camouflaged." It was crude, as airfields go, but quite adequate for the P-47s, or "Jugs" as they were nicknamed, clustered round the edge of the field. We wandered about and found Colonel Grosetta, the CO, in the Ops Room briefing his pilots.

Our group had only been operational since 9 May, but in this short month 513 Squadron had become well-blooded, paving the way for troop landings by strafing and dive bombing. A few attacks on the V-1 launching ski-sites, code named "Noballs," had been mostly ineffective.

After the day's missions ended, the CO had another briefing and let us tell our story. We would start some training in mock rocket attacks the next day with pilots not on ops. Airplanes in for servicing would also be equipped with the rocket gear before going back on line. Just as in Algiers, we'd work our way through all the pilots and aircraft until we could say we were ready for Operation Fireworks.

When we tallied all the equipment that had landed and what we could guess would be available in the near future, it was clear that we'd only have enough launchers for two on each side per aircraft instead of the four we wanted. In view of the paucity of our rocket supply, we'd have to limit live-firing training to one rocket per pilot.

When firing rockets, it is important to make a predetermined dive angle for best accuracy. We chose twenty degrees, the same as in our successful submarine attack. We planned to approach at two thousand feet to find and identify the target then drop down to a thousand feet and start the dive attack.

Colonel Grosetta impressed upon us that once the Jug was in a dive, it did not particularly like to come out of it. It would mush if you tried to haul it out too quickly and simply continue on its merry way. The dive we adopted would allow pilots about seven seconds to aim and fire at three hundred yards range and then ease out of the dive at a height of three hundred feet. All this seemed reasonable for seasoned pilots.

We set up a big aiming mark in the middle of the field and started dive-attack training. I wanted to mark out a big circle, as I'd used in Algiers, to take photos from the plane and get dive angle and range to fire but we didn't have time. Carl had a better idea.

As he himself had done at Inyokern in his own stint of pilot training, to check the pilots' dive angles, Carl made a "harp" with wires set at ten, twenty and thirty degrees and an eyepiece at the side. The pilot was told his dive angle over the aircraft radio and he learned as he flew. Much simpler and quicker than using my beloved circle.

In the middle of practice one morning Carl suddenly shouted, "Look out! Stop the dives!" A lone Spit approached from downwind very low and much too fast for a normal landing. But land he did—tail down on three points—going like an express train. He hurtled down the field and into the far hedge where he was summarily halted.

We ran over and could see all the fabric surfaces of his elevators were burned away. Only the tracery of ribs remained and the paint down the fuselage was darkened and blistered.

The Dutch pilot was scrambling out. He looked very groggy as we helped him away from the wreck, fearing a gas explosion. "What happened?" someone asked.

"I shot the bastard down," he said. "I got it! I blew it up but had to go right through the blast. It was a bloody V-1!"

One less to land on London, but it almost cost us a pilot. The Spit XII was a necessary price to pay and it could be mended.

The Dutchman fortunately wasn't badly hurt and was anxious to get back to his squadron, but we took him into the little cottage which served as the officers quarters to give him a cup of tea. "No thanks, but have you got a brandy?" he begged.

He told us his squadron was specifically assigned to V-1 targets. Usually they tried to get alongside the robot and use the airflow over their own wing tip to upset the balance of the flying bomb and turn it away from its path to London.

"But this one I had to shoot down, and got too bloody close," he recounted. "CO's going to be pissed off, losing a Spit. May I have another brandy, please?"

On 21 July, Hornsby and I took the first rocket-equipped P-47s over to Eastchurch with one live rocket apiece and let go at the targets. Results were very satisfactory. We hit the targets, and the warheads exploded on cue. We had agreed to keep our eyes peeled for incoming buzz bombs on the way back. Sure enough, we both spotted one streaking across a yellow field of mustard below. Our guns were loaded. "Yours!" I yelled to Hornsby, and down he went, throttle rammed right through the gate. I stayed at three thousand feet, hanging around for the next train in, so to speak. I almost missed seeing the second V-1 altogether and had to make a 180-degree turn and stand the Jug on its nose trying to catch up. Even so, I was much too late. The pulsing star of its exhaust drew away, leaving me standing—baffled and chagrined. Hornsby had no better luck. He had gained on his bird in the dive, but as he leveled off to stalk it, it slowly drew away and was gone.

GLOBAL UPDATE
July 1944

On 17 July, RAF fighter bombers machine gun a staff car with General Rommel, the Desert Fox, aboard. He is severely wounded but does not die.

A complicated plot to kill Hitler at his Rastenburg HQ in Prussia on 20 July fails. The bomb kills several senior officers, but Hitler is lucky to survive. Many die in savage retribution.

After Saipan, Guam is invaded on 21 July and falls twenty days later. At the same time, U.S. troops are also taking Tinian, the last island to fall in the Marianas. With the loss of these strategically important islands the government of dictator Tojo falls.

Toward the end of the training period, we were suddenly told our tactical mission had changed completely. Fixed V-1 launchers were abandoned when increased bombing attacks began knocking them out of action. Now coming into use were mobile launchers which moved after every use and were almost impossible to spot. They were spared our fiery storm. Our job was to be very close support for the American armies as they moved out of the beachhead where they were stalemated. The small fields surrounded by impenetrable hedges of the Bocage country of Normandy allowed the Germans to bring up a ring of troops and dig in, offering few targets for our fighter-bombers.

To break the stranglehold on the left flank, the British used the carpet-bombing technique just ahead of their troops at Caen. Aided immeasurably by Typhoon squadrons with eight rockets per airplane, they burst through immediately afterward on 18 July. American forces on the right, recalling a nasty experience using a similar tactic at Cassino in Italy, were reluctant to try it again. But with the devil driving, the successful demonstration at Caen encouraged them to go ahead with it. On 25 July, medium and heavy bombers laid down a very heavy carpet between Periers and St. Lô, right in front of the U.S. First Army. Over 2,500 aircraft participated. As soon as the bombardment ceased, they overcame the dazed Germans and broke through.

While the bombardment was in progress, Carl Anderson caught a ride over to Strip 3, at Cardonville in France, where our squadron was located. I picked up a Jug modified for rockets and followed him over. Grosetta drove us in his new Jeep to report to Major General Quesada, commanding the Ninth Tactical Air Force; his aide took us to the general's caravan and showed us in.

Pete Quasada shook Carl's hand and turned to me. "Yes, I remember you," he said. "We met when I was deputy to Air Vice Marshal Hugh Pughe Lloyd in Algiers." I was flattered that he remembered my introducing our own antisubmarine rockets to Coastal more than a year back.

"The rockets are from our own stables this time," Carl told him, "developed for the Navy, who send them with their best wishes. We brought Dixi along to help train the squadron since he's done it before. He didn't offer any resistance to speak of."

"Glad to have you with us again," said our commander. "I think Carl's rockets are just in time for a possible breakthrough at St. Lô, today or tomorrow. Happy hunting to you!"

As soon as we got back to the air strip, Grosetta put me to work. We went over to the ops tent and studied the ground situation immediately forward of our position and beyond the Villedieu area that had been carpet bombed that day.

"We are trying to improve direct communication with the First Army so they can call on our patrols for help where it's needed. Then we can go right in and remove the problem. I think it would be useful if you'd make a swing around the area and get familiar with the situation while it's still light. Don't buy any trouble. You can do that tomorrow."

At 7:00 that evening I took off as wing man to one of our pilots on an armed reconnaissance. We saw no tanks at all in the open, but we took on some moving armored trucks with some success. The eight 50-caliber machine guns in the Jug have a devastating hose of fire. I managed to set one truck aflame and send another off the road to overturn in the ditch. On the way back I saw several large tanks buried, hull-down with 88 mm guns trained down roads to the beach. They could taste rockets tomorrow.

The whole squadron was up before dawn. When there was enough light to see the targets, our first patrol of two P-47s with four rockets each was over the battle area. After that a patrol of two left every half hour or so all day long. Our job was to support the American tank column moving through the Montreuil area. The Army was truly breaking out.

"This is your first serious mission, Dixi," said our CO. "So I'm giving you Swanberry as wing man. He's an old hand and will take good care of you. Off you go, and good luck!" We were airborne at half past six. Earlier sorties took care of the buried tanks. They were evacuated when the first rockets came near.

We found the column and were directed by them to the road ahead where an enemy concentration was creating a nuisance. I twisted my neck around to see where Swan had got to. Not seeing him behind me, I yelled "Tally ho" and streaked off to the head of the column. I picked out a Panzer tank and came in fast on his flank as soon as I could get into position. I was too excited, and the pair of rockets missed over the top. When I came around again, the big brute had gone. It had completely disappeared so I took on a smaller Mark IV. This I also missed, but I must have scared him out of his pants because he took off through a convenient gate in the stone wall into an orchard and now cut a swath through the apple trees as fast as his tracks would carry him. I warily circled the scene below, and dammit, there was that bloody Panzer. He was inside the downstairs part of a house he'd barged straight into and all that showed were his track marks through the garden. The cunning fox! Probably one of Rommel's people. Perhaps the next flight would get him as he backed out of the kitchen.

Having wasted my rockets completely, I returned to the melee for a little gunnery. Carefully laying a bead on the rear of the roof of a Mark IV tank as it retreated down the narrow road, I gave it the longest squirt I could. Coming round once more, I was elated to see he had stopped with smoke and flames pouring from his open turret. First scalp. I left him to stew and picked out another for the same treatment. That fish got away, so I used up my remaining rounds on tank crews fleeing the scene on foot. I couldn't see Swan anywhere, and out of ammo, I steep-turned away with naught degrees on the compass and close to naught feet on the altimeter.

"Is Swan back?" I asked the intelligence officer in the debriefing tent.

"Not yet," he replied, "You're the first from your show. Now tell me all about it, and minimize the bullshit."

In the mess tent for breakfast I sat next to Grosetta. "Have you seen Swan?" I asked him.

"Not since you left," he answered. "You should know." Suddenly I realized Swan was in real trouble. No news came in while I was still in France. I heard later—goddammit—they found the place where he was shot down.

My next turn came at 10:00 A.M. and the Germans had

moved on to the Le Mesnil Amey area. I flew wing man to one of the other pilots, and we came into position without a scratch, although the light flak was a lot heavier from the fields flanking our targeted armored column.

I missed a Tiger with my first two rockets—right over the top again. The dive was too steep. In a second go around I hit his rear sprocket. It stopped him, to be sure, but he was by no means dead. Even disabled, he was too tough for my guns. I returned to lesser fry which seemed to be more my game.

An unwary Mark IV became a flamer with a long burst from my hammering 50-calibers going through the rear engine louvers, and no one survived. The second one I hosed down stopped, though it wasn't on fire. The lid flew open and the crew bailed out to run for cover.

I was feeling a bit better now about the wasted rockets and circled like a barracuda, just as hungry. I spied some fancy staff cars pulling away from a big house and lining up behind an armored car. I hung back to let them get underway and then approached from the rear as they gathered speed down a handsome tree-lined avenue. The 50s sang harshly, and the cars were smashed one after another. I got three of them, and only the one out in front was left. I was pretty low by now but only needed a second or two more. Squirt! Squirt! I got him and hauled back hard on the stick.

Grosetta was quite right. The Jug didn't like such treatment. It sank like a river rhino into the tops of the roadside poplars. A colossal bang predicted curtains. But no—the tough old bird just shook herself, began to lift, and we still flew.

"Wad jer think yar?" said my crew chief as I jumped out back at the field. "A goddamn wood chopper?"

"Why? What do you mean?" I asked.

When I reached the front of the port wing I saw what caused the remark. There was a huge dent in its leading edge and a leafy branch decorated the bomb rack behind.

"I'm damn sorry, Sarge," I said. "I guess that calls for drinks all round, and I'm grounded."

"Not to worry, sir," he grinned, "plenty more where this came from." With that, he and the rest of the crew got on the tail and shoved the stricken Juggernaut off the metal planking, out of the line of fire.

The rest of the squadron was on the top of the world. reporting many rocket kills against all types of tank. One fellow said he'd blown up an enemy column's lead tank and he and his wing man had a field day with those stalled behind. Their enthusiasm was good to see and to share. Calls coming in from the Army told much the same tale. They had picked up one downed pilot, who would have to stay inside the tank until a lull let him return. We hoped his rescuers would not press-gang him into staying with them or persuade him to desert to the iron cavalry in gratitude for his salvation. Unfortunately, a third pilot was missing too.

That afternoon I was given a new Jug and sent out for a third trip against part of the same column of ours, a little farther along the road. I got a small tank with a rocket and damaged another so badly that the crew abandoned ship and fled. As I approached a third vehicle, the crew was out and gone before I could fire.

I hailed my crew chief when I landed. "There she is, good as new!"

"No, sirree! See here?" he called from under the wing. I bent down to take a look and saw that a 20 mm Jerry slug had knocked off the bomb rack's rear support.

"Damnation! That's a bit of luck. You know, I didn't even feel it," I told Chiefy. "At least there's no damage to your precious ship."

"Our precious ship," he corrected. We were pals now.

Gross caught up with me, while I was filling out damage forms in debriefing. "Carl wants to drive forward as far as we can and take a gander at the damage done by the rockets," he said.

We took off down the cratered country road, following a

large-scale map crayoned in where we thought the front line was, heading south toward St. Lô.

The stench got worse as we neared the carpet-bombed terrain. Dead cows and horses lay in the warm sun with their legs pointing stiffly skyward and their bellies hugely distended. Lifeless soldiers from both sides lay waiting sympathetic disposal. In this business the wounded enjoy priority. "Good God!" said Carl. "What a dreadful waste." It was a grim sight over which a faint pall of dust hung, unable to settle. Throughout, the acrid reek of explosives, and everywhere, abandoned equipment, rifles, mess tins...and letters from home. Wrecked vehicles littered the road, only half-shoved aside. Many of them were burned out, but others had no visible damage at all. The German retreat after the bombing was close to a rout.

"Stop here a sec, Gross," I said. "I think I recognize where we are. Yes, there's the armored truck I sent off the road last night." Farther along were the remains of a string of tanks the boys had knocked out, mostly with rockets. The front tank, a Mark IV, was a direct hit as the pilot had reported, a heap of twisted steel, black and blue from the flames. The ones following had tried to drive around but had fallen prey to the waiting fighters above. Another tank in the line, also a direct hit, had lost its turret but looked otherwise untouched.

"There's no doubt in my mind," said Carl, grimly, "that our rockets have plenty of explosive, and the fusing is effective."

"The best thing," I added, "is that we've not had any damage to the Jugs from warhead bursts. Lots of damage from flak, yes, but none we could say were rocket warhead splinters." We drove on, but the noise grew ominous. We were coming too close to the front.

"Let's get back," said Gross, "I didn't volunteer for the poor bloody infantry! Had enough, Carl?" He wheeled the Jeep around and we retraced our tracks. As we drove along, we kept a quiet lookout for any sign of Swan's aircraft, but saw nothing. The only thing to give any cheer in this macabre scene was the steady drone of P-47s overhead on the way to battle or returning for more rockets. We waved them encouragement, for what it was worth.

In camp once again, we took a welcome bucket bath and then got down to a council of war.

"I've seen enough." Carl said. "What about you Dixi?"

"Yep, me too. The guys don't need any more advice from me, they're terrific with the rockets. I'd love to stay but I've shot my wad, dammit."

"We'll arrange to get you two back to the U.K. tomorrow," said Gross. "Let's eat, and then I want to introduce you to a local friend I met before you got out here." It was almost dark when we set out across the pierced-steel planking that made up the landing surface of our single strip. Once out on the road it was only a few minutes' walk to the stone cottage at the corner. No light showed. Gross knocked lightly on the window, and in a moment the door opened a crack. *"Oui, qui est là?"* came a voice.

"It's me—Colonel Grosetta."

"Aw! Come een, come een, *mon ami*. A moment, I get a light." A match spluttered as our host lit a kerosene lamp.

"I 'eard you," said Jean. "All zer day you fly!"

"Yes," said Gross, "I think we're now on the way to Paris. Today we flew thirty missions, and more tomorrow. We knocked out at least a dozen of your friends' tanks and a lot of their trucks."

"My friends you call them? Surely you mock me!" said Jean with feigned heat. "But zees calls for a little Calvados—a moment, if you please." He pulled a dresser away from the wall, raised a trap in the floor, and beckoned us to join him. We followed down a steep ladder into a small, chilly, and windowless cellar.

"Voilà!" said Jean, drawing a bottle from a stone recess. "Zees is one I have kep' to drink with my real friends. let me call Madeleine."

His pretty, dark-haired wife came to join us, and together we toasted the continued success of the Allies.

"You speak French, *mon Capitaine?*" asked Madeleine.

"*Mais oui, madame,* a little."

I told them how in 1916 my mother had joined my father in France, bringing my sister Debbie and me to live there.

"But the war?" Jean asked.

"Well, yes; but father commanded the British Engineers in Cherbourg and made his own orders. The Boches were a long way off, we had Irish passports, and father had a navy friend—captain of a destroyer—to fetch us from Dublin. We also lived in Bayeux and in Arromanches for a while, too."

"Then we are truly ancient neighbors?" burst out Jean enthusiastically. "Another toast, please, to our *vieux ami!*"

There is more heartfelt joy in a mutual celebration of deliverance from an evil foe than in a self-congratulatory orgy for the success of deliberate aggression. I hope so. Our unabashed expression of gratitude for a new-found safety was a subconscious grace we offered; two French people joined two from America—the New World—and one from old England, all descended at some remove from the Norman natives. We bellowed our national anthems raucously and with verve. As we sang the Marseillaise, the most moving of them all we empathized fully with the last line, "What an impure blood befouls our furrows." It was singularly appropriate.

The lack of a serious hangover the next morning bespoke the excellent quality of the apply brandy that we had lowered in such quantity the night before.

While the facts were fresh in our minds and the records still at first hand, I tried to help Carl pull his report together on the field effectiveness of the five-inch HVAR rocket in the close support role. We concluded that this weapon was truly formidable and eminently ready for war.

The squadron was to fly thirty-four more missions on the second day of the breakthrough. In those two days, twelve tanks were destroyed, thirteen more hit (one left on fire), and a number of trucks and armored cars wiped out. Nor were pillboxes and flak towers ignored. A few pilots complained that suitable targets were lacking in the later phases.

Coming just round the corner was the complete triumph of the rocket. The RAF Typhoons, piloted mostly by junior officers and sergeant-pilots, chopped up the bulk of the panzer force trapped in a huge pocket at Falaise. They were gallantly supported from the south by No. 513 Squadron, that I was about to leave. At that time it was the only P-47 squadron equipped with any rockets at all. Allied rocketeers had a field day, but casualties were heavy on all sides.

The aircraft rocket weapon, born on 25 October 1941, came into its own in Normandy.

In a letter dated 30 August 1944, Lieutenant General Carl Spaatz, commanding general, United States Strategic Air Forces in Europe, graciously commended the mission that had enabled No. 513 Squadron to be equipped, trained and placed on operational duty in two and a half weeks. He stated that "the success of the equipment had resulted in a requirement from the Ninth Air Force to equip all of their P-47s with the Navy rockets."

We packed our grips and piled into the small Cessna UC-78 that Gross had for communications. We also put in the back the brown paper bag containing six nicely ripened Camembert cheeses that Madeleine had pressed on us in the very early morning as we left their farm. They were definitely ready to eat.

It was getting hotter all the time in the little cockpit under the Plexiglas canopy. It was like being in a little greenhouse as we hopped over to Strip 13 at Bayeux, where Gross had business. By mid afternoon when we took off for the last time and headed north across the Channel, it was becoming a serious toss-up whether we could stand the atmosphere of the cheeses or if they would have to be tossed overboard.

The voting was uneven since Carl and I were the owners of

the treasures. Gross then threw the vote our way saying we were his guests and he couldn't be churlish; so we kept the smelly little things, but we opened the clear view panels as wide as possible. "Only an hour to go," said Gross, bravely, between his teeth.

On the ground at Ashford everything looked ghostly and deserted. We tried to persuade Gross to stay and have a final wee party with us, but he declined. "Got to get back to my chickens," he said, locking the canopy. So we waved him au revoir.

In the morning Carl called the American Embassy to find out where Charlie had got to. "Dr. Lauritsen is not in the country," said the secretary in the scientific office. "No," she added, "I'm sorry I'm not at liberty to say over the phone where he is." When we arrived in London, we found that Charlie had gone off to some remote spot in Scandinavia to inspect the remains of an errant V-2 he'd got wind of.

Carl and I were invited to a high-level scientific meeting at the Ministry of Aircraft Production to discuss that very subject. Every man and his dog was there who had anything to do with rocketry or newfangled weaponry. Though some still wondered if such weapons were operationally feasible, it was really a question of economics. But it didn't matter because the unbalanced German leader was guided by a different logic. the Allies would clearly overrun the V-1 launching areas before long; the second *vergeltung* (retaliation) weapon—the V-2—would now come into action and hang the cost. There was no active defense against a long-range rocket we knew of. They must be attacked at the source—the factory or the launchers.

In late Autumn the Nazis produced a revolutionary day fighter propelled by a liquid-fuel rocket to attack the B-17 formations.[2] The Me 163b-1 (*Komet*) had two 30 mm cannon with sixty rounds per gun. Fortunately its range was so limited it could only be used to defend specific targets, but for this task it was murderous. Major Späte had a test group at Leipzig to

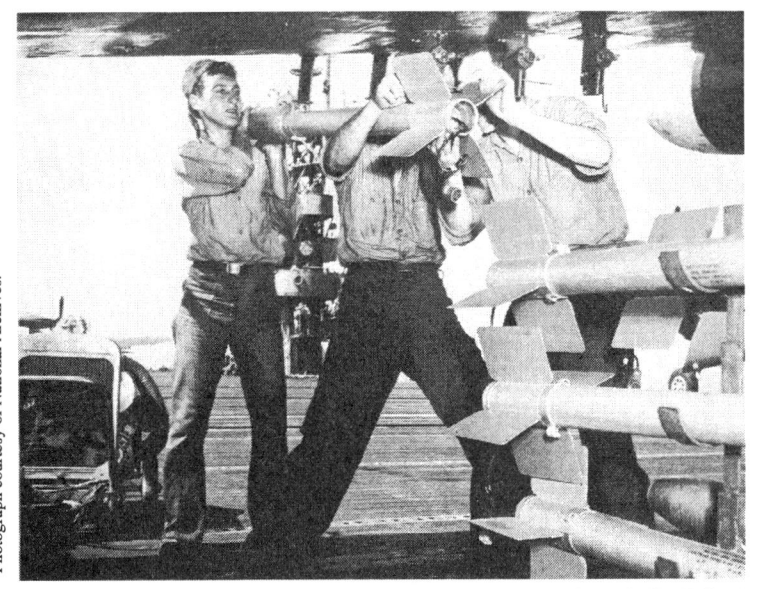

August 15, 1944—Mounting five-inch AR rockets on zero-length launchers of F6F (Hellcat) on carrier for invastion of southern France—Operation Dragoon. Photograph courtesy of National Archives.

1945—New five-inch High Velocity Aircraft Rocket (HVAR) mounted on B-25 bomber for close support of the Army or attack of shipping.

protect the Leuna synthetic fuel plants frequently under attack by the Eighth. On one occasion over Altenburg three bombers were destroyed by one Me 163B-1 in the same sortie.

GLOBAL UPDATE
August 1944

On 11 August, the Germans evacuate Florence, leaving the city undamaged.

The Allied invasion Dragoon—originally Anvil—of southern France between Cannes and Toulon starts on 15 August in two thrusts. Resistance is light and good progress is made.

The grand strategic plan calls for the British Second Army in Normandy to take a holding position south of Caen while the U.S. First Army breaks through at St. Lô and heads toward Paris. Gen. George Patton makes a second advance to seal off Brittany ports. Both Allied fronts now move forward—U.S. forces eastward, British and Canadian to the south. Hitler's armies advance west to cut First Army's communications from the beachhead, but the Allies trap a dozen divisions between 17 and 20 August in a pocket with a steadily closing mouth from Falaise to Argentan. Artillery and RAF rocket Typhoons annihilate eight divisions with the U.S. Ninth Air Force supporting from the south. The First Army reaches the Seine on 21 August intending to bypass Paris, but a resistance uprising brings in French troops to liberate the city on August 25. The Nazi commander surrenders to General Leclerc. General de Gaulle formally enters Paris the next day.

Rumania surrenders and joins the Allies on August 23.

We were having such a good time that it was almost as if Fate connived to help us stay in England a little longer. The C-54 bearing us back to Washington via Iceland struggled for hours through wretched weather and in the end we had to come back. Iceland was socked in solid. After waiting a suitable interval for the Atlantic to change its foul temper we tried again.

Carl departed for Pasadena as soon as we got in. My great gain was sharing the trip with such a superb person. Carl, one of God's great gentlemen, showed such humility, though he was indeed a Nobel superstar in the field of cosmic rays, and was a stalwart companion throughout an epic journey.

Eleven

"We've missed you," said Connie. "We really have, but I do hope you had a good time."

"Oh, come on," I demurred. "It's only been six weeks! Get all the chaps in along with some coffee, and let's have a powwow. It was a lively meeting. I gave them the highlights of the Rocket Mission. "A great exercise in cooperation between the U.S. Navy, the Air Corps, and the First Army, and to be sure, with the RAF," I added in summary.

Washington hadn't changed. How could I expect it to? It was still rush, rush, rush! I ran into Commander Campbell, RN, in the corridor. Dennis was on the staff at the commission, and we'd known each other for years. He was a colleague from the good old Boscombe days, and had been one of the early pilots to be on test flying duty for the aircraft being built for the Navy. We'd done a lot together on their armament. From his agile mind came the idea of expanding the inadequate size of aircraft carrier decks. "Why not add a small landing area swung off to the port side," he had asked, "and leave the forward area for normal takeoffs?" So simple, so obvious—after it had been thought of. Thus was born the canted deck that became standard on all new Allied carriers and many in retrofit.

I lay low for a couple of weeks, attending to my knitting in proper fashion. Then came the call of the siren yet again.

"It's Willy Fowler," purred the innocent voice of temptation, "A new naval chap, Chick Hayward, has arrived at Inyokern and is now in charge of development there. You must come over and meet him pronto. This is urgent. besides, we have a whole lot to tell you about your Uncle Tom's cousin."

"I'll be out there by 3 September, you old devil. You sure know my weak spot, don't you?"

By some good fortune I had a perfect excuse for going and did not have to invent one on the spur of the moment. It so happened that a certain Group Captain Rhys had to go out to the West Coast, and I myself still owed a visit to an electric gun-turret maker in St. Louis. Clearly, it was my job to be chauffeur.

On 1 September we were in St. Louis, and I called up the Emerson Electric Company to say we were safely down. "Just a moment for Mr. Symington," said the young lady answering the phone.

"Have you ever seen a baseball game? Because now's your chance. This is Stuart Symington speaking."

"Never had the pleasure," I said, "but I'd like to try."

"Get yourself a bite to eat; it's bit late to join us now. I'll be by for you in thirty minutes."

Rhys didn't want to come along, so I waited in the lobby for my host. Right on time in came a fellow, handsome as any film star, who bounded over and shook my fist. "I'm so glad to see you. Spreckles said you'd be calling in sometime. But you've left it far too long. By the way, bring your bags, we're expecting you to stay the night with us, if that's okay."

I was a bit overwhelmed by this turn of events but made a mental note to drop Spreckley a word of thanks when I got back. The air commodore was a senior armament expert who had made a number of special trips to the U.S. over the past few years. He was most able and a real charmer.

I got in the back of the car and was introduced to Stuart's wife, Eve, who was riding copilot with him in front. We drove rapidly to the ballpark and were ushered to a well-positioned box up behind the place where the batsman stood.

"How much do you know about baseball?" Eve wanted to know. "When Spreckles was with us we had such a job teaching him the game. He is such a dear. He said it was a bit like 'rounders' and nothing like cricket at all."

Bit by bit I began to get some idea of what it was all about. It was really quite exciting. When the batsman—man at bat, said Stuart—did manage to connect with the ball, I could watch it take off like a bullet, sailing away up into the stands to be seized by the lucky spectator it struck and hoarded away forever. We bought some popcorn and soon got into the Spirit of the St. Louis game.

The man at bat hit a longish ground ball, and all of a sudden everyone on the field seemed to be running about at the same time. A great cheer rose up followed by an even louder cry and then a perfectly deafening roar from every manjack in the stadium—except me. I hadn't seen exactly what happened, nor would I have understood. Everyone was standing, mostly on the seats, waving and yelling at the top of their lungs. I couldn't even get a word in edgewise.

"Fantastic!" Stuart shouted at me. "Did you see that? Did you get that?"

"Darling," interjected Eve, "of course he didn't. How would

Dixi know what a triple play was?"

That was the end of my baseball education—at the ballpark. Back home they went over the extraordinary event again and again. We retired soon afterward, as the night had stolen up on us too fast. It was quite late.

We made a quick but absorbing tour of the gun-turret plant, where even the workers' conversations with us were still mostly about last night's game. Rhys was sorry he hadn't joined us but he knew even less about baseball than I and would obviously have had no idea what a triple play was all about, poor guy.

We flew for ten hours that day. In view of my role as tour guide for Rhys, the cross-country trip needed careful planning. Visiting firemen must be suitably regaled. We were only a third of the way over this huge landmass when we left St. Louis. The little C-45 didn't have the legs to make the rest of the passage to the Coast in a day—well, not in the necessary comfort—so I figured three longish hops, each about three hours, the last one to be a real showstopper.

In the late afternoon our Beech lifted from the hot strip at Albuquerque, New Mexico, on the last leg. The light was already suffused with a delicate pink, making our flight over the Petrified Forest the more spectacular. Then came the Painted Desert and the Grand Canyon area. "If you won't accuse me of an awful pun," said Rhys, in some awe, "I'd say this is absolutely gorgeous!"

"Pun or no pun," I said, "I agree. It's unbelievable."

We flew along inside the magnificent chasm, just below rim level and were treated to a view that none of us will easily forget. I learned later that such flights were discouraged: forbidden may have been the word. I also heard about the pilot of a light twin-engined bomber who ran into one of the island buttes in the middle of the canyon. All on board were killed.

The last phase of my nefarious plot to overentertain had us spending the night at Las Vegas. Rhys was thereby introduced to a one-arm bandit that could only survive on a diet of solid silver dollars. The flight from Vegas to L.A. was late starting next day. The chauffeur and crew overslept after a rather late retirement. I dropped Rhys off at Burbank to go about his affairs and then jumped over to Alhambra, a small field hard by Caltech, much more convenient for the real purpose at hand.

I had dinner with Willy and Ardie Fowler at their house. There was, as usual, a great deal to say. "You go first, Willy," I begged. "You've heard most of my news from Carl, so do bring me up to date with your shenanigans."

"Okay. But first the bad news, and very bad news it is. We lost a pilot, Lieutenant Armitage, two weeks ago air-firing a Tiny Tim from an SB-2C. We'd fired three others successfully before, but on the second shot that day, he fired and just dived straight into the deck."

"What on earth?..."

"We're not quite sure yet," he said, "but it looks as though the huge blast from the igniter bent an elevator trim tab out of shape. It's a tragedy and a nasty setback. Tom Pollock fired the first one in the air two months ago, and more since. We didn't bargain for this." We moved from the table to more comfortable seats.

"We're going to fire a Tiny Tim on the ground in a day or two and try to pinpoint the trouble." He told me.

"I can't wait to see it, and to meeting Chick."

Much had occurred since my last visit, and the lab had made some excellent records of underwater rocket trajectories.[1] It was reassuring to note their research agreed with our early empirical observations. We went over the sorrows of Tiny Tim, the details of its lengthy ground trials, and the disaster in the air. It made for a gloomy discussion.

It goes without saying that we had a cookout later on. More profound thoughts and observations seem to be distilled from a juicy piece of steak or a rich hamburger than from any midday harangue at work; I know the drinks had nothing to do with it.

1944 to 1947—Capt. John Tucker Hayward, NOTS Experimental Officer.

Chick Hayward joined us. He was one after my own heart. Absolutely no nonsense, with a ready, open mind. Chick often seemed aware of a thought before it was spoken. I looked forward to time with him, as I always did with the rest of these delightful people.

They were ready for the Tiny Tim firing at Inyokern, so my crew chief and I flew the Beech across the now-familiar desert to Harvey field. Chick was waiting and Tom Pollock, too.

The rocket was pleasing to the eye, so nicely was it crafted, and I was enormously impressed. We stood back and held our breath. It departed with a satisfying roar that measured up well to the sheer size of the elegant brute. This was the first time I'd seen Tiny Tim in action and the test went off like clockwork. I voted Caltech another Oscar.

Chick drew me to one side. "I have a Corsair F-4U fitted with a local rocket sight. Dr. Babcock at Caltech dreamed it up. You ought to fly it tomorrow, and try it out with a few five-inch rockets. You've flown a Corsair before, I'm sure."

"No, tomorrow will be the first time if your offer still holds."

"You're on!" said the gallant commander, not batting an eyelid. "She's a pussycat." I appreciated his trust.

Chick showed me the taps on the Corsair in the morning. "Off you go," he said. And he was right—the aircraft was a sweetheart to fly and had no vice to beware of that I could detect.

The new sight was of some help but I didn't much like the "ladder reticule," which had rungs marked for different ranges to allow for the fall of the rockets. All well and good, but I still had to estimate range and then pick out the right "rung" to use. It would be too hard to use in battle, so we still needed a more automatic something.

I was forced to fly my desk in Washington for several weeks. The U.K. wanted reports, and arrangements had to be made for some upcoming visits.

A month after the Tiny Tim launch, Willy called. "Our

Corsair with the displaced launcher successfully gave birth in the air yesterday!" he said. "We think we have the blast problem licked!"

"Before you know it," I warned him, "your fledgling will be out of the nest and taking on those damned Japs!"

Chick Hayward confirmed it when we met in mid October at a fighter conference held at Patuxent Naval Test Center. It was a full week-long meeting of fighter aces from all the Allied Forces, and they had put together a collection of all fighter aircraft in service. Such a gathering of ace flyers and fighter aircraft of several nations must be unique in the annals of aerial dueling and will probably never be possible again.

I was glad to be able to gatecrash the show and also to meet Colonel Charles Lindbergh though I did not condone his pro-Nazi attitude earlier in the war. When I spoke to him at some length, he seemed mellowed and less sure of his one-time isolationism, for which he was vaguely apologetic. I liked him and admired him for the tribulations he had endured.

The pilots spoke of the special tactics they had developed in the many different theaters of conflict against the various nations who were our foes. The one pervasive message that came through at this very special congregation was a universal, deep love of flying. I'd always thought it might be a disease, but at the very least it can be an obsession. Perhaps a bit of each. Moreover, we would obviously never be cured.

Chick and I had a private competition to rack up the most new types of aircraft to add to our logbooks at the show. I got in a Bearcat F7F, a Mustang P-51D with a bubble canopy, a Harvard NH1 with new horizon instrumentation, and a Lightning P-38F with boosted ailerons. Unfortunately, we hadn't specified whether new variants of the same aircraft would count, and so we had to call the match a draw—a very close draw. Everyone who hadn't flown the Spitfire before fell in love with her. She was voted the belle of the ball.

GLOBAL UPDATE
August and September 1944

Wingate's Chindits (British) and Merrill's Marauders (U.S.) are waging quasi-guerrilla warfare in Burma, matching the jungle tactics of the enemy. These gallant but insufficient forces have had to wait until reinforcements came in under Admiral Lord Louis Mountbatten, who drives the invaders south to capture the key position of Myitkyina. He is now on the way to reopening the Burma Road and recapturing Rangoon.

The British First Army liberates Brussels on 3 September.

An armistice is declared on 4 September between Russia and Finland. The Soviets declare war on Bulgaria but sign an armistice four days later on 9 September.

On 8 September the first German V-2 rocket lands on London.

A deep Allied airborne strike is made on 17 September into the Netherlands.

Russia makes a penetrating move into Czechoslovakia from Poland on her successful advance against German panzers.

An important mission was due on our doorstep at the end of the month. From the ministry's letter, I gathered there would be five or six in the party, all specialists in incendiary bombs and chemical weapons.

Stan Curtis had drawn up a good timetable for the visit to cover meetings with their opposite numbers in Washington and include a prolonged trip to the Dugway Proving Ground in Utah. It would take several weeks to do everything they had in mind.

"I thought you'd like to fly them out to Dugway, yourself," said Stan, "It's a long way from Salt Lake City, the nearest commercial airport, and it might be better not to impose on Dugway to ferry them around."

"Nice work, Stan. Thanks a lot." He couldn't get away so I was left to shepherd the mission.

I was delighted to find the team was headed by Professor

George Finch, a member of the courageous third British expedition up Mt. Everest in 1924. George Mallory, the leader, and Andrew Irvine probably reached the summit; but they never came down again, and the mystery remains. George was later advisor to Sir Edmund Hillary on the first successful climb ever in 1953.

I felt particularly privileged to be leading Professor Finch around because it was he who taught me chemistry when I was an undergraduate. It was now my turn to be of service. Wg. Cmdrs. Mitchell and Howell, old RAF armament friends of mine, were there from the ministry and Doctor Wild and Mr. Elder, scientists at George's lab.

We piled into our C-45 at Bolling and struck out for the Wild West. November isn't the best time of year to cross the U.S.A. It's a large continent to begin with, the weather as different and individual as each state we crossed. By early winter the mountain ranges have grown tall with snow to add spice to a journey through them.

Outward bound from Topeka we crossed the eye-stretching plains of Kansas—as wide and as flat as an ocean with real waves rolling in the grass. "That's extraordinary," said George. "Look at those lines down there: every one of them running north and south—and east and west as well. Damn place is like an enormous chess board. What's it all about?"

"It goes back to the early days when land was given away to settlers in sections," I explained, every bit the new professor, basking under my minidegree in American history from Princeton, "A section is a square plot, a mile to a side—to this day. Over the years some have been combined to make larger tracts. The lines you see are roads running up and down and across. They're the edges of the old land holdings."

After a long, thrumming flight we approached the Continental Divide, looming in the dusk, and suddenly came upon Denver. The winking lights of the mile-high city were strangely at our level, and the runway seemed jacked up for our convenience, to save us having to let down to land. A choice place to bed down for the night, I thought. And it was, too. Denver is to be recommended for a good night's sleep. The air is crisp and clean, though a touch sparse.

As we trundled down the runway the next morning I wondered for a moment why our chariot was so slow in lifting off until I recalled we were already over five thousand feet up. Our eagle had lost some buoyancy. Like settlers before us, we chose to take the safety of a pass through the mountains at Cheyenne, and it was a relief to leave the jagged mountains behind as we came to Salt Lake City. We could now nose over into a long, fast power glide to perch finally on the desert floor at the army base, some seventy miles to the southwest.

GLOBAL UPDATE
October 1944

With the firing sites overrun, V-1s are launched spasmodically from twin-engine airplanes but to no useful purpose.

Abandoned by Russia, Polish Resistance forces in Warsaw surrender to the Nazis on 3 October after a heroic two-month struggle. Retribution is swift and barbaric.

General MacArthur's schedule for recapturing the Philippines is advanced two months. Landings are made on the east coast of Leyte with four divisions of the U.S. Sixth Army on 20 October. Vice Adm. Thomas Kinkaid's Seventh Fleet give direct support; the overall operation is covered by the massive Third Fleet under Adm. William Halsey. The huge naval force is the largest ever assembled and probably the last of such immensity. Potential loss of the Philippines presents a mortal blow to Japan. All that is left of her navy, ships and aircraft in harbors from Singapore to the Japanese Inland Sea, is brought into action. The Japanese use the last-ditch tactics of suicide and introduce special attack groups of Kamikaze pilots.

This becomes known as the battle for Leyte Gulf, the greatest sea fight of all time.[2] Japanese sea power is broken and the outcome of the war is clear.

After a late lunch we had a briefing on the program of trials for the next three days. So much was planned there didn't seem enough hours in a day, but the show went like clockwork. A lot of time was spent getting out to the observation points, making sure the area was clear, getting the bombing aircraft over on cue, and then going over to inspect the target damage when the fires were doused. I recalled how difficult it can be to stage such trials. Murphy's Law applies, I think.

After an extensive tour of most of the facilities, we had a limited demonstration of what could be expected from certain chemical weapons. Although the results were not new to the visitors, some of the measuring techniques were. Many of the Dugway people had already been to the U.K. and worked with their counterparts at Porton, our corresponding testing establishment, adjacent to Boscombe Down.

At this stage of the war, with the Germans in full retreat, there was serious concern that Hitler might, in a demonic panic, release poison gases or bacteriological agents against our advancing armies. The Germans did not hesitate to use gas at Ypres in 1915. Thus there was a surge of activity to bring chemical weapon research fully up to date and provide an adequate stockpile. More important was to have the best defense against such monstrous tools of war if needed. A beastly business.

The next stop for the team was a visit to the air weapons test center at Eglin AFB in Florida. We left the good people at Dugway and headed for Salt Lake City to refuel and file a flight plan. A cold front had passed through Dugway and was backed up on the Wasatch Range to the east of the city. We couldn't find the field under the fog, nor could I raise the control tower on the radio. Now what? I turned back over the lake and dropped to the surface. We were now acting more like a boat than a plane. Using the tallest landmarks sticking up through the white soup and the compass set to the bearing of the main runway, we headed in toward land. We could see ahead as long as we stayed at nought feet. Though there were no lights turned on at the airport and we were a bit off to the side when we crossed the threshold of the field, the runway was long enough to forgive the error. We had plenty of room without all my eminent charges having kittens on the spot.

The heavy cloud was raining on us as we taxied up to the tower. We went inside to report.

"I'm sorry, sir, but you can't land here. The field is closed," said the official behind the counter.

"You mean we should take off and go away?" asked a voice from some wag in our party behind me.

Of course, we did no such thing.

The weather wizards predicted that the fog and cloud cover would persist all day. "This front has enough energy, though, to be gone by the morning," said the chief tea-leaf reader.

We bussed into town for a hotel. It was fun to explore the place. The Tabernacle is a worthy monument to the early Mormons. It would have been good to hear the famous choir.

George Finch had taken to flying up in the second pilot's seat ever absorbed in the changing scene below. As we winged along a mountainous part of the trip, we crossed close to a snow-capped peak rearing abruptly before us. "Well," said the great climber as a lonely pine flashed by, seeming closer than it really was. "That's the fastest I've climbed a mountain in all my life and the easiest, too!" George is a remarkable person, with the spirit of the hills carved into his handsome face. Not a man of many words, but the few he uses are incisive and reflect deep vision. Later we flew over the phenomenal Painted Desert with its mile after mile of distorted terrain. He suddenly smiled and said more to himself than to me, "Yes, indeed, a veritable lunar landscape!" He put into words what we'd all be thinking.

Our last stop had been at Amarillo, and we left there late that blustery afternoon, heading east for Florida's Eglin AFB. We were dog-tired and fed up with running through a spate of bad weather. All we wanted to do was go to bed and Eglin was too far to fly without refueling. The pitch-dark night had already fallen as we passed north of Dallas. Up ahead and stretching right across our path we could see a line of severe thunderstorms revealed by continuous flashes of lightning.

I was worried. The weather reports we were picking up said the situation was getting worse. I decided we'd have to plop down somewhere and lay over for the night. While I was poring over the chart I felt Corporal Dedeere's hand on my arm. I lifted my earphone and leaned back into the gloom of the cabin so I could hear him. "Why don't we run down to the coast an' visit with my pa?" he suggest. "We've a farm near Beaumont, an' he'll be real glad to have us."

It was the first I'd known that we were so near his home, and it was typical of him not to have mentioned it. Nor did he say that he hadn't been home for a long time. He waited apparently, until it was of some help to us to say anything at all.

"Your father certainly doesn't want six strangers parked on him without warning," I protested.

"Nothing would please my ol' man more!" said Dedeere, and that was the end of that.

I called flight control on the radio. "This is Army 7162. Request change of flight plan to land Beaumont, Texas. ETA 2145 hours. Over."

"Army 7162. This is Sherman Radio. Affirmative. Over."

"Sherman Radio. Please have Beaumont call a Mr. Dedeere, that's D-E-D-E-E-R-E in local phone book and advise that his son with party of six—S-I-X—will arrive Beaumont 2145 to stay overnight. Over."

"Army 7162. Message received. Wilco. Have a pleasant trip. Out."

"Sherman. Many thanks. Out."

We banked and hurried south, skirting the storm. No longer threatening, the blinding flashes became a show put on for our amusement until at last we met the welcoming lights of the runway. We circled and with a sigh of relief made our landing.

Waiting for us was the genial, weather-beaten Farmer Dedeere and a neighbor, as tanned as he, each with a vintage car to drive us down to the farm. "Not too fancy," said the old man, "but they do go fine."

During the long drive toward the sea nothing was said of what awaited us. We tumbled out of the cars and crowded into the warm kitchen. There we found a dozen or more neighbors gathered from all around and a big table loaded with hams and chickens and cakes and beverages of all kinds.

They greeted us as though we had known them all our lives, and suddenly we weren't tired anymore. I cherish the warmth of that impromptu get-together. Soon we were all talking at once about everything under the sun and feasting in between.

It was the first time most of us had been in the U.S. This wonderful example of American hospitality was as true as the stories we'd heard. We were treated as if the party were being put on especially for us and began to feel less like visitors from Mars and more like true Texans.

Mr. Dedeere wanted to talk about his boy—was he doing a good job? He was then curious to know all about farming in England, assuming me to be an expert. What did we grow? What cattle were raised? Was it a good business? Did we have "critters in Washington" to bother an honest farmer?

When we got around to wild fowling, I felt on safer ground. "D'you want to see a real flight of geese?" he asked.

"Why, indeed I would," I replied.

"Okay. You be up at six tomorrow and we'll go. I bet you've never seen the likes of our dawn flight back in your country."

It was quite late by the time we were shown to our beds for the night. I shared a large, sweet-scented room with George. "What people!" he said as we turned out the light. "What incredibly kind people."

Six o'clock came round all too soon, but we had a date and a challenge to meet. Reluctantly George and I dragged ourselves out of bed. I'd told him about the Texan's claim, and he was eager to see the spectacle.

Half asleep, we stumbled down the stairs into the warm kitchen it seemed we had just left. "Well I'm blowed!" said George, ahead of me, and I echoed his sentiments as I, too, came into the room. Farmer Dedeere and his wife had spent the night on two thin mattresses laid on the hard floor in front of the fire. It was their own comfortable room they gave to George and me. "Is there nothing you nice people won't do for us?" asked George. They looked away, as though they hadn't heard him. We couldn't help feeling a little embarrassed.

Mr. Dedeere was almost dressed, so we slipped out into the cold of the predawn to wait for him. A faint light tinged the sky to the east, but we could scarcely see as we picked our way across a stubble field and climbed a small rise.

"This'll be a fine spot," whispered the farmer. "Now keep real quiet."

We paused in the shelter of a clump of bushes big enough to afford us cover. We didn't have long to wait.

"There!" he cried, pointing an arthritic finger out across the flats. "Just look!"

And as the stars paled and dawn stole up from the sea, a solid dark line detached itself from the barely discerned horizon and rose with the light. We could see fairly well now across the marshy land. The line thickened as it came nearer until suddenly it was upon us. We could now pick out individual birds by the hundreds. The noise of their flight was uncanny in its loudness. They passed over our heads, no more than fifty feet up, and were rapidly away. An amazing sight, not just to quicken the pulse of the hunter—or ex-poacher to be sure—but to fill him with certain awe. I have never seen, before or since, so many wildfowl in the air at the same time.

We got back to find everyone collected in the kitchen, sorry that they missed the extraordinary sight.

A cheery breakfast certainly dispelled any notion that Englishmen are grumpy at that hour and must take refuge behind a newspaper.

As we rose into the still, cool air of the early morning, we looked down upon the lingering mist nestling among the folded hills like memories caught in the convolutions of the mind. Whenever I see those shredded wisps of night against the dawn, remembrance of that brief encounter comes vividly to life. I savor again the moving, spontaneous demonstration of kindness to strangers who quite literally dropped in from the sky.

We were a subdued group as we winged our way eastward. I think the unexpected, wonderfully relaxed visit to a remote farm on the Gulf of Mexico lifted these scientists briefly from a pervasive gloom connected with the deadly hunt they were on. They had one of the foulest tasks any human could be asked to do: they must bend all thought to finding measures against attack by poisonous gas, plague, and incendiary burnings worse than at the stake. Turning from the farmer's uncomplicated routine of producing the earthy means of life, they must face again their agonizing search for defense from the noxious means of death. There was no escape from the task of cleansing the Augean stables—until our inhuman enemies and their putrid regime had been totally flushed away.

GLOBAL UPDATE
November 1944

Russia renounces her neutrality pact with Japan on 6 November.

Franklin D. Roosevelt is elected for a fourth term as president of the U.S.

The German battleship *Tirpitz* lies damaged in Tromsö Fjord. The RAF sends out twenty-nine Lancasters of No. 617 Squadron each with a twelve-thousand-pound Tallboy armor-piercing bomb and obtain three direct hits. The mighty ship turns turtle at her moorings with the loss of nineteen hundred of her crew. Only one bomber was lost. The air crew survived.

Preparatory to an Allied invasion of Japan, very heavy air bombardment is started by massive daylight raids of B-29 heavy bombers from Saipan, a distance of fifteen hundred miles away.

The chiefs in the chemical warfare and incendiary bomb business wanted a wind-up meeting with the Finch Mission on our return to Washington. The consensus was that the sub rosa branch of the armament department of dirty tricks was in good shape—effective, up-to-date, and with ample reserves of operational stores. George took the moment to firm up a return match in the U.K. for the coming year.

It was reassuring to find the sensitive field of chemical weapons was modern and active, but I sensed a general slacking-off in other areas of armament development. It was due, undoubtedly, to the rapid progress of the war toward defeat of the Axis forces in the European theater. The situation in the Pacific had turned about and was moving toward a final showdown with the Japanese. In reality major breakthroughs were coming to pass after five years of desperate struggle and all-out scientific development.

The jet engine was in production, making vastly greater air speeds possible. In July of 1944, the RAF got their first operational jet fighter, the Gloster Meteor, and used it against the V-1 buzz bomb with great success. The Luftwaffe had the Meserschmitt Me 262 twin jet in service only one month after the Meteor.

Bombs now weighed twelve thousand pounds or more, each, able to pierce twenty feet of concrete or sixty feet of earth.

Airborne radar permitted navigation and the aiming of guns and bombs in the dark and under all weather conditions. Thus, our air forces could be operational round-the-clock without let or hindrance.

Forward-firing rockets transformed air force tactics for close army support and for maritime use against ships and U-boats no deeper than periscope depth. The Germans had beaten us to the draw with small air-to-air rockets and were using them in salvos of twenty-four against U.S. daylight bombers. Soon they would have massive, long-range guided rockets for bombardment.

Only in these areas did the new-discovery effort remain at fever pitch. Development teams, sensing that the end was in sight, rushed to procure wartime funds that would soon dry up but were readily available for the nonce. Important new R & D could still command substantial support.

The Ministry of Aircraft Production decided to send Gp. Capt. John Baker-Carr, head of the rocket development branch to take stock of rocket R & D in the U.S.—firsthand. I called Willy Fowler with the news.

"We'll be delighted to see your guys over here," he said, "anytime, as long as they can play liar's dice."

"Okay, Willy. Many thanks." I answered. "We'll come commercial. I don't fancy this winter weather on our private airline. One of our planes is in dock, anyway."

"Chicken!" said Willy, with three thousand miles of safety net between us.

"No comment! We'll be there 25 November." I replied.

Baker-Carr, his aide, and I slept our way across by air and duly arrived at the L.A. International Airport on Saturday afternoon. We were immediately, mercilessly, and royally regaled by the joyous Caltech fellows until in exhaustion, we cried uncle and retired to our inn.

I got the impression that B-C fresh from war-deprived Britain, thought it all a bit much; but we did have a wonderful time that weekend and even got some useful work done between sips.

Chick Hayward blew in as we sat down for our first formal conference in Pasadena. "When are you coming over to

Inyokern?" he asked me. "We've a special present for you."

"What is it?" I wanted to know.

"You'll have to come and find out. We don't want you flying back without seeing it."

"Fat chance!" I said, "How about tomorrow?"

"You're on, Dix. Tom'll send a C-45 to pick you up."

Chick met us as the shuttle swung neatly around in front of the Inyokern flight offices. "Day's half gone," he grumbled, looking pointedly at his watch. "We've a lot to see, guys. Tom'll look after you, Dixi. Come on, let's go."

Tom took me over to a Corsair F4U sitting docilely on the apron and said, "Here's your present. You're sure you want to do this thing, now...oh, all right then! Go shoot that Tiny Tim at Strip L. And four or our new high-velocity rockets are on board as well."

"I bet Willy put Chick up to this," I suggested.

As we reached the fighter, I could see the huge thousand-

1944—"Tiny Tim" mounted on displacement launcher on Vought Corsair F4U ready for air firing.

pound rocket mounted between the wheels, up against the fuselage.

"The big baby is on a displacement launcher," Tom explained. "When you press the tit, the launcher will swing down and lower the rocket well away from the ship. As it reaches the bottom, it'll fire automatically. It's all over very quickly. You won't feel any trim change at all. But don't forget to bring this babe in tail up or she'll bite you! Good luck!"

I sensed no difference in takeoff; the Corsair managed the load with ease. I climbed to make a thirty-degree dive attack from a thousand yards, made one dummy attack, and then came in to fire. "Steady as she goes," I said to the Corsair, and let fly.

Tiny Tim made a noise for sure; I was surprised how little I heard, but the volcanic exhaust was most impressive. The shiny, sparkling torpedo seemed to hang a moment for admiration, as a thoroughbred is apt to do before a race, and then took off with a rearward kick as though the whip had fallen. It sped away with great acceleration to become a waning, pulsing sun. It was so huge I could follow it with ease all the way to the ground.

"How was it," Chick wanted to know, punching my arm in excitement, "eh?"

"You've just given me a Christmas present to beat all presents, old boy!" I told him, equally excited. "It was the greatest thrill of my life. Thanks a million!"

Tom had an F6F ready with eight five-inch rockets and a new Babcock sight fitted. "Fire them in pairs—all in one pass," he advised. "At ranges of three thousand yards down to one thousand. We'll keep score. Under fifty points and you pay the gas." The sight worked. Progressive allowances over the range markers were easy to make. Good progress, I thought, particularly since I didn't have to pay for the gas.

Chick flew us to L.A. International to connect with American Airlines and get rid of us.

"I wish we had your resources," said B-C as we said goodbye to this super guy.

"We're all in this thing together," was his simple reply.

1944—The NOTS-Caltech team. From left: Cmdr J. O. Richmond, Dr. C. C. Lauritsen, Capt S. E. Burroughs Jr., Cmdr J. T. Hayward, Dr. W. A. Fowler, and Dr. E. L. Ellis.

• • •

The year began to run away with itself and suddenly was gone. "Get Mr. McLellan on the phone, please, Connie. I must answer his call."

Steve came on the line. "We have your rocket sight finished and mounted in a Hellcat F6F—a gift from the Navy. When can you try it out?"

In mid-February the Washington weather is always mixed up. I couldn't possibly fly up to Long Island in that stuff. I took a train and changed in New York for Glen Cove.

Not only had Monsieur Alkan designed a sweetheart of a rocket sight, but he had also developed a cunning method of measuring the illusive angle of attack of the aircraft in flight.[3]

"Only one word can I use, Monsieur," I said. *Élégant!*" He gave me a Gallic bow and a happy grin.

The navy fighter was parked at Roosevelt Field. From there I made a number of flights to test it, and the Coast Guard was good enough not to report my low passes over the shore at the end of the dives. It was a neat device and deserved complete approval. With a preset range it was a real help for gravity drop. It would be interesting to see how much it improved accuracy with angle of attack fed in all the time.

Steve was pleased. "Now I'll call the bureau. They wanted to know when we'd be ready. They plan to have it flown to a carrier and delivered to the Royal Navy. The sight has been funded under some lend-lease subsection and rightfully belongs to you guys."

"Now I call that downright gentlemanly," I said. "I hope you kept a copy."

"Matter of fact," admitted Steve, "we're producing it already."

I got back to Washington to learn that my term at the British Air Commission was over, and I was to return home, forthwith.

London greeted me with more warmth than I really wanted and certainly more than I felt I deserved. Military Air Transport Service (MATS) dropped me off at the U.S. base at Bovingdon on 1 March. I borrowed a staff car and set off to report to the Air House. It was a Monday, when they say it always rains in England. Something to do with National Washing Day, probably. As we sloshed down Park Lane, wipers in high gear, there was an incredible, deafening blast, like a heavy bomb.

"What the hell was that?" I asked the driver.

"Probably a V-2, sir," he replied with studied nonchalance, "We've had quite a few drop in lately without so much as by-your-leave."

I'd heard these infernal machines of war were operational and being aimed at London. That widespread target forgave aiming errors, and the nature of the beast could ignore London's Monday weather. We stopped and looked around but could see nothing. That V-2 I found out later had almost landed on Marble Arch. It was a close call and a rotten sort of welcome.

After a quick visit home I returned to London Town to take up my new assignment. Baker-Carr and I swapped jobs. It was time he had a breath of fresh air away from our drab HQ and we made a simple direct swap. He left to be chief of armament development in the British Air Commission in Washington, and I became head of the Rocket Development Branch, Ministry of Aircraft Production, London. In a way it was full circle. After five years of intensive gun and rocket test flying in England and another year of development work in the U.S., I was now given—with Draconian justice—the job of organizing the development program for the child that I had reared from a newborn babe and which had shown such promise of a brilliant future.

Before he left, I went over the list of projects underway with Baker-Carr and became thoroughly familiar with the work in hand. I found that most of the projects on the rocket branch list at that time involved modifications to existing equipment or the adaptation of other weaponry for rocket propulsion. There was nothing very new, but I could understand that. It was bleak in England, just then.

I was much chagrined to find that the area of guided rockets I had started work on, initially to remove gravity drop, had been taken away from our branch and was now being handled by a brand-new separate group called the Guided Weapons Branch. It meant that I could no longer play with any steering mechanisms or control features on our rockets: we were limited to the field of unguided rockets. It was a bitter pill.

I got the boys together. Squadron Leader Clem Naylor was my senior aide and had been with the branch from its inception early in the war. He knew the business backward and all about the covert politics involved.

"Clem," I said, "I'd like to go over everything in hand to weed out any that can't blossom soon or look like duds. We'll start up new projects that will show real breakthroughs in the near future."

"We're going to run out of war before long," I went on. "Then it'll be hard to justify efforts that are only palliative. Let's go away and have a good look-see and meet again in seven days."

For my own part, I had a damn good think. It was a chance to review everything since the rocket took flight from a Hurricane in October 1941 and try and cut the cackle for the future. I brooded on the successful flights of the thousand-pound rockets in California. Firing Tiny Tim rounded out my test flying. Nothing could top that. I visited a Tempest squadron at Tangmere to try out our latest gyro gunsight, now modified for firing rockets. It did a fantastic job, and I thought it to be the best all-round sight for rocket aiming I'd used.

When we gathered again in my office, we pooled our ideas. Clem was all for better servicing of rocket weaponry in the field, including aircraft installations. Flt. Lt. Ambrose Eyre agreed but also wanted to see more effective warheads. Bachellier thought higher velocities would pay off more than anything else. The boys had done their work well and we drew up a fine new list.

We cleaned out our closet and filled it with different things which soon, such being the nature of things, would become tomorrow's rubbish and in turn be dumped.

It was with great joy that I heard from Lew Motley again. "Dix," came the long-silent voice on the phone, "The Farnborough boffins have at long last finished my 60 mm spin-stabilized rocket installation. It's mounted on a Mustang and ready to go. It has an automatic feed and is right down your alley."

Being the first to test-fly this new rocket and launcher at the Projectile Development Establishment in Wales on 7 June 1945 was a fitting swan song for me. The rockets came out of the spout flawlessly at four hundred rounds per minute, and sped down the range with uncanny accuracy. Future tests for some time to

April to June 1945—3.5-inch and 5-inch AR forward-firing rockets were used extensively by Marine Corps combat aircraft against Japanese strongholds on Okinawa.

1945—Marine F4U fighter fires salvo of five-inch AR rockets at machine gun stronghold on Okinawa.

come would be pedestrian by comparison. We now had the missing piece in a proper program. At last we had an air-to-air rocket to complete the range of unguided rocket weapons in our quiver.

Bells must have been ringing in the spinner rocket bailiwick because not too long afterward came also wonderful news from my good friends in Pasadena, California. Their second generation naval barrage 5-inch High Velocity Spinner Rocket (HVSR)[4] spawned from the prototype 4.5-inch version—first used in the Torch invasion of North Africa in November 1942—had racked up a new achievement to add to its many glories.

An intrepid U.S. Navy commander, Eugene Fluckey, one of the most daring and successful submariners of all time, was on his way home from his long final patrol in the southern Okhotsk Sea north of Hokkaido, commanding USS *Barb*. He had scrounged a twelve-round five-inch spin rocket launcher to mount on his fo'c'sle and as many rounds as he could lay his hands on—seventy-two in all. Adm. Lockwood, Commander Submarines Pacific, had signaled him to raise a rumpus, a trait for which Fluckey was well known, in that arena, to confuse the enemy and draw antisubmarine attention away from the narrow La Perouse Strait. The Strait was needed for safe passage of the nine submarines of three U.S. wolf packs returning to Guam from the Sea of Japan.

Gene Fluckey was the first and only person to fire rockets, or ballistic missiles as he more properly called them, from a submarine in World War II. In the early morning of 22 June 1945 he launched the first salvo of twelve HE rockets on Shari, a mining and lumber town on the north coast of Hokkaido. Great havoc and rapidly spreading fires lured three Jap hunter/killer frigates and an ASW group of planes away from the important Strait and gave a very plausible impression of strong U.S. forces in the area, hinting at new U.S. air attacks as well. This served Admiral Halsey's strike-force purpose admirably for his attacks on eastern Japan.

On 3 July 1945 *Barb* launched twelve rockets after midnight at the Shikuka Air Base destroying many buildings. The Japanese reported that five U.S. warships had attacked the base and that the defense strategy in the region should be reoriented urgently from anti-Russian to anti-U.S.A.

Shortly after, at midnight on July 25, *Barb* launched three full loads of ballistic missiles on Shiritori, an important industrial town in Patience Bay on the east coast of the large island north of Hokkaido. The raid produced immense damage to the Oji Paper Factory—the largest in Japan—and other factories, and left a raging inferno three miles long. A final "Rockets away!" later that night on Kashiho—forty miles south—spread the largesse and denied any favoritism. The islanders and Tokyo brass were now sure invasion was nigh, particularly since *Barb* had landed a party some fifty miles south of Kashiho two nights earlier and blown up a long military train and locomotive, with one hundred and fifty-two soldiers killed.

This whole escapade was so much in the glorious spirit of Sir Francis Drake in the days of Elizabeth I of England. It was a very apt last hurrah, too, for the prodigious efforts of the merry men of Pasadena—Caltech's superlative rocket team.

Two days after *Barb*'s fantastic patrol was over and she had tied up at Midway, the first atom bomb was dropped on Japan and the second one shortly after. It was all over.

Though the war was now certainly finished I hoped and prayed this did not mean that the heartwarming and vital friendship between our two nations was all over as well. This dreadful war had brought the American and the British to a new and deep understanding of mutual aims and interests. We held between us the key to eventual global peace. A peace on earth?

At first I thought the crested, engraved note waiting on my desk was an invitation to a cocktail party at the American Embassy but it wasn't. It was a formal letter from my friend

Colonel John Ackerman, Assistant U.S. Military Air Attaché, asking me if I could attend a presentation ceremony at his embassy.

"What's it all about?" I asked John, when I called him after sending my acceptance.

"We have a little medal for you, Dixi. And afterward we can raise a glass of bubbly together to celebrate the happy occasion!"

At the ceremony, I was greatly honored to receive the United States Legion of Merit, Degree of Officer, together with a glowing citations signed by President Harry Truman, himself.

It more than made my day. It went a long way toward making my war.

July 26, 1950—Fighter Command Conference at West Raynham. Conferees move out to observe twin-jet METEOR fighters.

July 26, 1950—Fighter Command Conference. METEOR fighter display. Left to right: Gp Capt H. W. Dean, A.F.C., Mr. Pepe Burrell, DeHavilland, Air Cdre H. V. Satterley, C.B., C.B.E., D.F.C., and Gp Capt E. E. Vielle, O.B.E.

Epilogue

I left the development of unguided rockets to attend the RAF Staff College at Bracknell, in the countryside west of London. It was a breath of fresh air and a whiff of elegant military education. Then back to the metropolis to sit for a couple of years on the bench of the august armament law court—the Ordnance Board. An imposing experience, where I enjoyed the screen of anonymous power—hid by the proceedings we issued—legislating for the performance and safety of air armament.

On 2 September 1948, I was posted to the branch of the Air Staff responsible for deciding the armament requirements for the RAF, looking ahead at least five years. Irony of ironies, I found the first line of air defense of the British Isles had been reposed, for some time, in a guided weapon system while manned fighters had been consigned to a back burner.

Even with my firm belief that the guided rocket would be the future weaponry of the RAF, I could never have supported this dangerous and fallacious policy at this time. It was premature in the extreme. Fortunately, wiser minds had now prevailed and the priorities of the two systems had recently been reversed.

As happened so many times before Hawkers were ready for this return to sanity. A new Air Ministry spec was written (F 3/48) around Hawkers completed plans for an advanced manned fighter: P 1067. Three prototypes were ordered in June 1948 and she was christened Hunter.

My job was to consolidate the armanent installation. We had a new 30 mm Aden cannon ready, designed at Fort Halstead, to replace the Hispano 20 mm in service since 1940. We were able to mount four in the nose of the jet. I'd always wanted to put all the cannon in a removable box—already synchronized with the gun sight—so that rapid rearmament could be affected. I was able to persuade my friends at Hawkers to try this idea.

This elegant fighter was one of the subjects of discussion at a Fighter Command operational conference in 1950 and the continued use of the manned fighter was widely supported.

The first prototype made its maiden flight at Boscombe in July 1951, and proved to be an immediate, outstanding success. Propelled by a single Rolls-Royce Avon jet engine with 10,000 pounds thrust, it had a speed of Mach 0.95 at thirty thousand feet or 716 miles per hour at sea level. It climbed to 45,000 feet in seven and a half minutes. The detachable gun-pack, together with a one-point refuelling system, made it possible to reduce the turn round time between sorties to only seven minutes.

The Hunter, like her predecessors from the Hawker stable of thoroughbreds, was a thing of rare beauty. She proved her true worth to the RAF for more than five years, over Europe and in the Middle East.

Naturally we kept the guided missle on the books—I still had faith, even though later on these things were sometimes referred to as misguided fissiles, with some truth to the insult. But that seems to be life.

Notes

CHAPTER 1 NOTES

1. This quotation gives the general gist of the conclusion of the Prime Minister's announcement and may not be exactly verbatim.

2. Bristol BLENHEIM, No. L 1495. Two Bristol Pegasus engines. Medium bomber. Speed: Max. 240 mph at 12,000 ft. Cruise 180 mph. Bombs: 1,000 lb. over 1,460 mi. Crew: Three. Defense: one Vickers "K" Drum-fed machine gun in mid-upper power turret and one fwd-firing fixed Browning gun; both .303 caliber.

3. R.F.D. Guilford's DAGLING Primary. Flying speed about 15 mph. Stall—or mush—at 8 to 10 mph. We tried streamlined fairings around our lightest pilot who then floated back and forth along the

ridge of the hill until we had to threaten murder most foul if he did not land back on the hilltop—*now!*

4. Avro Aviation Company. AVIAN. Cirrus engine, single bank, in-line. HP: 60. Empty weight about 700 lbs.

5. de Havilland TIGER MOTH (DH. 82). Developed from the most successful GYPSY MOTH (DH. 60). De H Gypsy Major engine, HP: 130. Two seater.

6. Armstrong Whitworth ATLAS. Bristol Jupiter engine. Army Co-op duties and light day bomber.

7. Hawker FURY. Rolls-Royce Kestrel V engine. HP: 695 at take-off. Two Vickers .303-caliber guns in fuselage within reach of pilot.

8. British Vickers machine gun: .303 caliber. Rate of fire: 750 rnds/min. Muzzle velocity (MV): 2,000 ft/sec. Belt feed. Projectile weight: .344 oz.

9. U.S. Browning machine gun: originally .300 caliber, changed for U.K. ammo to .303 caliber. RPM: 1,200. MV: 2,400 ft/sec. Belt feed. Projectile weight: .344 oz.

10. Hawker HURRICANE prototype, No. K 5083. Rolls-Royce Merlin C. HP: 800. Two-blade, fixed-pitch wooden airscrew gave 315 mph (increased to 340 mph in service). Eight x .303 Browning guns.

11a. Bayrische Flugzeugwerke, Heinkel, Arado, and Focke-Wulf. First three had Rolls-Royce Kestrel V engines. HP: 695 at takeoff. Focke-Wulf had a Junkers Jumo 210 A. HP: 610 at takeoff.

11b. Bf 109 for Bayrische Flugzeugwerke. Later incorrectly and widely called Me 109 because Willy Messerschmitt was the chief designer. This text follow the more widely used Me 109.

12. Rhein Metall-Borg Mg 17 machine gun, 7.92 mm (.311 caliber) RPM: 1,100. MV: 2,450 ft/sec. Projectile weight: .45 oz.

13. Handley-Page HINAIDI heavy bombers. Twin Bristol Jupiter engines. With 99(B) Squadron at Upper Heyford, Oxfordshire. The plane got its name from the airfield the squadron occupied in Iraq

when we had the defense of that protectorate after WW I. The Hinaidi took off at 80 mph, climbed and cruised at the same speed. Defense: one Lewis machine gun .303 caliber, drum feed in the nose and one mounted mid-upper; all guns hand-held.

14. Handley-Page HEYFORD heavy bombers. Twin Rolls-Royce Kestrel engines. Named after the base we occupied at Upper Heyford. Crew: four. Bomb load: 2,500 lbs. in lower wing center section, 1,000 lbs. external. Defense: .303-caliber Lewis guns in nose and mid-upper positions and one gun in retractable rotating "dustbin" amidships; all guns hand-held.

15. Supermarine SPITFIRE prototype, No. K 5054. Merlin C engine. HP: about 800. Two-blade, fixed-pitch wooden airscrew gave initial speed of 350 mph (improved to over 400 mph in service).

16. Hispano-Suiza 20 mm cannon. RPM: 700. MV: 2,100 ft/sec. Initially spring-loaded drum feed with 19 rounds. Projectile weight: 4.82 oz. (HE), 6.03 oz. (AP) or solid steel.

17. Vickers WELLINGTON heavy bomber. Initially two Pegasus engines. HP: 1,000 ea. Initial turrets were hand-operated mounts held between two louvered, sliding metal curtains, nose and tail.

18. JUNKERS Ju 87 (Sturzkampfflugzeug—"Stuka"). Inspired by U.S. Curtis F8C HELLDIVER. Single engine, single seat. Speed: 232 mph. Bombs: 1,100 lbs. over 200 mi. Very specialized vertical dive-bomber with dive brakes, fixed spatted undercarriage and screaming sirens.

19. Swiss Oerlikon MG FF 20 mm cannon. Developed from an ack-ack weapon, lightened, made smaller, given a higher RPM: 520. MV: 1,800 ft/sec. Ammo: 60 rnds/gun. Projectile weight: 4.82 oz. Suffered severe teething troubles, vibrating and seizing up after only a few rounds. It took many months to solve the problems. The Me109C had the two central synchronized guns and one more small caliber guns in each wing.

CHAPTER 2 NOTES

1. Hawker HART, No. K 2968. Rolls-Royce Kestrel engine. HP: 695

at takeoff. Two-seat light day bomber. Rear defense: one Vickers K gun, .303 caliber drum fed.

2. Hawker HURRICANE IIB. No. L 1574. Rolls-Royce Merlin II engine. HP: 1,000. Speed: 325 mph. Eight x .303 Browning guns.

3. The RAF used the same ammo as the British army rifle. The propellant was cordite or nitroglycerin, although almost all other armies had converted to nitrocellulose. Cordite is more stable in tropical conditions but is apt to detonate in a hot breech. The Browning breech in the American version was closed between bursts. It had to be held open for use in RAF planes because of the long bursts in aerial combat and very high rate of fire. The caliber was increased from .300 (U.S.) to .303 British Army/RAF rounds.

4. Hawker HURRICANE IIB. No. L 1695. Very early production model fitted with new ammo boxes designed by James Martin, chief designer and general manager of Martin-Baker Aircraft Co. In the first models ammo boxes lay along the length of the wings, at right angles to the guns so that the belts fed straight out into the guns. Fore and aft wing ribs severely limited the box size. The M-B boxes were parallel to the guns, giving a greatly increased ammo supply. The good flexibility of the flat ammo belt around the bullets permitted swan-necked feed chutes to curl the belts up and around into the breeches. Dru Drury worked out this clever technique with Jimmie Martin.

5. De Wilde .303-caliber ammo, a Belgian invention. Bought outright in early 1939. It had an explosive bullet, banned by the Hague Conference against personnel. On aircraft structures the prohibition did not apply. Design defects had to be corrected in secrecy before our tests. We found it satisfactory for service use, and we could still start production in time for the aerial duels to come. It proved to be the best we had in that caliber and contributed much to our later successes in air-to-air combat.

6. Intricate probability math included likely variables in a future dogfight: height, speeds, relative flight paths, "g" loads from steep turns and changes occurring. The calculations sought the "best chance of not missing"—a more subtle and fitting concept than the more obvious "best chance of hitting." They found the optimum size of a bullet hosepipe from all guns (cone of fire) for an inexperienced pilot should measure one degree—or a 30-foot diameter at a fighting range of one to two hundred yards. Only the "50% zone" of each gun,

where only half the bullets fall, was used because this area is practically constant. The 50 percent zone of the Browning gun is $^1/_3$ degree, i.e., $^1/_3$ of the desired hosepipe area. Thus the guns must be spread out by $^1/_3$ degree from the center to get the one degree coverage. The open pattern is achieved in practice by aligning the two inner guns (p4 and 5s, see below) dead on target. The other six are evenly spread around these two key guns with the 50% bullet zones just touching. The guns in the port wing are aligned on the corners of a vertical diamond and those of the starb'd wing on a similar diamond. The inner corners of the diamonds, p4 and 5s, are on the same spot (target center), as in the following diagram:

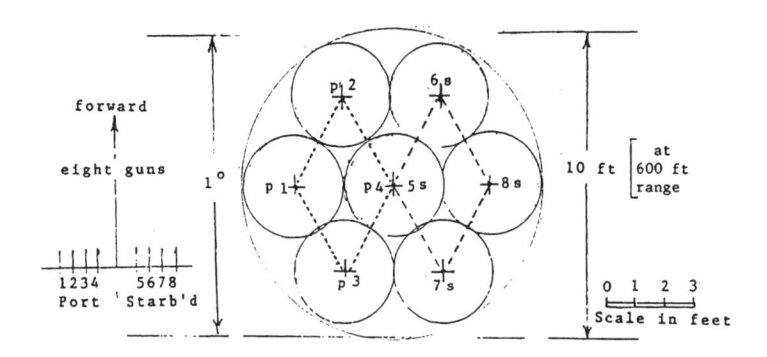

[Diagram: Eight-gun pattern showing circles arranged in diamond formation. Labels include "forward", "eight guns", "1234 Port", "5678 Starb'd", gun positions p1, p2, p3, p4, 5s, 6s, 7s, 8s, "1°", "10 ft", "at 600 ft range", and "Scale in feet 0 1 2 3".]

7. A routine gunnery training target (air-to-air towed banner) would be no good to record our group. There is not enough time to shoot at this moving target, with maximum crossing speed over the attacker's bows, needing constantly changing deflection of aim.

8. Blackburn ROC. No. L 3069. Perseus engine. Two-seat fighter with Boulton Paul electric turret with four .303 Browning guns.

9. Dr. Melvil Jones, Prof. of Aeronautical Science at Cambridge; Dr. R. Jones, Operational Research Lab; Sqn Ldrs Reggie Emson and Dru Drury; Fl Lt Dean.

10. A .303-caliber rifle was mounted vertically through the floor of a Blenheim bomber with a very high speed cinecamera aligned parallel and a searchlight pointing down as well. We flew level over the sea and fired one bullet at a time, the camera recording its point of

water impact. We did this at several altitudes and always under the calmest possible weather conditions, mostly at night.

11. Gloster GLADIATOR. No. K 6129. Bristol Mercury engine. Two Vickers .303-caliber guns in upper fuselage.

12. Fairey FANTÔME. Belgium. No. L 7045. Hispano-Suiza engine. A long, in-line Vee. No armament in this particular aircraft.

13. Barnes Wallis designed the R 100, one of a pair of huge, rigid airships built in the early 1930s to provide economic long-range transportation within the British Empire. The R 100 flew well across the Atlantic and back; but the sister ship, the R 101, government designed and built, crashed in France during a severe thunderstorm seven hours outbound on her maiden voyage to India. After the tragedy Britain canceled all further work with rigid airships.

14. Vickers WELLINGTON 1C (Wimpy). Medium-heavy bomber. Two Bristol Pegasus XVIII engines. HP: 1,000 each. Gross weight: 30,000 lbs. Speed: max. 235, cruise 165 mph at 12,000 feet. Bombs: 4,500 lbs. over 1,200 mi. 1,000 lbs. over 2,550 mi. Crew: six. Defense: two .303-caliber guns in front and rear turrets. Added later was a single free .303-caliber on each beam
Frazer-Nash turrets were driven by oil motors for rotation and elevation. Control was by small, close-placed "bicycle handlebars" to steer the turret for rotational control and by wrist twisting to move the guns in elevation. Fine control was achieved by throttling the oil flow through a keyhole slot, permitting only a slight flow at small handle movements and a much increased flow at larger movements. Ammo supply was mostly 1,000 rnds/gun.

15. Armstrong-Whitworth WHITLEY (Flying barn door). Heavy bomber. Early Marks had two Arm-Whit. Tiger engines. HP: 920. Defense: one free gun in nose, two in tail, all .303 caliber.
Whitley Mark V. Two Merlin X engines. Crew: five. Speed: Cruise 165, max. 202 mph. Bombs: 8,000 lbs. over 630 mi.; 3,500 lbs. over 950 mi. Defense: one .303 in nose; four .303 Browning power-operated Frazer-Nash rear turret with 1,000 rnds/gun.

16. HURRICANE No. L 1750 and SPITFIRE No. L1007. Within 10 days of each other Hawker and Supermarine sent test installations of one 20 mm Hispano-Suiza cannon mounted close under each wing. Each cannon had a coil-spring–operated drum of 19 rounds. MV: 2,400 ft/sec. Rate of fire: 700 rpm. Weight of projectile: 4.69 oz.

CHAPTER 3 NOTES

1. Hawker HURRICANE I. Merlin II engine. HP: 1,100. Speed: 325 mph at 17,500 ft. Range: 700 mi. at 200 mph. Ceiling: 36,000 ft. Climb to 20,000 ft. in nine mins. Eight x .303 Browning machine guns mounted in wings outside propeller disc. Early models had fixed-pitch airscrews and non-ejector exhausts, severely limiting their ceiling. Corrective modifications were started immediately.

2. Fairey BATTLE. Light bomber. One Merlin engine. HP: 1,050. Speed: 245 mph at 12,000 ft. Bomb load: 1,000 lbs. Crew: two. Defense: one hand-held Vickers K gun drum fed .303-caliber machine gun in a mid-upper mounting.

   Bristol BLENHEIM IV. Medium bomber. Two Bristol Mercury XV engines. HP: 920. Speed: max. 266 mph at 12,000 ft.; cruise 180 mph. Bombs: 1,000 lbs. over 1,460 mi. Crew: three. Defense: one Vickers K drum fed .303-caliber in upper power turret; one forward-firing fixed Browning .303 machine gun.

   Handley-Page HAMPDEN. Medium bomber. Two Bristol Pegasus XVIII engines. HP: 1,000. Ceiling: 20,000 ft. Speed: max. 243 mph; cruise 155 mph. Bombs: 4,000 lbs. over 1,200 mi. or 2,000 lbs. over 1,900 mi. Crew: four. Defense: single fixed and single free .303-caliber nose; single or twin free .303-caliber rear and mid-under positions.

3. Armstrong-Whitworth WHITLEY medium-heavy bomber. (See chap. 2, note 15.) Rear turret now with servo-ammo-feed.

   Vickers WELLINGTON IC (Wimpy). Heavy bomber. (See chap. 2, note 2.)

4. DORNIER Do 17 and Do 215, (flying pencil). Medium bombers. The oldest type and still about 300 operational. Two Jumo 211 engines. Bombs: 2,200 lbs.

   HEINKEL He 111. Medium bomber. Two Jumo 211 engines. Crew: three. Heavily armored. Heaviest bomb load: 4,400 lbs.

   JUNKERS Ju 88. Medium bomber. Two Jumo 211 engines. The best of the enemy bombers.

5. JUNKERS Ju 87, (Sturzkampfflugzeug-Stuka). Described in chap. 1, note 18.

6. The four-gun Frazer-Nash hydraulic power-operated rear turret became standard in all the heavies; 1,000 rounds per gun .303 Brownings.

7. A.W. WHITLEY, Mark V. (See chap. 2, note 15.)

8. The stern chase. Any attack except from directly astern or ahead requires an accurate estimate of the ever-changing amount to "lead" the target, i.e., aiming ahead along its flight line, as any skeet shooter will tell you. In an attack which starts on the beam of the bomber and is not limited to just a quick squirt but is pressed into close quarters, inevitably the attacking fighter gets "sucked" into a stern chase by the very speed of the crossing, fleeing bomber.

9. Shadow factory. Name given to the many skeleton aircraft factories set up at the beginning of the war, ready to pitch in without delay and build any design of aircraft needed in larger numbers or to undertake retroactive modifications.

10. Short and Harland, makers of superior flying boats for many years, made the STERLING III. Four 1,500 HP Bristol Hercules VI engines. Gross weight: 70,000 lbs. with armor. Crew: seven. Speed: cruise 200 mph; max. 270 mph. Bombs: 14,000 lbs. over 590 mi.; 2,010 lb. over 3,575 mi. Planned originally for 24 x 500-lb. bombs. Defense: two-gun nose and mid-upper, four-gun rear turrets; all .303 caliber.

11. Avro MANCHESTER. Two experimental Rolls-Royce Vulture II engines. HP: 1,760. Gross weight: 50,000 lbs. Crew: seven. Speed: cruise 185 mph; max. 258 mph. Bombs: 10,350 lbs. over 1,200 mi.; 8,100 lbs. over 1,630 mi. Defense: two-gun nose and mid-upper, four-gun tail; all .303 Brownings.

12. Handley-Page HALIFAX III. Four x Hercules XVI engines. HP: 1,500+ Gross weight: 65,000 lb. Crew: seven. Speed: cruise 225 mph; max. 277 mph. Bombs: 13,000 lbs. over 980 mi. 6,250 lbs. over 2,005 mi. Defense: two-gun nose, four-gun mid-upper and tail turrets; all .303 caliber.

13. Avro LANCASTER III. Four x Rolls-Royce Merlin 38 engines. HP: 1,300. Gross weight: 68,000 lbs. Crew: seven or eight with Pathfinders or with ventral turrets. Speed: cruise 216 mph; max. 266 mph. Bombs: 14,000 lbs. over 1,660 mi. Defense: two-gun nose and mid-

upper ventral, four-gun tail turrets, all .303 Brownings. The Lanc was the lightest of the four-engined heavies, yet it carried its bomb load over a greater distance than any of the others. Out of 15,000 heavies built during the war, over half were Lancs.

14. The company was called Power Jets, Ltd.

15. The official Air Ministry specification No. was E28/39.

16. de Havilland made a small single tailless day fighter, powered by a de Havilland jet engine. Fore and aft control problems of this advanced design could not be overcome before de Havilland's son, Geoffrey, the company test pilot was killed in the prototype. A twin-boom tail was added and solved the control problem.

17. BMW and Junkers both developed axial-flow turbojets, and in the autumn of 1938 the German Air Ministry asked Messerschmitt to design an airframe to be ready to accommodate the new engines. Design studies were ready by June 1939. A mock-up was ordered and approved 1 March 1940. Three prototypes with BMW 109-003A engines were ordered for the next summer, and though the first engine ran in 1940, it produced only 570 lbs. thrust instead of 1,500 lbs. as expected. The first Junkers Jumo model ran in late 1940 but had serious troubles. By mid 1941 BMW engines were up to 1,000 lbs. thrust, but two failed in flight test in November. Eight months later the Jumo 109-004 was ready with 1,850 lbs. thrust and was the first successful prototype to fly on jet power alone. It was called the Me 262 but had only minimal priority and did not go into production until early 1944 after Hitler had seen it fly. Even then he only authorized production as a bomber.

18. Westland Aircraft Co. WHIRLWIND. No L 6845. Two counter-rotating Rolls-Royce Peregrine engines. HP: 950 ea. Speed 450 mph. Four Hispano-Suisa 20 mm cannon at first with drum feed, 19 rnds/ gun; later with Mk I belt feed, 100 rnds/gun. W. E. W. Petter, designer of the Whirlwind, had incorporated many advanced ideas, not all entirely practical. For example, the engine throttle controls were hydraulically operated, but it was hard to keep them sealed under operational conditions, and engine synchronization could not be held. Much later, he went on to design some superlative aircraft, notably the English Electric Canberra medium bomber and the Lightning fighter, both jets.

19. In a twin-engined aircraft both engines rotate in the same direction for economy in production and logistics. The turning of the airscrews reacts on the aircraft to make it want to rotate in the opposite direction. As the airplane moves off from rest, this reaction is sensed as a strong tendency to swing in the direction of the wing that is being pressed down by the reaction. If the pilot does not anticipate the movement in time, he may inadvertently be swung off the runway or even make a complete ground loop. If a large wing-down swing occurs just after take-off it generally means curtains for that pilot.

20. Diagnosing my own problem with the "self-firing guns": the magazines on both had refused to work under the Russian climate conditions, but both agreed to function when back in warmer air. Each then loaded a waiting round into the open breach—to be promptly fired as the normal firing cycle was completed by a now warmed-up and happy-to-cooperate gun. The mechanisms of the other two guns had obviously misfed due to ice interference and snapped the rounds in two.

21. Medium twin-bombers:
Blackburn BOTHA, No. L 6109. Mid-upper twin-gun turret.

Lockheed HUDSON, No. N 7206. Emerson electric mid-upper turret. U.S. built and very successful with Coastal Command.

Bristol BEAUFORT No. W 6482. Mid-upper turret. Many airframe components common with the Beaufighter.

22. Blenheim. No. L 4838 with Wattisham squadron turret. A bomber squadron at Wattisham mocked-up two Browning guns in the mid-upper turret. Bristol used this concept for a new turret to be fitted retroactively. Unfortunately, in turns with more than one "g" download, the guns could not pull the belts from the ammo boxes below after the upper half of the belts had been used up. I tried two heavy springs below a free-floating floor (in the boxes) which was retained progressively by pawls as it rose, raising the ammo to where the guns could still cope.

23. Westland Lysander. No. L 4737. Perseus air-cooled engine. The gunner or navigator was housed in a huge rear cockpit with twin Vickers drum-fed K guns for defense. I tested this archaic equipment, feeling it was just a waste of time to do so. It was a pitiful installation. The Battle, with its fate hanging on but one K gun for rear defense, had a problem; but this was twice as bad—two

peashooters, each ready to jam or call for a fresh drum at *le moment critique*. There was only one thing to do, which I did post haste. I had fun designing a twin hand-held, belt-fed Browning gun replacement for the rear gunner, in the same way the K gun was replaced in the Battle and Blenheim. The change was accepted by Their Airships and fitted retroactively, we hoped to the joy of the backseat drivers.

24. Boulton-Paul Defiant No. K 8310 with one 20 mm gun in turret, drum fed, 19 rnds. each. The few Defiants in France with the four-Browning turrets were withdrawn from ops. It was too slow and too blind for escort. It was essentially a defensive airplane. Though the 20 mm gave a longer range, a single cannon was silly to take to war. It was only used for R & D trials.

25. This Short Stirling III was the model most used on ops. See details above at note 10 on this very heavy bomber.

CHAPTER 4 NOTES

1. Each gun had a "recuperator" mounted alongside each breech. This was a 12"-tall box, 2.5" wide—with rollers at the upper edges, parallel to the gun. The belt was fed into the gun and ammo looped down into the box by a third "dancing" roller, held down by a spring. The other end of the belt fed back into the long supply chute. When the gun fired, the dancing roller rose as the ammo belt was drawn into the gun. Near the top of the box the roller passed a switch that turned on the servo motor. The servo was set to feed the belt faster than the gun could consume it, so the dancing roller fell back into its box until it was near the bottom, where it activated a second switch to turn off the servo. The cycle repeated as the box was emptied and refilled. The gun was only conscious of being fed by a free belt without excessive loads.

2. Briston Aeroplane Co. BEAUFIGHTER. No R 2055. Two Bristol Hercules II, 14-cylinder, two-row, sleeve-valve radial engines. HP: 1,300 each. Speed: 335 mph at 17,000 ft. Armament: four x 20 mm cannon with 19-round drums mounted in floor of fuselage, very accessible to crew member; six x Browning .303-caliber guns in wings.

3. Hawker HURRICANE, IIB. No P 3811. R-R Merlin XX 12-cylinder V6-engine. HP: 1,850. Speed: 320 to 340 mph at 21,000 ft. Arma-

ment: twelve x Browning .303-caliber guns and two x 250-lb. or 500-lb. bombs.

4. *Chatellerault* 20 mm cannon belt-feed mechanism. Rounds were carried in a disintegrating-link belt drawn into the gun by a big sprocket roller driven by a coil spring. As the gun recoiled, a ramp on the gun pushed up a plunger in the bottom of the nonrecoiling feed thus winding up the spring one notch to recuperate the tension lost from feeding the fired round. The gun had to recoil at least 20 mm to raise the plunger enough to rewind the spring.

5. Motley 20 mm cannon belt-feed mechanism. Rounds were fed into the gun by a 3"-dia. worm gear set at right angles to the gun breech with a pitch of about an inch to accommodate the girth of the rounds. It ran across a bank of 12 hoppers mounted above, with eight rounds in each, progressively feeding them into the breech. When the aircraft was inverted the springs pushing the rounds out of hoppers were not strong enough to overcome the negative "g" force. Strengthening the springs would impose too much pressure on the feed screw in level flight—a no-win situation.

6. Hurricane IIC No. V7360. Four x 20 mm Hispano cannon; drum fed, 19 rnds/gun. Because of the bulk of the ammo drums, the guns had to be mounted on their sides and the ejection chutes forced to curve over through 90 degrees to discharge the spent cases.

7. Record of path of 20 mm empty case ejection from cannon.

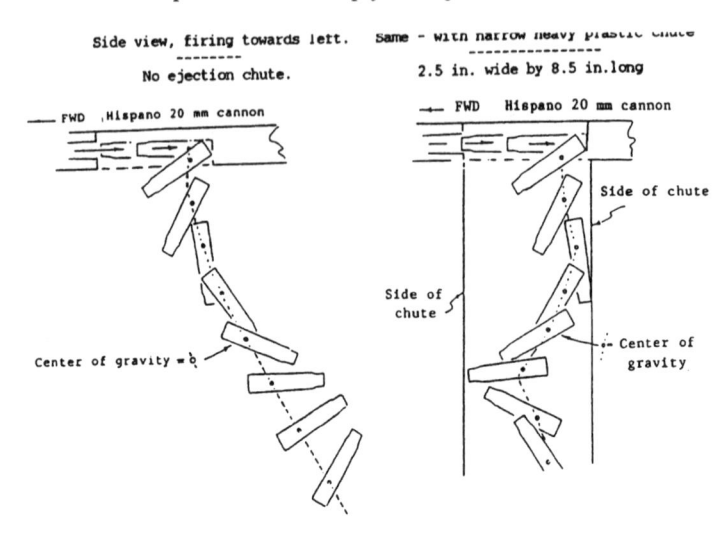

8. Spitfire IIB. No. R 6904. Merlin XII engine. HP: 1,175. Two x 20 mm Hispano cannon (drum fed) and four x .303 Brownings.

9. Hurricane IIC. No. Z2326. Four x 20 mm Hispano cannon, belt feed French *Chatellerault* design, British make, 100 rnds/gun. The dia. of the belt feed was smaller than the old drum, so the gun could be mounted upright and eject its empty cases straight down through the bottom of the wing. Because the multiple batteries of cannon worked so well in the Beau and the Whirlwind, we decided to start air firing right away and clear this important installation without delay. We ran into continual stoppages without any obvious misbehavior pattern to point to a solution. Every time one or another gun would jam when firing a full box of 100, but never from the old log-jam of empties in the chutes. All were caused by misfeeds and rounds failing to enter the breech.

The new feed was powered by a strong coil spring. The belt was drawn into the feed by rotating the feed sprocket handle until it was full and then adding two turns to give proper tension for feeding. The initial tension fed a round into the breech when the firing button was pressed and a small amount of spring tension was used up. However when the gun recoiled almost an inch within the mounting it rewound the feed spring one notch on a ratchet back to full tension. I began to detect a pattern. After each landing I noticed the jammed guns had lost most of the coil spring tension—resulting in misfeeds. This could only come from short recoils.

Disappointed, we went back to ground firing for a detailed study of our latest malaise. I fired each cannon alone, one shot at a time and measured the length of the recoil relative to the feed—which was anchored to the aircraft structure separately from the gun. It was crucial for this to be at least 20 mm. I let the cannon squash a piece of my daughter Ann's modeling clay between a flat spot on the gun and the forward face of the feed casing and measured the resultant gap—which was the length of the recoil. It was a sad commentary that even our children's toys had to be press-ganged into total war. The recoil was always less than when the gun was rigidly mounted on a test stand or—as was originally intended by the cannon designers—in a very solid part of the aircraft such as the V of an aero engine to fire through the prop boss. The installation in the Beau was solid. It was anchored to the very keel of the ship. In the Hurricane the somewhat short recoil with one gun firing alone meant some of the recoil was being absorbed elsewhere, though there was still enough recoil to recuperate the feed. The wing spar supporting the cannon and taking its full force of recoil must be bending and reducing the relative movement between gun and feed. When two guns were fired at exactly the same time in one wing, the recoils were even shorter in both guns. There had to be double the bending. To check I fired all guns at once, one shot from each, and all recoils were shorter. In several cases the recoils were too short to rewind the feeds. That seemed to offer the vital clue I was after.

At this stage of the game, the cannon had a muzzle brake at the end of the barrel with slots cut through at right angles to the barrel at a back angle to deflect the high-pressure gases behind the bullet as it left the barrel. This device "pulled" the barrel forward briefly as the gases burst through the canted slots and reduced the recoil force. I tried removing all four muzzle brakes and it seemed to do the trick. The stoppages were overcome and there was no obvious damage to the spars from the extra recoil forces previously absorbed by the muzzle brakes. In the air the heavier recoil was noticeable but acceptable.

Most of the ammunition could now be expended, but there were still some instances when a feed would lose tension and cause a misfeed. There was also a large steel spring around the barrel that bore on the main spar to absorb recoil. I reduced the initial compression on the springs on all guns by progressively unscrewing the retaining nuts. It helped a bit but some guns still failed. The more load on the spar, the more erratic the failure pattern.

With four guns in action and more so in a long burst the problem was much more complicated. Each gun had its individual rate of fire—differing slightly from another. In addition, the particular rate varied according to the care taken in cleaning, the temperature of that gun bay, and so on. Thus, all guns would initially fire almost exactly at the same time, but during a prolonged burst thereafter, the two guns in each wing got more and more out of phase with each other and hammered the spar in an irregular manner. The spars had to be stiffened to take more of the brunt of the ever-changing loads from the pair in each wing. Sidney Camm, God bless him, was convinced this time without a fight and set to work with all speed to beef up the wings' spars. The muzzle brakes were consigned to the scrap heap, and weaker recoil springs became standard.

10. As with the Whitley, the snaky belts were assisted by motor-driven sprockets in several places, but with the much larger supply, the loads on the belts were almost too much. We showed the Avro reps details of our feed "recuperator," and they agreed to include the device in their system as well.

11. The rear turret in the Manchester had tall, flat sides that blended with the sides of the back of the fuselage. The turret wall behind the gunner was curved to a circle drawn on the turret center of rotation. I got turret drawings from the Frazer-Nash rep and cut out the plan view in cardboard. I laid this over a same-scale plan view of the aft end of the bomber on my office floor and stuck a pin through the center of rotation. When I rotated the model, it was obvious where the problem lay. As the corner of the curved turret wall emerged into the slipstream, it created a bulge that was a perfect aerodynamic "Clark Y" airfoil section, highly efficient and used on the wings of many early aircraft. It created a maximum effect at 15 degrees, where we had most trouble. Naturally, this airfoil, appearing suddenly on the vertical face at the back of the long fuselage would suck the tail over in that direction. See diagram below.

Plan view of rear four-gun turret in Manchester showing airfoil section created when turret rotates through 12 degrees.

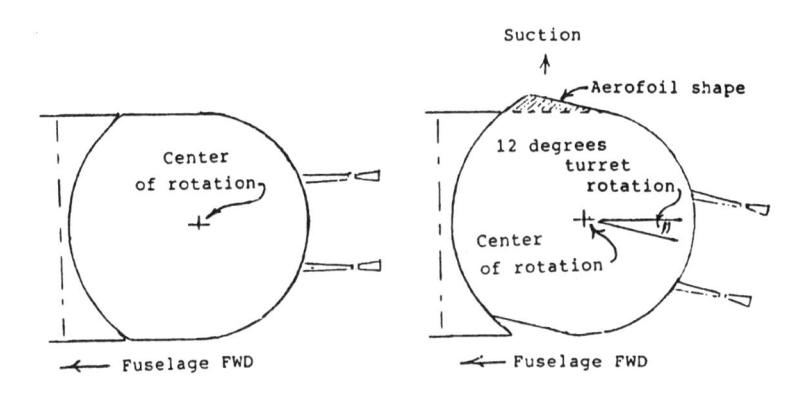

12. The vertical deflectors we tried forward of the turret were designed to destroy the unwelcome sideways lift. See diagram below.

Plan view of rear four-gun turret in Manchester showing left: one shape of spoilers tried unsuccessfully and, right: the final successful faired deflectors shown on following page.

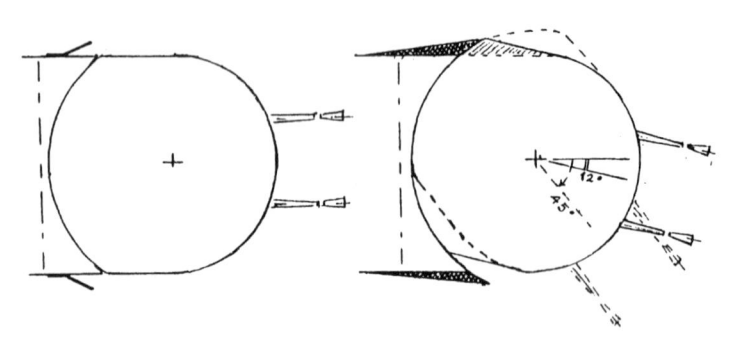

13. *Knickebein* (dog leg)
    Similar to Lorenz blind-landing technique and used existing equipment in aircraft. When on course, pilot heard a continuous steady tone; if he strayed one way he heard dots(…)and the other way he heard dashes(---). When at the target, a crossing beam told the bomb aimer to release the bombs.

14. *X-Gerat* (X tool)
    More complex, needed special equipment and training. Pilot flew on a beam to target and crossed three other beams. No. 1 alerted crew "target coming up." No. 2 told bomb aimer to punch a clockwork device. No. 3 told him to punch device again. One clock hand then stopped and the second went on to release bombs automatically. More accurate than *Knickebein* and harder to jam. A special *Gruppe* was trained to drop incendiaries as aiming points for the following bombers.

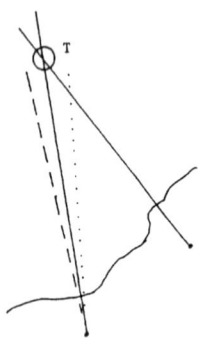

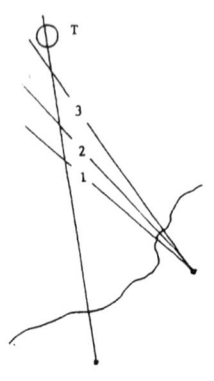

15. The *Bismarck,* a very powerful battleship, and her escort the *Prinz Eugen,* an eight-inch-gun cruiser, were holed up at Brest for some time. Two of our battleships *King George V* and *Prince of Wales,* and

the battle-cruiser *Hood* were at Scapa Flow ready to take on the pair of them. We learned they were moving out. Soon after, the Germans left the Kattegat, paused in Bergen Fjord, and were next sighted sailing west by cruisers patrolling north of Iceland. Some eighteen British capital ships in the Atlantic area, with at least two dozen destroyers, were given orders to join battle. The U.S. president was also told so the U.S. navy could be on the lookout and warn us if they got past our cordon around the south of the Denmark Strait.

The *Prince of Wales* and the *Hood* intercepted the enemy at dawn on 24 May, and at a range of fourteen miles the *Hood* opened fire. The *Bismarck* replied, starting a serious fire on the *Hood* and with the fifth salvo blowing her up. Fifteen hundred men perished. The *Prince of Wales*, though outgunned, continued the fight, inflicting severe damage to the *Bismarck* but had to break off under smoke. All the big ships in the vicinity turned to the chase; late that evening the *Bismarck* turned on them, and there was a small scrap. This was but a ruse to permit the *Prinz Eugen* to escape and make her way home to Brest. Aircraft from the carrier *Victorious* put a torpedo into the German under her bridge. She almost got away in the miserable weather, but on the evening of the 26th more aircraft attacked with torpedoes, inflicting fatal damage. The next morning two battleships took her on and silenced all guns; but it needed a cruiser, the *Dorsetshire*, to send her to the bottom with torpedoes. It was an important victory.

16. Bishop's design was based on the revolutionary, very successful de Havilland 88 Comet built specially for the 1934 MacRobertson race from Mildenhall, England to Melbourne, Australia—which it won. The name of the DH 88 should not be confused with the later four-jet airliner, also called Comet.

17. The military derivative was the DH 98, or MOSQUITO: W4052. Two R-R Merlin engines. Speed: 370 mph. The fighter version had four x 20 mm cannon, 100 rnds each with belt feed and four x .303 Browning guns with 1,000 rnds each.

18. Hawker TYPHOON IB No. R7579. Napier Sabre IIa 24-cylinder, liquid-cooled engine. HP: 2,200. Speed: 435 mph at 17,000 ft., 400 at sea level. Range: 1,300 mi. Four x 20 mm cannon, 150 rnds/gun belt feed, and eight x 60-lb. HE warhead rockets or two x 1,000-lb. bombs.

19. U.S. DOUGLAS, A-20, or Havoc. No. AH444. Two Cyclone

engines. Forward firing four x 20 mm cannon, magazine feed.

20. U.S. Consolidated B-24, or LIBERATOR. No. AM 991A. Four Cyclone engines. Four x 20 mm cannon, magazine feed for forward firing.

21. U.S. Bell AIRACOBRA. DS 173. Allison engine. One 37 mm low-velocity Colt cannon firing through prop boss, two x .50 and two x .30 machine guns in nose.

22. HURRICANE, IIB, Z2885. Merlin XX, 12 cylinder Vee, liquid-cooled. HP: 1,850; four x 20 mm cannon, drum fed, 19 rnds/gun. Bombs: two 250 or 500 lb., one under each wing.

CHAPTER 5 NOTES

1. HURRICANE, IID, Z 2326. Merlin XX, 12 cylinder Vee, liquid-cooled. HP: 1,850. Two Vickers 40 mm cannon, hopper fed, 15 rnds/gun, armor-piercing shot or light-case explosive shell.

2. Double-base powder is made by combining nitroglycerin and nitro-cellulose. Also called cordite, it is cast under mild heat into sticks of the desired diameter and length and with the required shape and size of central bore. No solvent remains in cordite. See also chap. 2, note 3 and below: note 6.

3. The rocket, code U.P. (unrotated projectile) later called R.P. (rocket projectile), came on the scene as a prime potential for the urgent need to provide close support in Egypt for attacking Rommel's tanks. It was easy to adapt armor-piercing shot from the 25-pounder field gun to screw onto the front of the R.P. motor. This is how it was tested for almost a year. The head weighed 25 lbs., the motor 35.5 lbs. With a burning time of 1.25 sec., it had a velocity of 1,500 ft/sec at burn out.

4. HURRICANE, No. L 1760. First experimental aircraft rocket installation to be fired on 25 October 1941 from Thorney Island airfield; two singles from the ground and two singles from the air all with 25-lb. solid-steel warheads.

5. A second warhead was under development for use especially against ships. It was a semiarmor-piercing 60-lb. steel shell strong enough

to pass through one-in. steel plate and burst 20 ft. behind. Here lay the first weapon which would increase the caliber of firepower for fighter-bombers to the equivalency of a six-in. shell with a striking velocity of 1,000 ft/sec.

6. The propellant was cordite, cast into a long tube, three-inch diam. with a one-inch hole. It fitted snugly inside an outer steel tube. On firing, a bag of gunpowder at the front of the cordite tube was lit, blasting an ignition flame back through the tube. But the speed of the flame through the web from inner wall to the outer did not reach the steel case uniformly. Slivers of unburned cordite were ejected at the last moment causing off-center thrust to force the rocket off course. With a circular hole in the center of the cordite stick the inside surface area is obviously much less than the outer surface, thus burning had to keep up with an increasing surface area. The boffins worked on a star or cruciform internal shape with an area equal to the outer surface. This improved accuracy.

7. Fired from twelve-foot rails, only 90 mph was added to the rocket speed before release. Better than nothing, perhaps, but no great shakes. I wondered if the difference was that important in view of the severe flexing of those drag-inducing bedsteads.

8. HURRICANE IIC, No. Z 2326. Merlin XX engine. HP: 1,850. Two Rolls-Royce (BH) 40 mm cannon of an original, unique design with an oil hydraulic system to absorb the powerful recoil; 12 rnds/gun as against 15 rounds with the Vickers (S) gun.

9. As the Eighth worked up we helped all we could. Some early experience was afforded by including an all-U.S. crew with RAF 226 Squadron flying A-10, Bostons in daylight attacks on railroad yards at Hazebrouk. To form a first-hand opinion of the RAF methods, General Fred Anderson of the Eighth flew on a number of occasions with us at night on bombing missions deep into Germany.

10. North American MUSTANG I. P-51. Single-seat day fighter. No. AG 359. Allison V-1710-30 (F3R) engine. HP: 1,100. Armament: Two .50-caliber U.S. MG 53-2 Browning machine guns in the fuselage (below the engine) firing through the prop; one .50-caliber MG 53 and two .30-caliber MG 40 guns in each wing. This version was used mainly for low-altitude tactical reconnaissance.
Later models had Rolls-Royce Merlin 61 engines and then Packard-built Merlin 61s, 1,520 HP, making them excellent high-altitude

fighters with two-speed, two-stage superchargers and intercoolers with a range of 1,000 miles plus 530 miles with long-range tanks. Speed: 437 mph at 25,000 ft.

A close-support version carried six x .50 Browning guns or four x 20 mms cannon in the wings outside the prop disc plus two x 1,000 lbs. bombs or eight x British 3.5-inch rockets, and later, ten x 5-inch high-velocity U.S. rockets or two x 40 mm cannon. Probably the best fighter available to the Allied forces in the latter stages.

The Mustang was the first fighter aircraft to employ a laminar-flow wing, with maximum thickness well aft that resulted in greatly reduced drag.

CHAPTER 6 NOTES

1. I took Hurricane BP 173 with two Vickers 40 mm cannon to fire solid armor-piercing shot and high explosive shells, with a couple of different fuses. Pete had a Hurricane with four 20 mm cannon. The ground crew flew in B Flight's Wellington bomber.

2. Drawings of the landing craft (tank), LC(T) were sent to the U.S. with the firing trial report and the vessels put into production for coming major amphibious landings.

3. In history's first ironclad ships, the Koreans under Yi Sunsin drove Hideyoshi's fleet from Chinhae Bay. Japanese losses at Midway were all 4 carriers, 1 cruiser, 250 aircraft, and about 1,000 men killed. The U.S. force lost the carrier *Yorktown*, a destroyer, 150 planes, and 300 men.

4. Focke-Wulf, Fw 190A. BMW 801D-2 engine, 14 cylinder, air-cooled two-row radial with methanol/water injection. HP: 1,700. HP: 2,100 with M/W 50 boost. Two x 13 mm MG 131 machine guns in upper cowling; two x 20 mm cannon MG 151 in wing roots; and one x 20 mm MG 151 cannon in each wing.

5. One long mirror about 6 ins. x 2.5 ins., facing the pilot, tipped back at 45 degrees was located across the cowling just above the dashboard; a second mirror about 9 ins. x 4 ins. was at the top of the windscreen but facing ahead at 45 degrees.

6. HURRICANE IV, No. BP 173. Merlin 24 engine. HP: 1,620. This Mark had as standard four x 20 mm cannon, two within each wing,

outside the propeller disc. It could also carry beneath the wings: two x 500 lb. bombs, or two x 40 mm cannon, or eight rockets (a total of two more than in all the prototype rocket trials).

7. Bf 109, (Me 109), No. DG 200. Now in RAF Museum at Duxford. Single-engine day fighter. Daimler-Benz DB 605A engine. Crew: one. Weight: 7,491 lbs. Ceiling: 37,890 ft. Cruise speed: 260 mph. Max. speed: 386 mph. Range: 620 mi. Armament: one x 30 mm or 20 mm cannon plus two x 13 mm machine guns.

8. Heinkel 111, No. AW 177. Twin-engine medium bomber.

9. Bf 100, (Me 110), No. AX 722. Twin-engine night fighter; Daimler-Benz DB 605B engines. Crew: three. Weight: 22,000 lbs. Ceiling: 26,250 ft. Cruise speed: 250 mph. Max. speed: 342 mph. Range: 1,305 mi. Armament: two x 30 mm cannon and two x 20 mm cannon in nose, twin 7.9 mm machine guns in rear.

10. Junkers 88, No. HM 509. Twin-engine night bomber or fighter. Two Junkers Jumo 211J engines. Crew: two or three. Weight: 27,225 lbs. Ceiling: 32,480 ft. Cruise speed: 263 mph. Max. speed: 307 mph. Range: 1,230 mi. Armament: three x 20 mm cannon and three x 7.9 mm machine guns in nose; one x 13 mm machine gun in rear of cockpit.

11. BEAUFIGHTER T.F. X, EL 329. Two Hercules XVII engines. HP: 1,725. Speed 310 mph at sea level. Four x 20 mm cannon in original bomb bay; eight x rockets under wings; one manual .303-caliber machine gun in mid-upper dorsal position.

12. HURRICANE IID. No. BP 173. I got to thinking: if the Beau's datum was wrong we should surely check all our forward-firing aircraft as well. What about our old favorite, Hurricane BP 173? Pete flew her past the hangars with a thick white ribbon painted down the length of her—we checked the films. The Hurricane datum was two degrees nose down at our attack speed. As they say in that Mecca of sailing harbors in Massachusetts, USA, "Light dawns over Marblehead." The revelation about the Hurricane meant that with the 40 mm cannon aligned with the manufacturer's datum—our normal drill— there was a component of the aircraft speed upward on the path of the shell, which according to our 12-in. slide rule accounted exactly for the five-feet "gun jump" at the target that we had met in 1941. Tongue in cheek, we quietly issued an addendum to our original

report, making sure that a copy was sent to Vickers to be shown to the quack who tried to pacify and mislead us.

13. MARTIN-BAKER fighter. Designed by Jimmie Martin to be easy to maintain and service under the worst field conditions. It was an elegant, robust aircraft with a widespread undercarriage for ease of operation in/out of rough fields. Captain Baker, Jimmie's partner and test pilot, had made a few flights and had nothing but praise for its performance.

14. Hawker TYPHOON 1A, No. R 7617. Napier Sabre engine; 24 cyl horizontal. HP: 2,200. Speed: 420 mph at 23,000 ft. Armts: 12 x .303 Browning machine guns initially; four x 20 mm cannon plus eight x 3.5-inch rockets later.

15. Fairey SWORDFISH. No. DK747. Bristol Pegasus XXX engine. HP: 750. Fleet Air Arm torpedo-bomber. Speed: max. 139 mph at 5,000 ft; cruise 125. One 18-in., 1,610-lb. torpedo or one 1,500-lb. mine plus two 250-lb. bombs; or three Mk VII depth charges; or eight 3.5-in. rockets, 60-lb. HE or 25-lb. AP warheads.

16. Officially, the correct head against ships, e.g. a U-boat, is the 60-lb. light-case HE head we had already started to test. Designed for the job, it is strong enough to penetrate the structure of a ship, say one-in.-thick steel plate, and burst about ten feet inside where it will do the greatest damage. With this warhead, only a direct hit on exposed parts of a surfaced U-boat would be effective. The pressure hull is a twenty-foot-diameter, one-in.-thick steel tube easily able to withstand the burst of a near miss. On the other hand, our armor plate trials showed the solid steel armor-piercing warheads designed for tanks would easily punch three-in. holes in the pressure hull; and in steep dives much more of the sub would be vulnerable.

17. The 25-lb. armor-piercing shot taken from the 88 mm field gun had been intended for tanks: now it was to be used for submarines. The 60-lb. light-case HE head designed specially for antishipping now had a prime role attacking tanks and for close support of army targets. It was an unbelievable switch. The 60-pounder would still be used against normal shipping.

18. This important 4.5-in. barrage rocket was spin-stabilized like Lew Motley's 60 mm dream child—a fundamentally different approach to inherent stability from our 3.5-in. fin-stabilized aircraft rocket. Lew and I cried in our beer with envy when we learned about it.

CHAPTER 7 NOTES

1. The rocket with 60-lb. warhead had a motor weighing 36 lbs.—a total of 96 lbs. It hit the target at about 950 mph. The 250-lb. bomb was the obvious place to start. The bomb, less rear fins, i.e., warhead for our maxi-rocket, weighed 200 lbs.—over three times the 60-lb. warhead. We needed four rocket tails to give it equal performance. Luckily, four rocket tubes would fit neatly into the round area of the bomb base where the rear cone was fastened; the rocket then weighed some 345 lbs. with a 200-lb. warhead and a speed at the target of 1,060 mph.

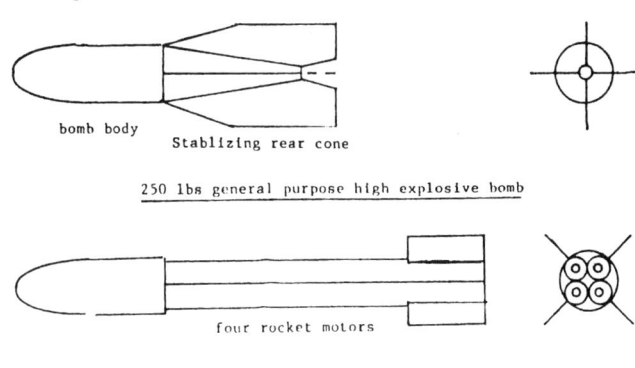

bomb body
Stablizing rear cone
250 lbs general purpose high explosive bomb

four rocket motors
345 lbs prototpe rocket-propelled bomb

2. The next size up is the 500-lb. bomb with a warhead of 430 lbs. We needed seven rockets to give it enough push, and the larger bomb base accepted that number in a small honeycomb of seven motors, six spaced evenly around one in the middle. The striking velocity of this 680-lb. monster was about 940 mph.

685 lbs prototype rocket-propelled bomb

bomb body

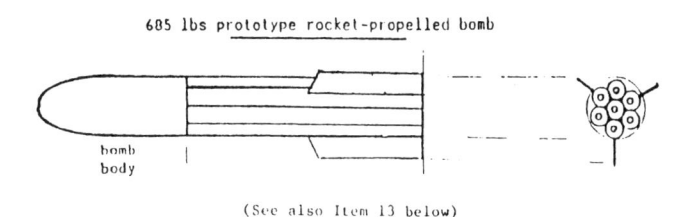

(See also Item 13 below)

3. The boffins insisted we needed rocket guide rails to overcome the windage factor. "Like a nice long gun barrel to guide a bullet," explained Bill Cook dangling a sort of red herring before me. I wanted no rails at all, but then the full effect of any offset from the slipstream would be felt, for sure. Would the aircraft speed alone be sufficient to stabilize the initial aim of the rocket without rails? Short rails would add a hundred miles an hour to the rocket speed over and above that of the aircraft before the rocket was free, but how much would that improve the overall accuracy? I seemed a lone voice worrying about changing attack angle of the aircraft at different speeds and dives. It was an area of great uncertainty and hard to allow for. I thought a rocket with an entirely different form of stabilization was needed to solve the problem.

4. I had the skillful Thomason build me a forward, wraparound nozzle for the rocket to deflect the burning gases from around the front of the tube toward the tail, surrounding it with a solid curtain of high speed exhaust gases to protect it from deflection by any difference in the ambient airflow. One of the patient boffins tried to explain: "The push on the rocket is not at the rear gas jet, it's up front just behind the warhead. Your design doesn't change that a bit." He missed my point. I wanted our baby protected from an antagonistic outside world—permitting it to go where it was pointing. We weren't listening to each other.

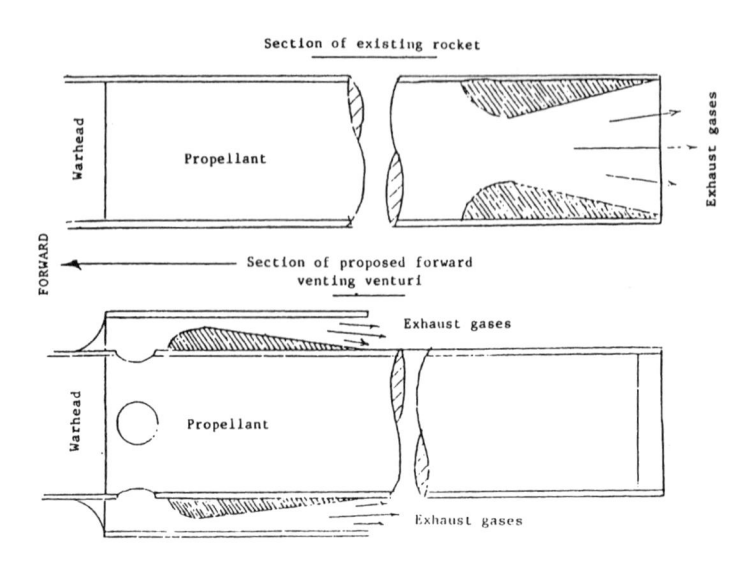

5. The steel launching tubes were six inches in diameter and seven feet long. Spiral rails, one inch deep were mounted on the inside walls all the way down. The span of stabilizing fins was cut back to just under one inch from the original four-inch span. The rocket was pushed into the tube, with the body riding on the spiral rails and the narrowed fins bearing on the edges of the rails. As the rocket pushed its way out of the tube, the rails gave it a slow spin that canceled the fluctuations of the line-of-thrust caused by the final offset burning of the propellant so bemoaned by Cookie.

6. It would be of no avail just to attach a pair of wings at the initial center of gravity: that point moves forward as propellant is burned. It would also be impossible to make each wing lift evenly. A roll would ensue, causing a swift turn toward the dropping wing. In addition, any wing will develop a different coefficient of lift with changing acceleration of the supported vehicle and rockets accelerate more as the weight of propellant diminishes. I needed time to sleep on the whole harebrained scheme. Feedback was the battle cry.

7. When long-range streamlined monoplanes came on the scene pilots found that extra range can be coaxed by "getting the plane up on the step." This is achieved by trimming the plane out in precise level flight by the auto pilot at about 90% power and then gingerly reducing power to normal cruising—about 75%. Little speed is lost and height is maintained.

8. "Gee." Radio pulses were sent out simultaneously from three stations wide apart in England. By exact timing of their arrival at the aircraft it could fix its position within a mile. "Oboe" was a more accurate and jam-proof version but still limited to line-of-sight operation and did need a dangerously long time on a straight line for the final fix.

9. "Sunflower seed." This rocket with a fast burning time of about a quarter second could reach 4,000 feet above the B-17 in 4.5 sec. With a light shell carrying two lbs. of TNT fused to burst at that height, the lethal area was large.

10. B-17 turret. The gunnery bits and pieces were removed and the turret locked in rotation and elevation. Four 12-ft.-long steel launching tubes were mounted vertically, canted four degrees forward to compensate for the slipstream. They were open at both ends, sticking out 12 in. at the top, where an armor steel plate replaced the perspex,

and out of the bottom of the fuselage. It was a point-blank aim. The tubes could be reloaded in the air and the rockets fired singly or in salvo as experience dictated.

11. The Dam bombs. This circular, rotatable bomb was designed by Barnes Wallis for the specific purpose of breaching dam walls and had been tested by Charles Dann a year before at Boscombe and elsewhere. It was carried in modified bays of Lancasters to be dropped from a height of 60 ft. It was given a backward spin just before release, and after dropping, skipped across the water, slowed down by the backward spin until it hit the dam wall, where it rolled down the inner face to burst at the proper depth to breach the retaining wall.

12. We used fully operational Sunflower Seed rockets with live HE warheads. At 6,000 ft. above Cardigan Bay we fired one rocket from each tube, timing the bursts above. Each left with a sledgehammer blow on the armor plate but all functioned to perfection. We landed to examine the B-17—all was well. At 20,000 ft. we repeated the single shots finally firing a few salvos of four. I noticed every man tucked his head in as the combined blast slammed on the protective plate. It was an angry weapon. Reloading all four tubes was fast and easy to do in flight.

13. 750 lbs. Hybrid bomb-body/multiple-tail rocket with plenum chamber for equalizing pressure in all seven motors.

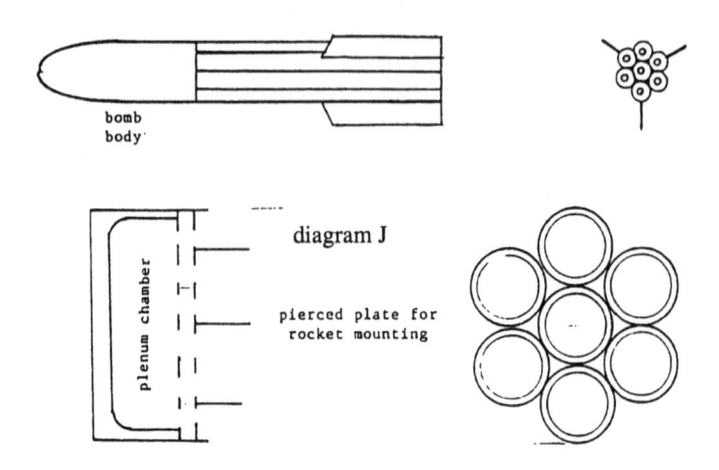

diagram J

bomb body

plenum chamber

pierced plate for rocket mounting

CHAPTER 8 NOTES

1. The shorter the flight time the less time the rocket has to fall away to earth. Flight time is shortened by giving it more speed and doing it sooner. These simple facts of life call for more propellant and one that burns more quickly. They both steal from the payload, and the compromise that must be struck results in a flight time much longer than that of a comparable caliber gun shell. The design system was the wrong way round. A rocket accelerates from rest in relation to the aircraft to attain a striking velocity of about 1,200 ft/sec, with the heavier 60-lb. head. On the other hand, a shell from our gun starts off with a velocity out of the barrel of over 2,000 ft/sec, and this speed is not much reduced by the time it reaches the target.
   At 300 yards, a heavy rocket drops 60 feet, while a gun shell falls only five feet. I thought the situation to be unacceptable, and somehow or other a remedy would have to be found.

2. The drones were propelled by a very slow-burning rocket with enough power to sustain level flight and at the same time give a long endurance.

3. A possible snag was that the little beasts were constantly accelerating during burning and so developing increasing lift (unlike the constant speed drones Lines already made), and therefore apt to climb on the way to the target. But on the other hand, the center of gravity was also moving forward as the propellant burned, which should help to keep the nose down. This gave us a neat, built-in automatic feedback system for elevation control.

4. I wondered if the girdle should rotate freely around the rocket body and thus develop a signal to be sent to wing ailerons to correct the roll. But the rocket itself was prone to roll on its own from chronic indigestion of the propellant. We would need a neutral reference.

CHAPTER 9 NOTES

1. Early work by a small rocket group in the East with Dr. Clarence Hickman, Capt. Leslie Skinner, U.S. Army, and Lt. Harold Baker at Indian Head produced a 4.5-in. rocket with minimal funds and backing. The propellant used was not entirely free from bursts. It had small folding fins and was launched from a tube. The weapon had a

high dispersion.
Length: 33 ins.; diameter: 4.5 ins.; all-up weight: 35 lbs.; warhead weight: 12 lbs.; max. velocity, less aircraft speed, 1,000 ft/sec.; burning time: 0.17 sec.; propellant: 60% nitrocellulose, 40% nitroglycerin cast in 10 hollow sticks 16.5 ins. long.

2. I told of our early problems with angle of attack in our Hurricane trials with 40 mm cannon, now a factor even more important with rockets. We'd been wondering how to measure it to feed into a rocket sight and I mentioned that Robert Alkan was now hot on the problem at the navy facility at Specialties, Inc. on Long Island.

3. This first standard operational U.S. Navy rocket was propelled by a new solventless cordite similar to the British, with a cruciform shaped hole all the way down the middle to give evenness of burning and help prevent motor bursts. It had a steel motor and carried a solid armor-piercing head or a newly designed 60-lb. explosive head. Its velocity was 20 percent higher than its British sire.

4. This brand new design of rocket had a heavier stick of solventless cordite propellant in an aluminum motor and a newly designed 60-lb. HE head. It was 50 percent faster than the early British version with a similar weight of warhead. The time of burning was about the same, just over one second.

CHAPTER 10 NOTES

1. TINY TIM, "the 1,000-lb. rocket." Specs laid down 24 Feb. 1944. Warhead: 590-lbs. bomb body with 150 pounds of TNT, 0.02 sec. base fuse delay. Four grains of extrudable, solventless powder: total weight 149 lbs. Nozzle exhaust in base of rocket motor: 24. Velocity at burn-out: 800 ft/sec.

2. In spite of the pioneering work of Dr. Goddard, the U.S. was tardy in the development of rocket-engined planes. Germany started in 1935 with experiments using exotic fuels such as hydrogen peroxide and potassium permanganate and by 1937 had brought in Lippisch's tailless glider as a test bed. Two years later Lippisch's team joined Messerschmitt, and the prototype fighter became the Me 163. The project moved to Peenemunde in late 1939, and being long-term research, was put on hold. A 1,650-lb. thrust HWK R.II Walter engine fitted to a refined airframe, Me 163 VI, began tests in August

1941 with Luftwaffe General Udet's influence behind it. In October it flew at 624 mph but it took two years to iron out aerodynamic problems and functioning snags of the radical motor and a further year to form an operational unit under Major Späte with Me 163B-1s, now called *Komet* (late 1944). Its range was only 50 miles and endurance 8 mins., shortly to be increased to 12 mins. Early models were trolley launched and skid landed. Later an undercarriage was fitted in the Me 163D but too late for use in ops.

Russia first began to develop a rocket-driven fighter in 1939. Three aircraft makers tested flying models in 1942 with some success, but there the work stopped.

In 1944 in the U.S., Northrop started work on the MX 324 to be a rocket-propelled ramming fighter, but it was too late for the war.

CHAPTER 11 NOTES

1. Caltech work verified that the weapon would penetrate a submarine pressure hull after passing through 80 ft. of water. A new nose shape was invented to reduce the severe upward turning moment on the rocket at water impact. A short nose cone sat on a second, steeper, chopped-off cone. The rocket continued on a straight path underwater. "We like it to curve upward," I said, "If we miss short, the rocket will turn up a little and not go too deep and pass underneath the pressure hull, which is only twenty feet in diameter. The upward force developed by the original ogive nose shape breaks our aluminum motors at impact," explained Willy Fowler. "Yours are steel motors."

2. All during August of 1944 Adm. William Halsey's juggernaut fleet has prowled through the Philippine islands, wreaking havoc on the remains of the Japanese air force heavily assembled here. The light response of the Japanese, supported by air intelligence, leads Halsey to believe that opposition to landings will not be strong and a fleet action is unlikely. The planned invasion of the islands is advanced two months and moved forward many hundreds of miles west and north to Leyte. Japan guessed the invasion would be in this area, but its fleets are widely separated: 7 battleships, 13 cruisers, and 19 destroyers at Singapore under Admiral Kurita. The rest are in home waters: 2 battleships, 6 cruisers, 4 emasculated carriers under Admiral Ozawa. Those ships faced almost four times that number in the U.S. fleets: Admiral Halsey's Third Fleet of 6 battleships, 5 cruisers, 16 carriers, and 58 destroyers; and Vice Adm. Thomas Kinkaid's

Seventh Fleet with 6 battleships, 16 escort carriers, eleven cruisers, and 86 destroyers. Five of Kinkaid's battleships are ones rescued from Pearl Harbor, his carriers are "baby flattops" converted from merchant men for support of amphibious operations. They were slow, unarmored, and had minimal ack-ack guns. Each carried 18 to 36 planes.

More than 700 U.S. ships of all kinds sailed into Leyte Gulf at daybreak, 20 October 1944. Battle is joined between the huge but very unequal navies at dawn on 23 October when two gallant U.S. submariners meet Kurita in the Palawan Passage. The *Darter* sinks the flagship *Atago,* a heavy cruiser and a second one, while the *Dace* blows up the cruiser *Maya.* The next day in the Sibuyan Sea, Kurita is badly hurt by air attack from U.S. carrier planes that sink one of his two heavy battleships, *Musashi,* and damage the *Yamato.* After noon Kurita turns about to run west. Without air cover, he has lost 1 super-battleship, 4 cruisers, and 4 destroyers. His retreat is misinterpreted by Halsey, who has discovered the spoof carrier fleet off the north cape of Luzon. The Third Fleet sails north to destroy Admiral Ozawa's fleet that has lured him away from continuing the attacks on Kurita.

In the meantime a second battle is fought in the Suriago Strait, where Admiral Nishimura loses 2 battleships, a cruiser, and 3 destroyers. Admiral Shima, his classmate at the naval college, following behind collides with Nishimura's sinking cruiser. Having lost a light cruiser, himself, he turns to save his skin. Thus ends the ignominious Battle of Suriago Strait.

The next day in the Battle of Cape Engano with Halsey, Ozawa loses all 4 of his carriers, 1 of his cruisers, and 2 destroyers before he, too, turns tail for home. Halsey loses the carrier *Princeton* from a sneak Japanese dive bomber. In a rescue attempt the cruiser *Birmingham* receives a blast that kills and maims over 600 men.

A fourth battle occurs the next day. Kurita has reversed course again to reappear unexpectedly from the west. He has the soft carriers at his mercy. The few aircraft from the escort carriers and destroyers rush in, breathing like dragons and making smoke. In a desperate conflict of pigmies versus giants, the brave tin cans' torpedoes and aircraft bombs pique and confuse Kurita. He thinks he is coming up against the formidable Third Fleet. He has lost 2 cruisers and another is badly damaged. Kinkaid loses 3 destroyers, a jeep flattop and over 100 planes. Kurita turns north to escape along the route he came, and at the end of the battle off Samar, Japan's navy effectively commits hari-kari. What will become known as the Battle of Leyte Gulf is over.

3. It was a ³/₈-inch aluminum tube pointing forward straight into the airstream with the front end capped into in a rounded shape and the rear end streamlined. The tube was divided internally into two chambers by a horizontal diaphragm. Minute orifices were drilled in the top and bottom of the rounded nose. Directly into wind, the pressure in the two chambers was the same. As soon as the angle of attack changed, a differential pressure was created between the chambers. This was measured and calibrated to give the angle of attack.

4. The 5-inch HVSR had a much longer range than the original 4.5-inch version. Ranging was achieved by setting the elevation of the Mk 51 launcher, fixed azimuth:

Elevation:	30°	35°	40°	45°
Range:	4,500 yds	4,900 yds	5,150 yds	5,250 yds
Drift Allce:	0.5° left			3° right

Launcher carried 12 rounds. All fired within 4.5 seconds.
Electric impulse fuse. High-capacity high-explosive head with 9.6 lbs. HE or twice the load of a 5-inch gun shell. Time of flight: 30 sec. to max. range.

Bibliography

Bridgewater, William, and Sherwood, Eliabeth J. eds. *Columbia Encyclopedia*, 2nd ed. New York: Columbia University Press. 1950.

Burchard, John E., ed. *Rockets, Guns and Targets*. Boston: Little, Brown and Company. 1948.

Christman, Albert B. *Sailors, Scientists, and Rockets: History of the Naval Weapons Center, China Lake, Vol. I,* Naval History Div. Washington: U.S. Printing Office. 1971.

Churchill, Winston S. *The Second World War,* 6 vols., Ft. Lauderdale: Cassell. 1960.

Collier, Richard. *1940 The Avalanche*. New York: Dial Press. 1979.

Dean, Hubert W. *RAF Pilot's Flying Log Book*. Form 414.

Deighton, Len. *Fighter: The True Story of the Battle of Britain*. New York: Alfred A. Knopf. 1978.

Fluckey, Eugege B. *Thunder Below! The USS Barb Revolutionizes Submarine Warfare in World War II*. Champaign: Univ. of Illinois Press. 1992.

Forrester, Larry. *Fly for Your Life*. New York: Bantam Books, Inc. 1956.

Gardner, Charles. *Allied Air Striking Force*. London: Hutchinson & Co. (Publishers) Ltd. 1940.

Gerrard-Gough, J. D. *History of the Naval Weapons Center, China Lake, California. Vol. II. The Grand Experiment at Inyokern*. Naval History Div. Washington: U.S. Printing Office. 1978.

Bibliography

Gilbert, James. *The Great Planes.* New York: Ridge Press, Grosset & Dunlap, Inc. 1970.

Green, William. *Famous Fighters of the Second World War.* New York: Hanover House. 1958.

Hamond Medallion World Atlas. Maplewood New Jersey. Hamond Inc. 1971.

Hastings, Max. *Bomber Command.* New York: Simon & Schuster. 1989.

Howard, Frank, and Gunston, Bill. *The Conquest of the Air.* New York: Random House. 1972.

Middlebrook, Martin, and Everitt, Chris. *The Bomber Command War Diaries.* New York: Penguin Books. 1990.

Reader's Digest. *Illustrated Story of World War II.* Pleasantville NY: The Reader's Digest Association, Inc. 1969.

Revie, Alastair. *The Bomber Command.* New York: Ballantine Books.

Scherman, David E., ed. *LIFE Goes to War.* New York: Simon & Schuster. 1977.